TRANSCULTURAL ARTIFICIAL INTELLIGENCE AND ROBOTICS IN HEALTH AND SOCIAL CARE

TRANSCULTURAL ARTIFICIAL INTELLIGENCE AND ROBOTICS IN HEALTH AND SOCIAL CARE

IRENA PAPADOPOULOS
Research Centre for Transcultural Studies in Health, Middlesex University, London, United Kingdom

CHRISTINA KOULOUGLIOTI
Research and Innovation Department, University Hospitals Sussex NHS Foundation Trust and Research Centre for Transcultural Studies in Health, Middlesex University, London, United Kingdom

CHRIS PAPADOPOULOS
Institute for Health Research, University of Bedfordshire, Luton, United Kingdom

ANTONIO SGORBISSA
Università degli Studi di Genova, Genova, Italy

Academic Press is an imprint of Elsevier
125 London Wall, London EC2Y 5AS, United Kingdom
525 B Street, Suite 1650, San Diego, CA 92101, United States
50 Hampshire Street, 5th Floor, Cambridge, MA 02139, United States
The Boulevard, Langford Lane, Kidlington, Oxford OX5 1GB, United Kingdom

Copyright © 2022 Elsevier Inc. All rights reserved.

No part of this publication may be reproduced or transmitted in any form or by any means, electronic or mechanical, including photocopying, recording, or any information storage and retrieval system, without permission in writing from the publisher. Details on how to seek permission, further information about the Publisher's permissions policies and our arrangements with organizations such as the Copyright Clearance Center and the Copyright Licensing Agency, can be found at our website: www.elsevier.com/permissions.

This book and the individual contributions contained in it are protected under copyright by the Publisher (other than as may be noted herein).

Notices

Knowledge and best practice in this field are constantly changing. As new research and experience broaden our understanding, changes in research methods, professional practices, or medical treatment may become necessary.

Practitioners and researchers must always rely on their own experience and knowledge in evaluating and using any information, methods, compounds, or experiments described herein. In using such information or methods they should be mindful of their own safety and the safety of others, including parties for whom they have a professional responsibility.

To the fullest extent of the law, neither the Publisher nor the authors, contributors, or editors, assume any liability for any injury and/or damage to persons or property as a matter of products liability, negligence or otherwise, or from any use or operation of any methods, products, instructions, or ideas contained in the material herein.

ISBN: 978-0-323-90407-0

For information on all Academic Press publications visit our website at
https://www.elsevier.com/books-and-journals

Publisher: Stacy Masucci
Acquisitions Editor: Rafael E. Teixeira
Editorial Project Manager: Kyle Gravel
Production Project Manager: Maria Bernard
Cover Designer: Christian J. Bilbow

Typeset by TNQ Technologies

Contents

Contributors ix
Foreword by Tetsuya Tanioka xi
Foreword by Matthias Rehm xiii

1. The fourth industrial revolution and the introduction of culturally competent concepts and values for AI technologies in health care
Irena Papadopoulos

1.1	Introduction	1
1.2	The fourth industrial revolution	3
1.3	The importance of cultural competence and the need for culturally competent socially assistive robots	6
1.4	The underpinning values, transcultural ethics, and cultural dimensions for culturally competent robots	10
1.5	Applying values, principles, definitions, components, and dimensions	13
1.6	Case study: Mrs. Christou story	13
1.7	What you will find in this book	16
1.8	Conclusion	19
1.9	Reflective questions	19
References		19
Further reading		20

2. A beginner's guide to how robots work
Antonio Sgorbissa

2.1	Introduction	21
2.2	Writing computer programs	22
2.3	Dealing with the complexity of the real world	26
2.4	Once again: "why can't the robot do that?"	31
2.5	Conclusion	39
References		39

3. What the literature says about social robots and AI technologies in health and social care
Christina Koulouglioti and Irena Papadopoulos

3.1	Introduction	41
3.2	Humanoid and animal-like socially assistive robots	42
3.3	Surgical robots and robots used in rehabilitation	44
3.4	Usefulness, appearance, and other cultural characteristics influencing acceptability	45
3.5	Views of nurses and other health professionals on the use of SARs	48
3.6	Enablers and barriers to the implementation of SARs	50
3.7	Conclusion	51
References		52

4. The ethics of socially assistive robots in health and social care
Linda Battistuzzi and Chris Papadopoulos

4.1	Introduction	59
4.2	Ethical frameworks for socially assistive robots in care	60
4.3	Ethics in the CARESSES project	62
4.4	Robots, care recipients, and caregivers: ethical considerations	63
4.5	Governance and legislation	72
4.6	Conclusion	74
4.7	Appendices	75
References		78

5. A workplan to develop culturally competent robots: the CARESSES case study
Antonio Sgorbissa

5.1	Introduction	83
5.2	Building social robots for everybody and everywhere: a contemplation of what is missing	85
5.3	The CARESSES case study told as a radio drama	89
5.4	Preparing the work plan: the path from scenarios and guidelines to artificial intelligence, from technological development to end-user evaluation	102
5.5	Conclusion	104
References		104

6. Stories and scenarios for the development of a culturally competent socially assistive robot for health and social care
Irena Papadopoulos and Christina Koulouglioti

6.1	Introduction	107
6.2	The use of stories	109
6.3	Writing stories for cultural groups	109
6.4	Explaining and discussing the construction of scenarios and their content	113
6.5	Discussion	129
6.6	Conclusion	130
6.7	Reflective questions	130
References		130

7. From stories to scenarios and guidelines for the programming of culturally competent, socially assistive robots
Irena Papadopoulos and Christina Koulouglioti

7.1	Introduction	133
7.2	Theoretical underpinnings	137
7.3	The observation study: the processes used for the development of observation tools	141
7.4	Creation of the observation tools and how to use them	143
7.5	Video recordings	147
7.6	Summary of selected example results	152
7.7	The ADORE model	153
7.8	Examples of the final guidelines produced	154
7.9	Evaluation of the videoed encounters of robot with actor-users	159
7.10	Conclusions	161
7.11	Reflective questions	163
References		163

8. From guidelines to culturally competent artificial intelligence
Antonio Sgorbissa

8.1	Introduction	165
8.2	Representing knowledge	166
8.3	How to embed cultural competence into robots	173
8.4	Conclusions	188
References		189

9. Development of a fully autonomous culturally competent robot companion
Carmine Tommaso Recchiuto and Antonio Sgorbissa

9.1	Introduction: autonomous robots revisited from Shakey to Boston dynamics legged robots	191
9.2	Yet some more words about 24/7 autonomy and robustness	194
9.3	A seemingly autonomous robot: the CARESSES case study	203
9.4	Cultural competence everywhere and the cloud hypothesis	209
9.5	Conclusion	214
References		214

10. The CARESSES trial and results
Chris Papadopoulos

10.1	Introduction	217
10.2	Trial design	218
10.3	Trial feasibility	225
10.4	Quantitative results and interpretations	230

10.5	Study limitations	241
10.6	Reflective questions	243
References		243

11. The role of culturally competent robots in major health disasters
Irena Papadopoulos and Runa Lazzarino

11.1	Introduction	245
11.2	The need for transcultural AI robotics in major health disasters	247
11.3	Developing a transcultural AI robotics strategy for major health disasters	264
11.4	Training and preparing for transcultural AI robotics in major health disasters	265
11.5	Conclusion	268
11.6	Reflective questions	269
References		269

12. Future gazing
Irena Papadopoulos and Antonio Sgorbissa

12.1	Introduction	277
12.2	My time-machine is parked in 2025: how technology will develop in the near future	280
12.3	Let us now gaze a little further into the future	285
12.4	The urgent need for training and engagement of health and social care staff	286
12.5	Conclusion	288
12.6	Reflective questions	288
References		289

Index **291**

Contributors

Linda Battistuzzi DIBRIS Department, Università degli Studi di Genova, Genova, Italy

Christina Koulouglioti Research and Innovation Department, University Hospitals Sussex NHS Foundation Trust and Research Centre for Transcultural Studies in Health, Middlesex University, London, United Kingdom

Runa Lazzarino Research Centre for Transcultural Studies in Health, Middlesex University, London, United Kingdom

Chris Papadopoulos Institute for Health Research, University of Bedfordshire, Luton, United Kingdom

Irena Papadopoulos Research Centre for Transcultural Studies in Health, Middlesex University, London, United Kingdom

Carmine Tommaso Recchiuto DIBRIS Department, Università degli Studi di Genova, Genova, Italy

Antonio Sgorbissa DIBRIS Department, Università degli Studi di Genova, Genova, Italy

Foreword by Tetsuya Tanioka

I was invited in October 2021 to provide a Foreword of this excellent book on TRANSCULTURAL ARTIFICIAL INTELLIGENCE AND ROBOTICS IN HEALTH AND SOCIAL CARE. I am privileged and honored by this invitation. The book aligns my team's program of research focused on Nursing Robots, Robotic Technology, and Human Caring, particularly for older persons, and it shares the general spirit of the Transactive Relationship Theory of Nursing (TRETON) I proposed in the last years.

An outstanding feature of the book is the focus on different cultures and the evaluation of different ways of communicating, influenced by transcultural dynamics, in the development of robotics and artificial intelligence (AI). The importance of these aspects can be intuitively captured by knowing that in Japan, for example, some Japanese people may think that a nonhuman creature or object may be enshrined and possess a soul: this can explain the memorial and funeral services for the dog-shaped robot AIBO that was held in Japan in 2018.

I agree with the authors that AI embedded in healthcare robots shall be capable of exhibiting different human facial expressions, appropriate language, and behavior in consideration of people's cultural backgrounds. It is critical that the robot is able to respond to a person's emotions and feelings who may also benefit from the fact that such capabilities are expressed by the robot in an anthropomorphic body. Since knowing a person is a multidimensional process, the robot and the persons it assists can better appreciate, support, and affirm each other if they mutually understand each other. From this perspective, to develop a caring robot, not only the robot should focus on communicating with people, but also assess and improve its abilities to "communicate well" with people (and other robots): Successful communication will heighten mutual understanding and may also influence persons to interact with robots as if they had "emotions" and a "soul." However, to realize a highly versatile AI allowing different people and robots to interact with each other in a gratifying way, it is necessary to create a large-scale database from multimodal data, possibly trained with machine learning algorithms. If we want to create socially and culturally competent robots, it is fundamental that the database includes a representation of characteristics influenced by cultures such as beliefs, values, customs, gestures, facial expressions, behaviors, and many others.

Given the current capabilities of robots, they are relegated to be only human assistants. Moreover, when there are no humans nearby, these robots are simply considered "objects." If robots are intended to "care for" humans, it becomes necessary to create fully autonomous and culturally competent robots. Moreover, if we want robots to become essential partners in health care, nursing staff engagement is both urgent and necessary. The growing use of robots in health and social care will produce increasing research on human—robot interaction. However, it is critical to ensure that scientific research in this field follows well-defined research design patterns such as the Intentional Observational Clinical Research Design, which may guide researchers to conduct rigorous investigations on human–robot interactions.

Given these premises, this book becomes essential reading for researchers, practitioners, and enthusiasts of the future of human–robot interactions in health and social care. Dr. Irena Papadopoulos, Dr. Christina Koulouglioti, Dr. Chris Papadopoulos, and Dr. Antonio Sgorbissa are sharing their forward thinking and experiences that will move nursing and healthcare practice into the future.

Tetsuya Tanioka, RN; MA, MSN, PhD, FAAN
Professor
Department of Nursing Outcome Management,
Institute of Biomedical Sciences,
Tokushima University, Graduate School
Tokushima, 770-8509, Japan
Board Member, Anne Boykin Institute,
Florida Atlantic University, Boca Raton, FL 33431, USA

Foreword by Matthias Rehm

Culture plays a vital role in our everyday behavior, providing us with heuristics for the "right" behavior in dynamic social contexts. At the same time, these heuristics present templates for analyzing the behavior of others. Thus, if our communication partner uses a different heuristic, the "wrong" template seen from our perspective, misunderstandings are likely to emerge.

Some 15 years ago, we started a new research program investigating the role of culture as a parameter influencing the interaction with technology like virtual agents or robots. At that time, the idea of enculturated or culture-aware systems was very much in its infancy. There was no data available describing behavior in different cultures apart from anecdotal information or random samples of situative culture-specific behavior. Not a good basis to develop a system that should be able to adapt to different cultural heuristics. While we were interested in general behaviors in interpersonal communication like first meeting encounters, it became quickly clear that specific contexts have their own cultural heuristics, and thus to develop culture-aware technology, it would be relevant to focus on the context of use of these technologies.

Over the last few years, the CARESSES project has done a marvelous job in investigating cultural behavior in the specific context of care giving and implementing their findings in socially assistive robots. The project is an excellent example of the need for real interdisciplinary research considering perspectives from all involved stakeholders.

This book serves an important purpose as it aims at making the topic and the results accessible to the people that deliver care and are often neglected in the development of socially assistive robots, although they will have to integrate such systems into their work routines.

So far, social robots in care are a discourse rather than a reality and two of the reasons are addressed in this book: (i) missing acknowledgement for the socio-cultural difference in care across countries and (ii) misguided expectations of care personnel based on slim knowledge about robotics technology. During the 12 chapters of this book, the reader will get a closer understanding of the cultural heuristics in care and how they matter for delivering care and the reader will also get a deeper understanding of the challenges of current robotics systems and their promise for supporting care personnel in their demanding work.

I hope that this book will become standard literature in care education and will help paving the way for more meaningful integration of intelligent technology in the care context.

Matthias Rehm, Professor MSO
Department of Architecture, Design, and Media Technology
Human Machine Interaction | Aalborg U Robotics
Coordinator Human Robot Interaction
Aalborg University, Aalborg, Denmark

CHAPTER 1

The fourth industrial revolution and the introduction of culturally competent concepts and values for AI technologies in health care

Irena Papadopoulos

Research Centre for Transcultural Studies in Health, Middlesex University, London, United Kingdom

LEARNING OBJECTIVES

- To introduce the purpose of this book and outline the content of its various chapters;
- To introduce the fourth industrial revolution and its impact on humanity and more specifically on health and social care;
- To discuss the need for AI technologies including SARs in the health and social care domains;
- To provide the theoretical concepts, definitions, values, components, and dimensions of cultural competence which can provide the framework for culturally competent AI technologies including SARs.
- To provide a case study example to illustrate the application of the framework in human—robot interactions.

1.1 Introduction

In this chapter, I introduce the authors' motivation to write this book as well as our philosophical stance regarding our views of the pragmatic state of AI and robotic applications in general, but particularly in the health and social care practice. I also introduce and briefly explore the impact that the fourth industrial revolution (4IR) is having on human societies and how the health and social care services are responding to the potential offered by artificially intelligent (AI) robotics and other AI devices. The need for culturally competent AI technologies is discussed, and the reader is introduced to the CARESSES project, which provides the binding thread that connects all the chapters in this book. Finally, I briefly introduce all the subsequent chapters.

The motivation for this book is based on the realization that the flurry of interest and developments in AI technologies, including socially assistive robots (SARs), is galloping at a high speed into our societies and increasingly into the lives of many people. Governments across the world are publishing policies and strategic plans, embracing the huge changes they wish to make. Generous funding for these developments is being provided in an attempt to keep up with the large scale of innovations. The health and social care sectors across the world are increasingly recognizing the usefulness of the new technologies, which are invariably viewed as positive solutions to many of these sectors' challenges. Adopting SARs in a human-orientated sector, such as that of health and social care, requires the acceptance of them by the potential users. Part of our motivation is to provide the existing evidence that explains the public's attitudes (positive and negative) and fears about SARs and other AI devices. We believe that this book will provide enough knowledge, primarily to health and social care workers as well as other individuals who wish to be informed, on key issues, in a pragmatic and accessible way.

In this brief introduction, we wish to provide the reader with a position statement regarding our stance about our views of AI technologies, specifically SARs in the health and social care practice. We believe that the current enthusiasm about these developments is often, but unintentionally, exaggerated. The published literature, the mass and social media often give the impression that research in progress, or the use of an AI prototype in trials and evaluations, indicate their imminent market availability for purchasing and deployment. For example, you will read in this book about the various robotic devices used during pandemics such as the COVID-19, or other major health disasters such as the Ebola epidemic. In this book, we took care to emphasize that even though we have described the robots or the platforms used, these were often experimental and most of them have not been made available for wider use. We believe that the production of a purchasable socially assistive, preferably culturally competent robot, meeting all the safety and other international regulation standards, that is widely available for deployment, does not represent the current reality.

As mentioned above, the reader will find references to the CARESSES project throughout this book. The authors were among a multidisciplinary team of European and Japanese scientists who conducted this award-winning EU-Japanese funded project during 2017—20. The acronym "CARESSES" stands for Culture-Aware Robots and Environmental Sensor Systems for Elderly Support, whose goal was to design the first care robots that can adapt the way they behave and speak, to the culture of the person they assist.

Finally, it is important to note that the reader will encounter different writing styles in this book. The book honors the differences in the included topics, which ranged from very technical to very philosophical. Whatever the differences in style, the authors endeavored to provide content that the reader will find interesting, easy to read, accurate, authentic, visually pleasing, and stimulating.

1.2 The fourth industrial revolution

1.2.1 What is the fourth industrial revolution and how it is affecting human societies

In 1956, the scientist John McCarthy coined "AI" (Artificial Intelligence) as "the science and engineering of making intelligent machines." In 2011, the term "Industrie 4.0" was used by a German project which promoted the computerization of manufacturing. In 2015, Klaus Schwab introduced the phrase "Fourth Industrial Revolution" in an article published by the magazine "Foreign Affairs," titled "The Fourth Industrial Revolution. What it Means and How to Respond." https://www.foreignaffairs.com/articles/2015-12-12/fourth-industrial-revolution.

Today, the 4IR refers to the ongoing automation of traditional manufacturing and industrial practices, using many technologies, such as machine learning and data science, to increasingly autonomous and intelligent systems.

According to Schwab (2016), the 4IR began at the turn of this century, building on the digital revolution. This new era is already changing how we live, work, and communicate. It is reshaping all aspects of government, such as education, health care, and commerce. It can change our relationships, our opportunities, and our identities as it changes the physical and virtual worlds we inhabit and even, in some cases, our bodies. In the future, it can also change the things we value and the way we value them.

The 4IR is enabling us to live longer due to advances in medicine and better living conditions. The United Nation's Department of Economic and Social Affairs report "World Population Prospects 2019" predicted that the population will expand from 7.2 billion in 2019 to 9.8 billion by 2050. The report also predicted that by 2050 there will be 2.1 billion adults over the age of 60, and that the number of older adults will be higher than children under 16 for the first time in history. https://population.un.org/wpp/.

As a result of the advances in technology, societies and governments need to rethink jobs, careers, health, and education systems to name but a few challenges. We are also now beginning to experience living in super diverse societies which require understanding, sensitivity, acceptance, transcultural communication, and transcultural ethics, if we are to ensure that we do not only live longer but we have fulfilling lives.

We cannot stop demographic nor technological change from happening. But we can and we should try to ensure that both changes can be positive and for the benefit of humankind. Schwab (2016) urges us to work together to shape a future for all by putting people first, empowering them and constantly reminding ourselves that all these new technologies are first and foremost tools by people for people.

1.2.2 How is health care and nursing responding to the challenges of the fourth industrial revolution

The 4IR is now rapidly changing health and social care, with many robots and other AI devices being trialled or deployed in these domains.

The recent EU Parliament report "Opportunities of Artificial Intelligence" (Eager et al., 2020) listed the following health related AI opportunities:

- The acceleration of new drug identification and development, as well as repurposing of existing drugs;

- augmentations and improvements in diagnosis and treatment;
- improvements in fetal health;
- prediction and monitoring epidemics and chronic diseases;
- improvements in the provision of primary healthcare services; and,
- enhancements in medical research and drug discovery.

In addition, the report refers to the benefits and opportunities of AI which had also been evident in tackling the COVID-19 crisis, with AI technologies and tools used to understand the virus, accelerate medical research, detect and diagnose the virus, predict the virus' evolution and spread, providing personalized information and learning, and monitoring recovery.

At the 2019 conference of the Royal College of Nursing (RCN) delegates took part in a debate about the potential role of robots in health and social care (https://www.rcn.org.uk/magazines/bulletin/2018/may/robots-in-health-and-social-care RCN conference debate, 2019).

It was stated that robots are already serving various tasks in the field of medicine and surgery. AI and robotics are already present in numerous health contexts, carrying out tasks ranging from delivering behavioral training for people with learning disabilities, facilitating rehabilitation exercises, and providing reminders to eat or take medication. The conference asserted that robots are poised to become one of the most important innovations of this century and have the potential to fill identified gaps in current health provision.

Specific examples of how robots are being used were given by the delegates, such as the Robocat that was ideally designed to provide company for lonely, frail, and elderly patients as well as reminding them to eat their meals, take their medication on time and locate lost items such as spectacles. However, the conference questioned the level of its success in implementing these tasks. Another example was the Hybrid Assistive Limb, a wearable appliance that allows poststroke patients to exercise without the need for environmental support during rehabilitation. Reference was also made to NAO, a programmable humanoid robot with the objective to support a number of different human/robot interaction tasks that may improve the medical conditions of patients in hospital and home care environments. It was reported that small robots were also used to improve the social and communication skills of autistic children, as well as improving the well-being of children having bone marrow transplants, while confined alone in an immuno-compromised state.

During the debate, speakers shared their views regarding the challenges posed by robots in care settings, such as safety, data protection, staff and patient acceptance, reliability, appropriate personalization, and the potential for the creation of health inequalities.

The safety issues are very prevalent in the nursing literature. In particular, the concerns about the possibility for robot hardware to be hacked, which could result in sensitive data being held to ransom or, even worse, patients being harmed as a result. Other ethical considerations will undoubtedly become more apparent as usage increases. Nursing literature also suggests that despite the useful advancements in robotics and AI, robotic assistance should not replace health care professionals. One of the delegates at the RCN conference urged the audience to define, refine, and protect the unique selling point of human contact while still being able to benefit from changing technologies. Another raised the important issue of the nursing need to prepare and look into how it is going to shift as a profession to keep up with these changes.

In 2019 The long-awaited Topol report was published. The report was commissioned by Health Education England. https://www.hee.nhs.uk/our-work/topol-review.

Titled "Preparing the healthcare workforce to deliver the digital future" the report suggested that the healthcare landscape in the UK is changing, as is the workforce. The NHS staff will need to have digital skills and digital literacy in order to be able to deal with new ways of working. Values of patient-centered care will need to be central to these efforts. Continuous investment in specialist skills, as well as appropriate leadership and planning will be needed to achieve the outcomes required to deal with the changes brought about by the 4IR.

In particular the Topol report recommended urgent action that:

- Employers must ensure that support for staff to develop and enhance digital literacy is built into training programs, career pathways and placements.
- Future healthcare professionals also need to understand the possibilities of digital healthcare technologies and the ethical and patient safety considerations.
- Education providers should ensure genomics, data analytics, and AI are prominent in undergraduate curricula for healthcare professionals.
- Professional, Statutory, and Regulatory Bodies and practitioners need to identify the knowledge, skills, professional attributes, and behaviors needed for healthcare graduates to work in a technologically enabled service and then work with educators to redesign the curricula for this purpose.
- Education providers should both offer opportunities for healthcare students to intercalate in areas such as engineering or computer science, and equally attract graduates in these areas to begin a career in health, to create and implement technological solutions that improve care and productivity in the NHS.

The European Commission's report titled "National strategies on artificial intelligence: A European perspective" was also published in 2019. https://knowledge4policy.ec.europa.eu/ai-watch/united-kingdom-ai-strategy-report_en.

It too emphasizes the key relevance of policies on formal education and training, reskilling and upskilling opportunities, and networking between academia, industry, and the public sector.

To conclude the first part of the chapter, the sources used to explore the changes and challenges brought about by the technological developments stimulated by the 4IR, the following points are provided:

- Health and social care sector must engage in the debate and the developments of 4G (now 5G) technologies;
- Intelligent robots will never replace human carers but can assist them and enable them to be even more caring and culturally competent and compassionate;
- Professional healthcare education (particularly nursing) must urgently review their curricula and start planning and developing learning which prepares the workforce to deal with the changes and challenges brought about by the 4IR, the decreasing pool of healthcare staff, and the huge demographic challenges.

> **Key points**
> - The 4IR is impacting on our lifestyles, our values and our identities
> - The 4IR is enabling us to live longer
> - The 4IR is rapidly changing health and social care
> - Health and social care workers need to be urgently trained to be able to deal with the 4IR changes

1.3 The importance of cultural competence and the need for culturally competent socially assistive robots

The key message of this book is that culture is not only an undeniable foundation of humanity, it is also an essential part of every individual, group, and nation. Human beings share many cultural values and beliefs but crucially the way they interpret, enact, experience, and prioritize these values and beliefs, is unique to each individual, group, and nation. For example, most humans value life, love, family, health, justice, and so on. However, the way we understand and express love, life, health, etc. will differ to some degree. This uniqueness defines and explains our personal cultural identity. The concept of cultural identity is considered to be a fundamental symbol of a person's existence and sense of self. It is expected that our cultural identity is respected, as to ignore it, or even worse to be hostile to it, would violate our personal integrity and human rights.

1.3.1 Definition and need for cultural competence in health, social, and robotic care

Understanding the significance of culture and cultural identity is essential for the development of cultural competence, especially in relation to health and social care. Papadopoulos (2006, pp. 11, 2018:1) defined cultural competence as "the process one goes through in order to continuously develop and refine their capacity to provide effective health [and social] care, taking into consideration people's cultural beliefs, behaviors, and needs." Although the notion of cultural competence has been around since the middle of the 20th century, it is only recently that this has become mainstream, not only in health and social care but in many other domains such as commerce, education, the justice system, environment, hospitality, etc. Closely linked to the notion of cultural competence are racism and inequalities worldwide, which have highlighted the suffering that can result from ignorance of cultural differences at personal, local, national and international levels. It is fair to say that many international organizations, such as the United Nations (UN), the UN Educational, Scientific and Cultural Organization, the World Health Organization, the European Union (EU), and so on, have produced policies and strategies which promote cultural competence.

There is now a huge corpus of published literature by researchers and practitioners in health and social care which provide evidence of the benefits of having a culturally competent organization and workforce. Among the benefits, researchers list the following: (a) higher levels of adherence to prescribed therapies, due to culturally competent treatment plans (McQuaid & Landier, 2018); (b) higher levels of satisfaction with care received, due to culturally sensitive communication and care delivery (Brunett & Shingles, 2018; Govere & Govere, 2016; Tucker et al., 2011); (c) fewer complaints as patients reported being listened to and had their cultural needs responded to (Brooks et al., 2019); (d) improvements to access of care and reduction in health disparities (White et al., 2019), (e) strengthened patient safety (Brach et al., 2019).

Echoing the above benefits, Dr. Jose Leon, in an article entitled "Older Adults and Cultural Competency," published on the website of the National Center for Health and the Aging, summarized the key reasons why cultural competence is important for the growing aging populations of the United States of America.

Cultural competence is

1. Expanding quality and effectiveness of care through addressing the patient's unique sociocultural experience and language needs.
2. Improving health outcomes and well-being through culturally competent care that promotes the identification of individual needs which are subsequently appropriately responded to.
3. Increasing the effectiveness of the older patient-provider communications which results in less suffering and fewer medication errors.
4. Expanding provider understanding of patients' beliefs, culture, and social values thus enabling the provision of quality care to a diverse population.
5. Fostering mutual respect and shared-decision making as providers work with patients to select treatments that take into account patients' health-related values, and treatment preferences.
6. Strengthening patient and provider satisfaction as culturally competent services have the potential to improve health outcomes, increase the efficiency of clinical and support staff, and result in greater client satisfaction. https://www.healthandtheaging.org/older-adults-and-cultural-competency

In 2014, the seminal Lancet Commission on Culture and Health was published (Napier et al., 2014). The report assessed why cultural competence matters in health, the nature of cultural competence (how people communicate across cultural divides), the adverse effects of health inequality (how culture can unequally limit opportunities to become healthier), the structure and function of communities of care (how collective activities around health either succeed or fail), and the social conditions that undermine or improve human wellbeing (how personal health relates to the presence or absence of social trust). Following a lengthy and detailed critical analysis of all concepts and issues linked to cultural competence, the authors summarized their findings under the following 12 themes, in need of immediate attention:

1. Medicine [healthcare services] should accommodate the cultural construction of well-being
2. Culture should be better defined
3. Culture should not be neglected in health and healthcare provision

4. Culture should become central to care practices
5. Clinical cultures should be reshaped
6. People who are not healthy should be recapacitated within the culture of biomedicine
7. Agency should be better understood with respect to culture
8. Training cultures should be better understood
9. Competence should be reconsidered across all cultures and systems of care
10. Exported and imported practices and services should be aligned with local cultural meaning
11. Building of trust in health care should be prioritized as a cultural value
12. New models of well-being and care should be identified and nourished across cultures.

The authors of the Lancet Commission believed that these points were imperative to the advancement of health worldwide and were the greatest challenges for health.

The difficulties in recruiting, training, and retaining health and social care staff have been debated for a number of years. In order to address the workforce challenges as well as the growing number of old and very old people, new solutions are being searched for and proposed. Digital, robotic, and artificial intelligent technologies have been gradually positioning themselves as useful solutions which could respond to these challenges.

In 2017, the CARESSES European-Japanese consortium commenced the process of developing the first culturally competent SAR (CCSAR). The team strongly believed that cultural competence would be as important to a robot carer/companion as it is to a human carer. The evidence provided above regarding the need and benefits of a culturally competent human carer should also apply in principle to a personal assistive robot. Bruno et al. (2017) stated that today, it is technically conceivable to build robots that reliably accomplish basic assistive services. However, the services provided by these robots are rigid and invariant with respect to the place, person, and culture. The consortium believed that if service robots are to be accepted in the real world by real people, they must take into account the cultural identity of their users in deciding how to provide their services.

1.3.2 Components of cultural competence

In the previous section, the concept of culture and its unequivocal link to health was discussed. In this section, the components or constructs of cultural competence taken from the Papadopoulos model of transcultural nursing and cultural competence will be defined (Papadopoulos 2006, pp. 10–21). These definitions informed and guided the CARESSES project in its quest to develop the first culturally competent robot.

Cultural awareness. Cultural awareness is the degree of awareness we have about our own cultural background and cultural identity. This helps us to understand the importance of our cultural heritage and that of others and makes us appreciate the dangers of ethnocentricity and stereotyping. Cultural awareness is the first key construct of the model referred to above, and the first step for the development of cultural competence.

Cultural knowledge. Meaningful contact with people from different ethnic/cultural groups can enhance knowledge around their health beliefs and behaviors, as well as raise understanding around the problems they may face such as health inequalities, marginalization, exclusion, and stereotyping. This is the second of the four key constructs of the model.

Cultural sensitivity. Cultural sensitivity, the third key construct, entails the crucial development of appropriate interpersonal relationships. Relationships involve trust, acceptance, compassion and respect, as well as facilitation and negotiation. Culturally sensitive communication is of immense importance in all the above processes.

Cultural competence. This has already been defined above. However, it is useful to provide this complementary definition, about the final key construct and stage of a process leading to cultural competence. The capacity to provide effective care taking into consideration people's cultural beliefs, behaviors, and needs is the result of knowledge, attitudes, and skills which one acquires during her/his personal and professional life and to which she/he is constantly adding. The achievement of cultural competence requires the synthesis of previously gained awareness, knowledge, and sensitivity, and their application in the assessment of clients' needs, and the subsequent care diagnosis and care giving.

It is important to add that a culturally competent practitioner is one that in addition to the knowledge, attitudes. and skills mentioned is willing and able to address and challenge prejudice, discrimination, and health inequalities. The Papadopoulos theory (2006) places equal importance on the impact of family, group, societal, and institutional structures which can be both enabling and disabling to people's health and well-being. Culture and structure are the two sides of the same coin and must therefore be given equal consideration. For example, healthcare policies and systems designed by people who are culturally incompetent can be unintentionally discriminating thus resulting in health inequalities.

Key points

- Culturally competent care and services are crucial in the 21st century multicultural societies
- AI technologies, especially SARs should be culturally competent in order to increase their acceptance
- Health and social care workers need to be reassured about the security of their jobs and if necessary be reskilled and upskilled

---

1.3.3 Definition of culturally competent socially assistive robots

A review of the literature on personal, social and assistive robots revealed that the issue of cultural competence has been largely underaddressed, and much work is still needed to pave the way to culturally competent robots. The pioneering CARESSES project was set up to respond to this challenge. This book draws heavily from the CARESSES research to provide its thinking, processes, guidelines, and final results, all of which constitute the first map in this robotics/AI domain that can help future researchers to expand the work on culturally competent robotics and AI devices. The CARESSES project has added cultural competence to the glossary of the social robotics discipline while managing to amplify the debate about the usefulness, capabilities, ethics, acceptability, effectiveness, and efficacy of AI SARs. The

CARESSES team also believes that cultural competence will allow SARs to increase their acceptance by being more sensitive to their users' needs, customs, and lifestyles, thus having a greater impact on the quality of users' lives.

I have defined a CCSAR as a robot that has knowledge of the culture-generic characteristics of its user, while being able to adapt its behavior to gain and use culture-specific knowledge in order to respond sensitively to the users' needs, preferences, and ways of living. To achieve this, the robot should be aware of factors such as the age, education, family structure, religion, and cultural heritage of the user (cultural awareness). In addition to the robot's programmed culture-generic knowledge, the robot should be able to assess the needs of the user to obtain culture-specific information. The process of the robot's assessment will be described in Chapter 6 and its implementation in an Artificial Intelligence program in Chapters 8 and 9. If the user has a health problem the robot should take into consideration the user's cultural values, beliefs, and attitudes about health and illness, as well as their selfcare practices (cultural knowledge). The robot should be sensitive about the user's attributes like language, accent, interpersonal skills, communication skills, ability to trust others, and to be compassionate to others (cultural sensitivity).

1.4 The underpinning values, transcultural ethics, and cultural dimensions for culturally competent robots

This section will present some of the underpinning values, transcultural ethics, and cultural dimensions for culturally competent robots which researchers need to bear in mind, particularly in the early stages of their work. Developing culturally competent AI/robotic devices requires a multidisciplinary and possibly a multinational effort. Such work is complex and requires a long-term commitment. It is of outmost importance that the project leader/s enable the team members to reflect on their own individual cultural values and learn about the cultural values of the other members. The team must establish a common value platform while at the same time respecting the diversity of values within the team. The values, ethical principles, and cultural dimensions described below are offered as guidance for the team working relationships (human to human), and for their installation in their products.

1.4.1 Human values and how these relate to SARs

Culture. All human beings are cultural beings. Culture is a human construct and in itself a human value. It represents the embodiment of the shared way of life of a group of people that includes beliefs, values, ideas, language, communication, norms, and visibly expressed artifacts such as customs, art, music, clothing, food, and etiquette. Culture influences individuals' lifestyles, personal identity, and their relationship with others, both within and outside their culture. Cultures are dynamic and ever changing as individuals are influenced by, and influence their culture, by different degrees.

Cultural identity. Identity refers to an image with which one associates and projects oneself. Cultural identity is important for people's sense of self and how they relate to others. When a nation has a cultural identity, it does not mean that it is uniform. Identifying with a particular culture gives people feelings of belonging and security.

Transcultural. Grounded in one's own culture but having the culture-generic and culture-specific skills to be able to live, interact, and work effectively in a multicultural environment.

Transcultural Health and Nursing. The study and research of cultural diversities and similarities in health and illness as well as their underpinning societal and organizational structures, in order to understand current practice and to contribute to its future development in a culturally responsive way. Transcultural nursing requires a commitment for the promotion of antioppressive, antidiscriminatory practices.

Diversity. Valuing diversity means being respectful and responsive to a wide range of people unlike oneself, according to any number of distinctions: race, gender, class, native language, national origin, physical ability, age, sexual orientation, religion, professional experience, personal preferences, and work style.

Caring/Nursing. Caring is an activity that responds to the uniqueness of individuals in a culturally sensitive and compassionate way through the use of therapeutic communication. Nursing is a learned activity aiming at providing care to individuals in culturally competent way.

Health/Well-being. Health refers to the state of well-being that is culturally defined and practiced. It reflects the ability of individuals (or groups) to perform their daily roles and activities, in culturally expressed and beneficial ways.

Illness. Illness refers to an unwanted condition that is culturally defined and culturally responded to.

Culturally Competent Compassion. The human quality of understanding the suffering of others and wanting to do something about it using culturally appropriate and acceptable caring interventions which take into consideration the cultural backgrounds of both the receiver and the giver of compassion as well as the context of this exchange.

Autonomy. To govern oneself, to be directed by considerations, desires, conditions, and characteristics that are not simply imposed externally upon one, but are part of what can be considered one's authentic self. (Stanford Encyclopedia of Philosophy. https://tinyurl.com/6b2aswk6).

Confidentiality. In health and social care, confidentiality is about privacy and respecting someone's wishes. It is also about the strict adherence to the professional codes and to any laws which protect the privacy of the individual.

Justice. Linked to equality, ethics, religion, and law, justice is a very complex concept or virtue, which in its broadest sense is the principle that people receive that which they deserve. The application of justice may differ between cultures.

1.4.2 Transcultural ethical principles

The principles of transcultural ethics (TE) are

(a) TE recognize the challenging nature of everyday multicultural ethical issues;
(b) TE acknowledge the limitations of approaches to ethics which focus solely on abstract thinking ignoring contexts (cultural, situational, historical);
(c) TE draw attention to the complexity of diverse human experience and relationships;
(d) TE accept that there is much uncertainty and unpredictability in everyday life and that humans are fallible; and,
(e) TE celebrate the values of moral diversity.

(Papadopoulos, 2006, pp. 65–84).

TE also acknowledges the following universal ethical principles as they relate to SARs. These principles are further expanded upon in relation to culturally competent SARs in Chapter 4:

- Informed consent for all requests of participation, involvement or in being the recipient of interventions which may affect one's physical, psychological, social, cultural, cognitive, and spiritual well-being.
- Privacy: AI sensors used in smart devices will not compromise a person's privacy.
- Harm: The robot will not harm the client in any way.
- Confidentiality: Any data collected by a robot and/or an AI device will be stored according to data protection laws and be safe, in order to avoid compromising the client's confidentiality.

1.4.3 Hofstede's cultural dimensions

In the 1970s, the social psychologist Geert Hofstede got access to a large survey database about values and related sentiments of people in over 50 countries around the world. After lengthy and complex statistical analyses, he identified and defined four dimensions of culture; in later years and after more research, he added two more dimensions (Hofstede, 2011).

Hofstede defined culture as "Culture is the collective programming of the mind that distinguishes the members of one group or category of people from others" (Hofstede, 1991, p. 5).

His framework is used extensively by researchers across the world to understand the cultural differences across countries as well as the effects of a society's culture on the values of its members, and how these values relate to behavior. The six cultural dimensions are

1.4.3.1 Power distance

Power distance refers to the extent to which inequality and power are tolerated.

1.4.3.2 Individualism versus collectivism

Individualism indicates that there is a greater importance placed on attaining personal goals. Collectivism indicates that there is a greater importance placed on the goals and well-being of the group.

1.4.3.3 Uncertainty avoidance

The uncertainty avoidance is the extent to which uncertainty and ambiguity are tolerated.
A high uncertainty avoidance indicates a low tolerance for uncertainty, ambiguity, and risk-taking while a low uncertainty avoidance indicates a high tolerance for uncertainty, ambiguity, and risk-taking.

1.4.3.4 Masculinity versus femininity

The masculinity/femininity dimension considers the preference of society for achievement, attitude toward sexuality equality, behavior, etc. Masculinity characteristics are distinct gender roles, assertiveness, and emphasis on material achievements and wealth-building. Femininity characteristics include fluid gender roles, modesty, nurturing, and quality of life.

1.4.3.5 Long-term orientation versus short-term orientation

The long-term orientation/short-term orientation is the extent to which society views its time horizon. Long-term orientation focuses on the future and involves delaying short-term success or gratification, in order to achieve long-term success. Short-term orientation focuses on the near future, involves delivering short-term success or gratification, and places a stronger emphasis on the present than the future.

1.4.3.6 Indulgence versus restraint

The indulgence/restraint dimension deals with the extent and tendency for a society to fulfill its desires. Indulgence indicates that a society allows relatively free gratification related to enjoying life and having fun. Restraint indicates that a society suppresses gratification of needs and regulates it through social norms.

1.5 Applying values, principles, definitions, components, and dimensions

The case study presented here provides an example of a woman who moved, at a young age, from a very small and strongly collectivist country to a large and predominantly individualist one. It illustrates some of her values, such as her strong family orientation, the expectations she has about her family, her dietary and work habits, and so on. The table that follows Mrs. Christou's story provides a detailed analysis of how she and a humanoid SAR are dealing with their early encounters. In the first column of the table, the dialogue between Mrs. Christou and the robot is provided. The second column gives details about the skills which the robot is using, while the third column explains the culture specific components of the encounter, using the main constructs of the Papadopoulos framework. Finally, the fourth column locates the dialog with the notion of the culture-generic elements of the encounter, using the Hofstede's cultural dimensions.

1.6 Case study: Mrs. Christou story

Mrs. Christou is a 75-year-old Greek Cypriot who migrated to the UK when she was 20 years old from a small village in Cyprus. She joined her brother who owned a large fish and chip shop where she worked until she retired. She married and had five children, four sons and one daughter. Her husband, also a first-generation Greek Cypriot, died soon after the birth of their youngest child. Mrs. Christou recently moved in sheltered housing when her brother sold the fish and chip shop and the flat above it, where she had been living since arriving from Cyprus. A year previously she suffered a stroke which had left her with a slight weakness on one side of her body and with slight memory problems. She was hoping to go and live with one of her children but none of the four daughters-in-law agreed to that. Since her own daughter has three young children and works full time, Mrs. Christou reluctantly agreed to move into sheltered housing. She feels very sad that having worked hard to bring her children up and to give them a good education, they were not able to look after her in her old age. Since arriving at her new accommodation, Mrs. Christou has had one fall, but luckily she did not break any bones. She is a stubborn woman who insists she can take care of herself. "I want to cook my Greek food and make my Greek coffee as I have always done" she says proudly. However, she often forgets to take her tablets; she also forgets where she puts her things and spends hours looking for them. She admits to feeling lonely and sad as she always had lots of people to talk to before moving to the sheltered home. When she was offered the opportunity to have a robot which could talk to her and keep her company, she was happy to accept it, although a bit apprehensive. "I'll treat it like one of my grandchildren" she declared.

Scenario: Mrs Maria Christou	Robot skills	Culture-specific	Culture-generic
First encounter—Introductions ROBOT: Hello Mrs. Christou (speaks with a female voice, gives her a Robot's hug) Mrs. Christou (M): Hello (smiles and hugs the robot) ROBOT: Would you prefer me to call you Maria? M: No. I prefer you to call me Kyria (Greek for Mrs.) Maria. That's how one calls an older woman in Cyprus. What is your name? ROBOT: I don't have a name yet. Would you like to give me a name? M: I will call you Sofia after my mother, God rest her soul (CROSSES HERSELF). S: Thank you. I like it. I am honored to be called after your mother. I have been given a map of your house. Can I go round and familiarize myself with it? M: Yes, go ahead. I hope you have a better memory than mine!	**SPEAKING** (asking and responding to simple questions) **MOVING** (moves hands, walks, hugs) **SPEAKING** (Catching key words and reacting) **MEMORISING** (compares prestored information to new specific information which it stores)	*Cultural awareness* The Robot is learning about Mrs. C's personal characteristics, her cultural background and cultural identity. She expects the robot to treat her older age status with some respect. This is why she asks the robot to call her Kyria Maria not just Maria. *Cultural awareness* She names the Robot after her mother a common custom used to name one's children. Mrs. M. shows her respect to the dead through signs of her religiosity.	**POWER DISTANCE (PD)** *(Although there are no Hofstede scores for Cyprus the Greek Cypriot culture is very similar to that of Greece, thus the its scores have been used)* Greece's PD score is 60 which means that hierarchy should be respected and some inequalities are to be expected and accepted.
Home and family SOFIA RETURNS AFTER THREE MINUTES M. How do you like my home Sofia? You see I have all the things I need. I brought most of them from my flat. S. This is a nice place you have here. Do you have a family?	**MOVING** (walks) **MEMORIZING** (building and storing a map of the house) **SPEAKING** (asking and responding to simple questions)	*Cultural knowledge* Kyria Maria is seeking feedback and praise from Sofia regarding her home and provides information about her family as well as her role within the family. Sofia learns about the position of the Greek	**MASCULINITY** At score of 57 Greece is a medium ranking Masculine society—success oriented and driven. Men consider it a personal honor to take care of their family. In

1.6 Case study: Mrs. Christou story

—cont'd

Scenario: Mrs Maria Christou	Robot skills	Culture-specific	Culture-generic
M: Yes, I have four sons and a daughter. They are all married. Giorgos is the oldest and he is married to Eleni. They have two sons. Next is Petros who is married to Karen; she is English. They have one son and one daughter. (CONTINUES TALKING BY PROVIDING DETAILS ABOUT FAMILY MEMBERS). I love my children and grandchildren very much! both my granddaughters are named Maria, and one of my grandsons is named Marios! (BIG PROUD SMILE) can you see all their photographs on the sideboard? I also have a brother who is older than me, and married. May God look after them and give them many more years of life (SHE CROSSES HERSELF). We are a close family. S: It must be nice to have such a big family. M: Yes it is Sofia. You will meet some of them I am sure, as most days one of them will visit me. They want to make sure that I have everything I need and I am not too lonely. Every Sunday one of my children will take me to their home for lunch and maybe for a "peripato" (an outing) or to church.	**MEMORIZING** (compares pre-stored information to new specific information which it stores)	women of Kyria Maria's age. She grew up in a male dominated society. Although adopting some of the UK's ways of life, she was able to work with her brother, who supported her so that she could care for the children and have a clean and tidy home. The robot (Sofia) matches this with prestored knowledge about the names of her children and the culture-generic knowledge about the position of Greek Cypriot women of her age. *Cultural knowledge* Kyria Maria likes to talk about her family, providing personal details. Family is the most important thing to her and even though she lives on her own now, she expects to be involved in the lives of her children and grandchildren. The robot understands this, asks for details and memorizes all of them.	Collectivistic and Masculine cultures, the success of a member of a family gives social value to the whole in-group. **COLLECTIVISM** At a score of 35 Greece is a collectivist culture, "we" defined, which means that people from birth onwards are integrated into the strong, cohesive in-group (especially represented by the extended family; including uncles, aunts, grandparents and cousins) which continues protecting its members in exchange for loyalty.
Finding out about Mrs. M's health S: How do you feel today Kyria Maria? M: I feel OK Sofia but it's time for my tablets. S: What are the tablets for? M: For my diabetes. S: How often do you take them? M: Twice a day: Morning, and evening. But sometimes I forget to take them or I just miss one on purpose. I don't think I really need so many tablets. S: OK. I Will remind you!	**MEMORIZING** (compares prestored information to new specific information which it stores) **SPEAKING** (catching key words and reacting)	*Cultural knowledge* The robot learns that Kyria Maria values her health and partly adheres to her medical regime. The robot requires information about Kyria Maria's health from her carers	

(Continued)

—cont'd

Scenario: Mrs Maria Christou	Robot skills	Culture-specific	Culture-generic
Empowering S: Are you on a diabetic diet? M: Yes, but I don't think I need to be. My Greek diet doesn't have much sugar. I eat lots of salads and boiled vegetables, beans, peas, lentils … It's the fish and chips I used to eat all the years I worked in the fish and chips shop which gave me the diabetes. But I don't eat them anymore. S: Greek food is great, but perhaps you should follow the specific diet that the doctor recommended, don't you think so? (TOUCHES Mrs. M'S HANDS) M: No, because this diet is for English people. S: How about asking your daughter's opinion about this? (LEANS HEAD FORWARDS) M: Ok, let's see what she says. S: I can call her if you want. M: No, she is coming to see me tomorrow. But enough about diets and tablets. We only live once and at my age, I don't have to be too careful. Let me cheer you up by singing you a nice Greek song my mother used to sing many, many years ago. (STARTS SINGING).	**SPEAKING** (asking for yes/no confirmation) **SPEAKING** (catching key words and reacting) **PLANNING** (a sequence of actions; empowering)	**Cultural knowledge** Sofia is learning about what it means to Kyria Maria to have diabetes. The robot is learning about her eating habits, her strong belief in the Greek diet (almost ethnocentric), and her opinion regarding the cause of her condition (this is her explanatory model about her health problem) *Cultural sensitivity* Sofia shows sensitivity and respect to Kyria Maria's views by not contradicting them or correcting them. It is respectful of the fact that these are Mrs. M's cultural habits and is sensitive in the ways of encouragement by suggesting to ask a family member that Mrs M trusts.	**LONG TERM ORIENTATION** This dimension describes how every society has to maintain some links with its own past while dealing with the challenges of the present and future. Greece has an intermediate score of 45 which indicates a preference toward time-honored traditions and norms while also taking into consideration the changes in society. **INDULGENCE – RESTRAINT** At an intermediate score of 50, Greece has no clear preference between indulgence and restraint.

1.7 What you will find in this book

Chapter 2 makes the reader aware of the complexity of building intelligent robots with the ambition of clarifying common misconceptions about Artificial Intelligence. Starting from the basics of computer programming explained simply, the chapter shows that Artificial Intelligence (AI) is nothing more than a computer program designed in such a way to address the diversity of situations that a robot may encounter when interacting with people and the environment. Specifically, the concept of "robustness" of a program is introduced, clarifying why robotic researchers aim to design robust AI programs: that is, robot programs that work well in almost all real-world situations and not only under well-specified and favorable conditions. Next, two popular approaches in the literature to enable robots to deal with the complexity of the environment are described and commented on. Finally, the chapter discusses why making a robot capable of operating reliably in a world that is inherently noisy and dynamic is so hard, and any attempt to build such a robot might incur the risk of frustrating people's expectations.

Chapter 3 draws content from three literature reviews to provide an overview of mainly the different types of humanoid and animal-like robots used in healthcare settings. The factors that influence the acceptance of SARs by health and social care potential and actual users, family caregivers and healthcare professionals will be discussed with a special emphasis on culture. In addition, the most current evidence on the views of healthcare professionals and the factors that impact on the implementation of these robots in health and social care environments will be presented.

Chapter 4 examines some of the key ethical considerations regarding the roll-out and implementation of SARs in care settings. The chapter provides readers with an overview of some of the main concerns that have emerged in the literature on ethics in SAR along with opportunities to reflect on the ethical challenges associated with the use of robots in the care of older adults. This includes issues of autonomy, dignity, informed consent, privacy and data protection, attachment and deception, false expectations, health inequalities, safety, responsibility and labor replacement, and the implications of such issues for care recipients and caregivers.

Chapter 5 will start by introducing the hottest research topics in the Social Robotics field. The reader will understand why Social Robotics is necessarily multidisciplinary, as confirmed by the most prominent international publications ranging from Computer Science to Psychology, from Philosophy to Human-Robot Interaction. Next, we will briefly overview how people's expectations concerning social robots have been forged by books and, most of all, movies. In doing so, we will provide our opinion about what social robots are currently missing to "invade our world." Finally, this chapter's last and longest part will introduce the EU-Japan CARESSES (Culture-Aware Robots and Environment Sensor Systems for Elderly Support) project. We will use the project as a case study to provide the reader with a rough idea of the challenges faced by any innovative, interdisciplinary research project aiming to develop SARs. Also, CARESSES will constitute a reference for the following chapters, in which we will formulate hypotheses and propose our solutions to make robots capable of exhibiting culturally competent behavior.

Chapter 6 describes in detail the processes involved from the development of stories leading to the production of scenarios that would lead to the eventual construction of the guidelines for a culturally competent, AI, SAR. The authors used a systematic approach, involving multiple layers for developing the initial stories and the scenarios.

Chapter 7 describes in detail the processes involved from the development of theories and tools which were used to collect and analyze data to help the production of and evaluation of the interim and final guidelines. The chapter introduces the ADORE model which enables the robot to capture culture-specific information about the user thus avoiding the use of stereotypical culture-generic information. The Cultural Iceberg Trigger theory is also introduced and explained. This theory enables the researchers to explore and capture the enactment of behaviors which represent the human subconscious cultural values, beliefs and perceptions. Both theories were used to develop tools for data collection and analysis of an observation study which is discussed in this chapter. The construction and content of the guidelines is discussed, and examples of the guidelines are provided. The chapter concludes with a description of the evaluation processes used to inform any necessary refinement of the guidelines and prepare the robot for the final trial with human users conducted in care homes for older people (see Chapter 10).

Chapter 8 introduces cultural knowledge representation: how to encode the knowledge required to interact appropriately with people who belong to different cultures in a computer program. First, a review is provided of the most popular solutions adopted by roboticists to encode knowledge in a formalism that robots can automatically process. Second, a discussion follows on how guidelines provided by experts in Transcultural Nursing can be translated into a computer Ontology and how Artificial Intelligence programs can automatically process cultural knowledge to produce an engaging verbal interaction with people. Third, we show how tools for probabilistic reasoning may be used to learn more about a person during the interaction to cope with individual differences and avoid stereotyped representations of people's cultures.

Chapter 9 addresses the problem of producing fully autonomous, intelligent robots: that is, robots equipped with sensors, actuators, and intelligent programs allowing them to perceive the environment, make decisions, and act without being teleoperated or following "a script." First, we provide a brief review of today's robotic technology by discussing why most robots shown in the media should be viewed as outstanding examples of "mechanics and control" that, however, are neither intelligent nor autonomous. Then, we follow the steps from creating a prototype in a research lab to deploying a robot operating 24/7 in the "real world:" we discuss the technological challenges and propose smart solutions to achieve the biggest impact with the slightest effort. Finally, we illustrate some ideas for the future.

Chapter 10 describes the final stages of the CARESSES research project which aimed to develop and evaluate a culturally competent artificial intelligent system embedded into social robots to support the wellbeing of older adults residing in long-term care settings in England and Japan. The chapter describes the aims of the trial phase of this project and the trial design including the methods used for screening, recruitment, data collection and ethical considerations. It then presents the key quantitative results of the trial pertaining to perceived cultural competence, mental and physical health-related impact, user satisfaction and attitudes. An assessment of the trial feasibility is also described as well as the trial's key methodological limitations.

Prompted by the 2020 corona virus pandemic, Chapter 11 draws evidence from research studies regarding the huge changes in the practices and methods for providing nursing, medical, and spiritual care in massively prohibitive working environments. Examples of AI and robotic devices used during the pandemic will be discussed in the spirit of constructive reflection and contemplation. The reported un-preparedness for an effective, efficient, and humane response to such major health disasters and hazards will be discussed, and suggestions for the future will be given. The training needs reported by health and social care workers will be analyzed in the light of the technological challenges staff are required to cope with.

The 12th and final chapter will stimulate debate about the future of AI social robotics and technological developments. The chapter analyses current trends and tries to guess how AI technology may develop in the near future. Technical challenges, ethical issues, regulations, and society's preparation for the proliferation of intelligent machines are discussed. Recognizing the importance of individuality and cultural identity, as well as the current concerns about the possible threats that AI robots may pose for humanity, the chapter speculates on how future AI robots could be not only efficient and complementary to humans, but through advancements in cultural competence and moral appreciation, they could help in the enhancement of humanity and protect the planet.

1.8 Conclusion

This chapter has provided brief insights into the birth of the 4IR and its huge consequences for health and social care. It has also introduced the theoretical concept and values related to cultural competence. The chapter has plotted the readers' journey through the rest of the book, in order to familiarize themselves with the key ethical and societal issues as well as the science and practices behind the developments, the implementation and the impact of the AI and robotics technologies which will continue being part of everyone's life in health and illness.

1.9 Reflective questions

- Reflect on some of the benefits and impact of the 4IR on society in general, and on your professional life in particular.
- Reflect on your values and concerns regarding AI technologies and how these affect your acceptance of such technologies in your work environment.

References

Brach, C., Hall, K. K., & Fitall, E. (2019). *Cultural competence and patient safety*. PSNet. https://psnet.ahrq.gov/perspective/cultural-competence-and-patient-safety. (Accessed 4 July 2021).

Brooks, L. A., Bloomer, M. J., & Manias, E. (2019). Culturally sensitive communication at the end-of-life in the intensive care unit: A systematic review. *Journal of Australian Critical Care, 32*(6), 516–523. https://doi.org/10.1016/j.aucc.2018.07.003

Brunett, M., & Revis Shingles, R. (2018). Does having a culturally competent health care provider affect the patients' experience or satisfaction? A critically appraised topic. *Journal of Sport Rehabilitation, 1;27*(3), 284–288. https://doi.org/10.1123/jsr.2016-0123

Bruno, B., Young Chong, N., Kamide, H., Kanoria, S., Lee, J., Lim, Y., Kumar Pandey, A., Papadopoulos, C., Papadopoulos, I., Pecora, F., Saffiotti, A., & Sgorbissa, A. (2017). Paving the way for culturally competent robots: A position paper, RO-MAN2017. In *IEEE international symposium on robot and human interactive communication, Lisbon, Portugal* (pp. 28–31). https://doi.org/10.1109/ROMAN.2017.8172357

CARESSES: The quest for a culturally aware robot (2017-2020). http://CARESSESrobot.org/en/project/.

Eager, J., Whittle, M., Smit, J., Cacciaguerra, G., Lale-Demoz, E., et al. (2020). *Opportunities of artificial intelligence. Policy department for economic, scientific and quality of life policies directorate-general for internal policies*. EU Parliament. https://www.europarl.europa.eu/RegData/etudes/STUD/2020/652713/IPOL_STU(2020)652713_EN.pdf. (Accessed 4 July 2021).

Govere, L., & Govere, E. M. (2016). How effective is cultural competence training of healthcare providers on improving patient satisfaction of minority groups? A systematic review of literature. *Worldviews on Evidence-Based Nursing, 13*(6), 402–410. https://doi.org/10.1111/wvn.12176

Hofstede, G. (1991). *Cultures and organizations. Software of the mind*. New York: McGraw-Hill.

Hofstede, G. (2011). Dimensionalizing cultures: The Hofstede model in context. *Online Readings in Psychology and Culture, 2*(1). https://doi.org/10.9707/2307-0919.1014. Online Readings in Psychology and Culture (ORPC). http://scholarworks.gvsu.edu/orpc/vol2/iss1/8. (Accessed 4 July 2021).

Leon J. (n.d.). Older Adults and Cultural Competency. The National Centre for Health and the Aging. https://www.healthandtheaging.org/older-adults-and-cultural-competency.

McQuaid, E. L., & Landier, W. (2018). Cultural issues in medication adherence: Disparities and directions. *Journal of General Internal Medicine, 33*(2), 200–206. https://doi.org/10.1007/s11606-017-4199-3

Napier, A. D., Ancarno, C., Butler, B., Calabrese, J., Chater, A., Chatterjee, H., Guesnet, F., Horne, R., Jacyna, S., Jadhav, S., Macdonald, A., Neuendorf, U., Parkhurst, A., Reynolds, R., Scambler, G., Shamdasani, S., Smith, S. Z., Stougaard-Nielsen, J., Thomson, L., … Woolf, K. (2014). Culture and health. *The Lancet Commissions, 384*(9954), 1607–1639. https://doi.org/10.1016/S0140-6736(14)61603-2

Papadopoulos, I. (Ed.). (2006). *Transcultural health and social care : Development of culturally competent practitioners*. Edinburgh: Churchill Livingstone Elsevier. ISBN 13: 978 0 443 10131 1.

Royal College of Nursing (RCN). (2019). *Conference debate on the potential role of robots in health and social care*. https://www.rcn.org.uk/magazines/bulletin/2018/may/robots-in-health-and-social-care.

Schwab, K. (2015). *The fourth industrial revolution. What it means and how to respond*. Foreign Affairs https://www.foreignaffairs.com/articles/2015-12-12/fourth-industrial-revolution.

Schwab, K. (2016). *The fourth industrial revolution: What it means, how to respond*. World Economic Forum. https://www.weforum.org/agenda/2016/01/the-fourth-industrial-revolution-what-it-means-and-how-to-respond/. (Accessed 4 July 2021).

Stanford Encyclopedia of Philosophy. Autonomy. https://tinyurl.com/6b2aswk6.

Tucker, C. M., Marsiske, M., Rice, K. G., Nielson, J. J., & Herman, K. (2011). Patient-centered culturally sensitive health care: Model testing and refinement. *Health Psychology, 30*(3), 342–350. https://doi.org/10.1037/a0022967

White, J., Plompen, T., Tao, L., Micallef, E., & Haines, T. (2019). What is needed in culturally competent healthcare systems? A qualitative exploration of culturally diverse patients and professional interpreters in an Australian healthcare setting. *BMC Public Health, 19*, 1096. https://doi.org/10.1186/s12889-019-7378-9

Further reading

European Commission. (2019). *National strategies on artificial intelligence: A European perspective*. https://knowledge4policy.ec.europa.eu/ai-watch/united-kingdom-ai-strategy-report_en. (Accessed 4 July 2021).

NHS. (2019). *The Topol review. Preparing the healthcare workforce to deliver the digital future*. Health Education England. https://www.hee.nhs.uk/our-work/topol-review.

United Nation's Department of Economic and Social Affairs. (2019). *World population Prospects 2019*. https://population.un.org/wpp/. (Accessed 4 July 2021).

CHAPTER 2

A beginner's guide to how robots work

Antonio Sgorbissa

DIBRIS Department, Università degli Studi di Genova, Genova, Italy

LEARNING OBJECTIVES

- To understand the basic principles of how a computer program works.
- To understand how an Artificially Intelligence program can be used to control an autonomous robot.
- To understand a key concept in Robotics, that is, the capability of a robot to exhibit a predictable and "robust" behavior in the presence of a world that is necessarily noisy, unpredictable, and dynamic.

2.1 Introduction

"Why can't the robot do that?"

This is one of the questions that robotic researchers are asked more frequently when showing the results of their work in public events or exhibitions. When repeatedly asked a question like this, researchers' reactions may be very varied: some of them will patiently explain that even simpler things may be complex for robots, some will just lose their temper. Try yourself and pay attention to reactions the next time when you will have the chance.

A quick answer to the question above is that robotic researchers find it more interesting to solve challenging technological problems rather than paying attention to what users would like to see and hear. In doing so, they tend to underestimate many vital factors to improve the user's experience: this is why big companies include multidisciplinary teams where psychologists, content writers, animation experts, ethicists work side by side with engineers, possibly with the involvement of end-user communities. From the point of view of a robotic researcher, the reply to the question "Why can't the robot do that?" is relatively straightforward, and it is hard for them to believe that people don't get it: the robot "can't do that" because adding new functionalities requires time for finding a solution that exhibits the desired behavior, implementing the solution as a computer program, testing the program to guarantee that it works safely and reliably. It is not possible to just "explain a robot" to do something: a human can tell another human the right way to do something because of our superior cognitive capabilities, which make us capable of learning new skills quite quickly through explanation or demonstration. On the opposite, the hard part of making robots is to embed the desired functionalities into them, which may require an incredibly high amount of resources: this is not something that can be achieved just by telling the robot the rules to behave appropriately.

However, the above is not the only possible answer. To provide a thorough response to the question "Why can't the robot do that?," it will be necessary to follow the longer path: we need to start from the basics of computer programming (hopefully, in an interesting and entertaining way). After reading the rest of this chapter, readers will have acquired the fundamental principles to understand how robots work. This will be crucial to be aware of the basic concepts and the terminology adopted throughout the book and avoid false ideas and expectations about what robots can or cannot do.

Let's put on our roboticist's hat and move forward.

2.2 Writing computer programs

In the rest of this book, we will never stop repeating that Artificial Intelligence (AI) is nothing more than a computer program, "made of the same substance as a word processor," to paraphrase Shakespeare.

A computer program is a sequence of instructions that, taken together, tell the computer what to do: instructions are executed one after the other by the so-called Central Processing Unit. Somebody suggests the metaphor that a computer program is similar to a recipe: as like as a cake recipe describes in detail all the steps that are required to prepare a cake, starting from mixing ingredients to baking the cake and then garnishing it, in the same spirit a computer program describes all the steps that are required to obtain output data (metaphorically, the cake) starting from input data (the ingredients).

However, the recipe metaphor has some limitations. To better understand, imagine a hypothetical program to compute a special kind of cake called "area of the triangle." Hopefully, everybody remembers the formula to calculate the area of a triangle as "base times height divided by two," which in computer programs is typically written using the expression "area = base*height/2." The symbols "+," "-," "*," and "/" are used for the four algebraic operations: addition, subtraction, multiplication, and division. According to the cake metaphor, one might say that the program instructs the computer to prepare the "area of the triangle cake" (yummy!) starting from the initial ingredients: "base" and "height." What makes a computer program very different from a cake recipe is that recipes typically assume that the initial ingredients should not be modified, whereas computer programs are designed to work with input data that may vary (triangles with a different base and height, in the example above). If you read in a cookbook that the pesto recipe requires basil, garlic, parmesan cheese, extra virgin oil, coarse salt, and pine nuts to be mixed in a particular order, you are usually not supposed to use the same recipe to prepare something different by doubling the quantity of oil or salt (unless you double all quantities proportionally), or switching garlic with onions or olive oil with vinegar. Adapting recipes can be done, but it is not everyone's cup of tea and requires the greatest care if you want to succeed with your guests. On the opposite, computer programs typically define a general procedure (computing the triangle area) that is expected to work with different values of the base and the height. Working with every possible triangle is precisely the reason why a computer program is designed for. Nobody is interested in a computer program that can compute only areas of triangles with a specific base (say, 3 cm long) and a specific height (say, 4 cm long) since the result would always be the same (invariably 6 cm^2: no fun at all). If we want a computer program to be useful, it shall have the capability to compute the area of any possible triangle, with any possible base and height, and return output results that are coherent with input data and our knowledge of plain geometry.

As an aside, it should also be noticed that writing a computer program that works for any possible combination of input data is relatively straightforward in this example, but not all problems are as simple as computing the area of a triangle. This specific problem is easy to solve because the area of the triangle is clearly defined by the mathematical formula "area = base*height/2," whose behavior is well known and can be predicted with no exceptions. However, when we start talking about AI programs, predicting the robot's behavior under any possible combination of input data is much more challenging. Consider a robot equipped with microphones for speech acquisition and a program for language processing, whose objective is to properly reply to the user's questions: in this case, the input "ingredients" are the words pronounced by the user, and the output is the reply of the robot. How can robotic scientists be sure that the robot will reply correctly to any possible combination of input data, that is, to any possible question that the user will ask? What is the mathematical formula that produces an appropriate answer in this case? Or think about a robot equipped with cameras that needs to reach a destination by finding a safe path in a room filled with people and furniture: in this case, the input "ingredients" are the coordinates of the destination as well as the position in the space of all people and pieces of furniture detected by cameras. How can robotic scientists be sure that the robot will succeed in finding a path to any possible destination for any possible number and location of people and pieces of furniture? What is the mathematical formula for computing a path in any given environmental situation?

Since guaranteeing these things is extremely hard, if not impossible, robotic scientists can never be 100% sure of the results that the program will produce: they are happy if the program behaves as desired in a subset of real-world situations that, taken together, cover almost 100% of the cases. Put in other words, there may be situations in which the program does not work well, but the probability for this to happen shall be extremely low. When the program has these desirable properties, they also say that the program is "robust." Creating robust programs requires a long work of theoretical investigation and experimental testing.

To represent computer programs in an easily understandable way (remember that an AI is just a computer program like a word processor or an Internet browser), it is pretty typical to use a diagram like the one in Fig. 2.1A, also referred to as a flowchart. Learning to read flowcharts is not too complex: the two circles Start and End correspond to the first and the last instructions to be executed by the computer; rectangles correspond to operations that the

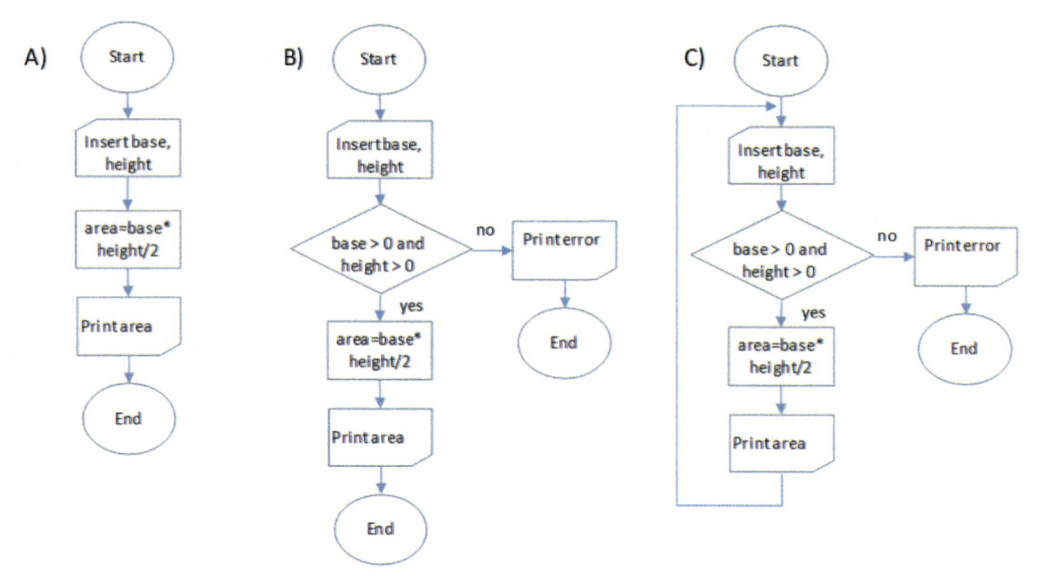

FIGURE 2.1   Three computer programs described as flowcharts.

program shall perform (computing the area of a triangle, sending audio to the speakers, or moving a wheel); a rectangle with a missing top-left corner instructs the computer to stop and ask the user to insert data (e.g., the base and the height of the triangle whose area shall be computed); a rectangle with a missing bottom-right corner instructs the computer to visualize results, for instance on a screen (e.g., the area that has been computed); arrows define the sequence in which operations shall be executed. Then, for example, the program in Fig. 2.1A instructs the computer to wait for input data "base" and "height" to be assigned a value by the user. Next, it computes the area depending on the inserted values. Finally, it prints results as an output on the screen. It shall be outlined that the flowchart cannot be directly interpreted and executed by the computer: this kind of graphical representation owes its success to being easily understandable by humans and the fact that it does not require special programming skills. To produce a program that can be executed by a computer, the flowchart shall be rewritten with a proper programming language (you may have heard of Basic, C++, or Python) using a well-defined vocabulary to translate blocks into instructions. Since the logic of the flowchart is the same as the one of the program, and the aim of this book is not to teach the reader how to program, flowcharts are more than appropriate for our purposes. If you want to know more about programming, there are many books for beginners, such as (Thomas and Hunt, 2019).

Flowcharts (and programs) put at the disposal of programmers at least another couple of fundamental instructions, which are used for "flow control": that is, to force the program to follow different "flows of execution" depending on external factors. To understand why this is needed, please remember that, even in the elementary example that we have introduced so far, there may be unexpected situations that need to be handled with care. For instance, what would happen if the user inserts a negative value for the base or the height? From knowledge of plain geometry, we know that triangles with a negative base or height cannot exist, and therefore, in this case, the area should not be computed. Moreover, to alert the user that something unexpected is happening, it would be good to visualize some sort of error message if a negative value is inserted. As an aside, this reveals that our simple program to compute the area of the rectangle was not very "robust" after all: at first glance, the mathematical formulation "area = base*height/2" seemed appropriate for any possible value of the input data, but it is now evident that it works only with one-fourth of the possible input combinations: the flowchart allows the user to insert any number for the base (positive and negative) and any number for the height (positive and negative), but only the situation in which both the base and the height are positive leads to a proper computation (out of four possible cases). Thus, three times over four, this program will fail!

To deal with a situation like this, we need a "conditional block," which is represented as a diamond in Fig. 2.1B. Conditional blocks are characterized by a condition to be checked that can be true or false and two departing arrows instead of one, corresponding to two different flows of execution depending on the condition being true or false. In the example, the condition to be checked is "base >0 and height >0." If both values are positive, the condition is true, and the program shall follow the arrow labeled with "yes" leading to the usual result; otherwise, the program shall follow the arrow labeled with "no," and print the error message accordingly.

Finally, in most situations, we are more interested in writing programs that repeatedly perform a sequence of operations until the user explicitly stops them, instead of programs that immediately terminate their execution after just one operation. For instance, we may like our program to compute the area of many triangles instead of only one. A reasonable way to do this is to allow the user to repeatedly insert new values for the input base and the height and compute the corresponding area until he or she is bored to death and explicitly asks the program to terminate. This is the behavior we are familiar with when talking about programs: word processors and videogames do not terminate their execution after letting the user insert just one word or using the joypad only once, but they repeatedly process inputs until the user explicitly quits the program (and hopefully goes to dinner). To write computer programs like these, it is necessary to introduce the concept of "cycles" (or "loops"). Cycles, differently from conditions, do not require adding any new block in the flowchart: they can be created by simply arranging arrows to properly determine the program's execution flow. For instance, a cycle can be added to the flowchart in Fig. 2.1B to obtain the flowchart in Fig. 2.1C, whose behavior can be understood by following the arrows from the start block to the end block. As a first step, the user enters a value for the base and the height that, if they are both positive, lead to the computation of the triangle's area as usual. Then, arrows lead back to the input block, and the user is required to introduce a new base and a new height that, if positive, lead to the computation of the corresponding area, and so on. In this example, the loop could ideally continue forever: the program terminates if and only if the user purposely introduces a negative value for the base or the height, which leads the program to follow the arrow labeled with "no" when exiting from the conditional block and ultimately to the end block.

That's all, folks: we have introduced all the required elements to explain how an AI program to control a robot works.

2.3 Dealing with the complexity of the real world

2.3.1 Making robots autonomous

A robot comprises an electromechanical structure made of many parts, motors, or actuators to move these parts, sensors to acquire data from the surrounding environments, and on-board computers to control motors and actuators. The computers run programs that do not substantially differ from those shown in the previous section, at least in principle. Moreover, the robots we are considering in this book are sometimes referred to as "autonomous robots." Autonomous robots are robots capable of autonomously making decisions enabling them to achieve goals, which can either be assigned by people or be the consequence of previous decisions taken by the robot itself.

Consider the flowchart in Fig. 2.2A, describing a typical program controlling an autonomous robot that follows the so-called "Sense Model Plan Act" paradigm (SMPA). Following the same general principles of the program to compute the triangle area, the SMPA "program" requires the following activities to be repeatedly performed in sequence, as determined by the cycle in the flowchart, until conditions to terminate the program verify.

- Sense: the robot perceives the world through its sensors. For instance, it may detect the presence of people, walls, and furniture through cameras, laser, or sonar sensors, which are also capable of measuring the distance to the closest person or object in a given direction. Another example of "sensing" is acquiring data to recognize people's emotions, gestures, and activities or acquiring speech and translating it into a chunk of text.
- Model: the robot updates its internal representation of the world through the data acquired in the previous step. For instance, it builds a map of the environment using

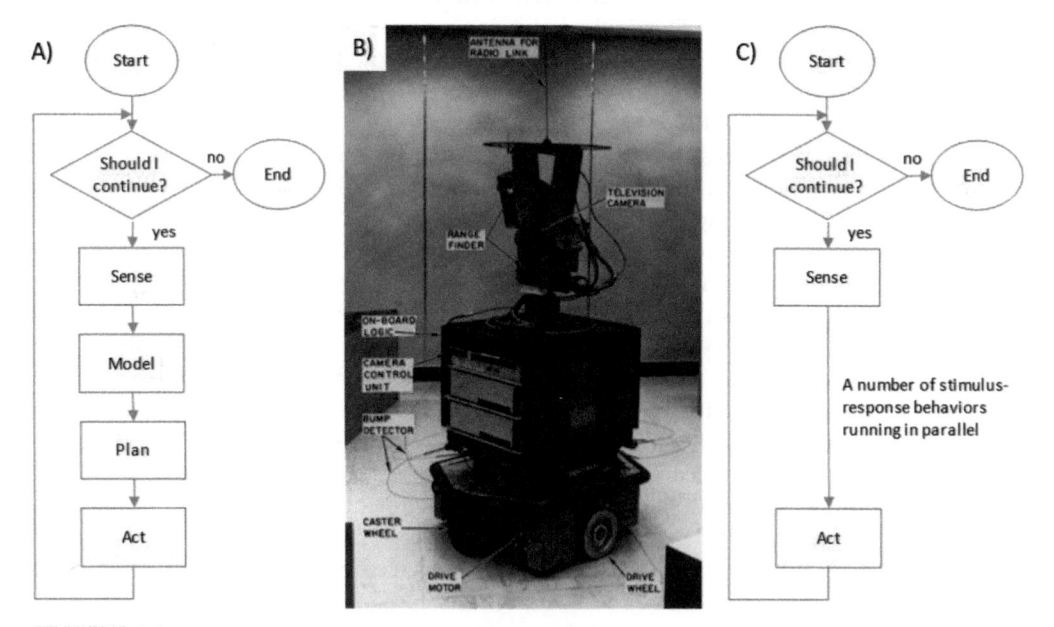

FIGURE 2.2 (A) Sense Plan Model Act architecture; (B) Shakey the robot; (C) Behavior-based approach.

distance measurements returned by sensors, where the space occupied by people and objects is represented in two or three dimensions. Another example of "modeling" is using the information acquired during the conversation with the robot to update the user's preferences or using sensor data to describe what the user is doing at any given time.
- Plan: the robot computes a sequence of actions to be performed depending on its current goal and the model of the world built in the previous step. For instance, it may compute a sequence of elementary motions leading from the current position to the destination by avoiding all people and objects on the map. Other examples of "planning" are choosing a proper sequence of movements of the arm and the hand to grasp and manipulate objects, figuring out the correct body posture and gestures to express emotions, or shaping the flow of the dialogue with the user to reach a shared objective.
- Act: the robot executes the first action in the plan and monitors its execution to check if it produces the desired effects, and then repeats the whole SMPA cycle from the beginning. Other examples of "acting" are moving arms, hands, the head, or the body; turning on and off smart devices distributed in the environments; translating a chunk of text into speech.

SMPA is a very old approach to robot programming: it was adopted by one of the first successful attempts to create an autonomous robot, "Shakey the robot" at Stanford University by Rosen and Nilsson, active from 1966 to 1972, Fig. 2.2B (Nilsson, 1984). Many researchers have put in discussion SMPA since the 1980: actually, the SMPA acronym itself was not used by Stanford researchers, but it was introduced by one of the fiercest detractors to this kind of approach, Rodney Brooks at MIT (Brooks, 1991), who later became one of the cofounders of iRobot, the company that created the cleaning robot Roomba. We will say more about Brooks' criticism of SMPA in the following section. Despite its limitations, from an educational perspective, SMPA is very useful to explain the fundamentals of how a robot program works: moreover, many robots still operate following, more or less closely, this approach.

Three things are worth being noticed in the SMPA flowchart.

First of all, the reader may observe that the blocks Sense, Model, Plan, Act are graphically represented using the same rectangles that we previously used to contain the formula "area = base*height/2." However, in the SMPA case, it is not straightforward to understand what these blocks are doing since the rectangles do not contain any explicit formula that can be used to compute outputs data starting from input data. For instance, if a robotic programmer wants to use a camera to detect the presence of people, how the block Sense shall look like? What formulas shall be written there? Since this is not a programming book, we are not providing these details here, but the reader shall always keep in mind that a macroactivity like Sense is necessarily composed of a complex sequence of blocks, where all the elementary instructions to acquire data from sensors and process them are ultimately described in extreme detail. But not here: for now, we are happy to represent elementary instructions as gathered into one block generically called Sense, and the same is done for the other macroactivities Model, Plan, and Act. A few more words about this will be said later in this chapter.

Second, it is imperative to keep in mind that each of the problems a robot needs to address (e.g., recognizing objects or computing a path from a start location to a destination) has no unique solution. Each task can be performed through many different methodologies, with each methodology requiring a different sequence of instructions to process the input data: finding the most efficient solutions to problems is one of the jobs of robotic scientists! However, here we purposely ignore this multiplicity of solutions and encourage the reader to focus on *what* computer programs achieve (e.g., recognizing a coffee machine from a chair, finding a path amid the crowd) rather than on *how* this is achieved. So far, to foster this attitude, we did not mention such tools as Neural Networks or Deep Learning (Schmidhuber, 2015), which frequently appear in the media as related to AI and Robotics. Indeed, we believe that emphasizing specific AI methodologies would be unfair since a portfolio of different tools to achieve similar objectives exist, not only Neural Networks: researchers switch between different tools daily since each of them may be more or less appropriate depending on the context.

Third, even if not explicitly represented in the flowcharts in Fig. 2.2A, we have already mentioned that every block in the SMPA sequence needs input data and produces output data, typically used by the following block in the sequence. According to this rationale, the Sense block operates sensors to acquire measurements, and the acquired sensor data are fed as an input to the Model block; the Model block uses sensor data to produce an updated representation of the world that is fed as an input to the Plan block; the Plan block analyses the current state of the world and plans a sequence of actions that are fed as an input to the Act block; the Act block processes the current plan and sends commands to motors and speakers to interact with people and the environment. However, in a robot program, data are not only acquired through sensors or passed from the previous block to the following one: the behavior of each block, and then of the robot itself, is typically fine-tuned depending on the value of additional factors that come from outside the SMPA loop. For instance, we may want to reduce the speed of the robot to guarantee safety while moving in a care home or select the appropriate language when talking to people of a given nationality: these additional factors play a crucial role and shall be taken into account, but they are not necessarily chosen by the AI of the robot. Indeed, it is very common that the moving speed or the language, to mention a few, is determined a priori by robotics scientists in a setup phase since they depend on external contextual or cultural factors that the robot may not be capable of inferring by itself.

As the reader now has an approximate idea of how an AI program for a robot works, it is worth mentioning that, recently, many commercial tools have been proposed for robot programming to enable nontechnicians to create effective robotic behaviors simply, usually with an emphasis on educational purposes. If you consider buying a robot, please keep this in mind: you do not need to be a computer scientist to do amazing things with robots. One of the most popular programming framework for people without technical skills is perhaps Choregraphe, that was developed for the humanoid robots NAO and Pepper. Choregraphe, as like other programming frameworks, allows the user to program the robot by using graphical tools that are conceptually similar to the flowcharts that we have just shown. The user has access to a vast library of basic blocks implementing many predefined behaviors for sensing, modeling, planning, and executing actions and can write complex programs just by linking these basic blocks. Preferences such as the movement speed or the speaking language can be set as well. A similar and very user-friendly programming framework was proposed by LEGO for its Mindstorm series, once again based on basic blocks to be composed into complex programs. Learning how to use these software programs is not too difficult, and the reader who wants to explore these topics more in detail is suggested to give them a try.

2.3.2 The behaviorist approach

The SMPA architecture, used as an illustrative example to describe a generic AI program to control a robot, was one of the first approaches to be successfully adopted by robotic researchers. Following this approach, the famous Shakey portrayed in Fig. 2.2B was able to move between different locations in a room using a rudimental vision system plus additional sensors to detect obstacles (Sense), memorize the location of goals and obstacles using logic (Model), plan a sequence of elementary motions using a reasoning program called STRIPS (Plan), and finally execute the planned motions by sending proper commands to the wheels (Act).

However, SMPA is not the only possible way to organize the different tasks that a robot needs to perform. Starting from the 1980, a branch of Robotics also known as "Behavior-based Robotics" challenged this vision: behavior-based roboticists, led by Rodney Brooks, argued that the world is too noisy and unpredictable, and sensor capabilities too poor, to enable robots to create a "mental model of the world" that could be of any use to perform a real task (Brooks, 1991). According to the detractors of the SMPA approach, the few examples of robotic systems that had succeeded so far (among which, the good old Shakey) owed their success to the fact that they operated in a "toy world," that is an environment carefully crafted for them. To be honest, if you watch Shakey's videos today, there is no doubt that obstacles look carefully painted to be easily recognized by sensors, the floor is flat and without the usual mess that you can find in ordinary houses, moving people or objects are absent, etc. Under these simplified conditions, behavior-based roboticists argue, controlling a robot is no more challenging than playing a chess game, something that AI can do very well. But the real world is not a chessboard! Elephants survive very well without being able to play chess, Brooks observes (Brooks, 1990). For this reason, researchers suggest a different solution in which perception (the Sense block) shall be directly coupled with action (the Action block), and no representation of the environment or complex plan shall be built: notice that the Model and Plan blocks are absent in Fig. 2.2C. Researchers suggest that AI should first emerge from the interaction with the physical environment rather than dealing with abstract problems: complex behaviors in Nature do not necessarily require complex cognitive activities but rather emerge from composing many simpler reactive stimulus-response behaviors in the absence of any internal representation of the world. The way how a colony of ants manages to find the shortest path from the nest to a nearby food source has nothing to do with road maps or GPS navigators, as the reader can imagine.

To see the difference between SMPA and Behavior-based approaches in action, think about a robot that needs to find a path from the entrance to the desk of a hotel, finding its way among obstacles that include furniture and people. Assume for simplicity, even if this is not required, that the floor is covered by square tiles. A typical SMPA approach first uses sensors to create a map of the hall, that is, localizing all obstacles and labeling some tiles as free, some as occupied by obstacles. Then it creates a sequence of moves from start to the goal by iteratively choosing the next free tile in such a way as to avoid collisions with obstacles. Finally, it executes the sequence of moves. After an initial delay to perform all the required computations, the result would be very similar to a board game, which is not a surprise since this approach to producing an "intelligent behavior" owes a lot to AI programs to play chess. Remember that chess is one of the first applications AI was thought for and, according to someone, one of the most intelligent things humans can do (Brooks and elephants would strongly disagree!).

A Behavior-based approach acts differently. No map is built, but the robot starts to move toward the goal with no delay: if it encounters an obstacle on its left (stimulus), it will steer a little to the right (response); if it encounters an obstacle on its right (stimulus), it will steer a little to the left (response). And what if the robot encounters an obstacle precisely in the center of its path? If the obstacle is a person, this person would likely move away to let the robot pass. If it's a table, we may have just encountered one of the most renowned problems of Behavior-based approaches: the robot does not know whether it should steer to the left or to the right, and therefore it is stuck there forever. Implementing a simple Behavior-based solution to deal with the problem above is not that challenging. For instance, the robot might perform small random movements whenever a deadlock occurs so that the obstacle will not be "precisely in the center of its path anymore," and it may be safely avoided on the left or on the right as usual. However, this is not the point: it is generally known that Behavior-based approaches can sometimes fail in achieving the goal because they lack advanced planning capabilities. Behavior-based approaches do not require heavy computations, are robust to noise because they do not need to create a coherent map, and can effectively react to a quickly changing environment. But they are not capable of solving complex, "chess-like" problems. Sometimes, you may hear researchers talk about "reactive behavior," or even "reactive planning" when referring to how Behavior-based robots address real-world situations. If you want to know more about how complex problems can be addressed through simple solutions, we invite you to have a look at Valentino Breitenberg's famous book "Vehicles" (Breitenberg, 1984).

Despite its limitations, robotic history shows that Behaviour-based Robotics, thanks to this innovative vision, managed to produce amazingly simple "robotic beings" able to operate in real-time in a noisy and dynamic real-world, in a way that nobody was capable of doing before. This is even more amazing as it happened when the sensing capabilities of robots and the computational power of computers were incomparably lower than today, thus making Behaviour-based approaches dominate the scene of robotic research for many years. Today, robotics researchers tend to think that a "good mixture" of SMPA-like and Behaviour-based approaches is more promising (Arkin & Balch, 1997; Gat, 1997). Indeed, it turns out that there are activities more efficiently performed in a Behaviour-based spirit (as it happens for obstacle avoidance) and other activities for which a world model is mandatory (as it happens for a robot that needs to understand its position in a building).

Most importantly, Behaviour-based Robotics taught researchers a key lesson: the need to build robots capable of operating in a noisy and dynamic, and hence unpredictable, world to achieve the ultimate goal of producing a real impact on society. Thanks to this lesson, robotic scientists have learned to give the maximum priority to designing "robust" robot programs that work well in almost all real-world situations and not only under well-specified and favorable conditions.

A side effect of this attitude is that most robotic scientists tend to raise their eyebrows when watching a video showing a robot interacting with objects that have been purposely chosen for their unique shape or color (to make them more easily recognizable). As an exercise, we challenge the reader to search for videos on the web and spot robots interacting with "red balls" and "yellow boxes," especially when researchers claim to have implemented complex cognitive capabilities emulating human beings. There are many.

When you find one, raise your eyebrow.

2.4 Once again: "why can't the robot do that?"

2.4.1 Writing computer programs for autonomous robots

We now have all the elements to reply to such questions as "why can't the robot do that?" or "can you teach the robot to do this?" that, from time to time, can become a more specific question such as "why doesn't the robot know Harry Potter?" or "can you teach the robot to come closer to me?" With some experience in showing robots during public exhibitions, it is possible to imagine many variants of these questions that visitors frustrated by a poor interaction with the robot may ask us to make us lose our temper. You are still wearing the roboticist's hat, do you remember?

"Why can't the robot do that?"

By considering the previous sections with attention, the reader will find out that an answer has been already implicitly given: the robot "can't do that" because researchers prioritize robustness, and they may have not yet found a solution that is robust enough for "doing that." They will never accept a solution that can work only in a minimal subset of cases. They will never spend their time programming a new functionality if they cannot guarantee that such functionality will work in almost all combinations of real-world situations. This is not just an elegant way to say: "the robot can't do that because it is difficult." Indeed, more profound reasons are subtended, which require recalling all the concepts that have been presented so far.

What real-world situations can challenge the robustness of a robot program, exactly?

In line with the current research trends, let's assume that we follow a hybrid SMPA/Behaviour-based approach, executing in parallel complex planning activities with reactive behaviors capable of dealing with the dynamicity and noisiness of the real world. If we focus on sensing or modeling, the reader may easily guess that a robust program shall guarantee satisfactory performance in object recognition with different lighting conditions or when objects may be partially occluded by other objects. It shall faithfully translate speech into text even when people speak with different accents, pitch, or volume, in the presence of background noise or a crowded room. If we focus on planning or acting, a robust program shall be able to find a path to the destination even in maze-like environments. It shall guarantee safety even when the speed increases or some unpredicted event happens, such as a person suddenly crossing the path. It shall carry on the dialogue in a coherent way whatever the user says, by replying with richer sentences than the frustrating answer "sorry, I do not understand." But how can robustness be achieved from a programmer's perspective? What will be ultimately written inside the flowchart describing a robot program capable of performing the macroactivities Sense, Model, Plan, Act (or a subset of them)? Given that real life is not a theatrical show and does not follow a "script," what technological solutions are required to handle the diversity of environmental conditions mentioned above?

This is a programmer's job, so let's take our programming tools out of the suitcase.

Following the examples shown in the previous sections, the reader should know what is needed to write a flowchart that handles different environmental conditions:

- Formulas with variable inputs, which we typically write inside rectangular blocks. An example considered so far is the formula to compute the area of a triangle, which works for all triangles whose base and height are positive (and not only for a subset of all possible triangles!).
- Instructions for flow control, which we typically write inside diamond-shaped blocks. An example considered so far is the instruction to check if the triangle's base and height are positive, enabling the program to follow different execution branches depending on their input values.

Believe it or not, from a technical perspective, the above list (plus instructions for getting inputs from sensors and sending outputs to motors, displays, or speakers) includes all the required programming tools to make the robot work in the presence of different environmental conditions. If we had the time and space, we could do that. For each macroactivity, we just need to write a considerable number of rectangular and diamond-shaped blocks. Rectangular blocks determine the most appropriate formulas to be computed, and diamond-shaped blocks determine the execution flow depending on what the robot is currently perceiving around itself and its current goals. If rectangular and diamond-shaped blocks are adequately chosen to cover the vast majority of possible situations, the system will be robust. Easy-peasy, isn't it?

But then, why the hell can't we use this mechanism to make a robust robot capable of talking about Harry Potter if somebody asks for this?

2.4.2 Robots in the wild

Suppose that, following this approach, we have introduced conversational capabilities in our robot, which has been specially designed as a companion for older people living in care homes. These capabilities have been programmed through a very complex flowchart that is ultimately made of formulas and instructions for flow control, carefully written to check all possible input sentences and produce an appropriate response. For instance, if the user says: "I want to call the Doctor," a conditional block may recognize the whole sentence between quotation marks or, more likely, detect the keywords "call" and "doctor," and may follow a branch of the flowchart with the ultimate goal of starting a phone call. If the user says: "I love football," another conditional block will likely detect the keywords "love" and "football" and execute a branch of the program that selects a random reply such as "Well, I love football too. What is your favorite team?" After some months of work, through a significant effort involving both engineers and creative content writers, we developed a conversational robot capable of understanding 10.000 keywords and producing the related answers. We conjecture that this shall be sufficient to guarantee a rewarding conversation with most people.

Hooray! We are ready to start a larger trial with recruited participants!

It is Thursday afternoon. We are ready to test our new robot in a care home starting from Monday, and we are currently showing how the system works to nurses and caregivers that will support the testing phase with residents. We are very proud of the system because we worked hard on it, and we came out with some innovative solutions. We might file a patent application or submit a scientific article to an International Journal soon.

Nurses and caregivers are very curious about how this cute robot works. A middle-aged caregiver is still a little worried because newspapers are publishing articles about how robots will steal jobs from health and social care workers in the next future. Luckily, this robot is "sooo cute!" and we were terrific in explaining to the audience that it cannot perform any physical tasks at all, thus being unlikely to substitute nurses or caregivers in their job, at least in the near future. Everybody is super happy to hear that no robot in the world is reliable enough to go to the kitchen and bring back a glass of water or a bottle of pills: houses are messy, and it's not easy to find and pick up objects.

"So, what's this thing for?" the cynic of the group asks.

We clarify that this robot we want to test is mainly designed to sustain a conversation with people, keep company, show movies on the screen, reminding the person of a visit, make a phone call, and things like that. To make our audience more familiar with it, we invite nurses and caregivers to have a conversation with the robot, if they want, to get a glimpse of how "this thing" really works. A young nurse makes a step forward. We invite him to say something to the robot, and he says: "Do you know Harry Potter?" The robot, very frustratingly, replies: "There are many things I can do for you. Do you want to talk with me about your daily routines?" Epic fail.

"Why doesn't the robot know Harry Potter? ... can you add Harry Potter, please?"

If the whole discussion about "robustness" is clear to you, that is, the fact that robot programs should work well in almost all real-world situations and not only in a minimal subset of cases, you are finally ready for the real answer to this question.

The real answer is that it is impossible to convince a robotic scientist that, at this point, changing the robot program to add knowledge about Harry Potter will improve the system. No matter how "epic" the failure was. The robotic scientist is not upset because of the request, his or her feelings are not hurt (well, indeed, they may be hurt, but this is not the point). Simply put, robotic scientists will hardly believe that this is a crucial thing to do. Of course, this is partly because robotic scientists have the tendency to underestimate many factors that are key to improving the user's experience. Robotic scientists seem not to care that Harry Potter fans will be frustrated because the robot does not know Harry Potter. Indeed, it would be wonderful if the robot might reply nicely when a Harry Potter fan proudly asserts: "I love Harry Potter." So why shouldn't we add a conditional block in the program to handle this possibility? Together with formulas with variable inputs, using conditional blocks is the appropriate way to address the diversity of possible events. We stated it many times!

Let's suppose that we have a heart. After some pressure, we agree to consider the nurse's request: we add a couple of blocks to the program by including a few possible replies that the program can randomly choose to address questions about Harry Potter. For instance, the robot may reply: "Harry Potter is the most famous wizard in the world!" or "He is the greatest broomstick flyer ever." From now on, everything will work fine with Harry Potter. But, one moment: what if another person asks about a different character taken from Harry Potter's world, such as Prof. Snape? No problem, we just need to add another couple of answers. And what if the user asks about Prof. Dumbledore? Hagrid? The Slytherin House? Quidditch? Harry Potter's creator, J.K Rowling?

Again, no problem: with some patience, we can add appropriate replies to the program to handle all of these requests. Suddenly we realize that not everybody is a Harry Potter fan! Many users, especially those in their fifties, may love to hear the robot talking about Star Wars characters like Luke Skywalker, Chewbacca, R2D2, and Dart Vader. Eighty years old may love to tell their memories about Long John Silver, Captain Nemo, Captain Ahab, and Mr. Hyde. After chitchatting with the robot about the books they loved to read and the movies they enjoyed watching, all these people may also be interested in talking about food and different kinds of food, sport, music, religion, politics. Shall we exhaustively add a new conditional block to handle all possible requests that the user may have, one after another? Will this process ever come to an end? Since we already know that it is impossible to plan everything because the robot and the user are not acting following a script, but everything is unpredictable as life is unpredictable, does this make sense at all?

The positions of different researchers are different and somehow controversial on how to address this kind of situation. Some researchers argue that it does not make sense, not even in principle, to iteratively add all the required knowledge by hand: they suggest that, to the end of handling the unpredictability and diversity of real-world conversations, methods are needed to automatically extract knowledge from existing data, such as conversations on Social Networks. Other researchers argue that approaches to autonomously learn how to talk from online resources are interesting but inappropriate if we want to keep control of what the robot says, which should always be accurate, safe, and ethically acceptable. They say that, in sensitive contexts, knowledge should ultimately be added by hand but by following criteria of some sort.

Whatever your position is, it should now be out of doubt that all robotics scientists will always look for general, "robust" solutions that address a problem in its entirety, rather than considering thousands of particular cases considered individually, one after another. Then, if we ultimately decide to add sentences by hand (about Harry Potter, Prof. Snape, Prof. Dumbledore, Luke Skywalker, Dart Vader, Long John Silver, Captain Nemo …), at least we should estimate the probability that a topic of conversation is raised by the user, before deciding to include it or not. Otherwise, this process might last forever! How probable is it that an older person living in a care home asks about Harry Potter? How probable is it that the same person will enjoy talking about World War II that he or she may have personally experienced? When wearing your roboticist's hat, you know that time spent in research is a valuable resource, that every modification to the system requires time not only for programming but also for repeatedly testing programs. Is it worth investing time on a specific topic of conversation that, when considering all possible users, may not have a significant impact in terms of subjective experience?

In Chapters 8 and 9, presenting technological solutions to design culturally competent robots, we will suggest some ideas to handle these problems from a broader perspective. For now, it is crucial to outline that these dilemmas arise whenever researchers face the problem of developing autonomous robots. As we repeatedly said, this problem is not related to conversation only but to any possible task that the robot has to perform. Once again, the robot "can't do that" because the real world is unpredictable, and therefore we cannot program a robot to act according to a script. We need to search for robust solutions addressing a problem in its entirety and not handling all cases individually!

FIGURE 2.3 Popular robots in the last 30 years: TRC Helpmate, Kismet, Pepper.

To conclude, it is worth reminding that, when designing robots that shall be our companions in everyday life (some examples of the last 30 years are shown in Fig. 2.3), many additional requirements emerge related to human−robot interaction. To address these requirements, researchers often stress the importance of taking inspiration from human behavior to produce robots capable of interacting with humans the same way humans do. One example is human-aware navigation in human-populated environments (Kruse et al., 2013). How should the robot approach people in the right way? How can a robot moving in the crowd keep the proper distance from people to avoid creating discomfort? Another example is human−robot cooperation. How can we implement robots with the same capabilities that humans have to reason not only about their own beliefs, goals, and intentions but also about other people's beliefs, goals, and intentions toward achieving shared goals (Scassellati, 2002)? How can the robot represent, recognize, and express emotional states and take them into account in the interaction (Breazeal, 2003)?

These are only some examples, and others will follow in the following chapters.

By considering the above list of exciting research areas currently explored in the robotics domain to enable a rewarding interaction with people, a final and more straightforward answer can be given to the question: "why can't the robot do that?"

Because there may be more important things to do before.

2.4.3 A few words about Neural Networks

This chapter might have ended with the previous section. However, we feel obliged to say a few words about Neural Networks.

Up to now, we almost completely ignored Neural Networks (Schmidhuber, 2015). Nowadays, these technologies are being paid great attention to by the media, up to the point that somebody might consider Neural Networks (and the so-called Deep Learning) synonyms of AI. However, they are not: in the previous sections, we clarified that different tools exist and are used by robotic programmers, no less frequently than Neural Networks, to solve specific problems related to sensing, modeling, planning, and acting. Neural Networks are only one of these tools.

Having said this, some robotic researchers would probably claim that many problems related to "robustness" can be easily solved using Neural Networks. "Programming the robot to address all possible situations by considering individual cases one after another is neither feasible nor convenient," they would argue with us, "and for this very reason using Neural Networks might be the optimal solution." They may be partially correct, and this section will clarify why.

Neural Networks are nothing more than a computer program, "made of the same substance as a word processor," to paraphrase Shakespeare again. For this reason, a Neural Network can ideally be implemented using the same approach we have proposed up to now: a flowchart with many rectangular blocks including algebraic formulas and diamond-shaped blocks including conditions to be checked. This is confirmed by the fact that programmers develop Neural Networks using the same programming languages to program word processors or videogames (Basic, C++, Python …). There's nothing exciting here. However, we will not describe Neural Networks using a flowchart: to show how a Neural Network works, it is easier and more common to visualize it as a net, whose structure is more similar to the regular structure of a fishing net than the free-topology of a road network, Fig. 2.4. Knots of the net are called neurons, which may not be a surprise since Neural Networks take inspiration from their biological counterpart. Neurons take inputs from other neurons along the direction of the arrows (or from the data to be analyzed), perform simple algebraic operations, and send outputs to other neurons (and ultimately produce output data). Researchers need to program the network structure, that is, how many neurons there are and how they are connected to each other, using a programming language. However, once the structure is defined, there is no need to program the network to perform a specific task: Neural Networks can be trained to do the right things by showing them examples of what to do. There's definitely something exciting here.

Think about the task of recognizing human faces in a picture, a typical sensing problem that can be crucial for a robot in a socially assistive scenario. Without using a Neural Network, programmers will likely start by considering how human faces "are made." At first, they will explore how a face can be decomposed into basic elements to be easily recognized by a computer program: the oval, the eyes, the nose, the mouth. Then, they will

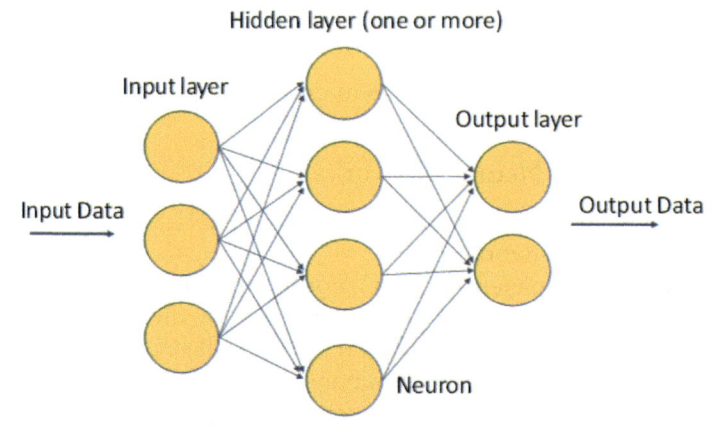

FIGURE 2.4 A typical Neural Network: the number of neurons and their connections may vary.

consider the visible properties of each basic element, that is, its shape, size, color, and position. Finally, they will evaluate how these properties may change their appearance depending on perspective, occlusions, and lighting conditions. As the reader can imagine, this process is very long precisely because researchers want to design "robust" computer programs, that is, capable of working in the vast majority of environmental conditions. After a tremendous effort, they may come out with a program that takes images of a given dimension in input (say 320 × 180 pixels) and provides a binary output: "this picture contains a face" or "this picture does not."

Designing a Neural Network requires operating in a completely different way. Consider again Fig. 2.4. The input neurons will be used to feed the network with the images to be checked: if we want to process images composed of 320 × 180 pixels, we need a corresponding number of neurons in the input layer. The output neurons will be used to output results, that is, "this picture contains a face," "this picture does not": we need only two neurons in the output layer. Between the input and the output layer, there may be a varying number of hidden layers, whose connections may vary depending on the type of network. As a curiosity, the presence of many hidden layers, that is, the "deepness" of the network, is at the basis of the terms Deep Neural Network and Deep Learning. Please notice that shaping the proper structure of the network is not trivial and very resource-consuming: researchers often start from networks that have been already "precooked" by other researchers and prove to work sufficiently well for their purposes.

Once the structure is defined, we only need to train the network by providing a sufficiently vast amount of paired data. Paired data shall include both images containing a face (fed to the input neurons) associated with the label "this picture contains a face" (fed to the output neurons) as well as images that do not contain a face with the corresponding label "this picture does not." The process is iterated many times until we have provided the network with a sufficiently vast number of cases to cover most situations (in the order of thousands or tens of thousands): faces with different shapes and skin colors, portrayed under different perspectives, with varying conditions of lighting, etc. During training, the network slowly learns: to do so, it modifies a few numbers associated with neurons (called "weights"; not shown in Fig. 2.4), so that the algebraic operations performed by each neuron will return a slightly different result. At the end of the learning process, if a sufficiently vast and varied number of cases has been used in the training phase, the network will be capable of classifying images as containing faces or not. Very importantly, the network will be capable of generalizing this process, that is, it will correctly classify also the images that have not been used during training! And what if we want to recognize coffee machines instead of faces? We just need to take the same network and train it again: this time, using thousands of coffee-machine pictures. It's a kind of magic.

Is this the key to achieve robust behavior without the need to write a program that explicitly considers all possible cases individually taken?

Classifying sensor data are relevant in many other robotic applications. For example, think about speech-to-text translation, which constitutes the basis for verbal interaction, or recognizing human gestures or activities using videos or multiple sensors distributed in the environment. However, classifying data are not the only possible task that a Neural Network can perform. Other kinds of networks can be used to generate plausible data starting from examples, by transforming things into something different: for example, younger people into older people, horses into zebras or apples into oranges (Wang et al., 2017). Some popular chatbots even use Neural Networks to produce sentences containing an appropriate reply to what the user is saying (Zhou et al., 2020). Remember? This problem gave us a headache when the nurse asked to know about Harry Potter. Despite the differences, all kinds of Neural Networks have similar training requirements: to work well, they need a vast amount of data to be used as examples, which may not be accessible to everybody. Indeed, this is one of the drawbacks of Neural Network: to train the network, you need data that can be available to big Internet colossuses but not to individual researchers that want to implement their own solutions. It is not by chance that the most popular services for image classification and speech-to-text translation, which often robotic researchers embed in their own solutions, are provided by Google, Microsoft, and Amazon.

Are Neural Networks the ultimate solution to make robust systems capable of performing well in a noisy and dynamic, unpredictable world? Yes and No.

The fact that Neural Networks are capable of generalizing from a vast amount of well-chosen examples is very appealing since they would spare us the effort of explicitly programming all possible situations to be addressed by hand. For example, providing a coherent reply whenever the user mentions Harry Potter and friends could be solved by letting the network learn from the vast number of conversations about Harry Potter on the Internet, such as forums or social media. However, this works well only when a sufficient amount of data is already at our disposal, which is not always true: in some other cases, for example, detecting user's activities such as eating, brushing own's teeth, or having a shower, data for training the network may not be available. Researchers produce and publish new datasets daily precisely for this purpose, but what happens if we want the robot to recognize something for which there is no dataset yet?

Also, think about the conversation. Who has control over what the robot is saying? A well-trained Neural Network can make the robot able to generate coherent replies based on what people write on forums, Twitter, and Facebook: how can we be sure that automatically generated answers will convey the right message and not contain offensive language? Can we let the network improvise in a sensitive context such as health and social care? We will say a few more words about this in Chapter 8: for the moment, consider that the problem is not limited to the conversation with the robot. Whenever Neural Networks learn from examples, they incur the risk of learning from bad examples. There are bad teachers everywhere, and many of them are on the Internet! Consider training a network to make decisions of some sort, either for recognizing a face in an image or selecting the best candidate for a job. If the examples used for training the network contain biases, the network will have the same biases. In all contexts where human decisions are influenced by gender, race, religion, culture, the network will be similarly affected. Researchers are working hard on this and may come out with terrific solutions soon for designing networks capable of making fairer decisions (Holstein et al., 2019) or, at least, networks that can explain why those decisions have been taken (Adadi & Berrada, 2018). The so-called research in Explainable AI (XAI) starts from considering that many AI technologies, including Neural Network, can produce impressive results. Still, the reasoning process followed to achieve those results may be obscure to the user, which is extremely dangerous.

We suggest considering all these elements to make informed decisions about the opportunity to use Neural Networks. Of course, Neural Networks' capabilities are unique, and they definitely deserve to be exploited to improve the system's robustness. However, the issues mentioned above are far from being a remote hypothesis, as they already created troubles for more than one public body and Internet company.

You don't want to be the next one.

2.5 Conclusion

This chapter has provided the reader without familiarity with computer and robot programming with the necessary bases to understand the most technological parts of this book in Chapters 8 and 9. Chapter 8 will discuss the problem of knowledge representation in detail, that is, how to provide the robot with the required cultural knowledge to interact with people culturally competently by avoiding stereotyped representations of people and cultures. Chapter 9 will discuss how to make a robot fully autonomous, that is, capable of interacting with people 24 h a day and 7 days a week with no external intervention, even in the presence of a real world that is necessarily dynamic and noisy and hence unpredictable. Whenever needed, the reader will be welcome to come back to read this chapter, which has laid the basis for thoroughly understanding the challenges posed by designing a fully autonomous, culturally competent robot for assisting older people by avoiding misconceptions or false expectations.

2.5.1 Reflective questions

- Robots need to operate in the real world, known to be noisy, unpredictable, and highly dynamic. So what do we mean when we say that a robot or an AI needs to be "robust"?
- Think about a simple program that asks the user to insert two numbers and returns the highest one. How can this program be described using a flowchart?
- Think about a task that, in your view, a robot for assisting older people should be capable of performing. What are the requirements in terms of sensing, modeling, planning, and acting? What do you think can be most challenging for a robot to perform that task?

References

Adadi, A., & Berrada, M. (2018). Peeking inside the black-box: A survey on explainable artificial intelligence (XAI). *IEEE Access, 6*, 52138–52160.

Arkin, R. C., & Balch, T. R. (1997). AuRA: Principles and practice in review. *Journal of Experimental & Theoretical Artificial Intelligence, 9*(2–3), 175–189.

Breazeal, C. (2003). Emotion and sociable humanoid robots. *International Journal of Human-Computer Studies, 59*(1–2), 119–155.

Breitenberg, V. (1984). *Vehicles: Experiments in synthetic psychology.* MIT Press Cambridge.

Brooks, R. A. (1990). Elephants don't play chess. *Robotics and Autonomous Systems, 6*(1–2), 3–15.

Brooks, R. A. (1991). Intelligence without representation. *Artificial Intelligence, 47*(1–3), 139–159.

Gat, E. (1997). On three-layer architectures. In D. Kortenkamp, R. P. Bonnasso, & R. Murphy (Eds.), *Artificial intelligence and mobile robots.* MIT/AAAI Press.

Holstein, K., Vaughan, J. W., Daumé, H., III, Dudík, M., & Wallach, H. (2019). Improving fairness in machine learning systems: What do industry practitioners need?. In *Proceedings of the 2019 CHI conference on human factors in computing systems* (pp. 1–16).

Kruse, T., Pandey, A. K., Alami, R., & Kirsch, A. (2013). Human-aware robot navigation: A survey. *Robotics and Autonomous Systems, 61*(12), 1726–1743. Cited 312 times.

Nilsson, N. J. (1984). *Shakey the robot*. Sri International Menlo Park CA.

Scassellati, B. (2002). Theory of mind for a humanoid robot. *Autonomous Robots, 12*(1), 13–24.

Schmidhuber, J. (2015). Deep Learning in neural networks: An overview. *Neural Networks, 61*, 85–117.

Thomas, D., & Hunt, A. (2019). *The pragmatic programmer: Your journey to mastery* (20th Anniversary Edition 2nd ed.). Addison-Wesley Professional.

Wang, K., Gou, C., Duan, Y., Lin, Y., Zheng, X., & Wang, F.-Y. (2017). Generative adversarial networks: Introduction and outlook. *IEEE/CAA Journal of Automatica Sinica, 4*(4), 588–598, 8039016.

Zhou, L., Gao, J., Li, D., & Shum, H.-Y. (2020). The design and implementation of xiaoice, an empathetic social chatbot. *Computational Linguistics, 46*(1), 53–93.

CHAPTER 3

What the literature says about social robots and AI technologies in health and social care

Christina Koulouglioti[1] and Irena Papadopoulos[2]

[1]Research and Innovation Department, University Hospitals Sussex NHS Foundation Trust and Research Centre for Transcultural Studies in Health, Middlesex University, London, United Kingdom; [2]Research Centre for Transcultural Studies in Health, Middlesex University, London, United Kingdom

> **LEARNING OBJECTIVES**
> - To gain a better understanding about the different types of robots used in health care;
> - To learn what currently nurses and other health professionals think about the use of robots in practice;
> - To gain a better understanding of influence that culture has in terms of the robots' acceptability, usability, and effectiveness;
> - To have an overview of what might facilitate or impede the use of robots in health care.

3.1 Introduction

As the use of care robots is accelerating within the health and social care domains, the debate about their benefits and possible negative consequences has also intensified. Some of the debate topics include questions such as "Are robots going to replace humans?" "Should we be placing the care of older adults in the hands of robots?" "What are the consequences regarding safety, privacy, and dignity?"

As mentioned in Chapter 1, the world is facing huge health and social care challenges due to a number of factors, such as the changing demographics, the shortages of health and social care workers, the more frequent and prohibitive major health disasters such as the recent

COVID-19 pandemic and so on. The latest briefing by the UK's King's Fund (The King's Fund, 2018) painted a gloomy picture about the UK NHS staff shortages. It stated that more than 250,000 shortages by 2030 are predicted, with a detrimental effect on the delivery and quality of care. Twenty percent of Nursing Associations from around the world have reported an increased rate of nurses leaving the profession during 2020 and the ICN (International Council of Nurses) estimates that around 13 million nurses will be needed in the near future to fill in the needs of the global population ("ICN," n.d.).

These challenges demand the reconceptualization of care delivery, and policy makers advocate harnessing the possibilities that artificial intelligence (AI) and robotic assistive technologies offer, in order to address current and predicted healthcare needs (The UK Government Office for The UK Government Office for Science, 2019). The European Commission (2020), states that AI is a strategic technology that offers many benefits to citizens, businesses, and societies, provided that it is human-centered, ethical and sustainable, and respects fundamental human rights and values.

This chapter draws content from three literature reviews to provide an overview of the different types of humanoid and animal like robots used in healthcare settings. The factors that influence the acceptance of socially assistive robots (SARs) by the potential and actual users will be discussed, with a special emphasis on culture. In addition, the current evidence on the views of healthcare professionals and the factors that impact on the implementation of these robots in health and social care environments will be presented and discussed.

3.2 Humanoid and animal-like socially assistive robots

Currently in healthcare practice, the use of AI is in its infancy and there is a long way ahead before it reaches its full potential (The Academic Health Science Network, 2018). The use of AI is one of the four main Grand Challenges described in the latest UK Government's policy papers (UK Department for business, Energy and Industrial Strategy, 2019) which provide an ambitious roadmap for the enhancement of AI, robotic autonomous systems, the integration of AI technology in the NHS and the provision of social care through robotic autonomous systems (Prescott & Caleb-Solly, 2017).

AI systems can be classified by their complexity in the following categories:

(a) "Low complexity: AI reasoning methods" such as clustering algorithms and decision trees;
(b) "Middle complexity: AI modules or components" such as text to speech modules, and image processing modules and
(c) "High complexity: AI applications" such as chatbots, autonomous vehicles, surgical or pharmacy robots, and care companion robots The Academic Health Science Network (2018).

Social robotic technology includes a large range of robotic applications which come in many different types and shapes. For example, we have humanoid robots such as Pepper and NAO, bartender robot Kime, but also animal-like robots such as Paro the robotic seal (Mervin et al., 2018) and Joy for All dog and cat (https://www.robopets.co.uk/). Even though there is no agreed universal definition for "social robots" (Henschel et al., 2021), an accepted unique characteristic of socially assistive humanoid robots is their ability to aid human users through social interaction, by using speech, movements, and gestures (Feil-Seifer & Matric, 2005). In other words, social robots are robots that can take different shapes and forms so we can have humanoid or animal-like social robots, but we use the term "socially assistive robots" when the social robot is designed to offer some form of assistance to the human user.

Sarrica et al. (2019, p. 11) analyzed the used definitions of social robots in published literature and found the following shared traits: *"social robots are physically embodied agents that possess human or animal-like qualities. They are described as autonomous or semi-autonomous, and perceive and respond to environmental cues, engage in social interactions, communicate, cooperate, learn, make decisions and perform actions. All these abilities become "social" in as much as they are enacted by robots and evaluated by humans according to the community's goals and social norms."*

The interpretation of the robot's actions and behaviors by humans based on current norms and conventions brings into light the importance of culture that we will discuss later. But first let us discuss some applications of humanoid and animal-like robots in health care.

The main body of literature about social robots comes from the use of animal-like robots. Over the last few years, robotic pets such as Paro, the baby seal robot (PARO therapeutic robot 2014), have been used in the care of patients suffering from dementia as a therapeutic tool.

The reviews of the current evidence from long-term facilities are very promising and demonstrate that Paro interventions have a beneficial effect on reducing agitation, anxiety and improving the quality of life of older adults with dementia (Abbott et al., 2019; Pu et al., 2019). Similar results have been reported from the use of robotic pet dogs with a positive effect on social functioning and a decrease on reported depressive symptoms and loneliness (Jain et al., 2020). Furthermore, research has found that the improvements in social interaction have a positive effect on mood and reduce the use for pain medication (Kang et al., 2020; Pu, Moyle, & Jones, 2020; Pu, Moyle, Jones, et al., 2020). In addition, reduction in anxiety had a positive effect on sleep (Jøranson et al., 2020). The use of Paro with patients suffering from dementia in an acute hospital setting has been limited, but the accounts of patients and staff indicate some promising future outcomes (Hung et al., 2021; Kelly et al., 2021). Paro, along with other animal-like social robots and humanoid social robots have also been used in affective therapy, in cognitive training and in physiological therapy among older adults with positive results that need to be replicated and further investigated (Abdi et al., 2018).

The CARESSES robot, based on the Pepper robotic platform developed by SoftBank Robotics, is the first *humanoid* socially assistive, culturally competent robot, which was created by the European/Japanese collaboration project "CARESSES" (details of this project are included in most of the chapters in this book). The culturally competent software and capabilities of the CARESSES robot were tested among 33 older adults living in care homes in England and Japan (see Chapter 10). Older adults had the opportunity to interact with the robot for up to 18 h over a period of 2 weeks. During the trial participants were divided into three groups: a) care as usual, b) care with a culturally competent robot, and c) care with a robot which was not programmed to be culturally competent. It was found that those who interacted with the culturally competent robot reported better scores on emotional well-being and a decrease on their level of loneliness. Despite the limitations of the experiment, the study provided preliminary evidence of the potential benefits that humanoid culturally competent social robots can have on the psychological health of older adults in care home facilities (Papadopoulos et al., 2021b). In other studies, using the Pepper robot has also been found to be an acceptable way to collect reliable PROM data (Patient Reported Outcome Measurement) (Boumans et al., 2019) and in a recent test of cohabitation with older adults in their home, Pepper was perceived as useful, especially in maintaining social relationships and as a link to the family and friends of the user (Fattal et al., 2020).

SARs can be used as care companions and for facilitating social interaction through games, quizzes, connecting to family and friends, or just chit-chatting with the user. These functions are considered especially important for tackling social isolation and loneliness (Pirhonen et al., 2020). In an acute hospital setting the humanoid robot NAO entertained patients by playing music, dancing, telling jokes, and exercising and the majority of patients enjoyed their interaction with it (Sarabia et al., 2018). A growing body of literature on interventions using NAO shows positive results in people with cognitive impairment and dementia but also with autistic individuals (Robaczewski et al., 2021).

In a recent review of the actual use of social robots during the pandemic, it was reported that social robots were used as a) substitutes in tasks where human-to-human interaction is required (e.g., delivering medicines, transportation, education, telemedicine); b) as safeguards to prevent contagion; and c) as well-being coaches (e.g., offering therapeutic and entertaining tasks to shielding people (Aymerich-Franch, 2020; see also Scassellati & Vázquez, 2020).The most recurrent robots were *Cruzr* (Ubtech), *Pepper* (Softbank), *Temi* (Robotemi), *Greetbot* (OrionStar), and the two top settings of deployment were hospitals and nursing homes (Aymerich-Franch & Ferrer, 2020) (Box 3.1).

BOX 3.1

Socially assistive robots —summary points

Key points

- SARs are autonomous or semi-autonomous, and perceive and respond to environmental cues, engage in social interactions, communicate, cooperate, learn, make decisions, and perform actions

- SARs can be used as care companions to alleviate loneliness and for facilitating social interaction
- The CARESSES robot, is the first *humanoid* socially assistive, culturally competent robot

---

3.3 Surgical robots and robots used in rehabilitation

Non-SARs such as advanced surgical robotic systems are now used routinely for a number of surgical interventions (Thomas, 2021; Wang, 2018). The latest generation of the *da Vinci* robotic system has been reported to offer numerous benefits for patients such as smaller incisions, reduction in infection risks, shorter healing time, and better diagnostics (Kucuk, 2020).

The COVID-19 pandemic (see more details in Chapter 11) highlighted the potential benefit of robotic surgery since it allows staff to maintain social distance from the patient and other staff (Kimmig et al., 2020; Vigneswaran et al., 2020). In addition, by decreasing the patient's length of hospital stay (Moawad et al., 2020; Quarto et al., 2020), the use of robotic surgery could be beneficial for the continuation of services. During the pandemic, many surgical operations had to be postponed due to the need of deploying medical staff to care for COVID-19 patients. In the UK, during April 2021 the NHS was reporting that 4.7 million patients were waiting for an operation (BBC News Health, 2021).

Various robotic systems have been used in the rehabilitation of patients after trauma, surgery, stroke, for individuals with congenital abnormalities, and certain neuromuscular or age-related disorders that impairs the movement of their upper and lower extremities (Zhao et al., 2020). There are several types of robotic systems designed and manufactured for both upper and lower extremity rehabilitation such as Mit-Manus (Krebs et al., 1999), Reharob (Fazekas et al., 2007), Armin (Nef & Riener, 2005), Medarm (Ball et al., 2007), L-exos (Frisoli et al., 2009), and Sarcos Master Arm (Mistry et al., 2005).

Lower limp exoskeleton robots integrate different technologies such as sensing and control, and they can be connected to the human body as wearables. They can stimulate normal gait as well as being able to drive the patient's limps to engage in robot-assisted rehabilitation training (Shi et al., 2019). Lower extremity robotic rehabilitation devices currently in use are the Lokohelp (Freivogel et al., 2008), Lokomat (Colombo et al., 2000), and the ReoAmbulator (West, 2004). The LokoHelp is an electromechanical gait device and trains neurological patients with impaired walking ability (Freivogel et al., 2008). LokoHelp has been tested in several training sessions, and results illustrate that this robotics rehabilitation system can be used in severely affected people with brain injury, stroke, or spinal cord injury (Freivogel et al., 2008). The other well-known robot-assisted gait trainer Lokomat, consists of a treadmill, a body weight support system, and a robotic gait orthosis. The studies illustrate that Lokomat provides effective training and high percentages of recovery potential (Colombo et al., 2000). The ReoAmbulator is also a body weight-supported treadmill robotic system (West, 2004). The use of robots in rehabilitation may reduce the patient—physiotherapist contact, as well as traveling for patients, which can be especially useful for those with reduced mobility (Leocani et al., 2020).

Despite the explosion of research on the use of robotic systems in rehabilitation during the last 20 years, the high cost of the technology, its complexity, and the relatively small incremental positive effect continue to hinder its widespread application (Weber & Stein, 2018). As a result, the number of commercialized robotic rehabilitation devices is still very low compared to the number of patients who may benefit from their use.

3.4 Usefulness, appearance, and other cultural characteristics influencing acceptability

As robots infiltrate our life, the field of human—robot interaction (HRI) is trying to understand what can make robots more desirable and acceptable. Surveys with users and the wider public, reported mixed views regarding their perceptions, and attitudes about the robots' benefits, desirability, acceptance, need, and other indicators. Some reviews on the use of robotic pets have revealed that not everyone likes to interact and engage with robots and some people actually dislike them (Abbott et al., 2019). Recent data from the European Union barometer showed that negative attitudes toward robots increased between the five-year period of 2012 and 2017. Negative attitudes were especially reported by women with lower education levels and for the use of robots in the workplace. However, responders from countries with a large population of older adults were more positive for the use of robots (Gnambs & Appel, 2019).

A meta-analysis of the factors affecting trust in HRI revealed that the robot's performance and attributes were the largest contributors to the development of trust (Hancock et al., 2011). Other teams have focused on the exploration of social eye gaze and its impact on HRI (Admoni & Scassellati, 2017) and found that people react more favorably to robots that are able to follow their conversation and the robot's gaze can track what is being said and done.

Understanding the acceptability of robots is especially critical for health care. Roboticists and social scientists understand that for SARs to be *accepted* by humans there is a need to be perceived as useful but also as easy to use, trustworthy, and likable. These topics are so relevant, that recent conferences on HRI tend to have special sessions entirely devoted to exploring the impact of different factors, especially on trust (Rossi et al., 2018).

Two main theoretical models have been used in research related to the acceptance of social robots. The Almere model of Hirt et al. (2021) is the most cited model of social robot acceptance and has been developed in the context of care facilities for older adults. The second model is the Shin and Choo (2011) acceptance of social interactive model that has been tested among students. Both models are based on the Unified Theory of Acceptance and Use of Technology (UTAUT) developed by Venkatesh et al. (2003). The UTAUT theory states that performance expectancy, effort expectancy, social influence, and facilitating conditions are direct determinants of intention to use a new technology and actual use. Vandemeulebroucke et al. (2021) found that acceptance of social robots is influenced by many factors, such as the users' perceived need for the technology, perceived usefulness and easiness to use, the users' previous experiences with technology, their age, level of education, expectations about what the technology can do, their attitudes and cultural background (Broadbent et al., 2009). In addition, a user's personality is also positively associated with acceptance, with those individuals with an open-minded, extrovert, and more agreeable personality type being more likely to accept the robot (Esterwood et al., 2021).

Appearance and the robot's interaction style play also a very important role in its acceptability. It has been found that users tend to like a humanoid robot that has some anthropomorphic characteristics, like head, eyes, hands, and legs but does look a lot like a human (Onyeulo & Gandhi, 2020) [Chapter 9 will further discuss the role of the robot's appearance, by introducing the so-called "Uncanny Valley theory]. Furthermore, acceptance is influenced by the type of interaction, with those having the opportunity to directly interact with a robot more likely to accept it, than those with an indirect interaction (have seen a demonstration or asked to observe) (Naneva et al., 2020; Sarda Gou et al., 2021).

Researchers have also found that robots that interact in a person oriented way and not a task oriented way have an effect on the user's self-efficacy and perceived agreeability. It has also been reported that users also experienced less frustration and interacted for longer periods with the person oriented robot (Latikka et al., 2019; Zafari et al., 2019). This is considered a significant finding since due to the novelty effect, the engagement with robots wears off quickly.

Robot use self-efficacy (RUSH) refers to the beliefs of users about their ability to use robots, and it has been found to be a separate construct from general self-efficacy (Turja et al., 2019). Most importantly, RUSH is related to the acceptance of the different types of robots. Significantly, it was found that users had stronger acceptance for the humanoid robots.

For the last 20 years, researchers have investigated how culture influences HRI and whether or not the display of culturally specific actions by robots improves HRI (Bruno et al., 2017; Lim et al., 2021). O'Neill-Brown (1997) first explained that the design of a robot needs to factor cultural variables and that a social robot should be able to detect verbal and nonverbal cultural communication patterns but also display appropriate responses. She proposed that in order to optimize interaction, the robot needs to match the user's communication preferences.

In our review of the literature (Papadopoulos & Koulouglioti, 2018), we found that culture influences the individual's attitudes toward robots, their perception, trust, and engagement. People from different countries and cultures do not exhibit the same behaviors toward robots and do not have the same attitudes or the same expectations. Current research work has examined participants from different countries and has used Hofstede's dimensions to understand their findings (Lim et al., 2021). The strongest findings are related to how one's cultural background influences their verbal and nonverbal communication with the robot. For example, how close or far (proximity) they will position themselves to the robot. The current evidence suggests that robots which are perceived to communicate (verbally and nonverbally) in a way that is close to the user's culture are more accepted and more likable. For example, robots that speak with the user's language or use gestures that the user is familiar with and most likely to use (e.g., Namaste hand gesture when greeting users from India or bowing when meeting someone in Japan). However, focusing only on what sociologists call cultural homophily (Basov, 2020) (how closely a robot's behavior can be aligned to the cultural expectations or norms of the human user) is not enough and cannot guarantee the user's acceptance. Many human users from different cultures that have the opportunity to interact with culturally aligned robots continue to report negative attitudes toward robots. Therefore, researchers call for the development of culturally adaptive robots. Robots that can make slight adjustments on actions and/or body and spoken language based on the individual user or user group (Lim et al., 2021).

Our work in the CARESSES project focused on the development of culturally competent SARs which is a further extension of the notion of adaptability. Details are described in later chapters (Box 3.2).

BOX 3.2

Factors influencing the acceptability of robots from human users

Key points

A number of factors have been identified as influencing the acceptability and desirability of the robot. These include

- The perceived need and usefulness of the robot
- The perceived user friendliness
- The robot's appearance
- The robot's cultural sensitivity and cultural competence

3.5 Views of nurses and other health professionals on the use of SARs

Another key to the successful use of the AI/robotic technologies is the understanding of the care workers' perceptions, attitudes, and views about the use of robots in care settings, as this can help with predicting how likely they might be to embrace their deployments in their workplace (Davis et al., 1989).

Our literature review revealed that overall, health and social care workers report mixed views regarding the use of robots in a healthcare setting (Papadopoulos et al., 2018). They raised concerns about the following issues which related to safety and acceptability (Broadbent et al., 2009, 2012; Louie et al., 2014; Zsiga et al., 2013):

- infection control,
- protecting the privacy of patients and staff,
- fears about being replaced by robots, and
- loss of the human to human personal care.

The reduction in human contact has been a major criticism. Nurses and other health professionals reported that they could accept robotic devices which were able to do chores, such as heavy lifting, moving patients, delivering materials (Turja et al., 2018), monitoring patients, reminding them about their schedule of the day or time for medication, while not approving a robotic companion role (Savela et al., 2018).

In contrast, other studies have shown that there are positive emotions and attitudes toward robots, and that robots have been received positively (Chen et al., 2020; Jayawardena et al., 2010; Louie et al., 2014; Stafford et al., 2010). This was notably the case where studies involved interaction with a robot which was designed to accommodate the preferences of older people (Jayawardena et al., 2010; Stafford et al., 2010). Similarly, the attitudes of health professionals toward the use of social robots for older adults in long-term care were significantly influenced by their awareness of social robots (Schutte, 2019). Most of them viewed social robots as beneficial and practical in psychosocial care for older adults (Chuan et al., 2020; Rantanen et al., 2018), and also as good devices for activating the patients' motor and cognitive skills (Łukasik et al., 2020; Chuan et al., 2020; Vänni et al., 2019).

In our work in the CARESSES project, after the trial was completed with the robot and older residents, we interviewed care workers in different participating sites on their views about humanoid SARs (Papadopoulos et al., 2021a). Semi-structured interviews were conducted between October 2019 and January 2020 with 23 care home workers in the UK. In line with previous research (Hebesberger et al., 2017; Melkas et al., 2020), we found that care workers had both positive and negative attitudes toward robots. Many participants responded positively and recognized the potential usefulness of SARs in the care home setting and in a rapidly changing society. By contrast, some participants were resistant to the use of robots, because they found the robot frightening, or because they were concerned that residents may also be afraid of it. In addition, participants identified that people from older generations (both staff and residents) may be less familiar with technology and therefore may be less accepting of the use of a robot. Furthermore, robots were seen as best placed working alongside carers rather than being carers in their own right, and participants suggested several ways in which robots could usefully assist them, for example, by providing companionship or monitoring the residents.

This finding was similar to previously published reports that also suggest that care home staff prefer robots to be assigned tasks that do not require the robot to take complete responsibility for caring for the older person, but instead support the care worker in the care they are already providing and engage with tasks that are considered secondary, for example, help the care worker by having a "fetch and carry" function, or be used as a hospitality guide by accompanying visitors to rooms and offices, or by providing useful general information (e.g., about the weather, the time, the date, the news, etc.) (Hebesberger et al., 2015; Niemela & Melkas, 2019; Turja et al., 2018). According to grey literature, in Japan human-like robots are already being utilized as supplemental healthcare workers in elders' homes across the country. Larger robotic machines are used to carry-out laborious physical tasks like moving patients, and smaller interactive robots are being used to combat loneliness and inactivity in the elderly population (Merkusheva, 2020; Hamstra, 2018).

Monitoring, providing reminders, raising the alarm in case of emergency and helping with contacting medical services were reported to be acceptable actions and were rated especially desirable from family members, health professionals, and the general public when humanoid robots are used in the care of people with Alzheimer's disease and related dementias (Yuan et al., 2021).

The literature reports that in Finland, healthcare professionals had negative attitudes toward the use of robots and thought that they could only be used in certain tasks such as lifting (Turja et al., 2018). Finnish care staff have also been found to be more fearful of the use of robots in the care of older adults compared to their Japanese counterparts who had more positive attitudes (Coco et al., 2018). Korean nurses reported that robots could be helpful in monitoring the patient and assisting with mobility, but they were concerned about the malfunction of the technology and that robots could interrupt the nurse—patient relationship (Lee et al., 2018). Pediatric nurses in Taiwan thought that robots could positively impact the care of pediatric patients and their families but may reduce employment opportunities for skilled nurses and may interfere with providing individualized patient care (Liang et al., 2019). Further, UK health professionals seem to have positive attitudes toward the use of social robots when used for older adults (Chuan et al., 2020) and toward the use of animal-like companion robots with older adults (Bradwell et al., 2020) (Box 3.3).

BOX 3.3

Views of healthcare workers about robots

Key points

- Health and social care workers reported mixed views regarding the use of robots in the workplaces
- Health and social care workers viewed a robot more positively if it could do the following:
  - Monitoring the patients, providing reminders, raising the alarm in case of emergency and helping with contacting medical services
  - Lifting patients and helping with their mobility
  - Helping the care staff
  - Fetch and carry things
  - Providing routine information to patients and visitors

3.6 Enablers and barriers to the implementation of SARs

Even though social robots are being used in different care settings, many questions remain unanswered, especially related to their effective implementation. A recent review on the use of Paro in the care of dementia patients revealed that a major gap in the research work is the fact that the implementation process is inadequately studied and that implementation theoretical models are not usually used. As a result, it is hard to identify whether the barriers or facilitators are related to the organization, the users or other stakeholders like families, clinicians, managers, or educators (Hung et al., 2019).

Belanche et al. (2020) presented a theoretical model for the implementation of service robots. The model explains that a) the design of the robot, b) the features of the customer, and c) the characteristics of the service encounters, dictate the performance of the robot. In other words, how well accepted the robot is; how satisfied the user is; and how loyal the user will be to the technology. Interestingly, the influence and importance of culture is recognized as a key factor for both the robot design and as a customer feature. In accordance with what we discovered in our reviews of the literature, the authors suggest that human users would most likely prefer a robot that exhibits features closer to their culture and that is also relevant to how natural the robots speak their language. The authors called for cross-cultural studies to explore how known cultural dimensions, such as the Hofstede's dimensions (Hofstede & Hofstede, 2005), influence attitudes toward robots, and to explore whether, for example, people from countries scoring high on uncertainty avoidance have more negative attitudes toward the robot, or those from individualistic societies have more positive attitudes.

In our systematic review of the literature (Papadopoulos et al., 2020) on what might hinder or facilitate the implementation of social robots in health care, we found that the main barriers seem to be related to the technical problems, previous experience with technology, robots' limited capabilities and negative preconceptions toward the use of robots in healthcare. Similar findings were reported from a recent implementation of a social service robot in a day care facility for older adults. Technical problems and attitudes toward the robots were the main problems that affected its effectiveness (Takanokura et al., 2021).

In contrast, the main enablers were related to how useful and easy to use the robot was, how enjoyable the interaction was and overall experience, whether or not the technology was personalized to the user's needs and how familiar toward the robot the user was. Other researchers looking into what characteristics and capabilities the users might like a social robotic dog to have, discovered that users preferred the manifestation of attachment, emotion, and personality (Konok et al., 2018). Familiarization with the robot is important for all health professionals, support staff, and families. A training session on social robots for professional recreational therapists revealed that after the sessions they felt more willing to engage with social robots, less fearful of making mistakes, and less intimidated (Eldridge et al., 2020).

Safety, safeguarding, privacy, and ethics were reported as main implementation influencing factors by healthcare professionals, family caregivers, and patients. A few studies have highlighted the importance of setting social and legal boundaries for robots in order to ensure safety and privacy of the caregivers and patients (Papadopoulos et al., 2020; Vänni et al., 2019; Coco et al., 2018; Maalouf et al., 2018) while Hirt et al. (2021), in their review of social robots interventions with people with dementia, raised the issue of the ethical application of such interventions. In their analysis, they found that researchers consistently failed to report how informed consent was obtained from patients with dementia, how they were involved in the development of the tested interventions or how the intervention was tailored to meet their specific needs. They called for a person-centered approach to ensure the ethical application of social robots in this vulnerable population.

The focus on person-centered care was also shared by the staff we interviewed during the post-CARESSES study. In fact, person-centered care and patient safety were central values when considering both the introduction of robots in care homes and the training that would be needed for their implementation. Participants wanted to ensure that there was no additional risk to residents and that the introduction of robots did not negatively impact on the care being provided to residents (Papadopoulos et al. 2021a).

Schmiedel et al. (2021) raised the issue of the organization's cultural values and how the integration of social robots needs to account for the fit between the cultural values that are embedded into the robots and the values of the organization that they are deployed in. According to the Consolidation Framework for Implementation Research (Damschroder et al., 2009), there are many factors that might influence implementation and they are organized in five domains: 1) the outer setting, 2) the inner setting, 3) the intervention, 4) the individual, and 5) the implementation process. The domain of "inner setting" refers to the cultural and structural characteristics of the organization where an intervention is being implemented. According to the framework, a successful implementation depends on understanding the culture, leadership, readiness, and resources available within the organization.

Currently, Koh et al. (2021) are conducting a scoping review focusing especially on the barriers and facilitators of the implementation of social robots among older people and adults suffering from dementia. While the results are not yet available, the COVID-19 pandemic has brought to the forefront the use of robots. The deployed robots used existing capabilities which due to the challenges imposed by the pandemic became very relevant. For example, the need to wear masks, to social distance, to disinfect, and to deliver products in a safe way became a paramount need and the deployment of robots useful. The pandemic called for the minimization of human to human interaction so robots were utilized to fulfill necessary tasks in a safe manner (Aymerich-Franch, 2020). Even though the utilization of robots during the pandemic was not vast, we are certain that many lessons will be learned from their quick deployment in certain environments. Was their use safe? Cost-effective? Useful? Or did it create more problems, additional cost, and required use of resources and a sophisticated infrastructure that still presents many disadvantages for their everyday use?

3.7 Conclusion

In summary, it is evident that the use of robots in health is expanding and developing fast. In regard to SARs, currently animal-like robots are mostly used in long-term care facilities and in the care for people suffering from dementia with many positive results. The use of humanoid robots and their application in health and social care continues to be limited. The COVID-19 pandemic accelerated the use of such robots in some settings but it is too early to evaluate the results and the long-term implications are unknown.

Views about robots remain mixed and are being influenced by many factors such as interaction with robots, the robot's capabilities, usefulness, and easiness of the technology. Nurses and healthcare professionals are willing to accept robots in supporting roles but worry about the patient's safety, privacy, and compromising the patient's quality of care. Culture seems to play a central role in acceptance of robots but current research has only explored the influence of culture on certain aspects of verbal and nonverbal communication leaving many unanswered questions.

Future explorations of the implementation of robots need to be guided by strong theoretical models that will enhance our understanding on the significance of organizational, individual, and contextual factors that can affect their successful implementation.

3.7.1 Reflective questions

- Taking into consideration your own cultural background and values, would you welcome a social robot in your department? Think of the reasons behind your positive or negative answer.
- Reflect on your work day. Can you think of three tasks that you would welcome the help of a SAR?
- Think about the patients that you care for (children, older adults, adolescents, adults) and your work setting (hospital, community, etc.). From your perspective, what are the main factors that could determine the success or failure of the implementation of a social robot in the care of your patients?

References

Abbott, R., Orr, N., McGill, P., Whear, R., Bethel, A., Garside, R., Stein, K., & Thompson-Coon, J. (2019). How do "robopets" impact the health and well-being of residents in care homes? A systematic review of qualitative and quantitative evidence. *International Journal of Older People Nursing, 14*. https://doi.org/10.1111/opn.12239

Abdi, J., Al-Hindawi, A., Ng, T., & Vizcaychipi, M. P. (2018). Scoping review on the use of socially assistive robot technology in elderly care. *BMJ Open, 8*, e018815. https://doi.org/10.1136/bmjopen-2017-018815

Admoni, H., & Scassellati, B. (2017). Social eye gaze in human-robot interaction: A review. *Journal Human Robot Interaction, 6*, 25. https://doi.org/10.5898/JHRI.6.1.Admoni

Aymerich-Franch, L. (2020). Why it is time to stop ostracizing social robots. *Nature Machine Intelligence, 2*. https://doi.org/10.1038/s42256-020-0202-5, 364–364.

Aymerich-Franch, L., & Ferrer, I. (2020). The implementation of social robots during the COVID-19 pandemic. ArXiv preprint. ArXiv:2007.03941.

Ball, S. J., Brown, I. E., & Scott, S. H. (2007). Medarm: A rehabilitation robot with 5DOF at the shoulder complex. In *2007 IEEE/ASME international conference on advanced intelligent mechatronics. Presented at the 2007 IEEE/ASME international conference on advanced intelligent mechatronics (AIM2007)* (pp. 1–6). Zurich: IEEE. https://doi.org/10.1109/AIM.2007.4412446

Basov, N. (2020). The ambivalence of cultural homophily: Field positions, semantic similarities, and social network ties in creative collectives. *Poetics, 78*, 101353. https://doi.org/10.1016/j.poetic.2019.02.004

BBC News Health. (2021). *4.7 million waiting for operations in England*. https://www.bbc.co.uk/news/health-56752599#:~:text=Around%204.7%20million%20people%20were,2007%2C%20NHS%20England%20figures%20show.&text=NHS%20England%20recently%20announced%20that,many%20people%20treated%20as%20possible.

Belanche, D., Casaló, L. V., Flavián, C., & Schepers, J. (2020). Service robot implementation: A theoretical framework and research agenda. *Service Industries Journal, 40*, 203–225. https://doi.org/10.1080/02642069.2019.1672666

References

Boumans, R., van Meulen, F., Hindriks, K., Neerincx, M., & Olde Rikkert, M. G. M. (2019). Robot for health data acquisition among older adults: A pilot randomised controlled cross-over trial. *BMJ Quality & Safety, 28*, 793. https://doi.org/10.1136/bmjqs-2018-008977

Bradwell, H. L., Winnington, R., Thill, S., & Jones, R. B. (2020). Longitudinal diary data: Six months real-world implementation of affordable companion robots for older people in supported living. In *Companion of the 2020 ACM/IEEE International Conference on Human-Robot Interaction* (pp. 148–150).

Broadbent, E., Stafford, R., & MacDonald, B. (2009). Acceptance of healthcare robots for the older population: Review and future directions. *International Journal of Social Robotics, 1*, 319–330. https://doi.org/10.1007/s12369-009-0030-6

Broadbent, E., Tamagawa, R., Patience, A., Knock, B., Kerse, N., Day, K., & MacDonald, B. A. (2012). Attitudes towards health-care robots in a retirement village. *Australasian Journal on Ageing, 31*(2), 115–120.

Bruno, B., Chong, N. Y., Kamide, H., Kanoria, S., Lee, J., Lim, Y., Pandey, A. K., Papadopoulos, C., Papadopoulos, I., Pecora, F., Saffiotti, A., & Sgorbissa, A. (2017). Paving the way for culturally competent robots: A position paper. In *2017 26th IEEE international symposium on robot and human interactive communication (RO-MAN). Presented at the 2017 26th IEEE international symposium on robot and human interactive communication (RO-MAN)* (pp. 553–560). Lisbon: IEEE. https://doi.org/10.1109/ROMAN.2017.8172357

Chen, S. C., Jones, C., & Moyle, W. (2020). Health professional and workers attitudes towards the use of social robots for older adults in long-term care. *International Journal of Social Robotics, 12*, 1135–1147.

Chuan, C., Cindy, J., & Wend, M. (2020). Health professional and workers attitudes towards the use of social robots for older adults in long-term care. *International Journal of Social Robotics, 12*, 1135–1147.

Coco, K., Kangasniemi, M., & Rantanen, T. (2018). Care personnel's attitudes and fears toward care robots in elderly care: A comparison of data from the care personnel in Finland and Japan. *Journal of Nursing Scholarship, 50*(6), 634–644.

Colombo, G., Joerg, M., Schreier, R., & Dietz, V. (2000). Treadmill training of paraplegic patients using a robotic orthosis. *Journal of Rehabilitation Research and Development, 37*, 693–700.

Damschroder, L. J., Aron, D. C., Keith, R. E., Kirsh, S. R., Alexander, J. A., & Lowery, J. C. (2009). Fostering implementation of health services research findings into practice: A consolidated framework for advancing implementation science. *Implementation Science, 4*, 50. https://doi.org/10.1186/1748-5908-4-50

Davis, F. D., Bagozzi, R. P., & Warshaw, P. R. (1989). User acceptance of computer technology: A comparison of two theoretical models. *Management Science, 35*(8), 982–1003.

Eldridge, L., Nagata, S., Piatt, J., Stanojevic, C., Sabanovic, S., Bennett, C., & Randall, N. (2020). Utilization of socially assistive robots in recreational therapy. *American Journal of Recreative Theraphy, 19*, 35–45.

Esterwood, C., Essenmacher, K., Yang, H., Zeng, F., & Robert, L. P. (2021). A meta-analysis of human personality and robot acceptance in human-robot interaction. In *Proceedings of the 2021 CHI Conference on Human Factors in Computing Systems* (pp. 1–18). https://doi.org/10.1145/3411764.3445542, Article No. 711

Fattal, C., Cossin, I., Pain, F., Haize, E., Marissael, C., Schmutz, S., & Ocnarescu, I. (2020). Perspectives on usability and accessibility of an autonomous humanoid robot living with elderly people. *Disability and Rehabilitation: Assistive Technology*, 1–13. https://doi.org/10.1080/17483107.2020.1786732

Fazekas, G., Horvath, M., Troznai, T., & Toth, A. (2007). Robot-mediated upper limb physiotherapy for patients with spastic hemiparesis: A preliminary study. *Journal of Rehabilitation Medicine, 39*, 580–582. https://doi.org/10.2340/16501977-0087

Feil-Seifer, D., & Mataric, M. J. (2005). Socially assistive robotics. In *9th international conference on rehabilitation robotics, 2005. ICORR 2005. Presented at the 9th international conference on rehabilitation robotics, 2005. ICORR 2005* (pp. 465–468). Chicago, IL, USA: IEEE. https://doi.org/10.1109/ICORR.2005.1501143

Freivogel, S., Mehrholz, J., Husak-Sotomayor, T., & Schmalohr, D. (2008). Gait training with the newly developed 'LokoHelp'-system is feasible for non-ambulatory patients after stroke, spinal cord and brain injury. A feasibility study. *Brain Injury, 22*, 625–632. https://doi.org/10.1080/02699050801941771

Frisoli, A., Bergamasco, M., Carboncini, M. C., & Rossi, B. (2009). Robotic assisted rehabilitation in virtual reality with the L-EXOS. *Studies in Health Technology and Informatics, 145*, 40–54.

Gnambs, T., & Appel, M. (2019). Are robots becoming unpopular? Changes in attitudes towards autonomous robotic systems in europe. *Computers in Human Behavior, 93*, 53–61. https://doi.org/10.1016/j.chb.2018.11.045

Hamstra, B. (2018). Will these nurse robots take your job? Don't freak out just yet. Available at: https://nurse.org/articles/nurse-robots-friend-or-foe/. (Accessed on: 8/02/2021).

Hancock, P. A., Billings, D. R., Schaefer, K. E., Chen, J. Y. C., de Visser, E. J., & Parasuraman, R. (2011). A meta-analysis of factors affecting trust in human-robot interaction. *Human Factors The Journal of Human Factors and Ergonomics Society,, 53*, 517–527. https://doi.org/10.1177/0018720811417254

Hebesberger, D., Kortner, T., Gisinger, C., & Pripfl, J. (2017). A long-term autonomous robot at a care hospital: a mixed-methods study on social acceptance and experiences of staff and older adults. *International Journal of Social Robotics, 9*, 417–429.

Hebesberger, D., Körtner, T., Pripfl, J., Gisinger, C., & Hanheide, M. (2015). What do staff in eldercare want a robot for? An assessment of potential tasks and user requirements for a long-term deployment. In *IROS workshop bridg. User needs deployed appl. Serv. Robots 28 sept. 2015 hambg.*

Henschel, A., Laban, G., & Cross, E. S. (2021). What makes a robot social? A review of social robots from science fiction to a home or hospital near you. *Current Robotics Reports, 2*, 9–19. https://doi.org/10.1007/s43154-020-00035-0

Hofstede, G., & Hofstede, G. J. (2005). *Cultures and organizations: Software of the mind ; [intercultural cooperation and its importance for survival]*. New York: McGraw-Hill.

Hung, L., Gregorio, M., Mann, J., Wallsworth, C., Horne, N., Berndt, A., Liu, C., Woldum, E., Au-Yeung, A., & Chaudhury, H. (2021). Exploring the perceptions of people with dementia about the social robot PARO in a hospital setting. *Dementia, 20*, 485–504. https://doi.org/10.1177/1471301219894141

Hung, L., Liu, C., Woldum, E., Au-Yeung, A., Berndt, A., Wallsworth, C., Horne, N., Gregorio, M., Mann, J., & Chaudhury, H. (2019). The benefits of and barriers to using a social robot PARO in care settings: A scoping review. *BMC Geriatrics, 19*, 232. https://doi.org/10.1186/s12877-019-1244-6

Hirt, J., Ballhausen, N., Hering, A., Kliegel, M., Beer, T., & Meyer, G. (2021). Social robot interventions for people with dementia: A systematic review on effects and quality of reporting. *Journal of Alzheimer's Disease, 79*, 773–792. https://doi.org/10.3233/JAD-200347

ICN: International Council of Nurses Policy Brief. The Global Nursing Shortage and Nurse Retention. ICN Policy Brief_Nurse Shortage and Retention.pdf. Accessed on 05/02/2021.

Jain, B., Syed, S., Hafford-Letchfield, T., & O'Farrell-Pearce, S. (2020). Dog-assisted interventions and outcomes for older adults in residential long-term care facilities: A systematic review and meta-analysis. *International Journal of Older People Nursing, 15*. https://doi.org/10.1111/opn.12320

Jayawardena, C., Kuo, I. H., Unger, U., Igic, A., Wong, R., Watson, C. I., … MacDonald, B. A. (2010). Deployment of a service robot to help older people. In *2010 IEEE/RSJ International Conference on Intelligent Robots and Systems* (pp. 5990–5995). IEEE.

Jøranson, N., Olsen, C., Calogiuri, G., Ihlebæk, C., & Pedersen, I. (2020). Effects on sleep from group activity with a robotic seal for nursing home residents with dementia: A cluster randomized controlled trial. *International Psychogeriatrics, 1*–12. https://doi.org/10.1017/S1041610220001787

Kang, H. S., Makimoto, K., Konno, R., & Koh, I. S. (2020). Review of outcome measures in PARO robot intervention studies for dementia care. *Geriatric Nursing, 41*, 207–214. https://doi.org/10.1016/j.gerinurse.2019.09.003

Kelly, P. A., Cox, L. A., Petersen, S. F., Gilder, R. E., Blann, A., Autrey, A. E., & MacDonell, K. (2021). The effect of PARO robotic seals for hospitalized patients with dementia: A feasibility study. *Geriatric Nursing, 42*, 37–45. https://doi.org/10.1016/j.gerinurse.2020.11.003

Kimmig, R., Verheijen, R. H. M., Rudnicki, M., & Council, for, S. (2020). Robot assisted surgery during the COVID-19 pandemic, especially for gynecological cancer: A statement of the society of European robotic gynaecological surgery (SERGS). *Journal of Gynecologic Oncology, 31*. https://doi.org/10.3802/jgo.2020.31.e59

Koh, W. Q., Felding, S. A., Toomey, E., & Casey, D. (2021). Barriers and facilitators to the implementation of social robots for older adults and people with dementia: A scoping review protocol. *Systematic Reviews, 10*, 49. https://doi.org/10.1186/s13643-021-01598-5

Konok, V., Korcsok, B., Miklósi, Á., & Gácsi, M. (2018). Should we love robots? – the most liked qualities of companion dogs and how they can be implemented in social robots. *Computers in Human Behavior, 80*, 132–142. https://doi.org/10.1016/j.chb.2017.11.002

Krebs, H. I., Hogan, N., Volpe, B. T., Aisen, M. L., Edelstein, L., & Diels, C. (1999). Overview of clinical trials with MIT-MANUS: A robot-aided neuro-rehabilitation facility. *Technology Health Care Offical Journal of the European Society for Medical Oncology, 7*, 419–423.

Kucuk, S. (2020). Introductory chapter: Medical robots in surgery and rehabilitation. In S. Küçük, & A. Erdem Canda (Eds.), *Medical robotics - new achievements*. IntechOpen. https://doi.org/10.5772/intechopen.85836

Latikka, R., Turja, T., & Oksanen, A. (2019). Self-efficacy and acceptance of robots. *Computers in Human Behavior, 93*, 157–163. https://doi.org/10.1016/j.chb.2018.12.017

Lee, J.-Y., Song, Y. A., Jung, J. Y., Kim, H. J., Kim, B. R., Do, H.-K., & Lim, J.-Y. (2018). Nurses' needs for care robots in integrated nursing care services. *Journal of Advanced Nursing, 74*, 2094–2105. https://doi.org/10.1111/jan.13711

Leocani, L., Diserens, K., Moccia, M., & Caltagirone, C. (2020). Disability through COVID-19 pandemic: Neurorehabilitation cannot wait. *European Journal of Neurology, 27*, e50–e51. https://doi.org/10.1111/ene.14320

Liang, H., Wu, K., Weng, C., & Hsieh, H. (2019). Nurses' views on the potential use of robots in the pediatric unit. *Journal of Pediatric Nursing, 47*, 58–64.

Lim, V., Rooksby, M., & Cross, E. S. (2021). Social robots on a global stage: Establishing a role for culture during human–robot interaction. *International Journal of Social Robotics, 13*, 1307–1333. https://doi.org/10.1007/s12369-020-00710-4

Louie, W. Y. G., Li, J., Vaquero, T., & Nejat, G. (2014). A focus group study on the design considerations and impressions of a socially assistive robot for long-term care. In *The 23rd IEEE International Symposium on Robot and Human Interactive Communication* (pp. 237–242). IEEE.

Łukasik, S., Tobis, S., Kropińska, S., & Suwalska, A. (2020). Role of assistive robots in the care of older people: Survey study among medical and nursing students. *Journal of Medical Internet Research, 22*(8), Article e18003.

Maalouf, N., Sidaoui, A., Elhajj, H. I., & Asmar, D. (2018). Robotics in nursing: A scoping review. *Journal of Nursing Scholarship, 50*(6), 590–600.

Melkas, H., Hennala, L., Pekkarinen, S., & Kyrki, V. (2020). Impacts of robot implementation on care personnel and clients in elderly-care institutions. *International Journal of Medical Informatics, 134*, 104041.

Merkusheva, D. (2020). 10 Humanoid Robots of 2020. Accessed on 04/02/2021. https://www.asme.org/topics-resources/content/10-humanoid-robots-of-2020.

Mervin, M. C., Moyle, W., Jones, C., Murfield, J., Draper, B., Beattie, E., Shum, D. H. K., O'Dwyer, S., & Thalib, L. (2018). The cost-effectiveness of using PARO, a therapeutic robotic seal, to reduce agitation and medication use in dementia: Findings from a cluster–randomized controlled trial. *Journal of the American Medical Directors Association, 19*, 619–622.e1. https://doi.org/10.1016/j.jamda.2017.10.008

Mistry, M., Mohajerian, P., & Schaal, S. (2005). An exoskeleton robot for human arm movement study. In *2005 IEEE/RSJ international conference on intelligent robots and systems. Presented at the 2005 IEEE/RSJ international conference on intelligent robots and systems* (pp. 4071–4076). Edmonton, Alta., Canada: IEEE. https://doi.org/10.1109/IROS.2005.1545450

Moawad, G. N., Rahman, S., Martino, M. A., & Klebanoff, J. S. (2020). Robotic surgery during the COVID pandemic: Why now and why for the future. *Journal of Robotic Surgery, 14*, 917–920. https://doi.org/10.1007/s11701-020-01120-4

Naneva, S., Sarda Gou, M., Webb, T. L., & Prescott, T. J. (2020). A systematic review of attitudes, anxiety, acceptance, and trust towards social robots. *International Journal of Social Robotics, 12*, 1179–1201. https://doi.org/10.1007/s12369-020-00659-4

Nef, T., & Riener, R. (2005). ARMin - design of a novel arm rehabilitation robot. In *9th international conference on rehabilitation robotics, 2005. ICORR 2005. Presented at the 9th international conference on rehabilitation robotics, 2005. ICORR 2005* (pp. 57–60). Chicago, IL, USA: IEEE. https://doi.org/10.1109/ICORR.2005.1501051

Niemelä, M., & Melkas, H. (2019). Robots as social and physical assistants in elderly care. In M. Toivonen, & E. Saari (Eds.), *Human-centered digitalization and services* (pp. 177–197). Singapore: Springer.

O'Neill-Brown, P. (1997). Setting the stage for the culturally adaptive agent. In *Proc. 1997 AAAI fall symp. Socially intell. Agents* (pp. 93–97).

Onyeulo, E. B., & Gandhi, V. (2020). What makes a social robot good at interacting with humans? *Information, 11*, 43. https://doi.org/10.3390/info11010043

Papadopoulos, I., Ali, S., Papadopoulos, C., Castro, N., Faulkens, N., & Koulouglioti, C. (2021a). A qualitative exploration of care homes workers' views and training needs in relation to the use of socially assistive humanoid robots in their workplace. *International Journal of Older People Nursing, e, 12432.*

Papadopoulos, C., Castro, N., Nigath, A., et al. (2021b). The CARESSES randomised controlled trial: Exploring the health-related impact of culturally competent artificial intelligence embedded into socially assistive robots and tested in older adult care homes. *International Journal of Social Robotics.* https://doi.org/10.1007/s12369-021-00781-x

Papadopoulos, I., & Koulouglioti, C. (2018). The influence of culture on attitudes towards humanoid and animal-like robots: An integrative review. *Journal of Nursing Scholarship, 50*, 653–665. https://doi.org/10.1111/jnu.12422

Papadopoulos, I., Koulouglioti, C., & Ali, S. (2018). Views of nurses and other health and social care workers on the use of assistive humanoid and animal-like robots in health and social care: a scoping review. *Contemporary Nurse, 54*(4–5), 425–442.

Papadopoulos, I., Koulouglioti, C., Lazzarino, R., & Ali, S. (2020). Enablers and barriers to the implementation of socially assistive humanoid robots in health and social care: A systematic review. *BMJ Open, 10*, e033096. https://doi.org/10.1136/bmjopen-2019-033096

PARO therapeutic robot | research papers [Internet]. (2014) [cited 28 November 2019]. Available from: Parorobots.com http://www.parorobots.com/whitepapers.asp.

Pirhonen, J., Tiilikainen, E., Pekkarinen, S., Lemivaara, M., & Melkas, H. (2020). Can robots tackle late-life loneliness? Scanning of future opportunities and challenges in assisted living facilities. *Futures, 124*, 102640. https://doi.org/10.1016/j.futures.2020.102640

Prescott, T., & Caleb-Solly, P. (2017). *Robotics in Social Care*. EPSRC UK-RAS Network. https://doi.org/10.31256/WP2017.3. ISSN: 2398-4422 (Online), ISSN: 2398-4414 (Print). https://www.ukras.org/wp-content/uploads/2021/01/UKRASWP_SocialCare2017_online.pdf

Pu, L., Moyle, W., & Jones, C. (2020a). How people with dementia perceive a therapeutic robot called PARO in relation to their pain and mood: A qualitative study. *Journal of Clinical Nursing, 29*, 437−446. https://doi.org/10.1111/jocn.15104

Pu, L., Moyle, W., Jones, C., & Todorovic, M. (2019). The effectiveness of social robots for older adults: A systematic review and meta-analysis of randomized controlled studies. *The Gerontologist, 59*, e37−e51. https://doi.org/10.1093/geront/gny046

Pu, L., Moyle, W., Jones, C., & Todorovic, M. (2020b). The effect of using PARO for people living with dementia and chronic pain: A pilot randomized controlled trial. *Journal of the American Medical Directors Association, 21*, 1079−1085. https://doi.org/10.1016/j.jamda.2020.01.014

Quarto, G., Grimaldi, G., Castaldo, L., Izzo, A., Muscariello, R., Sicato, S. D., Franzese, D., Crocerossa, F., Prete, P. D., Carbonara, U., Autorino, R., & Perdonà, S. (2020). Avoiding disruption of timely surgical management of genitourinary cancers during the early phase of the COVID-19 pandemic. *BJU International, 126*, 425−427. https://doi.org/10.1111/bju.15174

Rantanen, T., Lehto, P., Vuorinen, P., & Coco, K. (2018). The adoption of care robots in home care-A survey on the attitudes of Finnish home care personnel. *Journal of Clinical Nursing, 27*(9−10), 1846−1859.

Robaczewski, A., Bouchard, J., Bouchard, K., & Gaboury, S. (2021). Socially assistive robots: The specific case of the NAO. *International Journal of Social Robotics, 13*, 795−831. https://doi.org/10.1007/s12369-020-00664-7

Rossi, A., Holthaus, P., Dautenhahn, K., Koay, K. L., & Walters, M. L. (2018). Getting to know Pepper: Effects of people's awareness of a robot's capabilities on their trust in the robot. In *Proceedings of the 6th international conference on human-agent interaction. Presented at the HAI '18: 6th international conference on human-agent interaction* (pp. 246−252). Southampton United Kingdom: ACM. https://doi.org/10.1145/3284432.3284464

Sarabia, M., Young, N., Canavan, K., Edginton, T., Demiris, Y., & Vizcaychipi, M. P. (2018). Assistive robotic technology to combat social isolation in acute hospital settings. *International Journal of Social Robotics, 10*, 607−620. https://doi.org/10.1007/s12369-017-0421-z

Sarda Gou, M., Webb, T. L., & Prescott, T. (2021). The effect of direct and extended contact on attitudes towards social robots. *Heliyon, 7*, e06418. https://doi.org/10.1016/j.heliyon.2021.e06418

Sarrica, M., Brondi, S., & Fortunati, L. (2019). How many facets does a "social robot" have? A review of scientific and popular definitions online. *Information Technology and People, 33*, 1−21. https://doi.org/10.1108/ITP-04-2018-0203

Savela, N., Turja, T., & Oksanen, A. (2018). Social acceptance of robots in different occupational fields: A systematic literature review. *International Journal of Social Robotics, 10*, 493−502. https://doi.org/10.1007/s12369-017-0452-5

Scassellati, B., & Vázquez, M. (2020). The potential of socially assistive robots during infectious disease outbreaks. *Science Robotics, 5*. https://doi.org/10.1126/scirobotics.abc9014

Schmiedel, T., Jäger, J., & Zhong, V. J. (2021). Social robots in organizational contexts: The role of culture and future research needs. In R. Dornberger (Ed.), *New trends in business information systems and technology, studies in systems, decision and control* (pp. 163−177). Cham: Springer International Publishing. https://doi.org/10.1007/978-3-030-48332-6_11

Schutte, M. (2019). Socially assistive robots in elderly care. The attitudes of healthcare professionals towards the use of Socially Assistive Robots. Master thesis. University of Twente, Netherlands. Available at: http://essay.utwente.nl/79233/1/Schutte_MA_TNW.pdf (Accessed on: 15/02/2021).

Shi, D., Zhang, Wuxiang, Zhang, Wei, & Ding, X. (2019). A review on lower limb rehabilitation exoskeleton robots. *Chinese Journal of Mechanical Engineering, 32*, 74. https://doi.org/10.1186/s10033-019-0389-8

Shin, D. H., & Choo, H. (2011). Modeling the acceptance of socially interactive robotics: Social presence in human−robot interaction. *Interaction Studies, 12*(3), 430−460.

References

Stafford, R. Q., Broadbent, E., Jayawardena, C., Unger, U., Kuo, I. H., Igic, A., … MacDonald, B. A. (2010). Improved robot attitudes and emotions at a retirement home after meeting a robot. In *19th international symposium in robot and human interactive communication* (pp. 82−87). IEEE.

Takanokura, M., Kurashima, R., Ohhira, T., Kawahara, Y., & Ogiya, M. (2021). Implementation and user acceptance of social service robot for an elderly care program in a daycare facility. *Journal of Ambient Intelligence and Humanized Computing*, 1−10. https://doi.org/10.1007/s12652-020-02871-6

The Academic Health Science Network. (2018). *Accelerating artificial intelligence in health and care: Results from a state of the nation survey.* http://ai.ahsnnetwork.com/about/aireport/.

The European Commission. (2020). *A European approach to artificial intelligence.* Accessed on June 15th, 2021. https://digital-strategy.ec.europa.eu/en/policies/european-approach-artificial-intelligence.

The King's Fund. (2018). *The health care workforce in England: Make or break?.* https://www.kingsfund.org.uk/sites/default/files/2018-11/The%20health%20care%20workforce%20in%20England.pdf.

The UK Government Office for Science. (2019). *Future of an ageing population.* https://www.gov.uk/government/publications/future-of-an-ageing-population.

Thomas, L., n.d. Recent advances in robotic surgery.

Turja, T., Rantanen, T., & Oksanen, A. (2019). Robot use self-efficacy in healthcare work (RUSH): Development and validation of a new measure. *AI & Society, 34*, 137−143. https://doi.org/10.1007/s00146-017-0751-2

Turja, T., Van Aerschot, L., Särkikoski, T., & Oksanen, A. (2018). Finnish healthcare professionals' attitudes towards robots: Reflections on a population sample. *Nursing Open, 5*, 300−309. https://doi.org/10.1002/nop2.138

UK Department for business, Energy and Industrial Strategy. (2019). *Policy paper. The grant challenges.* https://www.gov.uk/government/publications/industrial-strategy-the-grand-challenges/industrial-strategy-the-grand-challenges.

Vandemeulebroucke, T., Dzi, K., & Gastmans, C. (2021). Older adults' experiences with and perceptions of the use of socially assistive robots in aged care: A systematic review of quantitative evidence. *Archives of Gerontology and Geriatrics, 95*, 104399. https://doi.org/10.1016/j.archger.2021.104399

Vänni, J. K., Sirpa, E., & Salin, E. S. (2019). Attitudes of professionals toward the need for assistive and social robots in the healthcare sector. In O. Korn (Ed.), *Social Robots: Technological, Societal and Ethical Aspects of Human-Robot Interaction* (pp. 205−236). Springer.

Venkatesh, V., Morris, M. G., Davis, G. B., & Davis, F. D. (2003). User acceptance of information technology: Toward a unified view. *MIS Quarterly*, 425−478.

Vigneswaran, Y., Prachand, V. N., Posner, M. C., Matthews, J. B., & Hussain, M. (2020). What is the appropriate use of laparoscopy over open procedures in the current COVID-19 climate? *Journal of Gastrointestinal Surgery, 24*, 1686−1691. https://doi.org/10.1007/s11605-020-04592-9

Wang, Z. (2018). Advances on the application and research of surgical robots. In *2018 11th international conference on intelligent computation technology and automation (ICICTA). Presented at the 2018 11th international conference on intelligent computation technology and automation (ICICTA)* (pp. 371−374). Changsha: IEEE. https://doi.org/10.1109/ICICTA.2018.00090

Weber, L. M., & Stein, J. (2018). The use of robots in stroke rehabilitation: A narrative review. *NeuroRehabilitation, 43*, 99−110. https://doi.org/10.3233/NRE-172408

West, G. R. (2004). *Powered gait orthosis and method of utilizing same.* https://patentscope.wipo.int/search/en/detail.jsf?docId=WO2004009011.

Yuan, F., Anderson, J. G., Wyatt, T., Lopez, R. P., Crane, M., Montgomery, A., & Zhao, X. (2021). *Assessing the acceptability of a humanoid robot for Alzheimer's disease and related dementia care using an online survey. ArXiv210412903 Cs.*

Zafari, S., Schwaninger, I., Hirschmanner, M., Schmidbauer, C., Weiss, A., & Koeszegi, S. T. (2019). "You are doing so great!" − the effect of a robot's interaction style on self-efficacy in HRI. In *2019 28th IEEE international conference on robot and human interactive communication (RO-MAN). Presented at the 2019 28th IEEE international conference on robot and human interactive communication (RO-MAN)* (pp. 1−7). New Delhi, India: IEEE. https://doi.org/10.1109/RO-MAN46459.2019.8956437

Zhao, P., Zi, B., Purwar, A., & An, N. (2020). Special issue on rehabilitation robots, devices, and methodologies. *Journal of Engineering and Science in Medical Diagnostics and Therapy, 3*, 020301. https://doi.org/10.1115/1.4046325

Zsiga, K., Edelmayer, G., Rumeau, P., Péter, O., Tóth, A., & Fazekas, G. (2013). Home care robot for socially supporting the elderly: focus group studies in three European countries to screen user attitudes and requirements. *International Journal of Rehabilitation Research, 36*(4), 375−378.

CHAPTER

4

The ethics of socially assistive robots in health and social care

Linda Battistuzzi[1] and Chris Papadopoulos[2]

[1]DIBRIS Department, Università degli Studi di Genova, Genova, Italy; [2]Institute for Health Research, University of Bedfordshire, Luton, United Kingdom

LEARNING OBJECTIVES

- To familiarize with some of the main ethical theories and approaches.
- To understand the main ethical considerations having to do with robots, care recipients, and caregivers.
- To understand how ethical challenges were handled within the CARESSES project.

4.1 Introduction

As more people live longer and fertility rates decline, the social and economic infrastructures designed to care for older adults are proving dramatically outdated. Care systems worldwide are buckling under the combined pressures of increased life expectancy and waning numbers of professional caregivers. The coronavirus pandemic has further added to the strain and, in many countries, has exposed vast inequities in care. In the UK, according to AgeUK, one of the country's most prominent older age charities, "The problems with social care are costing older people their dignity, safety, and their lives."(AgeUK, 2021). Finding viable solutions to the care crisis is thus an urgent ethical priority.

Arguably, robots may be one such solution. Proponents of care robotics suggest that robots could alleviate the growing care recipient-caregiver disparity by supporting formal and informal caregivers in repetitive or physically demanding tasks, freeing up time and energies for more significant interactions with care recipients (Vandemeulebroucke et al., 2018). For older adults with cognitive impairments, assistive care with robot technology may allow greater independence, resulting in their ability to live at home longer (Sharkey & Sharkey, 2010). Socially assistive robots also show promise in improving older adults' general mood and well-being, with studies reporting positive findings (Papadopoulos et al., 2021), including reductions in depression scores, and increases in quality of life scores (Abdi et al., 2018). Governments in several countries have therefore taken a favorable view of the possibilities that robots open up in the care domain and have directed significant funding toward initiatives dedicated to developing robots for elder care.

Critical views of care robots, however, have also emerged among ethicists, care experts and older age advocates. Scholars have expressed concerns about patient autonomy (Sparrow, 2016) and informed consent, quality of data management, human contact, infantilization, and equality of access (Sharkey & Sharkey, 2010; Sparrow & Sparrow, 2006). How these ethical issues should be prioritized and interpreted, and what strategies should be adopted to effectively handle them, largely remains to be understood (Wangmo et al., 2019).

What is already clear is that distinctions need to be drawn between robotic technologies and other innovations geared toward replacing human caregivers and those that are designed to support them in the delivery of improved care. Humans in need of care are entitled to compassionate, attentive help from others; at the same time, caring for others is at the very core of the human experience (van Est & Gerritsen, 2017). Thus, unless care recipients should prefer it, caring cannot be surrendered to robots. A reduction in human contact may only be acceptable if it is shown to ensure improved quality of care and to relieve the pressure on human care providers and care systems.

Certainly, robotic innovations need to be introduced with foresight and careful guidelines. As early as 2010, indeed, Sharkey and Sharkey (2010) predicted that "Robots and robotic technology could improve the lives of the elderly, reducing their dependence, and creating more opportunities for social interaction" (p27) as long as appropriate safeguards are in place. Standards and regulations will play a key role in harnessing novel technologies and ensuring they are beneficial to care recipients and caregivers alike.

The goal of this chapter is to provide readers with an overview of some of the main concerns that have emerged in the literature on ethics in socially assistive robotics along with opportunities to reflect on the ethical challenges associated with the use of robots in the care of older adults. This includes issues of dignity, autonomy, attachment and deception, informed consent, privacy, data collection, responsibility, stigma, and safety, and the implications of such issues for care recipients and caregivers. In the Appendix to the chapter, readers will find two case studies. The case studies will provide insights into real-world ethical complexities and are followed by reflective questions that will guide ethical analysis and encourage critical thinking.

4.2 Ethical frameworks for socially assistive robots in care

Technologies like socially assistive robots have far-reaching impacts on societies. According to philosopher of technology Peter-Paul Verbeek, "When technologies are used, they help shape the context in which they fulfill their function, help shape human actions and perceptions, and create new practices and ways of living." (Verbeek, 2008, p. 591). If robots can change the way we live and think and the relationships we have with each other, they must be designed in ways that uphold values of ethical importance (van Wynsberghe, 2013).

Before discussing the ethics of socially assistive robots in health and social care, we need to take a step back and briefly consider how we decide what is good and right. In order to establish what is ethically acceptable, people tend to rely on ethical theories, frameworks and approaches, some of which are based on traditions that emerged in various periods of human history but continue to be relevant and helpful today. Western philosophical traditions in ethics include

- consequentialism—ethical actions are those that maximize people's happiness or welfare; the focus is on the consequences of the act
- deontology—whether an act is morally good or right depends on whether it is in accordance with our duties as rational individuals living together in society; here what is emphasized is the nature of the act rather than its consequences
- virtue ethics—an act is ethical if it is consistent with what a virtuous person would do; instead of the nature of the act or its consequence, this approach emphasizes the character of the person who is acting
- rights-based ethics—humans have a fundamental moral right to choose freely what to do with their lives and to have those choices respected; ethical acts respect and promote this and other rights, such as the right to privacy, the right to the truth, the right not to be injured
- the fairness approach—an act is ethical if it ensures that everyone is treated equally, or if unequally then fairly, based on a defensible standard
- the common good approach—the good of individuals living in society is inextricably linked to the good of the community; ethical acts are those that contribute to the common good
- ethics of care—moral action revolves around relationships and the virtue of care; the emphasis here is placed on the importance of response to the individual rather than on generalizable standards.

In the context of health and social care, along with these theories and approaches, several ethical principles are often used as moral actionguides. The most widely referred to among these principles are respect for autonomy, nonmaleficence, beneficence, and justice (Beauchamp & Childress, 2019). Others include dignity, truth-telling, and solidarity. When considering the deployment of robots in care settings, respect for autonomy, safety, enablement, independence, privacy, and social connectedness may deserve greater attention than others (Draper & Sorell, 2017; Vallor, 2011).

On a transcultural ethics view, caregivers committed to culturally competent care will also need to develop the ability to recognize, affirm and enact principles across cultures, identifying common ground and negotiating divergences (Gallagher, 2006). The importance given to various principles and the priority assigned to them in specific situations, indeed, will be determined by a range of factors having to do, among other things, with the people involved, their lived experiences, their culture, and their values. In addition, individuals striving to uphold certain principles may find that such principles are interdependent, or that they conflict with each other. Responding to ethically challenging situations will often involve attempting to weigh and balance principles that are competing but equally important. Ethical theories, approaches, and frameworks will not always provide ready answers for the resolution of such challenges. Understanding theoretical approaches, however, can facilitate and support reflective practice. As Gallagher pointed out: "It is essential that caregivers are not complacent, can tolerate uncertainty and ambiguity and have the humility and honesty to engage in self-scrutiny and demonstrate a commitment to working toward ethical and cultural competence" (Gallagher, 2006, p. 82).

4.3 Ethics in the CARESSES project

In the CARESSES project (described in detail in Chapter 5), we understood that ethical considerations would require careful attention, both in terms of how the robot would be designed and of how the experimental phase of the project, in which the robot would be trialed with older adults living in care homes, would be conducted.

Human subjects research involving older adults living in long-term care facilities is often characterized by a range of ethical issues (Lingler, Jablonski, Bourbonniere, & Kolanowski, 2009a, 2009b; Maas et al., 2002). In the case of CARESSES, we expected that trialing robots in care settings could involve further ethical complexities. As one way to support researchers in handling ethically complex situations is to provide ethics training, we developed a research ethics training module that was administered to all the CARESSES researchers who were directly involved in the experiments. The training module employed case-based learning (CBL), an approach to learning and instruction that relies on stories to illustrate teaching points and issues (Bagdasarov et al., 2013a, 2013b). CBL presents study cases designed to replicate real-life problems, which learners are asked to solve by identifying analogies, building inferences, and forming decisions (Kalichman, 2014; Kolodner, 2014). The narrative, characters, and settings within cases are tools that enable learners to develop new understandings. Because cases can replicate the nuances of ethical complexities, CBL is extensively used in ethics education (Falkenberg & Woiceshyn, 2008). The core of the CARESSES research ethics training module was thus a series of ethical cases specifically designed for the project that described situations that could realistically emerge during the experiments with the robots (Battistuzzi et al., 2020).

To ensure that ethical considerations would equally be taken into account with regard to the design of the culturally competent robot, we developed a process geared toward embedding ethics within the design process itself. We began by identifying key ethical concepts in relevant ethical guidelines. We then applied those ethical concepts to the scenarios that described how the robot would interact with older adults belonging to different cultures and provided the groundwork for the system design. This straightforward approach highlighted the ethical implications of the robot's behavior early on during the design process and enabled us to identify and engage with ethical problems proactively (Battistuzzi et al., 2018).

The ethical concepts that underpinned this process were derived from the Alzheimer Europe position and guidelines on the ethical use of assistive technology (Alzheimer Europe, 2010). Based on literature reviews and consultations with experts and stakeholders, the Alzheimer Europe guidelines recognize that absolute recommendations, derived from specific sets of ethical principles, can be impractical, and acknowledge that "ethical decision making is a complex task, situations are rarely in effect identical and even those which seem to be so, involve different people who may have different perspectives and have different culturally determined assumptions" (Alzheimer Europe, 2010). The Alzheimer Europe guidelines, therefore, are not grounded in any particular ethical tradition, but emphasize the importance of several of the principles and concerns we have mentioned thus far, and which are discussed in further detail below.

4.4 Robots, care recipients, and caregivers: ethical considerations

4.4.1 Autonomy

The autonomy principle traditionally refers to an individual's capacity to be selfdetermining and to exercise choice without undue pressure, coercion, or other forms of persuasion (Beauchamp & Childress, 2019). This principle is based on the notion that all persons have intrinsic and unconditional worth, and thus, should have the power to make decisions for themselves (Guyer, 2003). Autonomy is often contrasted with paternalism, which occurs, for instance, when caregivers believe that they are better equipped or in a better position than care recipients to decide what is in their best interests and therefore make decisions on their behalf, or without respecting their wishes or seeking their informed consent.

Robotic technology under the control of a care recipient could empower them by promoting their autonomy. Socially assistive robots, which generally do not give physical aid, may be viewed as supporting and maintaining the autonomy and independence of care recipients because the suggestions, cues, and encouragement they provide can help them take care of tasks on their own and care for themselves (Battistuzzi et al., 2018). For example, a socially assistive robot instructed to provide reminders could have a greatly positive impact on a care recipient's sense of control and selfefficacy, reducing the likelihood of hazardous situations and promoting independence. Empowering care recipients in this way is likely to improve both their psychological and physical welfare (Sharkey & Sharkey, 2010).

The robot's assistance, however, should never exceed what is required and useful. Indeed, providing more support than necessary may result in the premature loss of capacities in older adults (Battistuzzi et al., 2018). Moreover, the right balance would need to be found between using robots to help care recipients retain their autonomy and independence and protecting care recipients from any harm that the robot could cause them. Although socially assistive robots may pose less of a risk than other types of assistive robots (such as a robotic wheelchair, or a robotic exoskeleton, for instance), striking this kind of balance is particularly complex with individuals whose cognitive and physical abilities are likely to decline over time (Sharkey & Sharkey, 2010). When faced with decisions about the use of robotic technology that require balancing the management of risk with the promotion of the person's autonomy, the ethical guidelines of Alzheimer Europe suggest "considering the real rather than hypothetical risks involved; the risks to the individual and not primarily the risks to the facility or establishment; considering potential benefits at the same time as potential risks; the fact that people have different perceptions of risk and levels of acceptable risk; and finally, the fact that it is unrealistic and even undesirable to try to eliminate every possible risk in the life of an older adult, even if their cognitive and physical capabilities are failing." (Alzheimer Europe, 2010).

4.4.2 Dignity

Although most of us have an intuitive understanding of what it is, dignity is a vague, slippery concept to define. At the core of human dignity, three elements can be recognized: (i) every human being, for the mere fact of being human, possesses an intrinsic worth; (ii) that intrinsic worth should be recognized and respected by others; (iii) the state exists for the benefit of individual human beings (Neuman, 2000). Scholars who have tried to clarify what dignity is also distinguish between inviolable or universal dignity, which is an inherent property of human beings and does not depend on their behavior, beliefs, or circumstances, and other forms of dignity, which can be held to varying degrees (Bostrom, 2008; Nordenfelt, 2004; Schroeder, 2010; Sharkey, 2015).

In health and social care, dignity is a pivotal concept and issue. Professional caregivers are expected to treat care recipients with dignity, and care recipients wish to be treated in a dignified manner (Clancy et al., 2020). Certain care practices may disregard the worth of human beings by, for instance, ignoring their individuality, overlooking their cultural differences, or belittling them. To preserve dignity, instead, support from a loving family has been found to be crucial (Tranvag et al., 2014). Care recipients' dignity and feelings of selfworth can also be enhanced by friendship and positive relationships with caregivers (Clancy et al., 2020). By acknowledging and responding to cultural backgrounds, values and differences with sensitivity and compassion, culturally competent care can further help care recipients feel respected and valued (Papadopoulos, 2006).

There are concerns that the introduction of robotic technologies in health and social care might lead to fewer opportunities for human contact, making care recipients feel objectified and that they are a burden to society (Sharkey & Sharkey, 2010; Zardiashvili & Fosch-Villaronga, 2020). Because robots are not capable of authentic compassion, empathy, or understanding, they would not be able to provide appropriate care. The inconsiderate application of robots in care settings could generate feelings of humiliation and a loss of selfrespect in care recipients (Sharkey, 2015).

Conversely, the careful deployment of robots could help older adults retain a feeling of control over their environment while reducing their dependence on others (Sharkey, 2015). Socially assistive robots in particular could enhance care recipients' ability to engage in various forms of social interaction and their access to valued experiences, thus providing more opportunities to connect with other people and improving their feelings of selfrespect and selfworth.

4.4.3 Informed consent and shared decision-making

Respecting an older person's autonomy and dignity requires that their ability to make free and informed decisions, particularly about their care, should be respected and actively promoted.

The importance of care recipients being able to make their own decisions is foregrounded in the patient-centered approach to delivering care (Richards et al., 2015). Respecting individuals and their choices, however, does not mean that care recipients will have absolute control over all decisions. Acknowledging that they have a right to lead an autonomous life, but at the same time may need support making certain decisions, the strategy of shared decision-making has emerged, in which care recipients, and formal and informal caregivers together engage in efforts to identify mutually acceptable goals of care (Barry & Edgman-Levitan, 2012; Sandman & Munthe, 2010). Shared decision-making recognizes that autonomy is always relational as the lives of human beings are situated in a web of relationships and mutual interdependencies, but it does not lessen the importance of always seeking the consent of competent older adults, or the assent of those with diminished capacity (Alzheimer Europe, 2010).

When contemplating the introduction of robots in health and social care, informed consent and shared decision-making are complicated by the realities of sophisticated technologies being offered to individuals whose cognitive capacities may be declining, and by the fact that the outcome of interactions between robots and humans is somewhat unpredictable. Consent will not be valid unless it is informed: agreement to the use of a robot without an understanding of its function and of the implications of that function (e.g., consenting to converse with a socially assistive robot without realizing that it might record conversations and sensitive, personal information) will not count as consent. The capacity to consent of older care recipients may vary from day to day or at different times of the day (Jacques & Jackson, 2000). A person may consent to robotic assistance but later have no recollection of what the robot is for (Astell et al., 2019). In this setting, consent should thus be considered a dynamic process, an ongoing conversation in which the care recipient's informed choice whether to use the technology or not is elicited time and time again. Specific training of those responsible for obtaining consent and the use of appropriate communication tools can help ensure that consent is truly sought (Alzheimer Europe, 2014), especially in the case of individuals with declining cognitive abilities.

Furthermore, consent must be voluntary and freely given, without any form of pressure or coercion. This is not always straightforward, as older people can be vulnerable, particularly if they reside in care homes. They may worry about retribution, or be inclined to give a socially desirable response, especially if they perceive themselves as being of lower social status than the person asking for consent (Perry et al., 2009).

4.4.4 Data protection and privacy

A key issue connected to the challenge of designing and deploying robotic solutions that are to be trusted in care settings is the management of data. Firstly, it is imperative that the artificial intelligence used in socially assistive robots is not underpinned by data and programs that are inherently biased toward some types of patient groups and not others. If this is not the case, a widening of inequalities could ensue, with the technologies working in an uneven manner, with some groups benefitting and others not. This is one of the main advantages of adopting principles of cultural competence toward the design of artificial intelligence, since an inherent aspect of this concept is the realization of value, knowledge, and sensitivity of all cultures, both in allocentric and in idiocentric terms. Therefore, the adoption of such principles during software design should protect against stereotyping and the reinforcement of whatever sociocultural biases the designers might themselves unconsciously plug in.

The second issue related to data management concerns the ownership and use of patient data that is generated during the application of robots in care settings. Understanding who owns such data is important toward understanding who can legally process and use such data, who can sell it, and who can control and restrict it in order to protect privacy and confidentiality. The type of data that socially assistive robots might generate could pertain to the user's particular background, their health status, and their particular individual preferences, interests, and values. This is likely to hold substantial value to many including the care recipient and their family (a personalized record of individual information could be emotionally powerful), clinical and professional staff (given its potential health-related utility) and businesses (who, e.g., might use such data to provide personalized adverts). Some argue that the most deontologically appropriate position should be for the user to own any data generated about him/her. Others, such as Bourke and Bourke (2020) argue that it is best to avoid the concept of individual data ownership altogether, and that we should instead adopt a society-centered approach whereby all parties through which such data flows commit to the moral management of data in order to strike a reasonable balance between privacy intrusion and public health gains.

The issue of privacy in social robotics also applies to the dynamics of social interaction. Given that social robots are designed to appear humanoid, with artificial faces and eyes, users may feel that the robot is watching them, particularly if the user has anthropomorphized the robot. This means that the user may feel uncomfortable with engaging in certain private activities such as getting dressed or going to the toilet. If this is not managed in a sensitive and appropriate way, it could impact upon user's health and well-being if it prevented the user from engaging in important activities to avoid feeling embarrassed.

4.4.5 Deception and attachment

Robots that are meant to interact with humans are often designed to display emotions, as this can improve their ability to communicate successfully with a person (Kirby et al., 2010). Robots that are used in assistive settings and imitate the behavior of a caregiver, displaying affection, humor, concern, or other emotions, raise the possibility that care recipients, especially those with cognitive impairment, might be misled about the robots' actual emotional capabilities (Sharkey & Sharkey, 2011). According to many scholars, this is a form of deception because the robot does not actually experience emotions and is misrepresenting its internal state (Fulmer et al., 2009; van Maris et al., 2020). In addition, a robot that imitates human emotions may place care recipients at risk if it leads those care recipients to perceive it in ways that were not intended by its designers or raises unrealistic or false expectations about it (van Maris et al., 2020). However, this type of imitation can be viewed as ethically permissible as long as the design of the robot is meant to help care recipients and there is evidence that interacting with the robot is beneficial (Coeckelbergh, 2011).

Research on attachment and robots has shown that humans can easily become attached to robots they spend time with, regardless of whether the robots behave in ways that are typically expected to encourage attachment (Scheutz, 2011). As socially assistive robots become more sophisticated, the likelihood of users developing emotional bonds with them increases (Collins et al., 2013). Whether it is acceptable for a robot to elicit attachment in care recipients is debated. Some experts say that the development of attachment is necessary for the robot to be fully effective in care settings (Birnbaum et al., 2016). However, robots in such settings typically need to be shared, which may lead to feelings of jealousy. Moreover, taking the robot away from care recipients that have become attached to it may cause them emotional distress (Sharkey & Sharkey, 2010; Coeckelbergh et al., 2016) as well as loss of therapeutic benefits (Feil-Seifer & Matarić, 2011). A recent experimental study on older adults and robots suggested that the connection between attachment, emotional deception, and excessive trust is especially important for older adults who are more vulnerable, for example, because of loneliness, as they may become more easily attached to the robot than other users (van Maris et al., 2020).

4.4.6 False expectations

As most people have no direct experience of interacting with a social robot, they will tend to draw their information and opinions about that robot from popular accounts in the media, in news sources, in science fiction literature, and in films (Horstmann & Kramer, 2020). These representations of robots form the basis of people's attitudes toward them, yet often mislead them as to what robots are and what they can do. Since the media tend to focus on success stories and underreport setbacks, people generally have inordinately high expectations about social robots (Horstmann & Kramer, 2019). Thus, reports and surveys have shown that robots are expected to be efficient, reliable, precise, rational, and perfectionist (Arras & Cerqui, 2005; Ezer et al., 2009; Horstmann & Kramer, 2020).

Misconceptions about robots may also derive from the fact that robots built to interact with humans often seem more intelligent and capable than they really are (Kwon et al., 2016). Because humans have a tendency to anthropomorphize human-like objects, including robots (Lemaignan et al., 2016), they also tend to generalize human mental models to those robots (Dautenhahn, 2002) and overestimate the robot's actual range of capabilities, at least initially. Human tendencies to misattribute intelligence, trustworthiness, and other positive characteristics to robots may result in false expectations and lead to misplaced trust, which can then quickly turn into disappointment and eventually mistrust.

Looking at social robots specifically, studies have found that people expect them to be able to converse and react in a sophisticated manner (Horstmann & Kramer, 2019). In health and social care, unrealistic expectations about a socially assistive robot can result in care recipients overrelying on it for support and assistance, or prioritizing its well-being over that of other people or their own (Fulmer et al., 2009). When overblown expectations are ultimately not met, this leads to negative outcomes like disappointment, mistrust, and rejection (Komatsu & Yamada, 2011).

4.4.7 Health inequalities

In December 2003, William Gibson, a famous science fiction author who coined the term "cyberspace," stated that, *"The future is already here. It's just not evenly distributed."* Gibson was referring to the fact that many of the technologies we could have only dreamed out about as children are now available, but that these technologies were not yet widely and evenly available to all. Gibson's statement served as a warning that if we are not careful and considered in our approach toward the design and implementation of such technologies, like robots in care, we may find such technologies deployed in a way that exacerbates existing health and social inequalities. In 2019, The Topol Review—an independent UK-based report on the issues and challenges ahead toward preparing the healthcare workforce toward a digital future, also highlighted how new technologies should "redress not reinforce inequalities" (p10) particularly among vulnerable and marginalized groups.

There is consensus among the scientific community that although technologies are becoming more sophisticated and powerful, and that innovations will and should continue to be strived for, these technologies should always be viewed as humanity's tools (Anderson & Rainie, 2018). In the spirit of Isaac Asimov's laws of robotics, the direction of power and control should always be in humanity's favor; it should be us who are applying these technologies in whatever way we so choose to deem ethically and morally desirable for the betterment of society, including health and social care. A reasonable approach toward working to achieve this is to ensure that the design and strategic implementation of such technologies are driven by those with expertise in the particular issues that are being targeted, both in terms of professional expertise and those who are experts through lived experience.

In the case of socially assistive robotics being used to enhance the health and social care, this should therefore involve a range of different clinicians who routinely work with such care recipients through their entire care journey and as such understand the problems of significance that need solving, and for which socially assistive robots could provide meaningful assistance. It should also include those who have lived experience of the particular issue being targeted. For example, if socially assistive robotics are to effectively reduce the feelings of loneliness, an issue that has been steadily increasing in prevalence for many years and worsened further due to the COVID-19 pandemic (Savage et al., 2020), then it is important that the voices of those who are experiencing—or have previously experienced—loneliness be listened to, and their insight valued and leveraged, in particular, as The Topol Review has highlighted, those voices from vulnerable and marginalized groups which are too frequently insufficiently heard. This would not only increase the likelihood of designing efficacious robotic solutions, in the sense of augmenting improved measurable user outcomes, but it would also crucially mean that these technologies are more readily accepted and trusted, both by the care recipients themselves but also the people engaged in caring who may well find themselves working alongside such technologies. The pursuit of acceptance and trust is key toward the production and implementation of ethical robotic solutions given that all users, care recipients and carers alike, should have the right to feel comfortable and happy to adopt and utilize such technologies beyond simply consenting to their use.

4.4.8 Safety and avoidance of harm

Among the most important objectives during socially assistive robotic interactions with users in care settings is the avoidance of harm, both physical and mental, and the promotion of safety. Indeed, robots, like all other interventions designed to improve health and medical care must subscribe to the core ethical principle of 'do no harm'. While the methods, strategies and principles toward achieving these outcomes are challenging and nuanced, they are nonetheless aspirations that must be carefully considered and prioritized given how particularly vulnerable those with care needs are toward experiencing physical and mental harm.

In terms of physical harm, there are several possible scenarios that a socially assistive robot will have to appropriately navigate. Perhaps the most obvious issue, is that a robot could be a large and heavy object that could cause significant injury. This is less of a problem for smaller table-top robots than robots specifically designed to provide physical assistance, and/or robots with sensors able to effectively map out and predict object movement in their environment, in order to prevent such risks and safely navigate around an individual.

Equally risky is the possibility of the robot autonomously providing advice or recommendations on medical and health-related matters. This is also the case with robots that suggest the user engage in a physical exercise and copy the movements of the robot. The risks associated with this possibility increase if the user perceives the robot to hold any type of expertise or authority on such matters. On the other hand, robots have the power to protect users from physical harms. For example, if a user was to experience a significant episode of poor health (e.g., a panic attack, an epileptic seizure, a fall), then the robot could be used to alert a carer to intervene (Wang et al., 2020). Further, robots that do not make reasonable health-related suggestions or recommendations during conversations may miss the opportunity to improve physical health. A reasonable approach to prevent such problems is to ensure that the user understands that any health-related or medical advice or suggestion that the socially assistive robot suggests or recommends should be treated with caution, and that the safest course of action is to consult with a medical or clinical professional. This could also be reinforced by statements to such effect by the robot during such conversations.

While the technology continues to improve its ability to provide safe and autonomous socially assistive care, a reasonable approach toward increasing user safety is to conduct live video surveillance while the robot is in the presence of a user, and so long as the care recipient has consented to surveillance. This might involve a technician and/or carer monitoring the video via a robot's on-board camera (if one were available) or an external wireless video-camera positioned safely away from the care recipient (and with the user being made fully aware of this). Then, if during monitoring, an accident were to occur, a carer could intervene.

One might expect that the risks associated with possible mental health-related harms from socially assistive robots be unlikely to occur given the primary goal of most socially assistive robots is social interaction, and as such the promotion of psycho-social, cognitive, and emotional well-being. Indeed, socially assistive robots that employ artificially intelligent systems, particularly those that embed principles of cultural competence, should be reasonably likely to promote and not impair mental health (Papadopoulos et al., 2021). However, in any conversation and social interaction, there is always a risk that the outcome may be negative and unanticipated. Effort therefore must be invested into understanding why an adverse reaction may have occurred, in order to continue to learn what changes and improvements to the artificial intelligence could ensue. This may also lead to learning for human carers should their investigation into what has occurred hold relevance for their practice during care.

4.4.9 Substitution for social contact

Another ethical issue is the concern that a socially assistive robot inadvertently acts as a substitute for forms of social contact that the user may otherwise have preferred to engage in, including regular social interactions and planned activities. This could result in the use of robots producing an overall net reduction in human social contact.

Therefore, prior to the introduction of a socially assistive robot and at intervals during ongoing interactions, it should be made clear to users that their robot is not intended to substitute meaningful existing and new human social contact. On the contrary, socially assistive robots should be designed with the aim of enhancing social capital and empowering relations. This may be facilitated through recommendations made during conversation or assisting the user to communicate with others, including formal and informal carers, through text messaging, audio/video calling, and/or setting up and facilitating interactions with others, for example, games of mutual interest (that may, e.g., be played using the robot's on-board tablet should one exist).

It should also be made clear to users that they should not ever feel obliged to remain with the robot if they prefer to go elsewhere or engage in any other social activities. This may become challenging should the user anthropomorphize their robot, a commonplace phenomenon within the realm of social robotics (Damiano & Dumouchel, 2018), during which humans attribute human traits to nonhuman entities such as robots (Złotowski et al., 2015), and treat nonhuman behavior as motivated by human feelings and mental states (Airenti, 2015). If this were to occur, the user may feel upset at the prospect of having to leave their robot alone while they proceed to enjoy other activities. Efforts to prevent anthropomorphism may be a potential solution; however, this must be weighed against the risk of the user objectifying their robot to such a degree that it inhibits use and thus the potential emotional and cognitive gains associated with engaging in meaningful conversations and social interactions.

4.4.10 Stigma

Stigma is an issue that, if left unchecked and unchallenged, will consistently worsen health and social care related outcomes. The term has its roots among the ancient Greeks who used it to represent the marks that were pricked onto their slaves to demonstrate ownership and to highlight their inferior social status. Goffman (1963) argued that stigma was a phenomenon that acts to highlight any attribute which socially discredits an individual, leading to doubts upon a person's character and abilities, in turn resulting in discrimination. This meaning carries on today; when someone is "stigmatized" they have been negatively labeled by others (usually with social, economic, and political power both clear and less apparent). This in turn influences society to perceive negative stereotypes and beliefs toward the stigmatized person or group, which leads to a range of harmful types of discrimination. This serves to damage mental health and wellbeing of those targeted by such labeling, and for some, the result is selfstigmatization and the "why try" effect, both of which are again detrimental to wellbeing (Corrigan et al., 2009; Maharjan & Panthee, 2019). Selfstigma occurs when the individual or group originally targeted by stigma becomes aware of the negative stereotype placed upon them and agrees with it. This then produces the "why try" effect, a psychological phenomenon by selfstigmatized individuals who experience reduced motivation toward achieving their life goals.

People with care needs are particularly vulnerable to stigma. This can be for many reasons including, for example, the attribute/behavior that has been socially and culturally negatively labeled which they carry may be very visible (e.g., openly talking to oneself), or the negative attribute/behavior has been deemed by society to be one that they are responsible for and possessed control over (e.g., the perception that obesity is one's own fault due to a lack of willpower (Tomiyama et al., 2018)).

For robots used in care, it is therefore ethically imperative that they are not designed or applied in a way that might reflect or reinforce existing social stigmas. Conversations and interactions around care needs should avoid judgments (even those well-intentioned may reinforce stigma) and instead focus on understanding and exploration. Interactions should also be designed in order to push-back against the possible stigmatized notion that people should not be receiving any socially assistive care or assistance from robots. To not do so would likely worsen the user's well-being further, particularly if any robot—human interactions were to trigger selfstigmatization and the why try effect.

4.4.11 Responsibility

Despite the best efforts of all those involved, whenever a robot is operated there is a risk of causing harm: a moving robot can bump into a person, a robotic arm can drop something heavy, or sharp onto someone. Although socially assistive robots tend to come into minimal contact with persons, as physical assistance is not what they are currently designed for, they can still malfunction, cause accidents, or cause mental harm as mentioned above. When this occurs, the question is: who is responsible for a robot's actions?

The issue of responsibility, which is one of the most widely debated within robot ethics, becomes especially complex if a robot has some degree of autonomy or is capable of behaving in ways that were not explicitly programmed (Harbers et al., 2017).

There is a broad consensus within the scientific and ethics communities that humans should always be responsible for a robot's actions (Coeckelbergh, 2020) and that autonomous systems should be auditable, to ensure that humans can be held accountable for what the technology or the system does (Bird et al., 2020). Some experts, however, have suggested that obligations that currently only apply to people and companies could also be applied to robots (Fosch-Villaronga, 2019). A European Parliament resolution of 2017, indeed, proposed that the most advanced robots could be granted the status of "electronic persons" (European Parliament, Committee on Legal Affairs, 2017). The proposal was opposed by prominent scholars who emphasized that conferring rights, obligations, and personhood to robots would be unnecessary and unhelpful, considering the difficulties involved in holding such electronic persons accountable (Bryson et al., 2017).

How responsibility should be allocated when it comes to robots with increasing autonomy has yet to be understood (Muller, 2020). One way forward, it has been suggested, might be to conduct further studies exploring any harms connected to the use of robots in different settings, in order to clarify whether such harms would justify the implementation of specific measures (Fosch-Villaronga, 2019).

Overall, it is not ethically acceptable to deploy a robotic system for tasks that predictably involve harmful human-robot interactions, and it is unlikely that robots can be held responsible (Fosch-Villaronga, 2019).

4.4.12 Labor replacement

When considering what constitutes an ethical implementation of robots in care settings, it is not only important to consider the impacts of such technology on the user but also the impact upon the formal care staff population. This is for many reasons, not least because any technological solution that produces negative consequences for care staff in terms of morale, selfefficacy, clinical competency and economic outcomes, means that any possible benefits associated with such technologies will be far offset by such costs. It also means that any possible patient-based benefits will likely to be short term, with the realities of reduced staff input, both in terms of quality and quantity of input, eventually taking hold.

If a consequentialist ethical approach to this issue is adopted, then it is most desirable to consider what set of circumstances would produce the greatest amount of positive consequences for all within care settings. This scenario would likely be one in which care staff are not replaced or undermined by socially assistive robots, but instead are applied together in a complementary way. For example, social robots could be used to keep users thinking, talking, and building social capital, both by conversing directly with the user but also acting as a digital bridge for communication with loved ones and other care recipients and friends. This would be particularly beneficial during periods of undesired isolation and loneliness. By doing so, users' cognitive and mental health should be supported, in turn making the daily tasks of care staff easier, with users being less resistant and more compliant. The robot's conversations with users could also enable new and precise prediction about health-related risks that staff could use for early intervention. With care staff perceiving positive changes in their care recipients as a result of both robots and care staff effectively working in tandem, their morale is crucially protected, which itself is key toward the overall quality of care provision (Picker & Raleigh, 2018). The wider implications of this scenario could be a renewed appeal associated with the care staff role, leading to increased interest and reduced workforce gaps, itself a critical need given the ever-increasing older adult population and thus demand for social care.

4.5 Governance and legislation

Key to the ethical design and implementation of social robotics used to assist the delivery of care is the adoption of legal and regulatory standards and policies that can uphold the ethical considerations outlined in this chapter. Regulations should focus upon ensuring that social robotics are harnessed and utilized in a way that as far as possible they safely and ethically benefit those who are the recipients of care and all those involved in the delivery of care. This means that standards should permeate through the entire framework and system of care, not just care recipients but also the individual carers, be it informal family carers or formal carers, as well as the organizations legally involved in the provision of such care.

One essential aspect of legislation should be to protect against robots replacing human carers. This is partly because robots cannot match the level of human skill involved in providing in many aspects of daily care such as bathing or dressing, either now or in the near future, and to attempt to do so would result in failure and harm. While social robots can, however, deliver effective culturally competent conversation and social interactions, a reality in which care recipients should only, or primarily, have socially assistive robots to converse with, is unlikely to be effective in relation to producing long-lasting positive psychosocial outcomes. Nor would it represent a desirable vision of the future, given that robotic conversations, as sophisticated as they may be, can never be underpinned with authentic human compassion, empathy and warmth, an understanding that would eventually become clear to all care recipients. Therefore, legislation must protect against the unnecessary and likely harmful replacement of human carers and instead promote the vision of social robotics used to assist, complement and bolster existing provisions of care.

Regulatory standards attempt to influence people and organizations who have a legal capacity to act. As such it is worth noting that existing robotic standards are not targeting robots per se, but rather the people and organizations involved in the design and implementation of such technology. Indeed, according to a report on civil law rules on robotics by the European Parliament, Committee on Legal Affairs (2017), until robots become or are made selfaware, Asimov's laws must be regarded as being directed at the designers, producers and operators of robots, since those laws cannot be converted into machine code (Point T under General Principles). However, given that robotic selfawareness could eventually occur, particularly for social robots, the eventual need for a separate category of governance for the robots themselves was also highlighted in this report: "ultimately, the autonomy of robots raises the question of their nature in the light of the existing legal categories or whether a new category should be created, with its own specific features and implications." However, the idea that autonomous robots could be legally granted their own "electronic personalities" to enable them to be held liable for damages was rejected in 2018 by a group 156 experts in artificial intelligence across 14 European countries in an open letter to the European Commission, warning that this would be inappropriate from a legal and ethical perspective.

International and national standards and legal statutes that begin to address this area have already been developed by, among others, the British Standards Institute, and, internationally, the Institute of Electrical and Electronic Engineers. These bodies have enabled the development of several regulations set out by the International Organization for Standardization (ISO) which have relevance and applicability to social care. These standards include the following:

- ISO 8373: This standard provides an overview of robotics terms and vocabularies, defining and differentiating between types of service and industrial robots;
- ISO 13482: This standard focuses on reducing the potential risks presented by robots that come into direct contact with people, and;
- BS 861: This standard addresses ethical hazards relating to the use of robots, and provides guidelines on the safe design, protective measures and information for the design and application of robots

In the United Kingdom, the Care Quality Commission (CQC), a body that acts as the independent regulator of health and social care in England, have recognized the increasing place that technologies, including social robotics, are having in care settings. Upon inspection and monitoring of care services, the CQC now question service providers to illustrate how the technology they utilize helps to promote good and outstanding person-centered care. Such illustrations must demonstrate that the technologies are safe, effective, caring, responsive to people's needs, and well-led, and that outstanding services will "Actively seek out new technology and other solutions to ensure that people live with as few restrictions as possible" (Care Quality Commission, 2018). However, these lines of enquiry are not specific to any particular technology and, therefore, as social robotics in care settings continue to evolve and become more commonplace, it is likely that independent quality assurance regulators such as the CQC will need to develop additional technology-specific lines of enquiry, such developments also likely to extend further within each particular category of technology. For social robotics, beyond conversational ability, these may or may not dispense medication, monitor falls, and/or provide exercise routines, to name only a few different types of possible functionalities. As such, it is likely that questions should be raised about the quality, safety, and ethics of each particular potential application. These specific functions may also need to be legally regulated differently. For example, robots that support individuals with their medication, either by reminding them or dispensing medication, may need to be regulated by national governmental agencies whose remit specifically aligns with medication. Whatever the case, a concerted and coordinated international effort will be needed if legislation is to be effective, as Merchant and Wallace (2015) argue, so that national partners may learn from each other and legally subscribe to common sets of principles and aspirations.

4.6 Conclusion

Robotic technologies may soon play a prominent role within health and social care. If introduced carefully, new healthcare applications of robotic technology can help ensure that care recipients are treated with the dignity and compassion they are entitled to, which current healthcare services often fail to provide today.

On the other hand, the implications of introducing this new technology in care settings are difficult to anticipate and may have broader impacts than expected (Zardiashvili & Fosch-Villaronga, 2020). Before robots become commonplace in care settings, answers need to be provided to crucial ethical questions about who chooses which technologies ought to be used, who will have control over the data they collect, and how they can be designed in ways that ensure they are inherently ethical (Astell et al., 2019). To date, intelligent assistive technologies aimed at health and social care have often been developed without a proactive consideration of ethical concerns resulting in a poor fit to users' needs, preferences, priorities, and values (Ienca et al., 2018). User-centered and value-based design approaches, instead, could attain improved usability and acceptance, and highlight the benefits and potential negative impacts of the technology, so that any ethical problems could be dealt with at an early stage (Battistuzzi et al., 2018). In addition, ensuring that cultural competence is embedded in the design of assistive robotic technologies could further support person-centered care practices that help treat care recipients with dignity, respect, and compassion (Bruno et al., 2017, 2019; Papadopoulos, 2006; Papadopoulos et al., 2021).

The successful application of socially assistive robots in care also requires more evidence on the benefits (or harms) it can provide to care recipients, meeting their quantifiable needs (Abdi et al., 2018; Papadopoulos et al., 2021), as well as a better understanding of how to integrate such technology in care settings in ways that will improve the job satisfaction of formal caregivers while mobilizing their professional knowledge and experience. This will likely involve further evidence gathering via rigorous research activity, ongoing listening exercises with all stakeholders involved, and training efforts geared toward ensuring that care staff has the skills and confidence to take advantage of robotic technologies and the benefits they may present (Turja et al., 2019), while appropriately navigating the ethical issues and challenges highlighted in this chapter.

4.7 Appendices

The case studies below describe situations that could realistically take place in the near future. They are meant to provide opportunities for reflection about ethically challenging situations that may arise if and when robots are incorporated in health and social care.

4.7.1 Case study 1 with reflective questions

You are working as a carer in a long-term nursing care home for older adults with significant physical and mental healthcare-related needs.

You are concerned about Daryl, a new resident who seems to be finding it difficult to make friends with the other residents in the care home, and who has told you that his only family, his son James, lives several hours away. You suggest to Daryl that a social robot might be something he could enjoy, thinking that it might be a useful way for him to connect with other residents and make friends. Daryl is reluctant and initially disagrees, but you are convinced he could benefit from it, so you bring him a social robot which begins to converse with Daryl in the privacy of his own room.

A week later, and Daryl seems a little happier. You enquire with him whether he is enjoying the robot. Daryl replies, "For the most part, yes. I've named him Gordon as he reminds me of someone who I used to work with who also told me off about certain things!" He adds that he is now communicating with his son James more frequently because he has found sending him messages easy and fun to do with the robot. He also adds that he has found the robot useful to lean against for balance when getting out of bed. However, he says that at times he felt uncertain whether he should continue talking with the robot or whether he should be spending more time with other residents, for example, joining them for the weekly sci-fi movie night which he thinks he would enjoy.

4.7.1.1 Reflective questions
1. What ethical issues can you identify in this case?
2. What actions could you have taken to prevent these issues from occurring?

Some answers and points to consider:

a. Ethical issue: Coercion and informed consent. Daryl was reluctant and did not formally agree to being provided with a robot. You believed that your choice for what is best for him to be more valuable and superior to Daryl's choice.
   What could you have done? You could have provided Daryl with your thinking about why you think a robot could help, together with clear information about the nature of the robot, and some training on how to use it. You should then leave Daryl with some time to think it over, and if he were to disagree, accept this.

b. Ethical issue: Physical harm. Daryl used the robot to lean against which posed a risk to his physical safety given that social robots are not designed to provide physical assistance.
   What could you have done? Participating in training about what social robots are, including what they can and cannot do, would have helped you to understand that social robots cannot provide physical assistance. You could also have explained this prior

to the commencement of use. Had Daryl consented to being remotely monitored for additional safety, you could have intervened when becoming aware of this. Finally, you could let the designers of the robot know that perhaps more could be done for the robot to make it clear to the resident that it cannot and should not be used for physical assistance.

c. Ethical issue: Substitution for social contact. Daryl has likely anthropomorphized the robot, having named the robot Gordon, for example. This raises the risk that Daryl might feel bad about leaving the robot to enjoy other activities that he had a desire to access. As a result, Daryl may have missed a good opportunity to build some human relationships.

What could you have done? You should frequently be reminding Daryl that he should feel no obligation to the robot and should prioritize his own well-being and desires first. If this means that Daryl genuinely prefers to continue conversing with the robot, then that is fine as it is his choice. However, if it means that Daryl would prefer to spend his time in some other fashion, then you should support him toward achieving this.

d. Ethical issue: Stigma. Daryl states that robot reminds him of someone he used to know, because he too, like the robot, made judgments about him. Judgments have significant potential to reinforce stigma which as a result could impact upon selfesteem and selfefficacy.

What could you have done? If you were aware that such judgments may occur prior to the robot being deployed, then you should have made Daryl aware of this and helped him prepare him for it, so to prevent any negative impact such statements might produce. After it had occurred, you should ask Daryl whether he would mind explaining what he meant by this, and to provide an example or two of the robot "telling him off." You could also inform the designer of the robot and its artificial intelligence so that the robot can cease doing this. If you believe that these judgments may be causing Daryl harm, then you could suggest a pause in use until this is addressed. Should Daryl wish to continue to use the robot, you may also wish to help Daryl to challenge these judgments, or to explain to him that he should ignore such statements.

4.7.2 Case study 2 with reflective questions

You are working as a professional caregiver in a nursing home for older adults with significant physical and mental healthcare-related needs.

Recently, you have been wondering about how best to support Francesca, who has been living in the care home since her husband Guido passed away a few months ago. Francesca has adapted rather well to her new life, but she tends to spend most of her time alone in her room looking at old pictures and reminiscing about the past. Since she has been showing signs of cognitive impairment, Francesca's family is worried about her feeling lonely but also that the lack of social interaction will accelerate her decline.

You decide to ask Francesca if she would like to spend some time with one of the home's socially assistive robots. The robot is programmed to be culturally competent and you think Francesca may enjoy chatting with it about Italian food, sports, and films. The robot could also give her something to talk about with other residents and help her make new friends.

Francesca agrees to try the robot and see how she likes it. On the day of Francesca's first session, you spend about an hour showing her how to operate the robot. You check that she is able to use the main functions and give her the chance to try the robot out on her own. Francesca seems a little nervous but she also appears to have understood everything and when you tell her the robot knows all about Italy, she is thrilled: "Nobody here has ever been to Italy or heard about my hometown," she says, "All they know about is Capri and Portofino."

After a few days, you meet Francesca in the lounge and ask her how she is getting along with the robot. "It isn't that much fun, really", she replies. "I thought we could talk about Italy and all the things I used to do there with Guido when we were young, but the robot kept interrupting me and asking me questions I didn't understand. Oh well, I'm old and no good with computers. I should have known I wouldn't be able to use the robot either."

Now try and answer these reflective questions:

1. What ethical issues can you identify in this case?
2. What actions could you have taken to prevent these issues from occurring?

Some answers and points to consider:

a. Ethical issue: Autonomy and informed consent. Francesca agreed to try the robot and you gave her appropriate instruction on how to use it. You did not, however, explain what the robot's limitations are and what Francesca should and should not expect from using it. Francesca's consent to use the robot was not truly informed.
   What could you have done? When showing Francesca how to operate the robot, you should have given her a more accurate picture of its capabilities and limitations, explaining, for instance, that robots cannot replicate the kind of conversation people share.
b. Ethical issue: Preventing psychological harm. By not explaining the robot's limitations, you exposed Francesca to a risk of distress. Not having a clear idea of what the robot can and can't do made Francesca think that the robot wasn't working properly because of her inability to operate it.
   What could you have done? When you showed the robot to Francesca, you should have clearly explained both its capabilities and its limitations. Then you could have emphasized that most people, including yourself, need plenty of time to learn to operate the robot comfortably, and perhaps shared an anecdote about your own difficulties with the robot. Also, you should have offered to provide more training and support if she liked.
c. Ethical issue: False expectations. Francesca overestimated the type of conversation she could share with the robot. The robot was not up to her expectations and she was disappointed, which might discourage her from spending more time with the robot.
   What could you have done? You should have asked Francesca what she imagined the robot could do. This would have given you the opportunity to understand her expectations and helped you give her a realistic picture of the robot's actual capabilities.
d. Ethical issue: Dignity. Not understanding what the robot can and can't do made Francesca feel incapable and may have hampered her feelings of selfconfidence and selfworth.

What could you have done? When Francesca first tried to use the robot on her own, after reminding her of what the robot can and can't do, you should have praised her efforts, provided plenty of positive feedback and reassured her that everyone needs lots of time to learn how to operate it comfortably.

e. Ethical issue: Self-stigma. Not having a clear picture of the robot's capabilities and limitations may have triggered the "why-try" response in Francesca, reinforcing her low technological selfefficacy and discouraging her from spending more time with the robot.

What could you have done? When you showed the robot to Francesca, you should have explained its capabilities as well as its limitations. After her first training session, you could have asked her how comfortable she felt using the robot. Had she reported some anxiety about her own ability to operate it, you might have pointed out how it is common for people, including yourself, to feel a bit anxious when learning to use something new, especially if it's a new type of technology, and offered more training and support if she liked.

References

Abdi, J., Al-Hindawi, A., Ng, T., & Vizcaychipi, M. P. (2018). Scoping review on the use of socially assistive robot technology in elderly care. *BMJ Open, 8*(2). https://doi.org/10.1136/bmjopen-2017-018815

AgeUK. (2021). *Care in crisis*. https://www.ageuk.org.uk/our-impact/campaigning/care-in-crisis/. (Accessed 4 June 2021).

Airenti, G. (2015). The cognitive bases of anthropomorphism: from relatedness to empathy. *International Journal of Social Robotics, 7*, 117–127. https://doi.org/10.1007/s12369-014-0263-x

Alzheimer Europe. (2010). The ethical issues linked to the use of assistive technology in dementia care. https://www.alzheimer-europe.org/sites/default/files/alzheimer_europe_ethics_report_2010.pdf

Alzheimer Europe. (2014). *Ethical dilemmas faced by carers and people with dementia. Luxembourg*. https://www.alzheimer-europe.org/Ethics/Ethical-issues-in-practice/2014-Ethical-dilemmas-faced-by-carers-and-people-with-dementia.

Anderson, J., & Raine, L. (2018). Improvements ahead: How humans and AI might evolve together in the next decade. Pew Research Center. https://www.pewresearch.org/internet/2018/12/10/improvements-ahead-how-humans-and-ai-might-evolve-together-in-the-next-decade/

Arras, K., & Cerqui, D. (2005). *Do we want to share our lives and bodies with robots? A 2000 people survey*. Technical report Nr. 0605-001.

Astell, A., Smith, S., & Joddrell, P. (Eds.). (2019). *Using technology in dementia care. A guide to technology solutions for everyday living*. Jessica Kingsley Publishers.

Bagdasarov, Z., Thiel, C. E., Johnson, J. F., Connelly, S., Harkrider, L. N., Devenport, L. D., & Mumford, M. D. (2013). Case-based ethics instruction: The influence of contextual and individual factors in case content on ethical decision-making. *Science and Engineering Ethics, 19*(3), 1305–1322. https://doi.org/10.1007/s11948-012-9414-3

Bagdasarov, Z., Thiel, C. E., Johnson, J. F., Connelly, S., Harkrider, L. N., Devenport, L. D., & Mumford, M. D. (2013). Case-based ethics instruction: The influence of contextual and individual factors in case content on ethical decision-making. *Science and Engineering Ethics, 19*(3), 1305–1322. https://doi.org/10.1007/s11948-012-9414-3

Barry, M., & Edgman-Levitan, S. (2012). Shared decision-making - the pinnacle of patient-centered care. *New England Journal of Medicine*, 780–781.

Battistuzzi, L., Papadopoulos, C., Hill, T., Castro, N., Bruno, B., & Sgorbissa, A. (2020). Socially assistive robots, older adults and research ethics: The case for case-based ethics training. *International Journal of Social Robotics, 13*(4), 647–659. https://doi.org/10.1007/s12369-020-00652-x

Battistuzzi, L., Sgorbissa, A., Papadopoulos, C., Papadopoulos, I., & Koulouglioti, C. (2018). Embedding ethics in the design of culturally competent socially assistive robots. In *2018 IEEE/RSJ International Conference on Intelligent Robots and Systems (IROS)* (pp. 1996–2001). https://doi.org/10.1109/IROS.2018.8594361

Beauchamp, T., & Childress, J. (2019). *Principles of biomedical ethics* (8th ed.). Oxford: Oxford University Press.

Bird, E., Fox-Skelly, J., Jenner, N., Larbey, R., Weitkamp, E., & Winfield, A. (2020). *The ethics of artificial intelligence: Issues and initiatives*. Brussels. https://www.europarl.europa.eu/RegData/etudes/STUD/2020/634452/EPRS_STU(2020)634452_EN.p%0Adf%3E

References

Birnbaum, G. R., Mizrahi, M., Hoffman, G., Reis, H. T., Finkel, E. J., & Sass, M. (2016). What robots can teach us about intimacy: The reassuring effects of robot responsiveness to human disclosure. *Computers in Human Behavior, 63*, 416–423. https://doi.org/10.1016/j.chb.2016.05.064

Bostrom, N. (2008). Dignity and enhancement. In A. Schulman, F. Daniel Davis, & D. Dennett (Eds.), *Human dignity and bioethics: Essays commissioned by the president's council on bioethics* (pp. 17–207) (Washington, DC).

Bourke, A., & Bourke, G. (2020). Who owns patient data? The answer is not that simple. *The BMJ Opinion*. https://blogs.bmj.com/bmj/2020/08/06/who-owns-patient-data-the-answer-is-not-that-simple/

Bruno, B., Chong, N. Y., Kamide, H., Kanoria, S., Lee, J., Lim, Y., Pandey, A. K., Papadopoulos, C., Papadopoulos, I., Pecora, F., Saffiotti, A., & Sgorbissa, A. (2017). Paving the way for culturally competent robots: A position paper. In *2017 26th IEEE international symposium on robot and human interactive communication (RO-MAN) Lisbon*. Portugal. Aug 28–Sept 1.

Bruno, B., Chong, N. Y., Kamide, H., Kanoria, S., Lee, J., Lim, Y., Pandey, A. K., Papadopoulos, C., Papadopoulos, I., Pecora, F., Saffiotti, A., & Sgorbissa, A. (2019). The CARESSES EU-Japan project: Making assistive robots culturally competent. *Lecture Notes in Electrical Engineering, 540*(August), 151–169. https://doi.org/10.1007/978-3-030-04672-9_10

Bryson, J., Diamantis, M., & Grant, T. (2017). *Of, for, and by the people: The legal lacuna of synthetic persons*. Artificial Intelligence & L.

Care Quality Commission. (2018). Innovative use of technology can help answer our five key questions. https://www.cqc.org.uk/guidance-providers/all-services/innovative-use-technology-can-help-answer-our-five-key-questions

Clancy, A., Simonsen, N., Lind, J., Liveng, A., & Johannessen, A. (2020). *The meaning of dignity for older adults: A meta-synthesis*. Nursing Ethics.

Coeckelbergh, M. (2011). Humans, animals, and robots: A phenomenological approach to human-robot relations. *International Journal of Social Robotics, 3*, 197–204. https://doi.org/10.1007/s12369-010-0075-6

Coeckelbergh, M. (2020). *AI ethics*. Cambridge, Massachusetts: The MIT Press.

Coekelbergh, M., Pop, C., Simut, R., Peca, A., Pintea, S., David, D., & Vanderborght, B. (2016). A survey of expectations about the role of robots in robot-assisted therapy for children with ASD: Ethical acceptability, trust, sociability, appearance, and attachment. *Science and Engineering Ethics, 22*(1), 47–65. https://doi.org/10.1007/s11948-015-9649-x

Collins, E. C., Millings, A., & Prescott, T. J. (2013). Attachment to assistive technology: A new conceptualisation. *Assistive Technology Research Series, 33*, 823–828. https://doi.org/10.3233/978-1-61499-304-9-823

Corrigan, P. W., Larson, J. E., & Rüsch, N. (2009). Self-stigma and the "why try" effect: impact on life goals and evidence-based practices. *World Psychiatry: Official Journal of the World Psychiatric Association (WPA), 8*(2), 75–81. https://doi.org/10.1002/j.2051-5545.2009.tb00218.x

Damiano, L., & Dumouchel, P. (2018). Anthropomorphism in human–Robot co-evolution. *Frontiers in Psychology, 9*. https://doi.org/10.3389/fpsyg.2018.00468

Draper, H., & Sorell, T. (2017). Ethical values and social care robots for older people: An international qualitative study. *Ethics and Information Technology, 19*(1), 49–68. https://doi.org/10.1007/s10676-016-9413-1

Dautenhahn, K. (2002). Design spaces and niche spaces of believable social robots. In *2002 11th IEEE International Workshop on Robot and Human Interactive Communication*.

van Est, R., & Gerritsen, J. (2017). *Human rights in the robot age*. https://www.rathenau.nl/sites/default/files/2018-02/Human%20Rights%20in%20the%20Robot%20Age-Rathenau%20Instituut-2017.pdf

European Parliament, Committee on Legal Affairs (2017). Report with recommendations to the Commission on Civil Law Rules on Robotics, 2015/2103(INL) 27 January 2017, 4.

Ezer, N., Fisk, A., & Rogers, W. (2009). Attitudinal and intentional acceptance of domestic robots by younger and older adults. In C. Stephanidis (Ed.), *Proceedings of the 5th international conference on universal access in human-computer interaction - UAHCI '09* (pp. 39–48). Berlin/Heidelberg: Springer.

Falkenberg, L., & Woiceshyn, J. (2008). Enhancing business ethics: Using cases to reach moral reasoning. *Journal of Business Ethics, 79*(3), 213–217. https://doi.org/10.1007/s10551-007-9381-9

Feil-Seifer, D., & Mataric, M. J. (2011). Ethical principles for socially assistive robotics. In *2011 IEEE Robotics & Automation Magazine, 18*(1), 24–31. https://doi.org/10.1109/MRA.2010.940150

Fosch-Villaronga, E. (2019). *Robots, healthcare, and the law: Regulating automation in personal care* (1st ed.). Routledge.

Fulmer, I., Barry, B., & Long, D. (2009). Lying and smiling: Informational and emotional deception in negotiation. *Journal of Business Ethics, 88*, 691–709.

Gallagher, A. (2006). The ethics of culturally competent health and social care. In I. Papadopoulos (Ed.), *Transcultural health and social care*. Churchill Livingstone.

Goffman, E. (1963). *Stigma: Notes on the Management of Spoiled Identity*. New York: Simon & Schuster.

Guyer, P. (2003). Kant on the theory and practice of autonomy. *Social Philosophy and Policy, 20*(2), 70–98.

Harbers, M., de Greeff, J., Kruijff-Korbayová, I., Neerincx, M. A., & Hindriks, K. V. (2017). *Exploring the ethical landscape of robot-assisted search and rescue* (pp. 93–107). https://doi.org/10.1007/978-3-319-46667-5_7

Horstmann, A., & Kramer, N. (2019). Great expectations? Relation of previous experiences with social robots in real life or in the media and expectancies based on qualitative and quantitative assessment. *Frontiers in Psychology, 10*.

Horstmann, A., & Kramer, N. (2020). Expectations vs. actual behavior of a social robot: An experimental investigation of the effects of a social robot's interaction skill level and its expected future role on people's evaluations. *PLoS One, 15*(8).

Ienca, M., Wangmo, T., Jotterand, F., Kressig, R., & Elger, B. (2018). Ethical design of intelligent assistive technologies for dementia: A descriptive review. *Science and Engineering Ethics, 24*(4), 1035–1055.

Jacques, A., & Jackson, G. (2000). *Understanding dementia*. Edinburgh: Churchill Livingstone.

Kalichman, M. (2014). Rescuing responsible conduct of research (RCR) education. *Accountability in Research, 21*(1), 68–83. https://doi.org/10.1080/08989621.2013.822271

Kirby, R., Forlizzi, J., & Simmons, R. (2010). Affective social robots. *Robotics and Autonomous Systems, 58*(3), 322–332. https://doi.org/10.1016/j.robot.2009.09.015

Kolodner, J. L. (2014). *Case-based reasoning*. Morgan Kaufmann.

Komatsu, T., & Yamada, S. (2011). Adaptation gap hypothesis: How differences between users' expected and perceived agent functions affect their subjective impression. *Journal of Systemics, Cybernetics and Informatics, 9*, 67–74.

Kwon, M., Jung, M. F. & Knepper, R.A. (2016). Human expectations of social robots. In *11th ACM/IEEE International Conference on Human-Robot Interaction (HRI)*, pp. 463-464. https://doi.org/10.1109/HRI.2016.7451807.

Lemaignan, S., Warnier, M., Sisbot, E., Clodic, A., & Alami, R. (2016). Artificial cognition for social human-robot interaction: an implementation. *Artificial Intelligence, 247*. https://doi.org/10.1016/j.artint.2016.07.002

Lingler, J., Jablonski, R., Bourbonniere, M., & Kolanowski, A. (2009). Informed consent to research in long-term care settings. *Research in Gerontological Nursing, 2*(3), 153–161. https://doi.org/10.3928/19404921-20090428-03

Lingler, J., Jablonski, R., Bourbonniere, M., & Kolanowski, A. (2009). Informed consent to research in long-term care settings. *Research in Gerontological Nursing, 2*(3), 153–161. https://doi.org/10.3928/19404921-20090428-03

Maas, M. L., Kelley, L. S., Park, M., & Specht, J. P. (2002). Issues in conducting research in nursing homes. *Western Journal of Nursing Research, 24*(4), 373–389. https://doi.org/10.1177/01945902024004006

Maharjan, S., & Panthee, B. (2019). Prevalence of self-stigma and its association with self-esteem among psychiatric patients in a Nepalese teaching hospital: a cross-sectional study. *BMC Psychiatry, 19*, 347. https://doi.org/10.1186/s12888-019-2344-8

Merchant, G. E., & Wallach, W. (2015). Coordinating technology governance. *Issues in Science and Technology, 31*(4), 43–50.

Muller, V. (2020). Ethics of artificial intelligence and robotics. In *The stanford encyclopedia of philosophy*. https://plato.stanford.edu/archives/win2020/entries/ethics-ai/

Neuman, G. (2000). Human dignity in the United States constitutional law. In D. Simon, & M. Weiss (Eds.), *Zur Autonomie des Individuums* (pp. 249–271). Baden-Baden: Liber Amicorum Spiros Simitis.

Nordenfelt, L. (2004). The varieties of dignity. *Health Care Analysis, 12*(2), 69–81.

Papadopoulos, I. (2006). The Papadopoulos, Tilki and Taylor model of developing cultural competence. In I. Papadopoulos (Ed.), *Transcultural health and social care: Development of culturally competent practitioners* (pp. 7–24). Churchill Livingstone, Elsevier.

Papadopoulos, C., Castro, N., Nigath, A., Davidson, R., Faulkes, N., Menicatti, R., Khaliq, A. A., Recchiuto, C., Battistuzzi, L., Randhawa, G., Merton, L., Kanoria, S., Chong, N. Y., Kamide, H., Hewson, D., & Sgorbissa, A. (2021). The CARESSES randomised controlled trial: Exploring the health-related impact of culturally competent artificial intelligence embedded into socially assistive robots and tested in older adult care homes. *International Journal of Social Robotics*, 1–12. https://doi.org/10.1007/s12369-021-00781-x. Advance online publication.

Perry, J., Beyer, S., & Holm, S. (2009). Assistive technology, telecare and people with intellectual disabilities: Ethical considerations. *Journal of Medical Ethics, 35*(2).

Picker, S. S., & Raleigh, V. (2018). The risks to care quality and staff wellbeing of an NHS system under pressure. The King's Fund.

References

Richards, T., Coulter, A., & Wicks, P. (2015). Time to deliver patient centred care. *BMJ, 350*, 530.

Sandman, L., & Munthe, C. (2010). Shared decision making, paternalism and patient choice. *Health Care Analysis, 18*, 60–84.

Savage, R. D., et al. (2020). Loneliness among older adults in the community during COVID-19: a cross-sectional survey in Canada. *BMJ Open, 11*, Article e044517. https://doi.org/10.1136/bmjopen-2020-044517

Scheutz, M. (2011). Architectural roles of affect and how to evaluate them in artificial agents. *International Journal of Synthetic Emotions, 2*, 48–65. https://doi.org/10.4018/jse.2011070103

Schroeder, D. (2010). Dignity—one, two, three, four, five; still counting. *Cambridge Quarterly of Healthcare Ethics, 19*(1), 118–125.

Sharkey, A. J. (2015). Robots and human dignity : A consideration of the effects of robot care on the dignity of older people. *Ethics and Information Technology, 14*(March 2014), 27–40. https://doi.org/10.1007/s10676-014-9338-5

Sharkey, A., & Sharkey, N. (2010). Granny and the robots: Ethical issues in robot care for the elderly. *Ethics and Information Technology, 14*(1), 27–40. https://doi.org/10.1007/s10676-010-9234-6

Sharkey, A., & Sharkey, N. (2011). *Children, the elderly, and interactive robots*. In 2011 *IEEE Robotics & Automation Magazine, 18*(1), 32–38. https://doi.org/10.1109/MRA.2010.940151

Sparrow, R. (2016). Robots in aged care: A dystopian future? *AI & Society, 31*(4), 445–454.

Sparrow, R., & Sparrow, L. (2006). In the hands of machines? The future of aged care. *Minds and Machines, 16*(2), 141–161.

Tomiyama, A., Carr, D., Granberg, E., et al. (2018). How and why weight stigma drives the obesity 'epidemic' and harms health. *BMC Medicine, 16*, 123. https://doi.org/10.1186/s12916-018-1116-5

Tranvag, O., Petersen, K., & Naden, D. (2014). Relational interactions preserving dignity experience: Perceptions of persons living with dementia. *Nursing Ethics, 22*(5).

Turja, T., Taipale, S., Kaakinen, M., & Oksanen, A. (2019). Care workers' readiness for robotization: Identifying psychological and socio-demographic determinants. *International Journal of Social Robotics, 12*, 79–90.

Vallor, S. (2011). Carebots and caregivers: Sustaining the ethical ideal of care in the twenty-first century. *Philosophy and Technology, 24*(3), 251–268. https://doi.org/10.1007/s13347-011-0015-x

Vandemeulebroucke, T., Dierckx de Casterlé, B., & Gastmans, C. (2018). The use of care robots in aged care: A systematic review of argument-based ethics literature. *Archives of Gerontology and Geriatrics, 74*(September 2017), 15–25. https://doi.org/10.1016/j.archger.2017.08.014

Verbeek, P. (2008). Morality in design; design ethics and the morality of technological artifacts. In P. Vermaas, P. Kroes, A. Light, & S. Moore (Eds.), *Philosophy and design: From engineering to architecture* (pp. 91–102). Berlin, Germany: Springer.

Wang, W., Ellul, J., & Azzopardi, G. (2020). Elderly fall detection systems: A literature survey. *Frontiers in Robotics and AI, 7*. https://doi.org/10.3389/frobt.2020.00071

Wangmo, T., Lipps, M., Kressig, R., & Ienca, M. (2019). Ethical concerns with the use of intelligent assistive technology: Findings from a qualitative study with professional stakeholders. *BMC Medical Ethics, 20*(1).

van Maris, A., Zook, N., Caleb-Solly, P., Studley, M., Winfield, A., & Dogramadzi, S. (2020). Designing ethical social robots-a longitudinal field study with older adults. *Frontiers in Robotics and AI, 7*(1). https://doi.org/10.3389/frobt.2020.00001

van Wynsberghe, A. (2013). Designing robots for care: Care centered value-sensitive design. *Science and Engineering Ethics, 19*(2), 407–433. https://doi.org/10.1007/s11948-011-9343-6

Zardiashvili, L., & Fosch-Villaronga, E. (2020). "Oh, dignity too?" Said the robot: Human dignity as the basis for the governance of robotics. *Minds and Machines, 30*, 121–143.

Złotowski, J., Proudfoot, D., Yogeeswaran, K., & Bartneck, C. (2015). Anthropomorphism: Opportunities and challenges in human-robot interaction. *International Journal of Social Robotics, 7*, 347–360. https://doi.org/10.1007/s12369-014-0267-6

CHAPTER 5

A workplan to develop culturally competent robots: the CARESSES case study

Antonio Sgorbissa

DIBRIS Department, Università degli Studi di Genova, Genova, Italy

LEARNING OBJECTIVES

- To understand what are the key research areas in Social Robotics, as well as differences and similarities with other robotics domains.
- To understand the steps required to build a robotic system and the complexity of a multidisciplinary project to develop a socially assistive robot.
- To understand the challenges that researchers have to face when planning to embed cultural competence into a robot.

5.1 Introduction

The International Journal of Social Robotics is a multidisciplinary scientific journal edited by Springer that publishes up-to-date research in the field of Social Robotics (which may be obvious, given its name). The journal gives visibility to research work performed in different robotic areas, typically exploring issues related to human—robot interaction: published articles include contributions from Neuroscientists, Psychologists, Cognitive Scientists, Social Scientists, and many others, including robot designers as well as experts in Artificial Intelligence (AI).

By inspecting the articles published online in April 2021 (at the time these words are being written), it turns out that the most recently published article is entitled "The CARESSES

Randomised Controlled Trial: Exploring the Health-Related Impact of Culturally Competent Artificial Intelligence Embedded Into Socially Assistive Robots and Tested in Older Adult Care Homes" (Papadopoulos et al., 2021). Previous articles in the list evaluate the effect on people of voice type and head-light color in social robots (Dou et al., 2021), measure the impact of "robotic hugs" to increase the time people is willing to interact with the robot as well as to disclosure themselves (Shiomi et al., 2021), explore the role played by emotions and our capability to cope with them in human—robot interaction (Spekman et al., 2021), analyze the level of attention during the interaction among children with cognitive impairment (Ismail et al., 2021). When inspecting the former 20 articles published online, we find two articles about "trust," a prevalent trend of research at the present time: one of the two articles explores the role played by "trust in robots" to enable a satisfactory and efficient human—robot interaction (Schneider & Kummert, 2021); the other one studies the interplay between emotional intelligence, gender, and trust (Law et al., 2021), and finally how it is possible to make people trust robot more by operating on some key aspects, including making robots able to learn user's preferences. The crucial role attributed by researchers to trust is not a surprise. As robots are expected to become more and more pervasive in our lives, it is reasonable to study the factors that can make people trust robots more. Or less, as "trust dampening" (i.e., reducing overtrust) may be crucial to avoid overestimating the robot's capabilities.

All these aspects, and several more, are addressed by researchers in Social Robotics from a multidisciplinary perspective. Typically, researchers in this field study how social relationships work among human beings (or animals), describe the observed behaviors through diagrams and mathematical formulas, mimic them with a robot, and finally trial the robot with human participants by measuring some variable of interest. A joint effort by different disciplines may be required to achieve this. Experts in Computer Science, AI, and Robotics may have the methodological and technological tools to implement a behavioral model into a piece of software. However, they may not know how to design a randomized trial to measure the impact of the robot on a construct of interest, say the person's quality of life. Psychologists may have clear in their mind the cognitive models that drive the robot's understanding of people's behavior. However, they may lack the required skills to implement such models through a set of computer tasks for sensor acquisition, knowledge representation and reasoning, planning, and motor control. Who is responsible for identifying the most promising application domains, robotic engineers or health and social care experts? Who is in charge of determining the robot's behavior to comply with the beliefs, values, preferences, habits, and customs of different countries and regions of the world: computer scientists or anthropologists; social scientists or researchers in Transcultural Nursing?

This chapter will first say a few words about current trends of research in Social Robotics. Next, it will discuss people's expectations concerning social robots and what social robots are currently missing to meet such expectations. Finally, it will introduce the EU-Japan CARESSES project as a case study to provide the reader with a rough idea of the challenges faced by any innovative, interdisciplinary research project aiming to develop Socially Assistive Robots (SAR).

5.2 Building social robots for everybody and everywhere: a contemplation of what is missing

Describing all the areas of research currently investigated in this field is impossible because of the vast amount of subareas to be considered. Everything that has to do with human beings and their social relations may produce a tentative attempt to replicate the same mechanism in robots. As an aside, this also makes it challenging to design a syllabus for a Social Robotics course. Defining the content of, say, a Robotic Manipulation course is almost straightforward: robotic teachers would mostly agree about the mathematical bases that students must possess to control a robotic manipulator. However, the same does not happen in Social Robotics, a field of studies whose borders are broad and fuzzy: nobody clearly knows what the priorities are in Social Robotics, but everybody knows they are many. Even worse, the topics that a hypothetical Social Robotics course would teach are likely to overlap with other teaching areas, up to the extent that Social Robotics students may have already acquired the same skills in other classes. For instance, all researchers would likely agree that enabling a natural conversation with the user is a prerequisite for a Social Robot to operate in an environment inhabited by human beings. However, conversational systems are already addressed in other subareas of Computer Science and AI, ranging from speech and Natural Language Processing (NLP) to automatic sentence generation. Perhaps, when teaching Social Robotics, the fundamental objective is not that students acquire specific skills. Instead, we should teach students to possess a peculiar attitude toward robotics, a novel perspective putting human beings and their needs at the center of research. We should teach them a Renaissance's openness capable of merging skills and tools from scientific and humanistic disciplines toward the ultimate objective of creating robots capable of establishing a bond with humans in the same way humans do.

Having this attitude in mind, we mention below some scientific questions worth being answered, with no explicit intent to cover all research topics under investigation in Social Robotics exhaustively.

What methods and algorithms can we implement for human–aware autonomous motion (Kruse et al., 2013) in a social environment crowded with people (e.g., a commercial center, a cruise ship, a hospital)? How can the robot negotiate the space with humans by taking sociocultural norms and safety constraints into account? How can the robot generate natural and human-like trajectories in the presence of obstacles to induce a sense of familiarity and trust in surrounding humans? How can the robot use verbal and nonverbal behavior (e.g., gaze direction, arm, and head gestures) to communicate with surrounding humans, for example, in the case of a narrow passage that requires the human and the robot to agree about a precedence order?

How can the robot infer the user's emotion and intentions (Lee et al., 2009) by relying on verbal and nonverbal signals (human body posture and movement, gesture, gaze direction, distance from the robot, pauses in speech, voice volume), given the available technology in sensing and recognition? Which is the role of known models in Neuroscience and Psychology, for example, the Appraisal Theory (Lazarus, 1991) and its variants? How can the detected attitude of the user be exploited to adapt the verbal and nonverbal behavior of the robot to interact with him or her most properly? How can the robot use the same models to express its own emotions to facilitate communication, rather than just interpreting the emotions of humans (Breazeal, 2003)?

What methods and algorithms can we implement to allow humans and robots to physically cooperate toward achieving a given task, such as passing each other an object, a task trivial for humans but still very challenging for robots (Moon et al., 2014)? For example, what is the best way for the robot to give the object to the human and vice versa so that the object handover is comfortable? What is the optimal approaching direction, distance, and direction of the arm holding the object? How to find a mutual agreement such that the agent holding the thing in its hands can safely release it?

Which methods and tools are required for human—robot verbal and nonverbal communication (Mavridis, 2015), ranging from NLP and human intent recognition to sentence generation? How can the robot learn to speak from thousands of sentences excerpted from human conversation, for example, taken from Social Media? How can we be sure that a system trained with human conversations will not learn an offensive language, prejudices, and biases? How can we overcome the limitations of "command-based" vocal interfaces and develop an open system capable of talking with the user about (almost) everything? How can we design systems for complex and purposeful dialog management that considers the current context instead of replying to users in a purely reactive fashion as most home assistants do?

What is the role played by Theory of Mind (ToM) in the interaction between humans and robots (Scassellati, 2002), that is the ability to attribute independent mental states to self and others in terms of beliefs, intents, and goals, to the end of predicting and explaining behaviors? How is it possible to adapt the robot's behavior to increase the human's trust in its robotic companion? How is it possible to restore trust in the robot after a failure?

And finally, what application domains can have the most significant benefit from Social Robots and are worth being explored?

From the previous examples, one might deduce that Social Robots are, after all, "just robots." Indeed, they very closely resemble the mental image of robots that people have in their minds: machines capable of interacting with humans in the same way humans do.

This is not a surprise: if the reader is not aware of the "real history" of Robotics that started at the beginning of the previous century, their mental image of robots is probably more forged by movies, comics, and Sci-Fi books rather than by photographs taken in factories or handbooks for engineers. The word "robot" was first used to denote a fictional humanoid in a 1920 play by the Czech playwright Karel Čapek, with the meaning of "servant": since then, human-like robots have started to populate movies and books. One prominent example is Metropolis by Fritz Lang (1927), where a robot is given the appearance of Maria, a rebellious teacher who leads mistreated workers against an oppressive power: the Maria-like robot has the task to ruin Maria's reputation among the workers to prevent the rebellion. Another notable example is Robby from Forbidden Planet, a benevolent and intelligent mechanical character that helps Earthmen land on a far-away planet: once again, Robby does not belong to the industrial domain but instead plays the role of a servant and has an anthropomorphic appearance. Moving forward in time, the reader probably remembers the two Star-Wars droids, C-3PO (humanoid) and R2-D2 (not humanoid). R2-D2 doesn't speak English, and therefore, its social interaction with humans is mediated by C-3PO, a so-called protocol droid that can speak over six million languages.

Yes, you understood correctly: a protocol droid. According to the Wookieepedia, "A protocol droid was a droid whose job was to aid sentients with their etiquette and relations with each other in the galaxy." We go so far as to say that a protocol droid is the non plus ultra of a Social Robot, not only concerning its human appearance but in the purpose itself for which it was built!

There are other notable examples: some are evil robots (e.g., The Terminator), some tend to be funny (e.g., the paranoid android Marvin from the Hitchhiker's Guide to the Galaxy), some are prone to philosophy (e.g., the bicentennial man, Roy the Nexus six from Blade Runner, and once again the above mentioned Marvin: the whole Hitchhiker's guide is a philosophical book about "Life, Universe, and Everything," after all). Some of these robots look very similar to humans. Some of them are indistinguishable from humans, which is very cost-effective from the point of view of special effects: movies with robots were produced long before Computer-Generated Imagery reached the current state of the art. Some of them look more "mechanic" in their appearance (Number five from Short Circuit). They are not always referred to as "robots," but they may sometimes be called differently depending on the technology according to which they have been built: besides robots made of plastic and metal (the evolution of appliances like fridges and dishwashers), in some movies we may find replicants (made by biotechnology and genetic engineering), cyborgs (half-humans and half-robots), androids (resembling humans, usually made from a flesh-like material). What is very important to notice is that, despite these differences, robots in fiction are almost always anthropomorphic (or sometimes zoomorphic), which gives them the possibility to "act" as their biological counterpart would do. There are no industrial manipulators in movies, books, and comics, or a very few of them: people love to see robots capable of acting in an expressive, human-like way because this makes it easier to attribute intentions, goals, beliefs, and emotions to them. Once again, ToM: once we learn to attribute mental states to things, either animated or unanimated, we cannot do without it anymore (if you want to know more about people's view about robots and what literature says about Social Robots and AI technologies in health and social care, have a look at Chapter 3).

Given all the elements presented so far, it is not surprising that Social Robots are the robots people have always longed for. However, if this is true, why are most robots operating in the real world not Social Robots? Why are there more industrial manipulators, vacuum cleaners, and lawnmowers than anthropomorphic robots assisting people in their everyday lives?

This question has an obvious answer and a less obvious answer. The obvious answer is that engineers develop robots to reduce labor cost so that entrepreneurs are willing to buy them: industrial robots are introduced in factories since they cost less than people (which is one of the greatest fears of workers). However, this cannot be the only reason: it would be equally convenient, from a purely economic perspective, to invest in robots capable of working in social environments as waiters, hostesses, or caregivers, just to mention a few. Then, the less obvious answer is that robotic researchers have primarily focused on factories because factories are simpler and more controllable environments than homes and other social settings where people live their everyday life. The reader may have a second look at Chapter 2 of this book, where we extensively argued that one of the biggest obstacles to introducing robots in the real world is that the world is complex and unpredictable. The more complex and unpredictable the environment is, the harder it is to develop "robust" robots capable of behaving correctly in almost all situations. Put yourself in the shoes of a robot: can you imagine a more complex and unpredictable environment than a place inhabited by humans, with hundreds of things everywhere continuously changing their location and everybody wanting something from you?

If this is the situation, what is the solution to make Social Robots "invade" our world? In December 2015, when we devised the CARESSES project, we identified two main aspects as having the highest priority.

First, we identified the primary need to create Social Robots that possibly have limited functionalities but can work autonomously 24/7 in social environments populated by people. In other words, we deemed it more critical for Social Robots to start doing small things by exhibiting robust behavior despite the complexity and unpredictability of the world around them, rather than mimicking complex human behaviors but in very controlled setups. We were aware that other researchers aim to design Social Robots capable of marvelous things: we thought it was time for Social Robots to start doing minimal things but do them for real.

Second, we deemed it essential to consider the cultural environment where robots are going to operate. An analysis of the scientific literature reports that cultural factors in Robotics have been investigated in the last decade (Rehm, 2013): previous researchers focused on individual features that can make the system more or less acceptable to people of different cultures, either concerning its appearance or its behavior (Rau et al., 2010), including verbal and nonverbal interaction (Rau et al., 2009) or social distance (Eresha et al., 2013). However, none of these earlier approaches aimed to define a general conceptual framework to make a robot culturally competent, that is, capable of adapting its verbal and nonverbal behavior depending on the person's cultural identity. Please, refer to Chapter 1 for such concepts as culture, cultural awareness, cultural knowledge, cultural sensitivity, and cultural identity.

We will now tell the story of CARESSES. This may look selfcelebratory; however, knowing about this project can be very helpful to make the reader aware of the challenges to be addressed when developing a complex robotic system requiring a multidisciplinary effort in a genuine Social Robotics spirit. Also, the rest of this chapter may work as a guide to better approach the following chapters, where we will formulate hypotheses and discuss solutions to make robots culturally competent.

In the following, we will sometimes refer to the key researchers involved in the project. To preserve anonymity, we will take inspiration from the TV serial "Money Heist" (in Spanish: "La casa de papel," The House of Paper), telling the story of a heist on the Royal Mint of Spain. If you have watched the TV series, you may remember that characters call each other using city names (Tokyo, Denver, Rio, Berlin) not to be identifiable. With a hint of humor, we will refer to CARESSES researchers using the names of the city where their institution's headquarters are. We use the academic title only the first time we mention a researcher.

So be ready to meet London, Genova, Örebro, Kanazawa, Luton, Paris, Chubu, Nagoya, London—Barnet. As you can see, the idea works only partially because there were two partners with headquarters in London in CARESSES. To avoid ambiguity, one of the two researchers has the suffix "Barnet" corresponding to the London borough where his offices are.

5.3 The CARESSES case study told as a radio drama

The following story is based on the ideas and the discussion that emerged while preparing the original CARESSES proposal, submitted for evaluation in Spring 2016 to the European Commission and the Ministry of Internal Affairs and Communication of Japan. However, the story we tell in the following did not happen precisely that way. For example, the phrases spoken by a character in our story may have been pronounced by another character, never been told, or be completely different. In addition, some ideas that we present here as included in the original project proposal may have emerged later during the project or even after the project's end.

Our only intention is to introduce CARESSES to the reader, hopefully by making things more engaging by adding a dash of drama.

5.3.1 Laying the ground

On November 27, 2015, around 1.30 p.m. (UK time), Prof. London from Middlesex University received a phone call. She had spent her morning trying to do some thinking and reading, in between all her other work. The phone call resulted from a brief exchange of emails to discuss a project proposal to be possibly submitted to the European Research Program H2020, in a Call specially dedicated to cooperation between Europe and Japan. Quite unusually, the project's objective was to design humanoid robots that might assist older people in their homes. Notwithstanding her long teaching experience in the Nursing field and her specific competence in health and social care in different cultures, she had never explored using robots to assist people. Was it possible to teach robots to take care of people at all? London had a strong passion for new and adventurous things for all her life, and therefore, she had immediately replied positively to the proposal. The idea seemed interesting and worth being explored.

The phone rang.

On the other side of the cable, Prof. Genova from the University of Genova knew that London had no previous experience in Robotics. Genova lived in Italy and had an academic background in the development of intelligent and autonomous robotic systems. Unfortunately, he was not very comfortable talking in English on the phone: the University of Genova is a medium-size University in Northern Italy, where most MS and Ph.D. students, postdocs, and researchers are Italian, and almost everybody speaks Italian there. Consequently, he was a little anxious: the concept he wanted to communicate to London needed to be fully understood. Genova needed her to say "yes."

She picked up the phone. After a few minutes, a small team was built.

The newborn team, which included AI and robotic scientists Prof. Örebro from Sweden and Prof. Kanazawa from Japan, was aware that the recent literature had already explored robots whose appearance or behavior matched people's cultural expectations. However, CARESSES had to be unique for the following reason: the project's primary goal was to explore general methods to program cultural competence into the very robots. Not only designers, engineers, and programmers were supposed to be culturally competent in customizing robots: the robots themselves would have acquired the capability of autonomously reconfiguring their behavior to the person's cultural identity.

Researchers realized that this ambitious goal raised several issues that they had to address.

From the scientific perspective, researchers committed to exploring cultural competence as a key feature to improve the acceptability of health and social care robots in society and studying how to make a robot culturally competent. This required investigating how to model different cultures in a language understandable by computer programs and how to use these models to guide the robot when perceiving the surroundings, planning things to do and say, and acting in the real world.

From the technological perspective, researchers committed to building a demonstration system based on a state-of-the-art humanoid robot specifically designed for social interaction with people and integrating the outcomes of the above scientific work into the robot.

From the testing and validation perspective, researchers committed to performing experiments with older care home residents. Experiments were needed to test the role of cultural competence in creating robots more sensitive to the user's needs, customs, and lifestyle, improving users' quality of life, reducing caregiver burden, and improving the system's efficiency and effectiveness.

The team, which in the meanwhile had become a consortium of seven research centers, one robotic company, and one care home network to adequately address all the issues above, also knew that a project like CARESSES might have created expectations and controversies in the media and the public. Therefore, researchers needed an adequate communication strategy to disseminate the project's findings. Finally, the team was aware that CARESSES might have posed significant challenges for project coordination. Indeed, the project involved a highly multidisciplinary team with partners that never worked together before and was funded by two different funding agencies from Europe and Japan with different customs and regulations, an excellent opportunity for a project focusing on cultural aspects, but not the most straightforward situation for project management!

"Things seem quite complex," Genova sighed. "To make some order, we need specific objectives and a proper Workplan to achieve them."

To this end, researchers had several meetings during Winter 2015 and Spring 2016, both in presence and video conference. Let's now attend one of these video conference meetings. Please remember that the following is a work of fiction: things never happened precisely this way.

5.3.2 Scientific objectives

"Objective 1," London said, "is to define the desired behaviour of a culturally competent robot. We will take care of it using our expertise in Transcultural Nursing," she proudly added. "The expected outcomes will be a set of scenarios describing the daily life of women and men of different cultures and a set of guidelines that will be used to determine the most appropriate robot's behaviour".

"What cultures will we consider?" Örebro asked, puzzled.

"English, Indian, and Japanese." London replied. "They are quite different cultures. Moreover, it should be simple to recruit participants when trialling the robot with people towards the end of the project. Many Indian people live in the UK."

"And, of course, many Japanese people live in Japan," Kanazawa concluded, smiling. He was the coordinator of the Japanese side of the project.

"Scenarios and guidelines," London continued, "will include a detailed description of what a person and his or her caregiver would do at different times of the day. Also, they will describe the objects and areas of the house relevant to different daily routines, and what the robot should do in every situation depending on the person's cultural background".

Dr. Paris, a chief scientist at SoftBank Robotics, observed: "So, perhaps, shall also we contribute to the definition of scenarios as robotic researchers? We know better than anybody else the actual capabilities of the Pepper robot. We made it!"

London approved, nodding. "We definitely need you for this. The second objective …"

"Objective 2," Genova wrote on his PC. Genova was going to be the coordinator of the whole project and was visibly anxious.

"… Objective 2," London continued, "will be aimed to define a procedure to avoid stereotyped representations of people and cultures. The guidelines we will produce can be used to determine the most appropriate behavior of the robot depending on the situation and the user's cultural background. Still, they cannot be applied rigidly: different people who may self-identify with the same culture will exhibit individual differences in their beliefs, values, preferences, and habits, even if they share a way of life under many aspects. Objective 2 is to establish a procedure allowing the robot to learn individual differences during the interaction with people. It is a fundamental objective," London concluded.

Genova took the floor. "Once the guidelines for a culturally competent robot's behavior are ready, we need to define a process to encode the guidelines into a database, or something like that. How can we call this database?"

"What about Cultural Knowledge Base?", Örebro suggested.

"Deal! We will use a Cultural Knowledge Base, programmed in such a way to allow computer scientists to encode guidelines produced by transcultural experts in a language understandable by the robot." Genova stared at the excited faces of his colleagues on his PC screen, constrained in small squared windows by the videoconference tool. "All these objectives require multidisciplinary expertise and tight cooperation. We all have a different scientific background here. I am afraid that working together may require a significant effort to establish a common vocabulary shared by all of us. Health and social care experts and engineers tend not to speak the same language, and we all make assumptions when talking about our work that may not be obvious to our interlocutors."

"Maybe, in the future, we might write a book about this experience," London intervened, "to reduce the distance between researchers of different disciplines having the same objective of building robots that can help people."

"I don't think we will ever find the time for this," Genova frowned. "Going back to the project, the procedure to avoid stereotypes by assessing personal preferences should also be implemented as a computer program."

"You mean Objective 2?" Örebro asked.

"Yes, Objective 2," Genova replied. "Programming the robot to acquire information during the interaction with the person will require, once again, a close interaction between transcultural experts, computer scientists, and robotics engineers. Indeed, to make the robot capable of learning the user's personal preferences during the interaction, we should consider that culture is not a rigid representation of people's beliefs, values, attitudes, and preferences. Is it correct, London?"

"Correct," she replied.

"Then," Genova concluded, "culture is probably better represented in a probabilistic sense. We shall find a formal way to express the idea that different persons self-identifying with a given culture will have different probabilities to be familiar with one or the other aspect that, to simplify things, are typically associated with that culture. For example, even if it is not that probable to happen, there are Italians that do not love pizza and football."

"Really?" everybody asked, laughing.

5.3.3 Technological objectives

Genova took the floor again. "It seems reasonable that Objective 3 shall be focused on implementing the Cultural Knowledge Base as a computer Ontology."

"A computer what … ?" asked Dr. Luton, intrigued. Luton was a researcher in Public Health and at the University of Bedfordshire. He loved all kinds of innovative technologies.

"A computer Ontology" Genova explained. "Ontologies can store information like a database but with more advanced functionalities. One of the things that make Ontologies very appealing is that, on the one hand, the knowledge stored in them can be automatically interpreted by computer programs and hence by robots. On the other hand, Ontologies are easily interpretable by humans that have no problems understanding what is written in them if they are not programmers. Well, after some training, of course."

London interrupted with excitement: "Then, Ontologies may provide the common language enabling transcultural experts and robotic engineers to collaborate in the implementation of guidelines into a computer program. Is it like that? I will learn how to write and read Ontologies!" She looked at Luton, winking. "We all should!"

Genova continued: "That is a great idea. But encoding guidelines in the Ontology won't be sufficient. As you suggested, we also need to implement an AI program for avoiding stereotypes by assessing personal preferences. This program will allow the robot to revise its assumptions, which have been initially made depending exclusively on the person's culture. As already agreed, we can do this by introducing a probabilistic twist about facts encoded in the knowledge base. We will not store just 'facts about different cultures' but facts that may be more or less probable."

"And then the robot should make educated guesses to understand what each person actually believes and values," London remarked.

Genova nodded: "That can be done and will be Objective 4. We will write AI programs that will use the information already in the Ontology to acquire new information about the person through educated guesses made verbally by the robot. Personalized information. Not about English, Indian, or Japanese people in general, but about you, you, and you!" Genova pointed theatrically at the different windows of the video conferencing tools showing his colleagues' faces.

Somebody approved, amused.

"And I have another idea. We might store in the Ontology not only facts. We might also encode 'chunks of sentences' to talk about such facts. The robot might then automatically compose these chunks of sentences to talk about culturally relevant concepts in a culturally sensitive way."

Örebro took the floor: "One moment. We are developing a robot, not a vocal assistant".

Paris smiled with an ironic look on his face.

Örebro insisted: "We need to equip the robot with other capabilities in addition to talking with the person about culturally relevant things. We are robotic scientists; we expect robots to perform actions in the real world. Think about the robot leading the way for the person to get to the bathroom, making a phone call, greeting guests, operating an air conditioner or a smart lamp, playing a video or a song, reading an audiobook. These are indispensable actions that a robot is expected to perform in a socially assistive scenario."

"Agreed," Kanazawa said.

"Don't forget that things are complex," Örebro continued, "because, when performing some of these activities, it may not be sufficient to perform just one action: in some cases, it may be necessary to execute a sequence of actions."

"A plan," Paris added.

"A plan. As an example, consider a person that gets back home at the end of the day. The robot is likely required to perform the following actions in sequence: wait for hearing the voice of the person entering the room, greet her or him, approach the person, ask if she or he needs something. I guess that robotic researchers in our team are familiar with the fact that robots can automatically compose plans through a piece of software called planner," Örebro paused, taking a breath.

"And then, Objective 5 ..." Genova smiled, taking a note on his PC.

"Objective 5," Örebro confirmed, "is to develop a culturally sensitive planner, i.e., a planner capable of producing sequences of actions that achieve a given goal while being appropriate to the cultural context in which the robot operates."

"Excellent," Genova commented, clapping his hand on the table.

"Let me make an example," Örebro gestured to wait, "depending on the customs and norms that hold in different cultural contexts, a culturally sensitive planner might tell the robot to give objects with one or two hands. We know that giving and receiving objects with two hands is considered more respectful in many Asian countries, do we? Or the planner might tell the robot to greet people with different gestures, such as waving the hand or bowing."

"Or by joining hands in front of your chest. Namaste," Paris interrupted him by showing to the webcam the typical Napalese gesture for greeting.

Örebro nodded. "Also, you may know that the amount of space that people feel it necessary to set between themselves and others during the interaction may depend on cultural factors."

"Of course. Proxemics studies these things," London specified.

"Our planner" Örebro concluded, "may tell the robot whether it should stay farther or closer to people when interacting with them. Depending on the culture of the person, of course. I am sure that London may suggest other daily routines and actions that are performed differently in different cultures."

"You can bet I can," London confirmed.

Kanazawa, who had remained almost silent until that moment, looked at Chubu and then Paris. "Ok, but there are more important things to do first. Aren't there? Robots that talk with people, robots that make plans - who does the dirty work?" He smiled. "We have decided not to develop a new robot but to buy a commercial platform, SoftBank's Pepper."

"Yes, because we do not have the time and resources to build a robot from scratch, starting from mechanics and electronics," Genova hastened to explain, worried.

"No excuses needed," Kanazawa stopped him. "Pepper is perfect for our purposes. Everybody seems to love it."

"Just my two cents," Örebro added. "If we can produce a culturally competent AI that works on a commercial robot like Pepper, the impact is more than if it works on a robot we purposely designed. After all, cultural competence has not to do with the robot's physical characteristics: if it is possible to teach cultural competence to every human being, why shouldn't it be possible to 'teach' cultural competence to every robot?"

Paris seemed very satisfied.

"Still," Kanazawa continued, "if we want Pepper to do something useful, we also need to develop those software components that robotics researchers" and here he looked at non-robotic researchers in the team, "sometimes call the 'low-level.'"

"The low-level?" Luton asked.

Kanazawa continued: "Objective 6 should be to develop that part of the software that is closer to the hardware and the physicality of the world. Or, if you prefer, that part of the software not dealing with 'high-level' cognitive activities such as knowledge representation, reasoning, or planning, but rather with sensorimotor tasks for acquiring data from sensors and controlling motors to perform actions. We need computer programs to use Pepper's sensors, such as microphones and cameras, to acquire new knowledge about the user during the interaction. We need computer programs that will lay the basis for verbal and non-verbal interaction with the user: speech acquisition, speech-to-text translation, speech synthesis, recognition of gestures, postures, and activities. My colleague Chubu on the Japanese side of the team has an interesting idea to recognize people's activities and habits. Prof. Chubu, can you please explain?"

"We won't use only sensors onboard Pepper," Chubu explained, "but also smart sensors distributed in the room. We will develop a smart environment making it easier for the robot to understand what the person is doing."

Kanazawa turned his gaze imperceptibly to Örebro. "Finally, we need computer programs to execute the actions that the planner has decided—for example, moving in-between locations of the environment, greeting the users, showing a video, starting a phone call, turning on a smart lamp. I am amazed that nobody remarked on this yet: we need a good variety of low-level sensorimotor capabilities as the basis for designing culturally competent skills. If the robot does not have the capacity to 'do something' in the real world, there is no way to 'do this something' in a culturally competent manner, right?"

Paris turned on his microphone: "Kanazawa hit the point. We need to put more emphasis on technological aspects if we want to succeed in making something useful for the scientific community and society." He paused to verify the effect of his words on the audience. "We need to explore how to integrate all software and hardware components, that is, computer programs and physical devices, into a proper 'software framework.' This framework will provide interfaces between the different components to allow the exchange of data between them. Be aware that integration is one of the most critical aspects of large cooperative research projects. Believe me. I have a long date experience in this. Integration always fails. Always." Then he laughed under his mustache, imitated in this by Örebro.

"Let's hope not," Genova commented, obviously worried.

Paris continued firmly: "We will see. There are many things to do, and we shall start as soon as possible. If your plan is to integrate research outcomes in the last year of the project, as many researchers do, we are doomed to fail. First, we need to choose a software framework for integrating all software and hardware components."

"What do you mean by 'software framework,' exactly?" Luton asked.

Paris raised his eyebrows: "Well, I suppose you know what an Operating System is, right? Windows, Mac OS, Linux …"

"Android, iOS … Got it!" Luton concluded the sentence.

"That's it. The ones you mentioned are Operating Systems for smartphones. But there are also Operating Systems specially designed for robotic applications. I also knew a framework to create smart environments developed during a previous European project. What's its name?" Paris asked himself. "The European Commission is usually happy if researchers show that they are re-utilizing the outcomes of previous projects."

"So, perhaps, should this be Objective 7?" Genova asked.

Paris approved: "Objective 7 should be the integration of the Pepper humanoid robot in the framework. Now I remember the name: universAAL. This will be followed by the integration of all the software components developed for knowledge representation, planning, as well as low-level sensorimotor tasks."

Kanazawa intervened: "Objective 7 shall also include integrating the Pepper robot with the standard for home automation ECHONET we use in Japan, which will ultimately enable the robot to control lights, air conditioners, or window curtains in Japanese smart-houses."

"This sounds great," Genova looked comforted, "Give me the time to write it down: ' … used in Japanese smart-houses for controlling light, air conditioners, or window curtains.' What about non-Japanese smart-houses?".

"We should find a solution to cope with this," Paris mumbled.

"This might be an opportunity for cultural exchange," Örebro observed, visibly happy. "Headline news: the European framework for smart environments meets the Japanese standard for home automation!"

"Bingo," Luton exclaimed.

"And now listen to Objective 8," Genova continued. "What about developing a 'Cloud version' of our system? After writing computer programs for culturally competent interaction with the person, we might move all our programs to the Cloud. We will execute them on third-party computers of Internet colossuses such as Google or Amazon."

"Should we pay a fee for that?" Luton asked.

"Yes, but consider the implications: once our solutions for culturally competent interaction are hosted somewhere on the Internet, every smart device equipped with a network interface, not only Pepper, not only robots, but also home assistants, smartphone apps and, why not, smart fridges, may acquire functionalities for culturally competent interaction."

London smiled excitedly: "This will be a revolution!"

5.3.4 Validation objectives

"I think it's my turn," Luton took a long breath, and a dog barked somewhere in his room. "We now need to talk about testing and evaluating our prototype of a culturally competent robot with care home residents in the UK and Japan in a randomized trial. Let me summarize what we have decided to do now: the robot will be Pepper equipped with software to store cultural knowledge, make culturally sensitive plans, perceive, and act with cultural competence. Correct?"

"Correct," Paris nodded.

"Then Objective 9," Luton continued, "shall be to develop the experimental protocol in detail. The general idea is that we will test the system in three cultural settings with English, Indian, and Japanese participants. Fifteen participants per cultural group. Each cultural group will include one experimental arm, interacting with the culturally competent robot, and two control arms, either interacting with a non-culturally competent robot or with no robot at all. I also think that we may need a specific objective focussing on screening and recruiting participants."

"Agreed. This will be Objective 10," Genova typed quickly on his PC.

"Notice that Objective 10 might reveal to be one of the most ambitious of the whole project", Luton pointed out, "we can ideally count on a vast population, at least in the UK, thanks to the involvement of the Advinia Health Care network …"

Luton turned his gaze to Dr. London–Barnet who looked back with pride.

"… but we know from the literature that recruiting participants for a trial with robots is extremely challenging, especially if participants are older care home residents. As I said, we have not prepared the experimental protocol yet. However, following a preliminary exchange of ideas I had with colleagues at the University of Bedfordshire, we will have to: find people living in care homes with the required cognitive capabilities; get their consent to participate in the study, which in our case may be quite time-demanding since participants will need to give availability for about 20 hours; deal with the schedules of care homes as well as with possible health-issues and personal schedules of participants."

"Wow, a lot of stuff," Kanazawa commented. "Please remember that we don't have a network of care homes in Japan as a partner of the project. We just have an agreement with one care home called HISUISUI that will kindly support us in performing experiments with residents. Prof. Nagoya, can we do these things in our care home in Japan as well?"

"The situation on the Japanese side of the project is different. We will do the best we can," Nagoya answered gently. She was a psychologist and knew very well how difficult it is to make tests with the frailer people.

"And that's not everything," Luton spoke again, "on the European side, we virtually have several residents that might be willing to participate, but logistic issues and costs can make things harder. Indeed, experimental sessions with the robot will likely need the presence of both technical and healthcare staff, which might be difficult to move all around the UK to chase participants nominated by Advinia's care homes managers."

"Trust me, we will cope with that," London—Barnet reassured him.

"Finally, Objective 11 will aim to measure the intervention's effectiveness through validated questionnaires and qualitative interviews," Luton prepared to conclude. "We will measure if the quality of life of the person improves using the robot, among others. And we will measure the cultural competence of the robot as the person perceives it."

"This is a fundamental objective," London—Barnet commented.

"It is." Luton confirmed. "In addition, achieving this objective will be crucial to pave the way for similar studies in the future. Indeed, since the trial will involve a small number of participants for each cultural group, it is hard to know in advance if statistically relevant differences between experimental and control arms will emerge. This uncertainty is also because nobody attempted a similar study evaluating the impact of a culturally competent assistive robot before. Because of this, we had no means to perform a power analysis to know the number of participants required to make statistically significant differences emerge."

"That's fine," London clarified, "our project will be a first step towards the development and deployment of culturally competent robots. A larger trial will have to follow before this might happen. Step by step."

"Step by step," other voices echoed her.

5.3.5 Dissemination and exploitation objectives

Genova stopped typing on his PC. "Congratulations to everybody for the work done! We now need to address a problem that deserves the greatest attention but is sometimes left in the background in large research projects. We all know that researchers put a significant effort into disseminating their results to the scientific community to the extent that publishing scientific articles may become their only goal. This concept is wonderfully expressed by a 'meme' populating Social Networks."

Örebro laughed to himself, apparently knowing the thing to what Genova was referring.

"The meme shows a poster entitled 'Types of robotics papers' and then reports some examples of papers with funny titles. 'Scary control system mathematics.' 'Summary of 30 papers so everyone cites mine.' 'We studied human-robot interaction in an application no one will ever use.' 'We applied machine learning to this solved problem, and it does almost as well.' 'It worked on the computer but not in real life.' 'Perfect results, in simulation.'

"I saw that one," Örebro, "the joke restates a key concept, that is, the fact that making robots work in the real world is extremely complex. So we should be very cautious about what we promise to do in the project."

"It also reminds us that researchers spend a large part of their time convincing other researchers that what they do is important," Genova added. "I am afraid we are no different and, therefore, Objective 12 will be focussed on writing and publishing scientific papers."

Signals of consensus came from the audience.

"However," Genova continued, "researchers have other duties. They need to make citizens aware of what they are doing, clarify what people can expect and not expect from their research, and finally, explain how they are spending the money received from the public to do what they are doing. Therefore, I firmly believe that we need Objective 13 to explicitly focus on communication actions to inform the media and the public."

"You don't have to convince us," London replied, considering Genova's statement as obvious, "our communication people are more than willing to send out press releases whenever we have a story to tell!"

"True," Luton confirmed.

"Communication is the key, but we need to be cautious. There's a lot of public debate around health and social care, and the use of robots is controversial. Some journalists may want to lure us into a trap", London—Barnet warned the audience with great composure.

While our characters reflect on the wise words of London—Barnet let's have a 5-min pause. This will also allow our characters to get a cup of tea or coffee, which they may need.

During the coffee break, let's jump to the future for a while. We are no more in 2015 now but in June 2021. The project has ended. You may have noticed that CARESSES researchers explicitly planned since the beginning to pay the greatest attention to communication actions to increase the awareness of the media, policymakers, and the public about the project's topic. The reader may still (hopefully) appreciate the CARESSES website and the nice animated video prepared to clarify the project's objective to the public. However, it shall also be remarked that things went far beyond initial expectations. Since the beginning of the project, the international press seemed very interested to know more about the project, and their interest continued throughout the whole project life cycle: the project repeatedly captured the attention of global media, including BBC, CNN, The Times, The Telegraph, Il Corriere Della Sera, the Italian, Japanese, Swedish and UK television, and many others. In 2018, the project was officially presented at the UK parliament and nominated "Project of the month" by the European Commission. The

EC Innovation Radar officially acknowledged its technologies as innovations. The project was included among the "UK best breakthrough" by the MadeAtUni Campaign in 2019 and among the "100 Italian Robotics & Automation Stories" in a report presented by Enel S.p.a. in February 2020. In December 2020, after its end, it was featured by BBC in its program "The big tech questions for 2021." Drawing conclusions about the reasons that made this success possible is not easy: it may depend on the fact that the project started at the right time and involved partners from a country, the UK, where health and social care-related issues are often on the front page, as our colleague London–Barnet observed. The importance attributed by partners to communication aspects, often underestimated by academic researchers, may have also contributed.

Whatever the reasons are, there's one thing you can say without fear of making a mistake. If you do not think communication is essential, it will hardly happen that people not working in your field will ever become aware of your work—which is unfair, given that you are doing this for them and with their money.

The coffee break has finished: time to get back to 2015.

"Finally," Genova resumed the discussion by sipping his American coffee from a large mug (unbelievably, Italians do not drink only Espresso coffee!) "Objective 14 will be to guarantee an appropriate exchange of information within researchers in the consortium. This will be crucial in all phases of research, especially in a complex multidisciplinary project like ours, ranging from developing scenarios and guidelines with the involvement of transcultural experts and computer scientists to testing and evaluation requiring tight cooperation between technical and health care staff."

London and Luton approved.

"We need repositories for storing data, reports, and other documentation." Genova clarified. "In addition, we need procedures for collaborative software development. I anticipate that, when developing and integrating hardware and software components into our prototype of a culturally competent robot, programmers located in Paris, Kanazawa, Örebro, or Genova may need to cooperate in writing different parts of the very same programs. If this happens, we need to prevent conflicts of any sort. For example, it would be unbearable if a programmer in timezone GMT+9 makes some changes to a program in the afternoon and another programmer in timezone GMT+1 deletes them in the morning."

"Oh, yes, and what's the problem?" Örebro said ironically.

"Or maybe, a programmer in Genova uses an older version of the program by ignoring the most recent updates of another programmer in Örebro." Genova felt a shiver run down his spine. "Can you imagine the mess if we do not establish clear procedures for this?"

"We have a long experience in industry-level programming. There are many tools for collaborative programming, and we habitually support our development partners that design applications for Pepper," Paris reassured him. "Genova, please also add Objective 15, aimed to prepare a plan for commercial exploitation of the project's outcomes. We don't know how far we will go, but I have good vibrations about this project. We shall be ready now for what's coming after the project's end if we want to have a real impact on society."

"If we want to do something good for people," London—Barnet concluded.

5.3.6 Project management and ethics

"We have almost finished," Genova spoke again, looking at Kanazawa. "Kanazawa and I will be the coordinators of the project. We think we need to fix an objective explicitly aimed to project management. Somebody might observe that project management is not directly related to research. However, everybody that has been the coordinator of a large research project with several partners would probably feel the opposite. In addition to dealing with administrative and financial issues, which administrative offices hopefully handle with minimal involvement of researchers, project management has the primary goal of putting researchers in the best conditions to work."

"Researchers can take the luxury to be anarchists," Kanazawa added, "but the coordinators cannot, unfortunately."

Genova continued: "Objective 15 will include keeping researchers updated about tasks to do and deadlines."

"As well as finding catchy email subjects and a proper balance in the number of emails sent for researchers not to ignore them," Örebro added.

"It will include scheduling regular meetings to agree on the next steps, recognizing risks, proposing mitigation plans and contingency measures if risks materialize. And finally, being creative and friendly to everybody so that everybody is happy to work, to create a bond that will last even beyond the project." Genova realized he was sweating.

London intervened with a reassuring look. "We all know that people work better when they like working together. So we need to keep a continuous and positive flow of ideas. Without it, maintaining the consensus of all researchers around objectives will not be possible."

"Also," Luton added, "since we are planning to make tests with human participants, it is essential that we comply with ethics requirements. An ethics committee will have to approve everything we do."

"Meeting ethics requirements will be Objective 16. Thanks, Luton. We should not underestimate this. Unfortunately, it happens all too often that engineers think that paying attention to ethical aspects is just a nuisance." Genova was starting to run out of air.

London stared at him: "You worry too much, Genova. We will all help you and Kanazawa."

"Let's hope for the best," he thought to himself.

5.4 Preparing the work plan: the path from scenarios and guidelines to artificial intelligence, from technological development to end-user evaluation

The previous section provided details about the objectives of the CARESSES project and paved the way to the next chapters of the book, in which the project will be used as a case study. We hope you liked the dramatization. If you want to know more about Objectives 1 and 2, have a look at Chapters 6 and 7. Check Chapter 8 for Objectives 3, 4, and 5, and Chapter 9 for Objectives 6, 7, and 8. Finally, Objectives 9, 10, and 11 will be addressed in Chapter 10.

However, please keep in mind that stating objectives is not sufficient: as mentioned above, managing a complex research project requires coordinating all activities to achieve those objectives. This included preparing a proper Workplan where the work to be performed was split into Work Packages (WP), smaller units of work assigned to different teams at different times, and ensuring that teams had the needed resources to perform their work according to such a plan.

CARESSES involved six participants from different EU countries and three participants from Japan, which you have just encountered. The Workplan to achieve the 16 objectives stated in the previous section included 10 WPs: each WP was led by the most entitled partner to complete the corresponding objectives, with the contribution of other partners. European and Japanese participants started to work collaboratively on the project on January 1, 2017, and the project lasted 37 months until January 31, 2020. The 7 WPs explicitly devoted to research are shown in Fig. 5.1. The Figure emphasizes that outcomes produced by a WP may provide an input to another WP and shows how the workload was distributed across European and Japanese partners.

When coming to implementation, the objectives described in the previous section were addressed by WPs as follows.

- WP1 (Transcultural Robotic Nursing) addressed Objectives 1 and 2 and was led by the University of Middlesex.

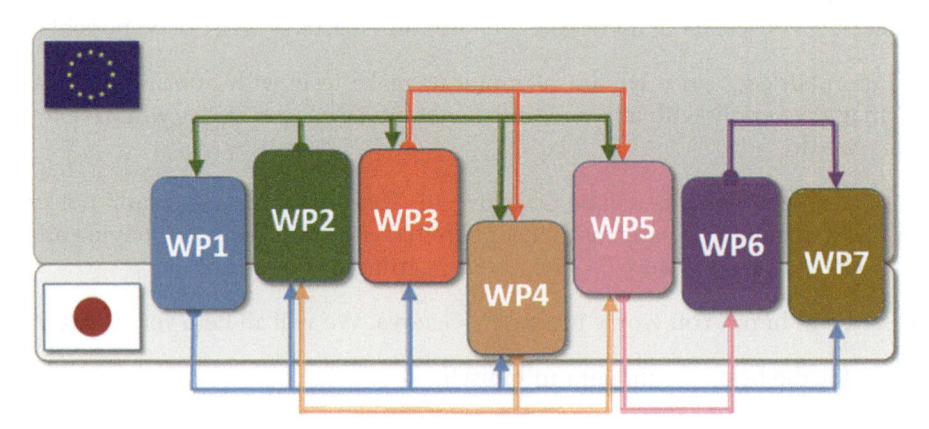

FIGURE 5.1 The CARESSES work packages.

- WP2 (Cultural Knowledge Representation) addressed Objectives 3 and 4 and was led by the University of Genova.
- WP3 (Culturally Sensitive Planning and Execution) addressed Objective 5 and was led by Örebro University.
- WP4 (Culture-Aware Interaction in a Smart ICT Environment) addressed Objectives 6 and was led by the Japan Advanced Institute of Science and Technology.
- WP5 (System Integration) addressed Objectives 7 and 8 and was led by SoftBank Robotics Europe.
- WP6 (Testing in Health-Care Facilities) addressed Objectives 9 and 10 and was led by Advinia Healthcare with the support of the University of Bedfordshire.
- WP7 (End-User Evaluation) addressed Objectives 11 and was led by the University of Bedfordshire.
- WP8 (Dissemination and Exploitation) addressed Objectives 12, 13, and 14 and was led by SoftBank Robotics Europe.
- WP9 (Project Management) and WP10 (Ethics Requirements) addressed Objectives 15 and 16 and were led by the University of Genova.

Finally, Fig. 5.2 reports the timeline of research WPs from one to seven by outlining the main milestones in the Work Plan: the delivery of guidelines and the first software release in October 2017, followed by an integration round in November; the release of the experimental protocol in June 2018, a new software release and a second integration round starting in July 2018; the pretrial in November/December 2019, followed by a revision of the experimental protocol and the software; the main trial from March 2019 to the end of September 2019.

The adventure has begun. The following chapters will describe in greater detail what we found during the journey.

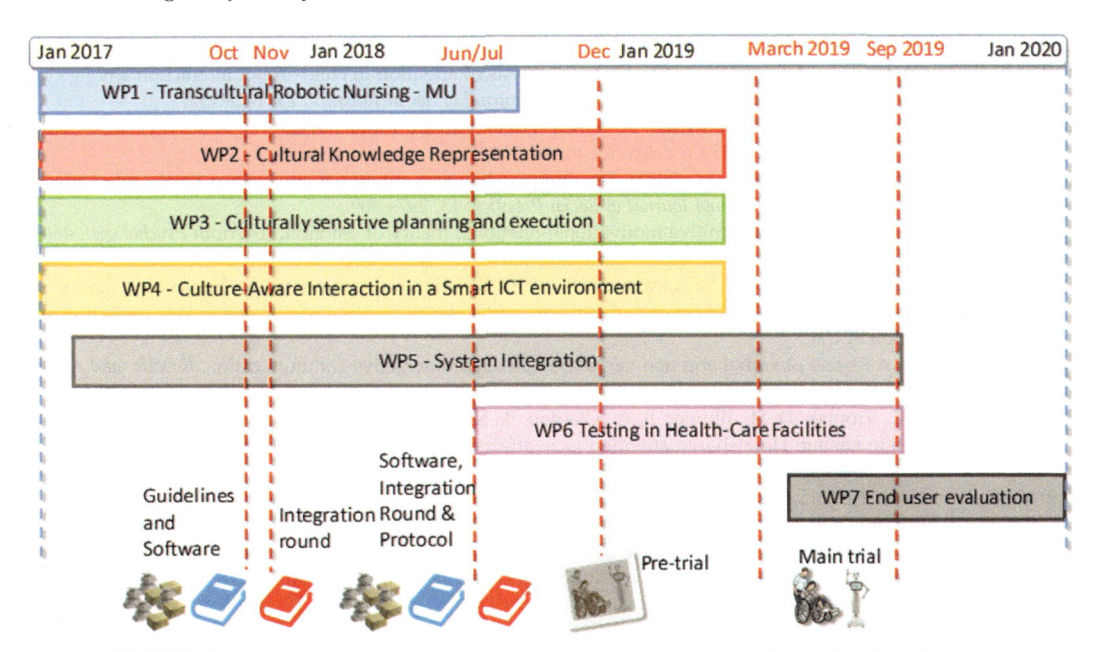

FIGURE 5.2 The CARESSES Workplan, showing Work Packages (WPs) and main milestones.

5.5 Conclusion

This chapter has introduced the field of Social Robotics and the objectives of the CARESSES project. CARESSES, whose objectives we discussed in detail, provides a case study to make the reader aware of the challenges raised by a complex robotic system requiring a multidisciplinary effort. Additionally, it will help the reader navigate the following chapters, formulating hypotheses and discussing our solutions to make robots capable of exhibiting culturally competent behavior.

5.5.1 Reflective questions

- What are the main objectives of Social Robotics?
- What are the main differences between industrial robots and SAR, both in terms of what the robot can do and the context in which it operates?
- Why designing a social robot is more challenging, in some respects, than designing an industrial robot?
- What are the most important aspects to be taken into consideration when developing a complex, multidisciplinary project?

References

Breazeal, C. (2003). Emotion and sociable humanoid robots. *International Journal of Human-Computer Studies, 59*(1–2), 119–155.

Dou, X., Wu, C. F., Niu, J., & Pan, K.-R. (2021). Effect of voice type and head-light color in social robots for different applications. *International Journal of Social Robotics*, 1–16.

Eresha, G., Haring, M., Endrass, B., Andre, E., & Obaid, M. (2013). Investigating the influence of culture on proxemic behaviors for humanoid robots. *RO-MAN, 2013*.

Ismail, L. I., Hanapiah, F. A., Belpaeme, T., et al. (2021). Analysis of attention in child–robot interaction among children diagnosed with cognitive impairment. *International Journal of Social Robotics, 13*, 141–152.

Kruse, T., Pandey, A. K., Alami, R., & Kirsch, A. (2013). Human-aware robot navigation: A survey. *Robotics and Autonomous Systems, 61*(12), 1726–1743. Cited 312 times.

Law, T., Chita-Tegmark, M., & Scheutz, M. (2021). The interplay between emotional intelligence, trust, and gender in human–robot interaction. *International Journal of Social Robotics, 13*, 297–309.

Lazarus, R. S. (1991). Progress on a cognitive-motivational-relational theory of emotion. *American Psychologist, 46*(8), 819–834.

Lee, C.-C., Mower, E., Busso, C., Lee, S., & Narayanan, S. (2009). Emotion recognition using a hierarchical binary decision tree approach. In *Proceedings of the annual conference of the international speech communication association* (pp. 320–323). INTERSPEECH.

Mavridis, N. (2015). A review of verbal and non-verbal human-robot interactive communication. *Robotics and Autonomous Systems, 63*(P1), 22–35.

Moon, A., Zheng, M., Troniak, D. M., Blumer, B. A., Gleeson, B., MacLean, K., Pan, M. K. X. J., & Croft, E. A. (2014). Meet me where i'm gazing: How shared attention gaze affects human-robot handover timing. In *ACM/IEEE international conference on human-robot interaction* (pp. 334–341).

Papadopoulos, C., Castro, N., Nigath, A., Davidson, R., Faulkes, N., Menicatti, R., Khaliq, A. A., Recchiuto, C., Battistuzzi, L., Randhawa, G., Merton, L., Kanoria, S., Chong, N.-Y., Kamide, H., Hewson, D., & Sgorbissa, A. (2021). The CARESSES randomised controlled trial: Exploring the health-related impact of culturally competent artificial intelligence embedded into socially assistive robots and tested in older Adult care homes. *International Journal of Social Robotics*, 1–12.

Rau, P. L. P., Li, Y., & Li, D. (2009). Effects of communication style and culture on ability to accept recommendations from robots. *Computers in Human Behavior, 25*(2), 587−595.

Rau, P., Li, Y., & Li, D. (2010). A cross-cultural study: Effect of robot appearance and task. *International Journal of Social Robotics, 2*(2), 175−186.

Rehm, M. (2013). From multicultural agents to culture-aware robots. *Lecture Notes in Computer Science,* 431−440.

Scassellati, B. (2002). Theory of mind for a humanoid robot. *Autonomous Robots, 12*(1), 13−24.

Schneider, S., & Kummert, F. (2021). Comparing robot and human guided personalization: Adaptive exercise robots are perceived as more competent and trustworthy. *International Journal of Social Robotics, 13,* 169−185.

Shiomi, M., Nakata, A., Kanbara, M., & Hagita, N. (2021). Robot reciprocation of hugs increases both interacting times and self-disclosures. *International Journal of Social Robotics, 13,* 353−361.

Spekman, M. L. C., Konijn, E. A., & Hoorn, J. F. (2021). How physical presence overrides emotional (coping) effects in HRI: Testing the transfer of emotions and emotional coping in interaction with a humanoid social robot. *International Journal of Social Robotics, 13,* 407−428.

CHAPTER 6

Stories and scenarios for the development of a culturally competent socially assistive robot for health and social care

Irena Papadopoulos[1] and Christina Koulouglioti[2]

[1]Research Centre for Transcultural Studies in Health, Middlesex University, London, United Kingdom; [2]Research and Innovation Department, University Hospitals Sussex NHS Foundation Trust and Research Centre for Transcultural Studies in Health, Middlesex University, London, United Kingdom

LEARNING OBJECTIVES

- To understand why we used stories and scenarios
- To become aware of the importance of creating conceptual diagrams to help with the development of stories and scenarios
- To understand the process of developing scenarios that could be used by robotic engineers and programmers

6.1 Introduction

This chapter is based on the work that the authors conducted during a multidisciplinary, international research project called CARESSES (Culturally Aware Robots and Environmental Sensor Systems for Elderly Support). The project aimed to develop artificially intelligent technology for the first culturally competent robot which we defined as a robot that recognizes general cultural characteristics, but it is also aware that these general characteristics take different forms in different individuals and therefore is able to respond appropriately to the user's cultural differences. (The CARESSES project—an EU/Japan collaboration—has already been extensively described in Chapter 5 and it is also mentioned in most of the subsequent chapters).

This ambitious project aimed to develop new capabilities for humanoid socially assistive robots catering to the needs of older adults from different cultural backgrounds. The new capabilities would include functions such as (a) communicating through culturally appropriate speech and gestures; (b) assisting in performing everyday tasks (e.g., reminding them to do a shopping list, suggesting menu plans, receiving visitors); (c) providing health-related assistance in a cultural sensitive way (e.g., reminding the person to take his/her medication, encouraging the person to engage in physical activity); (d) providing easy access to technology (e.g., Internet, video calls, smart appliances for home automation); (e) providing culturally appropriate entertainment (e.g., reading aloud, playing music and games, etc.); and (f) promoting health safety through information and raising the alarm when needed. The developed technology was subsequently tested in the UK and Japan among an older adult population of English, Indian[1], and Japanese cultural background.

Most nurses and health professionals are trained to provide care to patients from various cultures, religions, and beliefs. The importance of culture and the need for cultural competence in healthcare has been widely investigated in the last 5 decades by nursing and other health scientists and the relevant literature is growing (Hollins, 2018; Leininger, 2002; Papadopoulos, 2006).

We are encouraging you to stop for a minute and think about the last time you felt unwell, or the last time you "had a cold." Think of what you did to take care of yourself in order to get better and "restore" your health. One of the authors, for example, tends to do what she learned at nursing school but with a Greek twist. She will take some medication, drink plenty of fluids, drink tea with honey, and, before she goes to bed, she will call her mother and ask her to "xematiasei" which is a request to say a special prayer to get rid of the evil eye which may be responsible for her cold. Many Greek people believe in the "evil eye" and she is one of them. You will probably be taking similar actions but your selfcare routine will have its own cultural twists. Now you may ask, why is this important? Well, the way we think of illness and health and what we think can help us maintain and restore our health, affects our healthcare decisions, our interactions with healthcare professionals, our adherence to medical treatment and so much more. In other words, we cannot ignore culture even when we deal with the most common and universal situations like a common cold.

These ideas seemed simple but the more we thought about the robot's actions and behaviors the more we struggled with the *"how."* *How* were we supposed to capture the general cultural characteristics of the English, Japanese, or the Indian culture? *How* were we supposed to capture individual differences and preferences of a person with an English heritage? *How* were we supposed to communicate the notions of cultural competence to the software programming experts who were looking for something tangible that they could use with the robot? *How* could we ensure that we captured the breadth and complexity of cultural manifestations? *How* could we ensure that we did not stereotype the English, Indian, and Japanese cultures? Going back to the "common cold" example, many Greek people may share the "evil eye" belief or at least they are aware of it, but the challenge for our work was

---

[1] We are referring to Asian Indians.

that the technology had to be intelligent enough to recognize that not all Greek people will share this belief and therefore it may or may not come up in a conversation.

We needed a well thought out plan, a feasible and practical plan that others could understand and replicate. We also thought that a layered plan was most appropriate, in order to unravel all the critical elements of the project. Our plan, described below, included:

- The creation of stories (based on the cultures that we needed to address)
- The creation of guiding diagrams specific to the CAREESES aim to address the needs of older adults from diverse cultural backgrounds, who were mainly living in care homes
- The adoption of a strong theoretical framework
- The adoption of relevant ethical principles and
- The creation of specific scenarios that were based on the stories which could be used to identify and capture the robot's capabilities.

6.2 The use of stories

At the start of the CARESSES project, we produced "stories" upon which multiple scenarios were developed to describe in detail different examples of human–robot culturally competent interaction. But why did we use stories? And why do we recommend stories, as a starting point for the development of scenarios?

Storytelling is a powerful way to learn about others and ourselves. Stories create understanding and help us develop respect for people and situations that are different, unusual, or unknown (Stevenson, 2019). Storytelling has been used as a method to increase intercultural understanding for many years and for many reasons: through stories the reader can explore their own cultural roots but also experience diverse cultures; stories can provide insights into people's values and beliefs and through stories the reader can reveal the commonalities across cultures and the universality of certain situations when people from different cultures share similar conditions and emotions. Similarly the reader can empathize with the unfamiliar and the scary. https://www.teachingenglish.org.uk/article/storytelling-benefits-tips.

Educators in nursing and other health disciplines consistently use case studies as one method of teaching cultural competence. Such case studies are based on real patient cases (sometimes composite cases) which the students, under the guidance of their teachers, analyze them theoretically, then apply the learning in the clinical laboratory/simulation (in most cases), before applying the acquired knowledge and skills in the clinical environment with real patients. Educators rely on the production and use of stories so that their students can develop cultural awareness but also appreciation for the realities of diverse groups (Carter-Black, 2007).

6.3 Writing stories for cultural groups

The CARESSES project focused on older people from three different cultural groups: groups with English, Indian, and Japanese heritage. Acknowledging the importance of storytelling we embarked in creating stories for fictional characters: "Mr. and Mrs. Chaterjee" (Indian-Hindu), "Mr. and Mrs. Khan" (Indian-Muslim), and "Mrs. Smith" (English-Christian). Although stories and scenarios were developed for the Japanese heritage, this cultural group will not be included in this chapter.

The stories provided the vehicle through which we could explore and express the cultural influences on health, behaviors, customs, etiquette, and values. We utilized the Hofstede et al.'s (1991) and Hofstede & Hofstede (2005) national cultural dimensions theory to express (when appropriate), the well-known differences between UK, and India, on "power distance," "uncertainty avoidance," "individualism/collectivism," "long- and short-term orientation," "masculinity/femininity," and "indulgence and restraint." Our goal was to express these differences by the way the women and men in the stories expressed their emotions, values, behaviors, and ideas while interacting with their family members, friends, and carers, and while taking decisions or making choices. We also used the Papadopoulos expanded model of transcultural nursing and cultural competence (Papadopoulos, 2006) which provided the framework for understanding how individual cultural differences and similarities impact on health behaviors, attitudes to illness and health, expression of symptoms, family expectations during illness and health, and how therapeutic relations between user and carer can be formed and function in order to negotiate potential ways for restoring health and maintaining independence and happiness. These theories enabled us to make assumptions about the chosen cultural groups and identify the expected capabilities of culturally competent humans and robots. More information about these theories can be found in Chapters 1 and 7.

Taking into consideration the importance of the older adults' cultural backgrounds in the stories was very important. Martinson and Berridge's (2015) systematic review on successful aging, reported that researchers have criticized for years the lack of cultural breath in aging models, and urged the need to include subjective notions of successful aging from diverse cultural perspectives. Research has shown that migration to a different culture can challenge and influence the understanding of the concept of aging for older immigrants. Tan et al. (2010) also found that the idea of successful aging was culturally bound and was perceived differently for Anglo-Australians and for Chinese-Australians. Anglo-Australians regarded growing old gracefully as important, whereas their Chinese-Australian counterparts valued financial security and being active as important. Similarly, Belza et al. (2004) found that intervention programs targeting older adults from diverse backgrounds need to integrate culture-specific exercises in order to be successful.

These ideas, along with existing literature on gender roles, the importance of family and the aging process, influenced our stories, and the creation of original diagrams (Ali, 2015; Victor et al., 2011; Zubair et al., 2012). These diagrams (see below) helped us to conceptualize and systematically represent concepts related to activities of an ordinary day of older men and women. Below are examples focusing on an older person of Indian cultural heritage (Figs. 6.1–6.4).

First, we mapped out some key invisible pillars of the culture, that is, the values and beliefs around life, care, health, illness, and family (Fig. 6.1). Using existing literature, we also provided a few concrete examples of values and beliefs on the diagram. For example, Kent et al. (2020) described the connection of yoga, spirituality and prayer with positive emotional health among South Indians living in the US and Chattopadhyay et al. (2020) described how the use of yoga was chosen as a vehicle for managing type-2 diabetes among people in India since it was well fitted with the people's beliefs and culture. Another example comes from Sharma et al. (2012) who described how strong beliefs related to "suffering and death," "disclosure of information," and "duty to the family" challenge the decision making process for first and second generation of Asian Indians living in the US. These ideas are reflected in Fig. 6.1 to ensure that the stories captured the values and beliefs of an individual of Indian cultural background.

Then we considered some behaviors associated with health, care, avoidance of illness, and quality of life (Fig. 6.2). According to Rowe and Kahn (2015) who first introduced the notion of "successful aging," three areas are key: (a) keeping socially active and engaged, (b) maintain cognitive and physical function, and (c) avoid disability and disease. This model

6.3 Writing stories for cultural groups

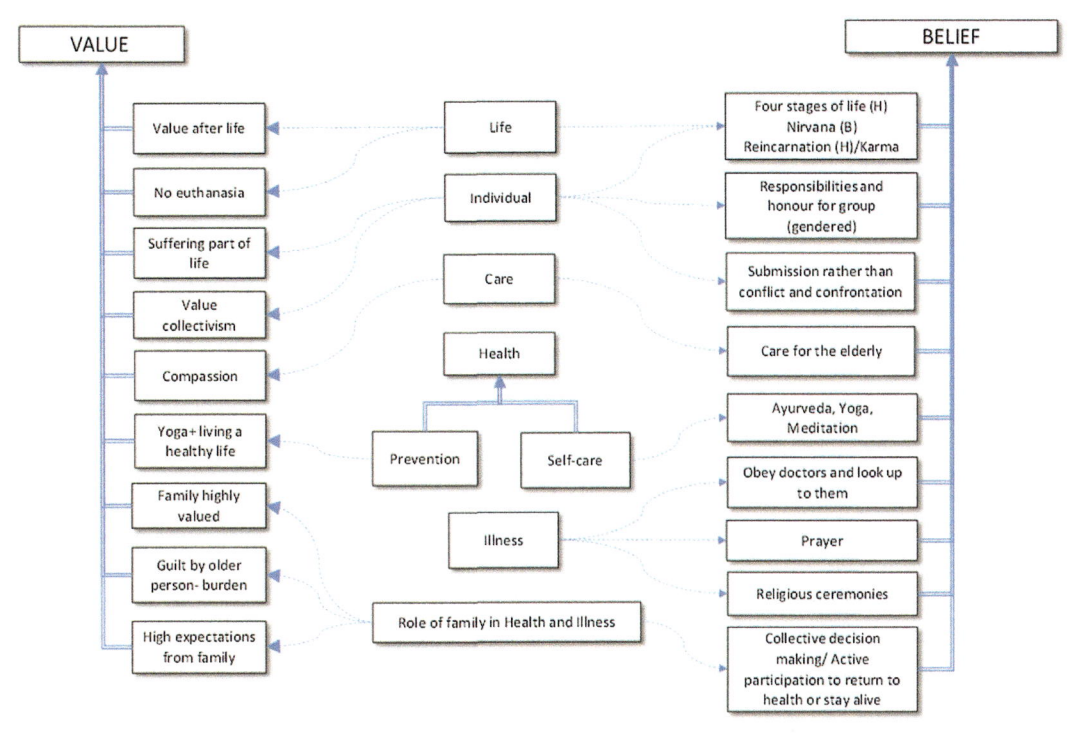

FIGURE 6.1 Values and beliefs (Indian scenarios).

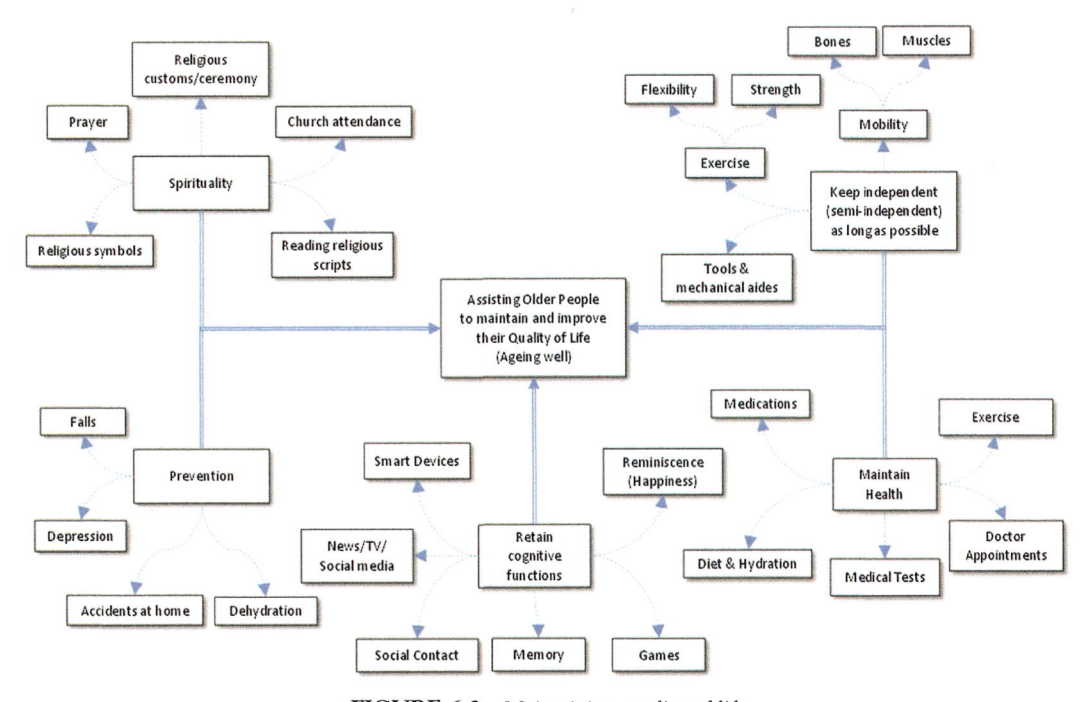

FIGURE 6.2 Maintaining quality of life.

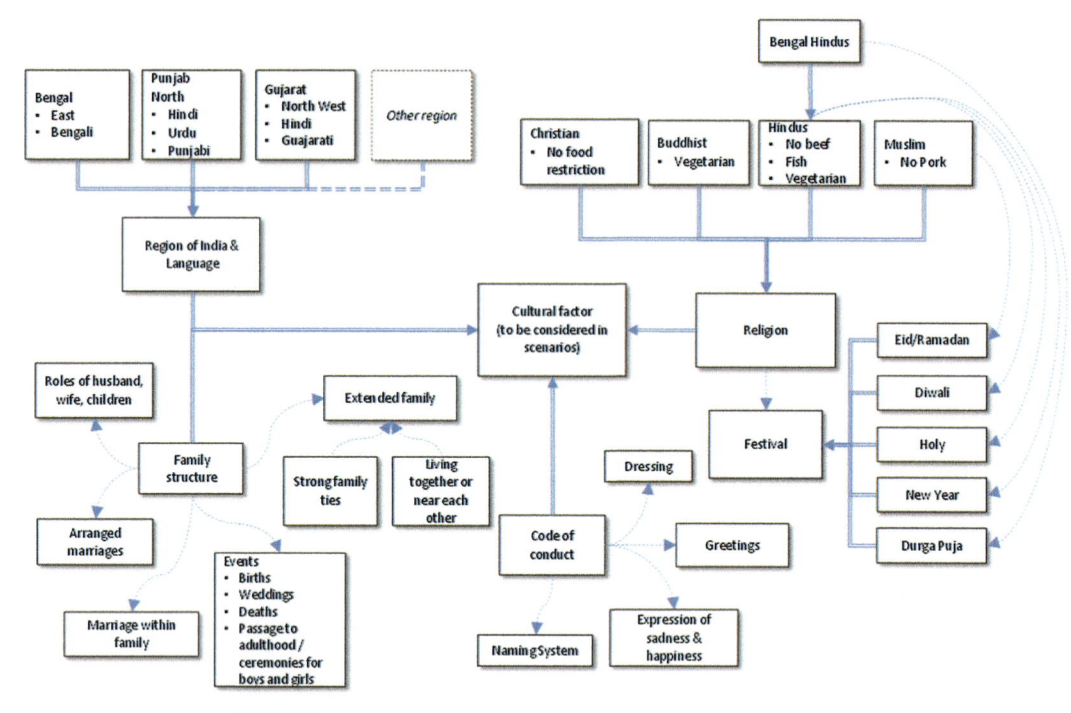

112   6. Stories and scenarios for the development of a culturally competent socially assistive robot for health and social care

FIGURE 6.3 Cultural factors to be considered (Indian scenarios).

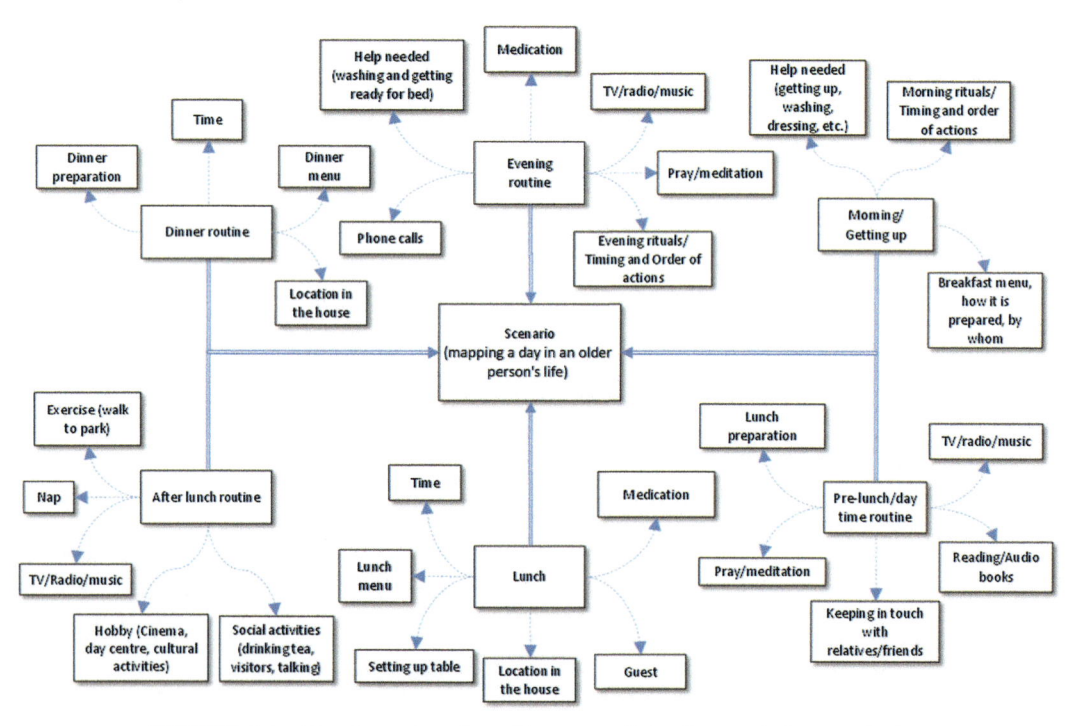

FIGURE 6.4 Mapping a day of an older person living in an assistive care facility.

was the basis for conceptualizing our ideas of aging well. The areas of prevention, retaining cognitive function, mobility, maintaining independence and health, along with the notion of spirituality (McCann et al., 2008) were included in our Fig. 6.2. In addition, examples from the current literature on prevention of Alzheimer's disease, which encourages regular exercise, games, and social interaction, as preventative factors were also included in our Fig. 6.2.

Focusing on our example of Indian culture, we then proceeded by mapping out key areas related to family and religion (Fig. 6.3). Our rationale for focusing on these two areas was mainly based on the diversity of the Indian culture. For example, even though a large part of the Indian population identify as Hindus (about 80% of the population), India has a large Muslim community (13% of the population), but also other religious groups such as Christians (2.3%), Sikhs (1.9%), Buddhists (0.8%), and Jains (0.4%) (https://worldpopulationreview.com/countries/india-population). In addition, India may have Hindi and English as the main official languages but many other languages are spoken across the subcontinent and there are large cultural differences across the regions. Focusing on the cultural diversity of the Indian culture was imperative in the process of developing culturally appropriate stories and subsequently culturally rich scenarios.

Lastly, we decided to divide the day into six sections to facilitate the mapping of most of the activities that may happen in an ordinary day of an older person (Fig. 6.4). Daily routines are powerful observable organizers of life and are also culturally bound (Fiese, 2006). For example, having or not having breakfast, the type of breakfast and the time devoted to this activity, how and where this takes place, all are affected by the person's cultural background but also by their individual preferences.

Stories helped us combine these ideas and also capture elements of a person's cultural identity (See two examples below in Tables 6.1A and 6.1B). Furthermore, our work was coherent with the guidelines in "BS 8611:2016:Robots and robotic devices. Guide to the ethical design and application of robots and robotic systems", published by The British Standards Institution (2016) and in particular with Guideline 5.1.5 "Respect for cultural diversity and pluralism" which states that *robot applications should take into account different cultural norms, including respect for language, religion, age, and gender by formal interaction with representatives of these groups*.

6.4 Explaining and discussing the construction of scenarios and their content

The development of the stories was followed with the creation of numerous scenarios. In total, 60 ($N = 60$) scenarios were developed. The scenarios were based on the stories and depicted everyday activities of older adults from English, Japanese and Indian heritage. The complete list of the scenarios can be found in http://CARESSESrobot.org/en/2018/03/08/CARESSES-scenarios-and-guidelines-available/.

The scenarios reflected the diversity in language, religion, food, festivals, ways of communicating, family relationships, expectations about health and illness, and ways of maintaining and restoring health. Separate scenarios were created for a person from each culture (both genders). For example, for a person's morning routine multiple scenarios were created, related to dressing, preparing and having breakfast, participating in health promotion activities and so on.

TABLE 6.1A Story of Mrs. Chaterjee.

Story 1. The story of Mrs. Chaterjee

Mrs. Sonali Chaterjee is a 75-year-old Indian, Hindu, lady from West Bengal. She was born in a city close to Kolkata and after completing her engineering degree in India she was married[1] and immigrated to the UK. Mrs. Chaterjee[2] is a Bengali *Brahmin*[3]. She highly values tradition and education and she likes to be treated with politeness and respect.	1. She had an arranged marriage 2. Usually a person's last name provides some initial information regarding the part of India they are coming from and in which cast they belong 3. Brahmins belong in the high cast
Even though she was educated, after marriage she devoted her energy in raising her family. She has a son and a daughter. Her husband died a few years ago. Both her children live relatively close and she sees them often. Mrs. Chaterjee has high cholesterol and a thyroid problem for which she takes regularly medication[4]. She also believes in homeopathy therefore she is also regularly taking some ayurvedic drops[5] for her thyroid problem. At the age of 30, she was diagnosed with retinitis pigmentosa (a genetic disease that affects the eyes)[6]. Through the years she started developing tunnel vision (losing her side vision) and she is slowly losing the ability to distinguish colors. In the last year, her eye condition deteriorated and she had to move into a care home.	4. Respect to western medicine 5. Ayurveda is a system of medicine with roots in the Indian subcontinent 6. Retinitis pigmentosa is a genetic disease that affects the eyes. This is a progressive disease for which unfortunately there is no cure
Her eye condition is creating a lot of stress and problems in her everyday life. Even though she didn't have a career she worked occasionally, people respected her. She would have help for the housework and cooking[7] but she would always make sure that everything was done properly. She always liked to have the oversight of every activity, and everything had to come to her first for approval (e.g., inspect the vegetables, fish, and meat for freshness). She cannot do that anymore and that frustrates her but she will not always express it. She also liked to cook for her family but that also is getting difficult. She is now having trouble cutting vegetables; she will frequently break or spill things and then feel embarrassed.	7. Common to have more than one helpers among middle class families
She likes to walk but now she hardly goes outside because she is scared of falling. She cannot always see the steps or uneven surfaces. A few weeks ago her grandchild came to visit and bend to touch her feet[8] but she couldn't see her and almost knocked her over. She was very sad about that.	8. Respectful way to greet an elderly loved one
Today she woke up with a little bit of cold. She calls her carer to help her make a hot drink. She would like to have some hot tea with ginger[9]. She also asks for some cloves to chew[10], they are good for the sore throat. Her good friend, Lila, comes over. She is still in her nightdress and robe but insists that she comes in. She needs to come in and have at least a cup of tea.[11,12]	9. Putting ginger in tea is believed to relieve cold symptoms 10. Similarly with chewing cloves, especially when you have a sore throat. 11. Visitors are welcome and need to be treated nicely, offering a snack or tea or coffee.

6.4 Explaining and discussing the construction of scenarios and their content   115

She goes in and gets dressed quickly. They start chatting in Bengali[13]. Her friend looks at her and comments on how beautiful she looks in her shawl[14]. She is cold; she needs something over her shoulders. She asks her carer to bring out some snacks and sweets[15]. She also asks her to make sweet masala tea[16], just the way her friend likes it. They sit comfortably and continue to chat. Her friend has a daughter around 25 and she is getting worried about her marriage[17].

After her friend leaves she goes to her bedroom to properly dress up. She has a beautiful selection of saris (silk, cottons, and from different parts of India) but after her husband died she only wears plain ones (predominantly white with a color border)[18]. She chooses one that her daughter bought her the last time[19] they went shopping together. She could also wear a pair of trousers and a blouse, or a salwar kameez[20] but she would like her granddaughter to see her in a sari and wearing a sari makes her feel better dressed. She opens her jewelry box and chooses a short simple necklace that her husband presented her on a wedding anniversary. She has a large selection of jewelry but they are now kept in a safety box (bank) and she only has a small selection at home (locked away and kept in a secret place in her closet, only her children know where). She has already given a lot of her jewelry to her daughter and daughter in law but she is keeping the rest for her grandchildren[21].

She will comb her hair nicely and just keep her stab earrings and two plain bangles in each hand[22]. She remembered dressing up …. She would choose a beautiful colorful sari, she would put on a short and long necklace, a bindi[23] and her sindur[24], and then of course make up and her favorite perfume. She does not do a lot of all that any more but at least she continues to color her hair which she does not keep very long[25]. She used to color her hair herself but now she needs to call a hairdresser/beautician[26] home every 6–8 weeks.

After dressing Mrs. C will light a scented stick to Lord Ganesha[27] and pray for the removal of obstacles and health for all her family/friends[28]. In the corner of her bedroom, she has a small table with a couple of small statues of Ganesha, Shiva and Durga[29]

The table is covered with a colorful cloth and on it there is a small tray with a small bell, a candle holder and an incense stick holder. She will spend a few minutes, standing or sitting on the floor, with her hands in "namaste"[30]. Today she will not make a "puja"[31].

12. Close friends may hug but it is not necessary. They will do a Namaste (hand gesture), take their shoes off and leave close to the door and then come in. To perform Namaste, place the hands together in front of the heart, close the eyes, and bow the head. It can also be done by placing the hands together in front of the third eye, bowing the head, and then bringing the hands down to the heart. This is an especially deep form of respect.
13. Common to talk with native language
14. Big scarf, if winter possibly woollen
15. Products purchased from a local Indian shop
16. Indian way of making tea … boil water, milk, some species and tea leaves
17. Role of astrology
18. Dresses and different ways of dressing. In addition, ways of dressing if you are mourning or widow (old widow, younger, etc.)
19. Way of showing her love and how important are her children
20. Salwar kameezs are worn mostly by Muslim ladies but Hindus also chose to wear especially younger because they are easier to wear and comfortable.
21. Importance of gold, for her security but also for the following generations … passing it on ….
22. Iron bangles are usually the symbol of marriage that she cannot take it off. In other parts of India a necklace with black and gold bids is the symbol instead of a wedding ring.
23. Forehead decorations that all women can wear.
24. Red powder spreads at the forehead but only for married women.
25. Long hair is a symbol of beauty and youth.
26. A beautician from the community will know to use herbal/henna coloring and possibly provide other services such as head massage or a facial or hand massage for less money.
27. The "elephant" God the patron of art and sciences and the removal of obstacles

(Continued)

TABLE 6.1A Story of Mrs. Chaterjee.—cont'd

Story 1. The story of Mrs. Chaterjee

It is now mid-morning, Mrs. C finished her exercise and she would like to have a cup of tea and listen to the news. She will make a simple cup of tea (using a tea bag) not the Indian way[32]. She used to read the newspaper along with her husband but now she will put the radio on and listen to the news. She likes to put on BBC or the Bengali channel, or the Indian TV[33] channel news. Then she will switch on her audiobook. She will listen for 20 min and then she will talk with her children on the phone. They have their regular time, and she or they will call every day.

After her husband died and because of her health problems (thyroid and high cholesterol) she has a light lunch. Usually dhal[34] and fish curry[35]. She has prepared enough dhal and fish curry for lunch and dinner and has kept them in two containers. Instead of bhat[36] she will make two chapatis[37] or maybe four and keep two of them for dinner. She takes out the ingredients and makes the dough. Then on the kitchen counter or table she will use the rolling pin to make perfect round chapatis. She will heat a frying pan and cook the chapatis without using any oil.[38]

She will put in two smaller bowls some dhal and fish curry and warm them up. She will sit at the table and with her left hand, she will first serve the dhal, then the fish curry. She likes eating with her hand (right hand only, serving with left)[39]. She may have some cucumber also and her homemade mango chutney. She will then have a glass of water and her medication for cholesterol.

After her light lunch now she is sitting comfortably in her armchair in the living room. The radio is on in the background. She has her feet on a stool and she is covered by her favorite soft blanket. She closes her eyes and meditates[40] for a while. She soon falls asleep. After half an hour she wakes up refreshed and looks for her slippers; she puts them on and takes a look outside. It is not raining and she has been told by her carer that it is not too cold outside today. She decides to go for a short walk in the garden. She struggles to put her coat on and grabs her walking stick which is hanging by the door.

After her nice walk, it is time for some tea. She takes the time to make a nice cup of tea[41]. She likes to have her tea with some tea biscuits or cake[42] brought by her son on his last visit.

28. Knowledge of all close family/friends birthdays, wedding anniversaries, death anniversaries, rice ceremonies, etc. Mrs. C makes an effort to always remember these special occasions and to pray for blessings of the family/friend's occasion
29. Different parts of India, place more importance to different gods. It is not uncommon even for Christian Indians to also have statues like that in their home or a small Buddha. This does not apply to Muslim Indian families.
30. "Namaste," place the hands together in front of the heart, close the eyes, and bow the head. It can also be done by placing the hands together in front of the third eye, bowing the head, and then bringing the hands down to the heart. This is an especially deep form of respect.
31. Puja" an offering to Gods made during prayer
32. Knowing the Indian way of making tea
33. Indian TV channels/radio
34. Lentils
35. Bengalis are very fond of fish curry and they prefer to have it every day if possible.
36. Rice (basmati)
37. Round bread made of flour and cooked on the fire.
38. Containers, rolling pins, etc. are brought from India
39. Common way of eating. Indians actually say that you cannot enjoy the food if you don't eat with your hand.
40. She may be holding a Japa Mala (praying string of beads) made out of 108 beads and she may recite the name of the God that she believes in (e.g., Guajarati's most probably Krishna, Bengalis most probably Durga) or she may say slowly the words: Buddham Sharanam Gacchami (a Buddhist mantra)

6.4 Explaining and discussing the construction of scenarios and their content   117

It is late afternoon now and her son just popped in to visit.

He calls her "Ma"[43], bends to touch her feet, she touches his head, and they hug[44]. He takes off his shoes[45], leaves them close to the door and they go in. They sit on the sofa close together. They start talking about his day. She asks about his work and the children. He asks about what she has done since he last visited. He shows her some of the latest photos on his smartphone from the children and family. He brings her glasses. They talk, and laugh. Then they take a selfie together and he also takes a photo of her. Before he leaves he helps her put her coat and hat on and takes her for a walk in the garden. He tells her that walking and exercising is good for her.

She asks him when he will visit her again and he reminds her that next week is Diwali[46] so he will be coming the day before Diwali to take her so that she can celebrate it with the family.

He has to go now, they hug, she touches his head, gives him her blessing, and they say goodbye.

On Sunday her daughter, son-in-law and granddaughter will be visiting for dinner. Now she needs to plan for dinner. She wants to make dhal (lentil dish), a cauliflower or maybe bindhi curry, (depending on what she can find), a simple chicken with potatoes curry and of course her signature mustard fish curry[47]. She needs to call the Indian grocery shop and place an order. She also needs to order the fish. She wants to make Hilsha fish and for that she needs to call another store. Her granddaughter is still too small to have Hilsha fish but it is her favorite dish and she cannot not have Hilsha. She asks her carer to help with the organization. (Calling the stores, ordering, making sure she has all the spices she will need, the specific cooking oil) Oh ... she also needs to order sweets, some sandesh and rasgulla[48].

The carers used to call her Mrs. Chaterjee when she first moved in the care home, but now they call her Mashi[49], a respectful way to address older Hindu women.

41. Boils the water, puts in some spices such as cinnamon and a couple of cloves, some sugar, milk, and tea leaves. She lets it boil and then closes the heat and lets it brew.
42. Fruit cake, made with different dried fruits and almonds.
43. Ways of calling mother: Ma or Ama or Ai, or Mata (depending on language)
44. Greetings
45. Entering the house
46. Indian festival of lights, usually in October or November, is one of the biggest festivals, celebrating the light over darkness, the good over evil.
47. Bengalis like to have a "full" table (many dishes). Fish is very important. Hilsha fish is a freshwater river fish that can be eaten all year around, is full of bones but especially loved.
48. Typical Bengali sweets
49. Auntie

TABLE 6.1B Scenario of Mrs. Chaterjee.

Scenario name	Mrs. Chaterjee—Lunch routine, eating
Time of the day	Lunch time
Human section	
General description	<....> Because of health problems (thyroid and high cholesterol) Mrs. C has normally a light lunch. Usually dhal[1] and fish curry[2]. She has prepared enough dhal and fish curry for lunch and dinner and has kept them in two containers. Instead of "bhat"[3] she will make 2 chapatis[4] or maybe four and keep 2 for dinner. She takes out the ingredients and makes the dough. Then on the kitchen counter or table she will use the rolling pin to make perfect round chapatis. She will heat a frying pan and just heat/cook the chapatis without using any oil.[5] She will put in two smaller bowls of dhal, fish curry, and warm them up. She will sit at the table and with her left hand, she will first serve the dhal, then the fish curry. She likes eating with her hand (right hand only, serving with left)[6]. She may have some cucumber also and her homemade mango chutney. She will then have a glass of water and her medication for cholesterol. 1. lentils 2. Bengalis are very fond of fish curry and they prefer to have it every day if possible. 3. rice (basmati) 4. round bread made of flour but it is not fried and can be made with wheat flour 5. containers, rolling pins, etc. are brought from India 6. common way of eating. Indians actually say that you cannot enjoy the food if you don't eat with your hand.
Functional areas of the house involved	F1. Kitchen F2. Kitchen table F3. Or dining table in another room
Relevant objects involved	O1. Brass utensils most probably brought from India O2. Possibly special frying pan for making chapatis O3. Plates/glass O4. Chairs/stools

6.4 Explaining and discussing the construction of scenarios and their content

Relevant persons (in addition to user and caregiver)	B1. No-one	
What a human (formal or informal) caregiver shall/can do in this scenario	H1. Assist with the warming of the food H2. Making the dough for the chapatis H3. Rolling the chapatis and cooking them H4. Bring everything at the table H5. Serve H6. Keep company H7. Bring the medication H8. Ask Mrs. C if she likes some music in the background. H9. Wash the dishes	
Cultural knowledge involved	C1. Indian way of cooking C2. Utensils used in Indian cooking C3. Dietary preferences based on region of India, caste and religion C4. Way of eating (use of right hand) C5. Way of serving C6. Indian music C7. Order food is served	
Which "qualitative" caregiver behavior is expected to be culturally dependent	D1. Time of eating D2. Type of food D3. Order of having the food. For Bengalis, dhal is offered first, and then the vegetable, then chicken or fish curry, you finish with chutney. D4. Appropriate utensils used D5. Type of music D6. If a guest is having lunch with Mrs. C, the guest is expected to eat and be served or be offered food multiple times. In addition many more dishes will have been prepared. D7. Indirect questioning	
Which behavior is "quantitatively" different depending on culture (volume and tone of voice, distance, velocity, etc)	1. Polite and soft tone of voice 2. Unrushed walking and eating 3. Being silent when needed	

(Continued)

TABLE 6.1B Scenario of Mrs. Chaterjee.—cont'd

Scenario name		Mrs. Chaterjee—Lunch routine, eating	
Time of the day		Lunch time	

Robot section

	Ideal tasks	Alternative/Surrogate tasks
What the robot shall/can do in this scenario Right: Alternative tasks	A1. Recommend dishes A2. Provide recipes A3. Remind Mrs. C of needed groceries A4. Locate things as needed (food, kitchen tools, medication) A5. Bring things as needed (food, kitchen tools, medication) to the table A6. Praise on eating a healthy and balanced diet A7. Suggest healthy food (e.g., salad) and to drink water A8. Keep company during lunch A9. Remind her to take her medication A10. Comment on how "good" the dishes look and congratulate her for her cooking abilities A11. Ask Mrs. C if she wants to hear some music and in case play Indian music	A3'. Knowing the recipes given in A2, ask Mrs. C if each of the needed ingredients is present and create a list on the tablet A3''. Ask Mrs. C if she wants to generate some reminders for missing ingredients A4'–A5'. Tell Mrs. C the positions of needed objects in the environment, knowing them a priori, or detecting them by using markers. A5''. Permanently attach a tray to the robot's chest to bring objects A10'. Provide general comments on dishes A11'. Ask Mrs. C if she wants to hear radio and the type of music. Then, reproduce the selected radio channel
Left: Robot motor capabilities required Right: Corresponding pepper API (if any)	1. Grasp objects 2. Carry lightweight items 3. Navigate autonomously in the house 4. Reach a target/person 5. Avoid unexpected static or moving obstacles/persons 6. Show feelings 7. Turn on radio/TV/cassette player 8. Operate appliance (by communicating with smart environment)	1. No dedicated module, it could be achieved with external libraries 2. Feasible if payload is < 300 g 3. ALNavigation 4. ALVisionRecognition, ALCloseObjectDetection, ALNavigation 5. ALMotion 6. ALLeds, ALRobotPosture, ALAnimationPlayer 7. ALAudioPlayer 8. For external devices, it could be achieved with a specific communication protocol It could be achieved with a specific communication protocol

Left: Robot perceptual capabilities required Right: Corresponding pepper API (if any)	1. Locate persons (distance and position) 2. Recognize obstacles/uneven ground 3. Recognize/Locate items 4. Retrieve/store information 5. Recognize persons/faces 6. Recognize actions	1. ALPeoplePerception 2. ALLaser, ALSonar 3. ALVisionRecognition 4. ALMemory 5. ALFaceDetection 6. No dedicated module, it could be achieved with external libraries
Left: Robot verbal capabilities involved Right: Corresponding pepper API (if any)	1. Ask yes/No questions 2. Ask multiple choice questions 3. Suggest/remind 4. List instructions 5. Context dependent chat 6. Encourage/praise 7. Report information	1. ALDialog, ALSpeechRecognition, ALTextToSpeech, ALTabletService 2. ALDialog, ALSpeechRecognition, ALTextToSpeech, ALTabletService 3. ALDialog, ALTextToSpeech, ALTabletService 4. ALDialog, ALTextToSpeech, ALTabletService 5. ALDialog, ALSpeechRecognition, ALTextToSpeech, ALTabletService 6. ALDialog, ALTextToSpeech, ALTabletService 7. ALMemory, ALTextToSpeech, ALTabletService
Which "qualitative" robot behavior is expected to be culturally dependent	1. Way of serving 2. Being discreet 3. Being silent when elders are speaking 4. Asks indirect questions	
Which behavior is "quantitatively" different depending on culture (volume and tone of voice, distance, velocity, etc)	1. Speaks with soft tone 2. Speaks in low volume 3. Walks in low speed 4. Stands not too close to Mrs. C	

In each scenario, interaction patterns that are prototypical of real-life situations were identified. The researchers first developed a template to capture the human and robot capabilities for each scenario. The structure of the template was divided in two sections: (a) the human section, and (b) the robot section (see examples in Tables 6.2A and 6.2B). The required information for each section was as follows:

6.4.1 Human section (light grey part of each table)

- scenario title,
- the time of day the scenario is taking place,
- a description of the scene, including cultural notes,
- the functional areas of the house involved ("F" item list),
- relevant objects involved ("O" item list),
- relevant persons ("B" item list),
- what a human caregiver can do ("H" item list),
- the cultural knowledge involved ("C" item list),
- which "qualitative" caregiver behaviors are culture dependent ("D" item list),
- which "quantitative" caregiver behaviors are culture dependent ("E" item list).

Regarding the "qualitative" and "quantitative" caregiver behaviors that are culturally dependent we focused on a few parameters that could be programmed in the robot. For example, tone of voice, proximity, speed, and gestures. It is well established in the literature that culture influences our body language and expressions such as how close or far we sit to another person, how we greet each other, our tone of voice and how that changes with the expressions of different emotions. We made an effort to capture as many as possible of these elements in the "Human section" of the table providing the software experts with a pool of elements that they could use for the programming of the robot.

The human section of the table was followed by the robot section that included:

6.4.2 Robot section (dark grey part of each table)

- what the robot shall/can do in this scenario ("A" item list, including a list of "surrogate" activities that the robot may perform to better meet technological constraints),
- robot motor capabilities required ("M" item list, including the corresponding functions in the programming interface of the humanoid socially assistive robot),
- robot perceptual capabilities required ("P" item list, including the corresponding functions in the programming interface of the robot),
- robot verbal capabilities required ("V" item list, including the corresponding functions in the programming interface of the robot),
- which "qualitative" robot behaviors are expected to be culturally dependent ("R" item list),
- which robot behaviors are "quantitatively" different depending on culture ("T" item list).

TABLE 6.2A Story of Mrs. Smith.

Story 2. The story of Mrs. Smith

Mrs. Smith is a 75-year-old English lady, a former school teacher who recently moved into sheltered accommodation in Cambridge UK along with her beloved cat named "tiger"[1]. Her husband died 2 years ago. She has only one son who lives with his new wife just over 3 h away by car.	1. Common for older adults to have pets
Mrs. Smith worked as a secondary school science teacher for nearly 40 years before she retired. Mrs. Smith has high cholesterol and a thyroid problem for which she takes regular medication. Recently, she developed cataract in both eyes which has affected her vision although the doctor told her they are not ready to be operated on. Her visual impairment has resulted in losing her confidence leaving her home and she tends to stay indoors more and more.	
Mrs. Smith always liked reading, something which she cannot easily do now and as a result she has to borrow audio books from the local library. She finds this fact frustrating and slightly depressing. Six months ago she had an accident by tripping over an uneven pavement, resulting in a fractured femur. Although she is now physically healed, she remains frightened in case she has another accident especially since her vision has deteriorated.	
Today is Sunday and her son is due to visit her. He tries to visit her every Sunday although he does not always have the time to do so. He occasionally telephones her although she never does because she does not want to bother him[2].	2. Family expectations
She has a boiled egg with toast around 9a.m. for breakfast[3] while listening to the news on the radio. She would really like to have some bacon and sausages but it is more difficult for her to make it. She would also like to read the newspaper as she always has done but of course her vision does not permit it these days.	3. Common foods for breakfast tea, toast, cereal/porridge, boiled eggs, fried/grilled bacon, sausage, baked beans, tomatoes
After breakfast, she gets dressed (she puts on a skirt and a nice blouse), sprays a little bit of perfume, combes her hair, and puts some make up on[4]. On Friday she had her monthly appointment with her hairdresser and she looks good. She had her hair colored and her nails done.	4. Dressing. Common for women of her generation to dress smartly and wear makeup irrespective of whether they will go out or not
Mrs. Smith was raised as an Anglican protestant. However, as an adult, and during her science degree, she challenged her faith and religious beliefs and decided to abandon religion. She does however, have strong humanistic values which she believes are compatible to Christianity and other religions such as Buddhism and Hinduism.	

(*Continued*)

TABLE 6.2A Story of Mrs. Smith.—cont'd

Story 2. The story of Mrs. Smith

She doesn't belong to any church groups nor attends mass. She likes to read or listen to audiobooks about religion especially those that combine her love of science and ethics with religion. She is also an avid viewer of TV programs that debate current ethical issues from religious and political perspectives.

She expects her son to arrive at 1p.m. and they will go to the local pub for Sunday roast lunch[5]. He arrives on time[6]. She puts on her coat, gloves, takes her handbag, umbrella and scrabble for them to play[7,8]. They spend the next couple of hours together and by 3p.m. they return to her home. He has to rush back so they hug and kiss (air kiss on one chick) and they say goodbye[9].

She comes in, takes off her shoes, puts on her slippers, sits on her armchair and covers herself with her blanket. She turns on the radio and soon she closes her eyes and takes a nap. Tiger snuggles up on her lap. She loves her cat, he is her closest friend and they have been together for almost 15 years. She loves to caress her cat and relax.

It is afternoon now and she is expecting her friend, Mrs. Brown. They had arranged this visit the last time they talked over the phone, a month ago[10]. It will be lovely to see her. They will have cream tea together[11]. Her friend brings in scones, cream, and strawberry jam and Mrs. Smith prepares tea. She will first put on the kettle and boil the water. She will take out her best China cups, cream holder, matching teapot, nice napkins, spoons/knives, and her favorite tea cosy[12]. She will slowly fill the tea pot with boiled water to warm it. She then empties the tea pot, refills it with hot water, and adds 3 tea bags. She will let it brew for a few minutes covering the nice teapot with the tea cosy.

They will sit at the table and talk about the old days when they were working together. They will also discuss her friend's recent holiday in Spain. They take a walk in the garden and after a couple of hours Mrs. Brown is ready to go. They give each other a formal embrace and they promise to talk soon on the phone and arrange another visit.
After her friend's departure Mrs. Smith turns the radio on and listens to some classical music.

It is time for dinner now and Mrs. Smith decides to have something light. She will have a ham salad[13] with some lettuce, cucumber, tomato, and a slice of bread with butter.

After dinner, despite her eyesight problems, she will watch her favorite TV program, "country file," feed Tiger, and take her evening pills.

5. Sunday roast lunch: usually will be beef, lamb or chicken with gravy, boiled vegetables and roasted potatoes, and Yorkshire pudding. Yorkshire pudding is not a sweet dish.
6. Cultural orientation to time
7. Common to share a board game such as scrabble
8. Not uncommon that the son visited without his wife
9. Greeting
10. Formal arranging of social visits
11. Cream tea: Afternoon tea with warm scones, cream and jam. Describe differences with "high tea" and "tea" which refers to light dinner.
12. Tea cosy is a tea pot cover normally knitted or made with thick woollen material designed to keep the tea warm in the pot.

13. Light dinner, often a cold salad or sandwiches

TABLE 6.2B Scenario of Mrs. Smith.

Scenario name	Mrs. Smith—after lunch routine, social activities (drinking tea, visitors, talking)
Time of the day	Early afternoon

Human section

General description	<.....> it is afternoon now and Mrs. S is expecting her friend, Mrs. Brown. They had arranged this visit the last time they talked over the phone, a month ago[1]. It will be lovely to see her. They will have cream tea together[2]. Her friend brings in scones, cream and strawberry jam and Mrs. Smith prepares tea[3]. She will first put on the kettle and boil the water. She will take out her China cups, cream holder, matching teapot, nice napkins, spoons/knife, and her favorite tea warmer. She will slowly fill the tea pot with boiled water and warm it. She will then pour in some fresh boiled water and the tea bags. She will let it brew covering the nice teapot with the tea warmer[4]. They will sit at the table and talk about the old days when they were working together. They will also discuss about her recent holiday in Spain. They will walk together in the garden and after a couple of hours Mrs. Brown is ready to go. They hug and they plan to talk soon on the phone and arrange another visit[5].	1. Formal arranging of social visits 2. Cream tea: Afternoon tea with warm scones, butter and jam. Describe differences with "high tea" and "tea" referring to light dinner 3. Relationships and expectations (what will visitor will bring or not) 4. English tea rituals, emphasis on the China used, tea pots, preparation of tea, tea warmer 5. Level of communication, exchange of details and information.
Functional areas of the house involved	1. Living room 2. Kitchen—cabinets, refrigerator
Relevant objects involved	1. Door 2. China cups, spoons 3. Tea pot 4. Tea warmer 5. Scones, cream, jam
Relevant persons (in addition to user and caregiver)	B1. Friend
What a human (formal or informal) caregiver shall/can do in this scenario	1. Open the door for visitor and greet appropriately 2. Welcome the visitor 3. Ask whether she would like to take her coat off 4. Take her coat and hang it or place it to the appropriate place 5. Help in the kitchen by getting the cups, plates, etc. 6. Help by making the tea 7. Help warm the scones 8. Help bring everything to the table

(Continued)

TABLE 6.2B Scenario of Mrs. Smith.—cont'd

Scenario name	Mrs. Smith—after lunch routine, social activities (drinking tea, visitors, talking)
Time of the day	Early afternoon

Human section

Cultural knowledge involved	1. English way of making tea 2. Cream tea, high tea, tea as light dinner; knowing distinctions 3. Scones, jam, cream, butter (appropriate foods for a cream tea) 4. China cups, tea pot, tea warmer, tea strainer 5. Organized visit well in advance 6. Expected to offer one item, for example, tea and maybe have some biscuits 7. What is expected from the visitor 8. Level of communication, topics of discussion 9. Organizing the next visit and marking their calendar
Which "qualitative" caregiver behavior is expected to be culturally dependent	1. Proper way of greeting 2. Properly addressing the visitor 3. Properly addressing Mrs. S 4. Distance from visitor and no-involvement in discussion 5. Helping in the kitchen, knowing where things are kept 6. Provide privacy 7. Knowing what cups/tea pot, etc. to use 8. Make the tea 9. Warm the scones 10. Washes dishes 11. Touching not desirable for nonfamily members
Which behavior is "quantitatively" different depending on culture (volume and tone of voice, distance, velocity, etc.)	1. Polite and soft tone of voice 2. Keep some distance for nonfamily members 3. Move gently and with low velocity 4. Smile

6.4 Explaining and discussing the construction of scenarios and their content 127

Scenario name	Mrs. Smith—after lunch routine, social activities (drinking tea, visitors, talking)	
Time of the day	Early afternoon	

Robot section

Left: What the robot shall/can do in this scenario Right: Alternative tasks	Ideal tasks	Alternative/Surrogate tasks
	A1. Open the door and greet the visitor (slight bow)	A1′. Open the door by communicating with the smart environment and greet the visitor (slight bow)
	A2. Welcome the visitor indoor, showing with the hand the way to the living room	
	A3. Take visitor's coat and suggest her to sit	A3′. Show the visitor where to hang coat and suggest to sit
	A4. Offer to take from Mrs. B (friend/visitor) the package that she has brought (assuming box with scones) and take it.	A4′. Suggest the visitor to put the box on the table
	A5. Inform Mrs. S that her friend has arrived	
	A6. Ask Mrs. S how it can help with the tea	
	A7. Locate things as needed (cups, scones, pots, spoons)	A7′+A8′. Tell Mrs. S the positions of needed objects in the environment, knowing them a priori, or detecting them by using markers.
	A8. Bring things as needed (cups, scones, pots, spoons)	A9′+A10′. Locate and indicate objects needed for preparing the tray, knowing their position in the environment, or using markers. Suggest Mrs. S to bring the tray with food to the table
	A9. Prepare a tray with tea and sweets	
	A10. Bring the tray in the living room	A8″+A10″. Permanently attach a tray to the robot's chest to bring objects
	A11. Comment about the food (e.g., Scones look delicious or recognize the brand/make of jam and comment if it is consider good?)	
	A12. Provide privacy to Mrs. S and friend	
	A13. Suggest Mrs. S to arrange another visit with her friend	
	A14. In case, retrieve her calendar, suggest a date and store the information	
	A15. Remind both of any occasions that they would like to celebrate or recommend things to do at the next visit	
Left: Robot motor capabilities required Right: Corresponding Pepper API (if any)	1. Coordinately move torso/arms/hands	1. ALMotion
	2. Coordinately move base/arms/hands	2. ALMotion
	3. Grasp objects	3. No dedicated module, it could be achieved with external libraries
	4. Carry lightweight items	4. Feasible if payload is < 300 g
	5. Carry heavyweight items	5. Not feasible
	6. Navigate autonomously in the house	6. ALNavigation
	7. Reach a target/person	7. ALVisionRecognition, ALCloseObjectDetection, ALNavigation
	8. Avoid unexpected static or moving obstacles/persons	8. ALMotion
	9. Open doors/windows (by communicating with smart environment)	9. It could be achieved with a specific communication protocol
	10. Show feelings	10. ALLeds, ALRobotPosture, ALAnimationPlayer

(*Continued*)

TABLE 6.2B Scenario of Mrs. Smith.—cont'd

Scenario name	Mrs. Smith—after lunch routine, social activities (drinking tea, visitors, talking)
Time of the day	Early afternoon

Robot section

	Ideal tasks	Alternative/Surrogate tasks
Left: Robot perceptual capabilities required Right: Corresponding pepper API (if any)	1. Locate persons (distance and position) 2. Recognize posture, gesture, movements 3. Recognize emotions 4. Recognize actions 5. Recognize persons/faces 6. Recognize obstacles/uneven ground 7. Recognize/locate items 8. Retrieve/store information 9. Recognize dialogue context 10. Have knowledge of the map of the environment	1. ALPeoplePerception 2. No dedicated module, it could be achieved with external libraries 3. ALMood 4. No dedicated module, it could be achieved with external libraries 5. ALFaceDetection 6. ALLaser, ALSonar 7. ALVisionRecognition 8. ALMemory 9. ALSpeechRecognition 10. No dedicated module, it could be achieved with different solutions
Left: Robot verbal capabilities involved Right: Corresponding pepper API (if any)	1. Ask yes/No questions 2. Ask multiple choice questions 3. Suggest/remind 4. Context dependent chat 5. Greet 6. Encourage/praise 7. Report information	1. ALDialog, ALSpeechRecognition, ALTextToSpeech, ALTabletService 2. ALDialog, ALSpeechRecognition, ALTextToSpeech, ALTabletService 3. ALDialog, ALTextToSpeech, ALTabletService 4. ALDialog, ALSpeechRecognition, ALTextToSpeech, ALTabletService 5. ALDialog, ALTextToSpeech 6. ALDialog, ALTextToSpeech, ALTabletService 7. ALMemory, ALTextToSpeech, ALTabletService
Which "qualitative" robot behavior is expected to be culturally dependent	1. Proper way of greeting 2. Properly addressing the visitor 3. Distance from visitor and noninvolvement in discussion 4. Helping in the kitchen, knowing where things are kept 5. Bring tray with tea and scones, etc. to the living room	
Which behavior is "quantitatively" different depending on culture (volume and tone of voice, distance, velocity, etc.)	1. Speaks in low volume 2. Speaks with soft voice 3. Move in low speed 4. Stands not too close to Mrs. C 5. Keeps acceptable distance from the visitor 6. Smile frequently	

6.5 Discussion

Unpicking the very specific human and robotic tasks involved in every scenario was a very critical process. We focused on *what ideally* a cultural competent human being could do in the specific scenario and what a robot could do ensuring at every stage that the technological constraints were taken into consideration. Therefore a list of desired robot capabilities were created but also a list of "surrogate" actions were listed taking into consideration the existing limitations. This critical iterative review of the scenarios by the whole CARESEES research team resulted in realistically implementable scenarios that could also be tested in the real world. The final aim was to develop a system with a portfolio of different capabilities for the robot that is able to deal with as many situations as possible in a culturally competent way. In Chapter 9, the reader can find out how these capabilities might be implemented on an autonomous, socially assistive robot.

The creation of these multiple detailed scenarios was followed by a series of steps to ensure the validity of the scenarios. Do the scenarios capture and reflect what they are supposed to? Do they capture the daily routine of an older adult? Do they capture the culture of the older adult? Do they express expected general cultural characteristics but also individual preferences? Had the ethical principles we committed to been followed? Do they provide opportunities for the robot to navigate challenging situations without using stereotypical answers?

Capturing this diversity was critical for developing a process for addressing the issue of stereotypes. In everyday human-to-human interactions, it may be difficult to avoid stereotypes, mainly because categorical thinking is often used to quickly assess another person. In fact, this process of categorization has been used in robotic programming (Wagner, 2012). However, stereotypes can be offensive, lead to misunderstandings, errors, and dissatisfaction with provision of care (Cooper et al., 2012). When humans use stereotypes in their interactions, they leave very little "room" for the other person to express and be themselves. For example, assuming that every English person would like to have "a cup of tea" and offering only the option of "tea" as a drink, limits the interaction. Assuming that every Indian person would be a Hindu or will be vegetarian or would not eat beef is incorrect and could be the cause of annoyance for a person being stereotyped. Cultural competence models such as the Papadopoulos (2006) recommends the use of open ended questions for the avoidance of stereotypes in everyday interactions as well as the verification of responses and actions before these are taken.

Validity of the scenarios was established by gathering data from multiple sources, multiple informants, and on multiple occasions. First, we observed and videotaped the daily routine of older adults in care homes in the UK. We were looking for cultural expressions and also for concrete evidence of what the daily routine really includes. Second, we asked external experts to review the videotapes and validate the observed cultural expressions and our interpretations. This validation enabled us to develop a preliminary set of guidelines. Chapter 7 provides a detailed description about the development, the testing and validation of the guidelines for the programming of a culturally competent robot.

6.6 Conclusion

Cultural competent interactions are highly desirable and valued in health care since they ensure the provision of person-centered care. When we consider the introduction of social robots in our lives, we should aim for the creation of the best possible technology and in this chapter we presented our layered approach for the development of the initial stages of such artificial intelligent technology.

6.7 Reflective questions

- Think about your daily routine. What does your morning or evening routine include? Can you find the elements in your routine that express your own cultural background?
- Look at the robotic capabilities (dark grey part of the scenario table) and think why it was important to program the robot to ask multiple choice questions and not only yes/no questions? Similarly, think why it was important for the robot to use "suggestions" and "reminders"? What ethical principle is transmitted through this action?

References

Ali, N. R. (2015). *Exploring older South Asian migrant (SAM) women's experiences of old age and ageing*. Doctoral thesis. University of Huddersfield.

Belza, B., Walwick, J., Schwartz, S., LoGerfo, J., Shiu-Thornton, S., & Taylor, M. (2004). Peer reviewed: older adult perspectives on physical activity and exercise: Voices from multiple cultures. *Preventing Chronic Disease, 1*(4).

BSI. (2016). *Robots and robotic devices. Guide to the ethical design and application of robots and robotic systems*. BSI 8611 https://shop.bsigroup.com/products/robots-and-robotic-devices-guide-to-the-ethical-design-and-application-of-robots-and-robotic-systems/standard.

Carter-Black, J. (2007). Teaching cultural competence: An innovative strategy grounded in the universality of storytelling as depicted in African and African American storytelling traditions. *Journal of Social Work Education, 43*(1), 31–50.

Chattopadhyay, K., Mishra, P., Manjunath, N. K., Harris, T., Hamer, M., Greenfield, S.,., & Prabhakaran, D. (2020). Development of a yoga programme for type-2 diabetes prevention (YOGA-DP) among high-risk people in India. *Frontiers in Public Health, 8*, 688.

Cooper, L. A., Roter, D. L., Carson, K. A., Beach, M. C., Sabin, J. A., Greenwald, A. G., & Inui, T. S. (2012). The associations of clinicians' implicit attitudes about race with medical visit communication and patient ratings of interpersonal care. *American Journal of Public Health, 102*(5), 979–987.

Fiese, B. H. (2006). *Family routines and rituals, Current perspectives in psychology*. New Haven: Yale University Press.

Galvin, J. E. (2017). Prevention of Alzheimer's disease: Lessons learned and applied. *Journal of the American Geriatrics Society, 65*(10), 2128–2133.

Hofstede, G., & Hofstede, G. J. (2005). *Cultures and organizations: Software of the mind; [intercultural cooperation and its importance for survival]*. New York: McGraw-Hill.

Hofstede, G., Hofstede, G. J., & Minkov, M. (1991). *Cultures and organizations: software of the mind, 2*. New York City: McGraw-Hill.

Hollins, S. (2018). *Religions, culture and healthcare: A practical handbook for use in healthcare environments*. CRC Press.

Kent, B. V., Stroope, S., Kanaya, A. M., Zhang, Y., Kandula, N. R., & Shields, A. E. (2020). Private religion/spirituality, self-rated health, and mental health among US South Asians. *Quality of Life Research, 29*(2), 495–504.

Leininger, M. (2002). Culture care theory: A major contribution to advance transcultural nursing knowledge and practices. *Journal of Transcultural Nursing, 13*(3), 189–192.

Martinson, M., & Berridge, C. (2015). Successful aging and its discontents: A systematic review of the social gerontology literature. *The Gerontologist, 55*(1), 58–69.

McCann, Mortimer, P., Ward, L., & Winefield, H. (2008). Successful ageing by whose definition? Views of older, spiritually affiliated women. *Australasian Journal on Ageing, 27*(4), 200–204.

Papadopoulos, I. (2006). *Transcultural health and social care: Development of culturally competent practitioners*. Edinburgh: Churchill Livingstone Elsevier.

Rowe, J. W., & Kahn, R. L. (2015). Successful aging 2.0: Conceptual expansions for the 21st century. *The Journals of Gerontology: Series B, 70*(4), 593–596.

Sharma, R. K., Khosla, N., Tulsky, J. A., & Carrese, J. A. (2012). Traditional expectations versus US realities: First-and second-generation Asian Indian perspectives on end-of-life care. *Journal of General Internal Medicine, 27*(3), 311–317.

Stevenson, N. (2019). Developing cultural understanding through story-telling. *Journal of Teaching in Travel & Tourism, 19*(1), 8–21.

Tan, J., Ward, L., & Ziaian, T. (2010). Experiences of Chinese immigrants and Anglo-Australians ageing in Australia: A cross-cultural perspective on successful ageing. *Journal of Health Psychology, 15*(5), 697–706.

Victor, C., Martin, W., & Zubair, M. (2011). Families and caring amongst older people in South Asian communities in the UK: A pilot study. *European Journal of Social Work, 15*(1). https://doi.org/10.1080/13691457.2011.573913

Wagner, A. R. (October 2012). Using cluster-based stereotyping to foster human-robot cooperation. In *Intelligent robots and systems (IROS), 2012 IEEE/RSJ international conference on* (pp. 1615–1622). IEEE.

Zubair, M., Martin, W., & Victor, C. (2012). Embodying gender, age, ethnicity and power in the 'field': Reflections on dress and the presentation of the self in research with older Pakistani Muslims. *Sociological Research Online, 17*(3), 21. http://www.socresonline.org.uk/17/3/21.html.

CHAPTER 7

From stories to scenarios and guidelines for the programming of culturally competent, socially assistive robots

Irena Papadopoulos[1] and Christina Koulouglioti[2]

[1]Research Centre for Transcultural Studies in Health, Middlesex University, London, United Kingdom; [2]Research and Innovation Department, University Hospitals Sussex NHS Foundation Trust and Research Centre for Transcultural Studies in Health, Middlesex University, London, United Kingdom

LEARNING OBJECTIVES

- To understand the primary purpose of developing guidelines for the programming of culturally competent socially assistive robots
- To learn about the theories used in this project and their role in guiding and underpinning the development of tools for data collection and analysis
- To become aware of the observation methodology used in the development of the guidelines for the programming of the robot and reflect on its complexity, innovation, and contribution
- To acquire some knowledge of the processes involved in the development and refinement of guidelines for the programming of culturally competent socially assistive robots

7.1 Introduction

As mentioned in previous chapters, the influence of culture on health has been well documented in the literature. Living in a multicultural society dictates the need to provide culturally competent health and social care. A culturally competent health professional recognizes the existence of cultural differences and—in most cases—can effectively communicate, intervene, and create a working environment that considers the social and cultural influences. This chapter presents a case study based on the work the authors undertook during the CARESSES project which aimed to develop the first culturally competent socially assistive humanoid robot to cater to the needs of older adults. The CARESSES project (Culture-Aware Robots and Environmental Sensor Systems for Elderly Support) was a European—Japanese collaboration and was funded by the European Union and by the Ministry of Internal Affairs and Communications of Japan, 2017—2020. The project included work on three cultural groups: English, Indian, and Japanese. This chapter presents the work undertaken by the European partner which relates to the English and Indian heritage groups only (more information related to the CARESSES project can be found in all chapters of this book but a more detailed and extensive description can be found in Chapter 5). In this chapter, we have used the case of CARESSES as a vehicle in order to provide the general principles and processes required for the development of guidelines for the programming of culturally competent, socially assistive robots (SARs). The reader may choose to adapt the same processes with a different cultural group.

In the field of nursing and other health professions, the human-to-human interactions can be guided through the principles of cultural competence which can assist healthcare professionals to navigate through difficult situations and provide appropriate and safe care (Papadopoulos, 2006). It is critical that the same principals be considered for the development of SARs, to enable them to execute their caring roles in a culturally competent way.

Robotics have acknowledged the importance of culture and O'Neill-Brown's (1997) influential piece on culturally adaptive agents called for the design of systems that are adaptable to the user and can communicate in a way that reflects the user's culture. Subsequently, other pieces of seminal work have been conducted in order to better understand how culture influences the human—robot interaction and on how to develop culturally aware robots and information technology systems (Endrass, 2014; Blanchard & Allard, 2010).

Acknowledging the importance of culture is a very critical step in the development of SARs and for further understanding the human—robot interactions. However, a major issue with any interaction between people from different cultures is the avoidance of stereotypes. Stereotypes often lead to misunderstandings and miscommunication but can also lead to the collapse of the communication due to the culturally insensitive nature of the messages being communicated or due to difference in cultural values or language barriers. The development of culturally competent skills can assist in the successful navigation through multicultural interactions and the avoidance of stereotypes. Therefore, SAR developers must be themselves culturally competent if they are to produce artificial intelligence (AI) software that are culturally sensitive and can avoid stereotyping.

Chapter 6 described in detail the processes involved for the development of stories and the production of scenarios, for the eventual construction of the guidelines for a culturally competent, artificially intelligent, SAR. Chapter 6 and this chapter provide step-by-step examples of the work the authors undertook during the CARESSES project, to achieve the goal of producing the first culturally competent humanoid robot. It is not the intention of this chapter to provide detailed results about the data collected during the observation and evaluation studies described in this chapter, but to provide a description of the processes involved in the development of theories and tools used to collect and analyze the data, for

7.1 Introduction

the production of the guidelines, their evaluation, and the final refinement of the guidelines for the programming of the robot. The technical aspect that underpin the principles, the encoding and operationalization of guidelines in the robot are discussed in Chapters 8 and 9.

The following flowchart (Fig. 7.1) which includes the processes we undertook to arrive at the final refined guidelines for the development of a culturally competent robot is intended as an advanced visual organizer for the reader.

As mentioned in the introduction, an important primary goal for the development of guidelines to be used in the programming of a culturally competent robot was to avoid, as much as possible, the stereotyping of people from different cultural groups. The literature confirms that there are more similarities than differences in human beings. Often the differences are very subtle, context specific, and difficult to observe, but they are very important as they define one's individuality as well as group belonging. The development of the

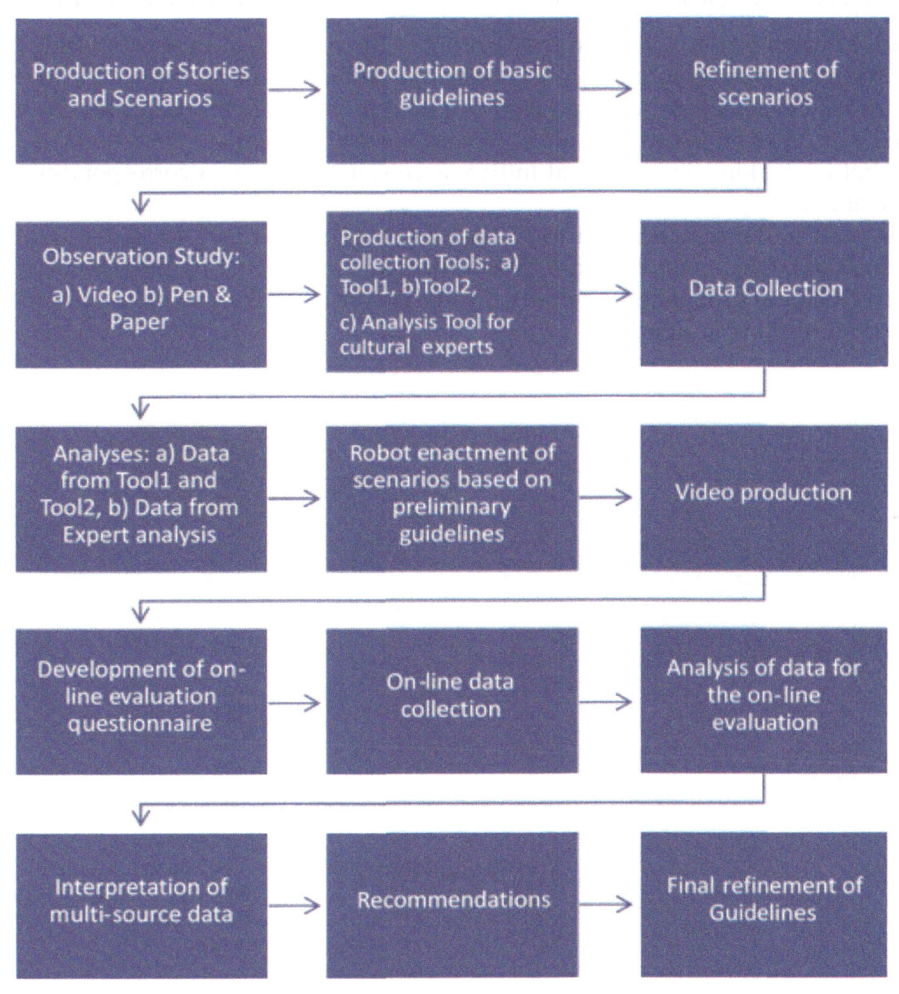

FIGURE 7.1 The development of guidelines: Processes and outputs.

guidelines began with the creation of scenarios (Chapter 6) which were based on the stories we wrote. These included both culture-generic and culture-specific information based on the researchers' prior work and knowledge, as well as personal and professional experiences, and many years of living and working in multicultural environments.

At the same time, we developed a conceptual framework for the production of guidelines (Fig. 7.2). The framework indicates how the generic and specific elements of culture would be combined in order to develop the guidelines. It is also important when developing tools and processes to follow an organizing framework for the presentation of guidelines that mirrors the way in which the software architecture and programs are designed. To achieve the required programming, structured templates were used to present the content of the guidelines in accordance with the structures, tools, and languages for knowledge representation (see Chapter 8). Guidelines were produced in the following knowledge domains: (A) Topics of conversation, (B) Goals, (C) Qualitative Behaviors, (D) Quantitative Parameters, and (E) Norms.

a. **Topics of conversations**, refer to the topics that the robot shall raise when chit-chatting with the user, in order to increase the sense of familiarity during the interaction and explore the person's individual preferences; the topics of conversation can also be presented as images on the robot's tablet to complement the verbal interaction (i.e., when the robot is speaking about typical Indian sweets, it may show a corresponding picture on its tablet);

b. **Goals**, refer to the activities that the robot shall suggest and perform (after asking for a confirmation), which may be more or less likely to be welcome by the user belonging to different cultural groups (e.g., helping during prayer or cooking is more relevant in some cultures than in others);

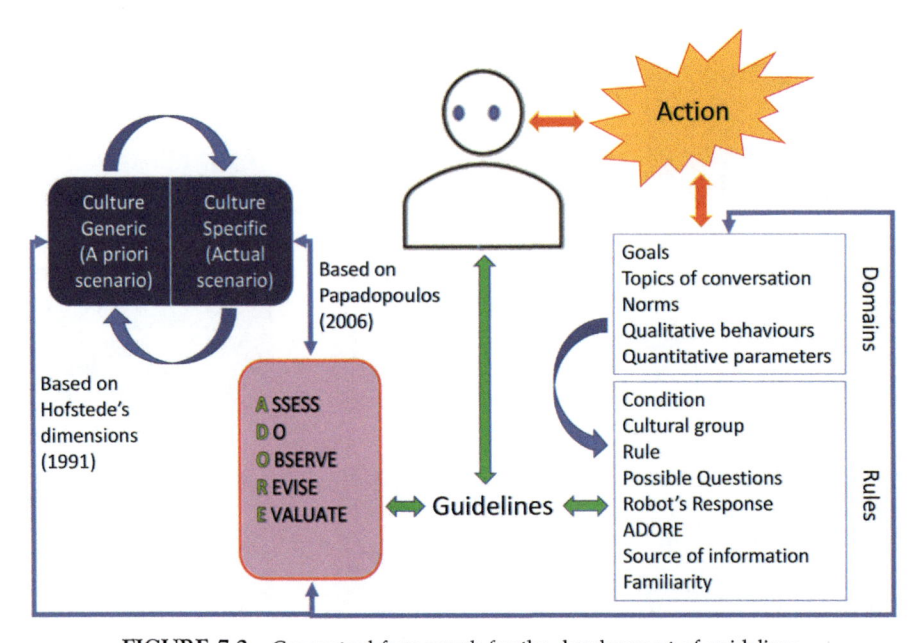

FIGURE 7.2 Conceptual framework for the development of guidelines.

c. **Quantitative parameters**, refer to the actual values of measurable parameters that determine the behavior of the robot during the interaction in a culturally sensitive way: for example, the volume and duration of pauses while speaking (which may vary for different cultures and daily situation, e.g., praying or having lunch), the distance during the interaction (e.g., according to how varies in different cultures), the frequency of gestures, etc;
d. **Qualitative behaviors**, refer to actions that may be more or less appropriate depending on the cultural identity of the person: this includes sensorimotor actions (such as different type of greetings or the handling of objects with one or two hands) as well as different suggestions that the robot may give the user when, for example, required to play a movie or a song (suggesting a Bollywood movie may not be appropriate for all persons), or even suggestions about different technological solutions such WhatsApp or Telegram messaging in Europe versus Line in Japan;
e. **Norms,** refer to situations avoided or preferred, depending on the cultural group and additional conditions (e.g., avoid asking intimate questions to users of English heritage, always ask permission from the user before taking an action).

For each domain of knowledge, numerous guidelines were developed using the following rules: (1) **Condition:** when and where this guideline apply, (2) **Cultural group:** for which cultural group (3) **Rule:** what the robot shall do; (4) **Possible Questions:** what the robot may ask to start the conversation; (5) **Robot's response:** what the robot may say in response to the user; (6) **ADORE:** Steps of the model involved in this rule are "Assess" "Do," "Observe" "Revise" "Evaluate" (explained in detail below); (7) **Source:** the sources of information which allowed a rule to be written were: Theory (T), Literature (L), Scenarios (S), Observations (O), Cultural Competence (CC), Design Choice (DC), Family (F) and Common Sense (CS); (8) **Familiarity:** the probability that this rule will be appropriate for a person self identifying with this cultural group, (which will be the basis to develop AI solutions allowing the robot to store knowledge in a non stereotyped way, as discussed in Chapter 8).

A simple example for the domain of "Topics of Conversation" is provided in Table 7.1, which deals briefly with the topic of "family."

Before we go any further into the presentation and explanation of the guidelines, we will discuss the theories and methods we adopted in order to produce the tools for an observation study we conducted, to gain the required real-life deep insights about the two chosen cultural groups of older adults, for whom the guidelines were developed.

7.2 Theoretical underpinnings

The development of the culturally competent guidelines for SARs was guided by the Papadopoulos (2006) conceptual model for transcultural nursing and cultural competence and her notions about the existence of culture-generic and culture-specific elements. These ideas were combined with Hofstede's (1991) national/cultural dimensions, and with the notion of the cultural iceberg attributed to Hall (1976).

The Papadopoulos et al. (1998) model of transcultural nursing was revised and expanded by Papadopoulos in 2006, who added the model's underpinning theories and defined the key

TABLE 7.1 Example of the guidelines template—topic of conversation.

Condition: When does the rule apply?	Cultural group: For which cultural group?	Rule: What does the rule say?	Possible Questions	Robot's Responses	ADORE: Assess Do Observe Revise Evaluate	Source: How was this rule produced?	Familiarity: How likely is the rule to hold for the specified cultural group
When robot-user first meet	Indian	Talk about family	Do you have a big family? Do they live close by? Do they visit you often? Who are the closest members of your family and what are their names? Can you show me some photos?	OK, I know that Indian names usually have a meaning. Tell me the meanings of the names of the people you mentioned.	Assess	S+L+F	High

conceptual terms of the model, including that of "cultural competence" (Papadopoulos, 2006). According to this model, a culturally competent person (or in this case a culturally competent robot) must possess adequate levels of cultural awareness, cultural knowledge, and cultural sensitivity and be able to combine these and implement the knowledge gained and associated practical skills in such a way that the patient or the service user can benefit in holistic and nurturing ways, which challenge discrimination and stereotypes.

Cultural awareness refers to the acquisition of knowledge and skills about culture, cultural identity, levels of heritage adherence, and avoidance of stereotyping, while cultural knowledge refers to an understanding of cultural health beliefs and behaviors, the similarities and differences between cultures and the inequalities which result from the power differentials between people of various cultures. Cultural sensitivity refers to the development of culturally appropriate and positive relations between people of different cultures. In addition, Papadopoulos and Lees (2002) proposed that health and social care professionals develop and use, throughout their careers, a set of culture-generic competencies that are applicable across cultural groups. These culture-generic competencies enable them to acquire culture-specific competencies, which are particular to specific groups and individuals within cultural groups. Since it is impossible for a person (or a robot) to be knowledgeable of all the cultural differences within and between cultural groups, the dynamic nature of the culture-generic and culture-specific notion of cultural competence allows a care giver with adequate culture-generic competence to gain cultural-specific competence by asking the relevant questions and verifying their understanding of the answers with the service user. In a later section of this chapter, we present the ADORE model, which we specially created based on these principles, which enable a robot to move between these two domains.

7.2.1 National and individual culture

Hofstede's (Hofstede, Hofstede, & Minkov, 1991) extensive research on the impact of culture on individuals resulted in the development of six cultural dimensions which were validated with thousands of workers in different countries. The cultural dimensions—which have already been introduced in Chapter 1—have subsequently been in hundreds if not thousands of studies as the benchmark classification of the following cultural characteristics of many nations: "power distance," "uncertain avoidance," "individualism versus collectivism," "long-term versus short-term orientation," "masculinity versus femininity," and "indulgence versus restrain." These dimensions underpinned the construction of the stories and scenarios we developed in this project and provided the a priori culture generic dimensions of the two cultural groups in our investigation: the English heritage and the Indian heritage.

Notwithstanding the usefulness of the national indices produced by the Hofstede's cultural dimensions, and the consensus on certain universal values as expressed in human rights codes and legislation, Papadopoulos (2006) has argued that at a cultural/ethnic group level, as well as at the individual level, cultural differences exist in terms of values, perceptions, and attitudes and their manifestations in decisions taken—including those related to self care practices, and the reactions to, and management of life course events, challenges, and so on.

7.2.2 The cultural iceberg theory

Hall (1976) viewed culture as an iceberg with only 5%–10% of it being visible above the water line. The visible or consciousness level elements are things such as food, dress, language, rituals, and other cultural behaviors which a person is conscious of, and an observer can see. Beneath the visible part of the iceberg lie the invisible or subconscious level elements, such as our values, feelings, philosophical and religious beliefs and principles, that we acquire through socialization from early childhood and adolescence, with further evolution during adulthood's life experiences. In order to understand a person's cultural identity and behaviors, including those related to family, health, self care, decision making, and those associated with feelings such as anger, happiness, sadness, kindness, patience and so on, one needs to investigate the components of the invisible, subconscious level. To produce the guidelines, we conducted an observation study which will be outlined in a later section of this chapter.

7.2.3 Daily routines and the hidden part of our consciousness

Of relevance to developing guidelines for programming culturally competent robots is the work of anthropologists Bossard and Boll (1950) who, more than 70 years ago concluded that rituals are powerful organizers of family life, and found that family routines are observable, patterned interactions that are repeated over time but are not the same for every individual or family. In other words, we may all have a morning, a midday, and an evening routine, but that routine, will not be the same for each one of us. As a result, observing naturally occurring everyday routines provides the ideal avenue of exploring culturally observable behaviors and their subtle differences among individuals from the same or different cultural background.

In addition, literature has demonstrated that routines of daily living relate to an individuals' health and well-being (Fiese, 2006). For example, it has been found that young children living in disorganized home environments characterized by lack of routines (Gregory et al., 2005) or by increased noise levels, crowding, and family instability (Brown & Low, 2008), had an increased likelihood of experiencing sleep problems and were less likely to have regular sleep routines (Koulouglioti et al., 2014). Among healthy adults, eating regular breakfast has been associated with reduced dietary fat intake and decrease prevalence of obesity (Guinter et al., 2020). Predictable everyday routines are considered essential for preventing distress among patients with dementia or memory loss (https://alzheimersproject.org/the-importance-of-routine-and-familiarity-to-persons-with-dementia/ and https://www.dementiauk.org/get-support/understanding-changes-in-behaviour/coping-with-distress/).

Therefore, a caring robot should be both aware and knowledgeable about the visible and hidden factors of culture and how to use these in order to reduce its user's distress and contribute to the promotion of physical and mental health. However, currently it is not feasible for a robot to autonomously learn about the visible and hidden factors of culture, due to the limitation of its perceptual and cognitive system. For this reason, this work is currently performed by experts, who encode the knowledge in robots using appropriate tools for knowledge representation.

7.2.4 The cultural iceberg trigger theory

In terms of observing and documenting the hidden elements of the culture, we hypothesized that unexpected events can disrupt a person's everyday routine and can trigger the hidden subconscious elements to produce responses reflecting one's culture, which surface to the consciousness level as observable behaviors. Our observation study aimed to identify triggers which stimulate a subconscious response, and to capture the subsequent observable behaviors. Fig. 7.3 provides a visual representation of our hypothesis.

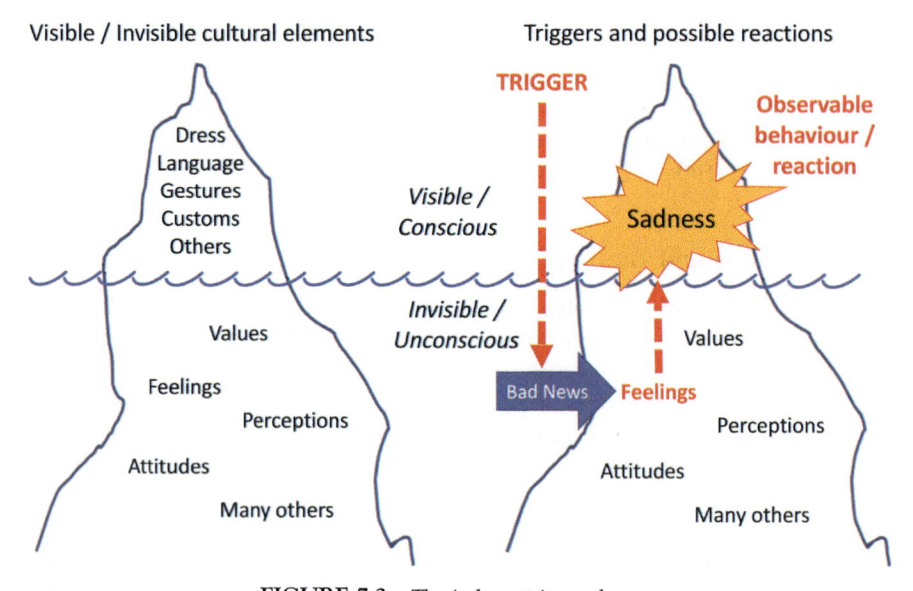

FIGURE 7.3 The iceberg trigger theory.

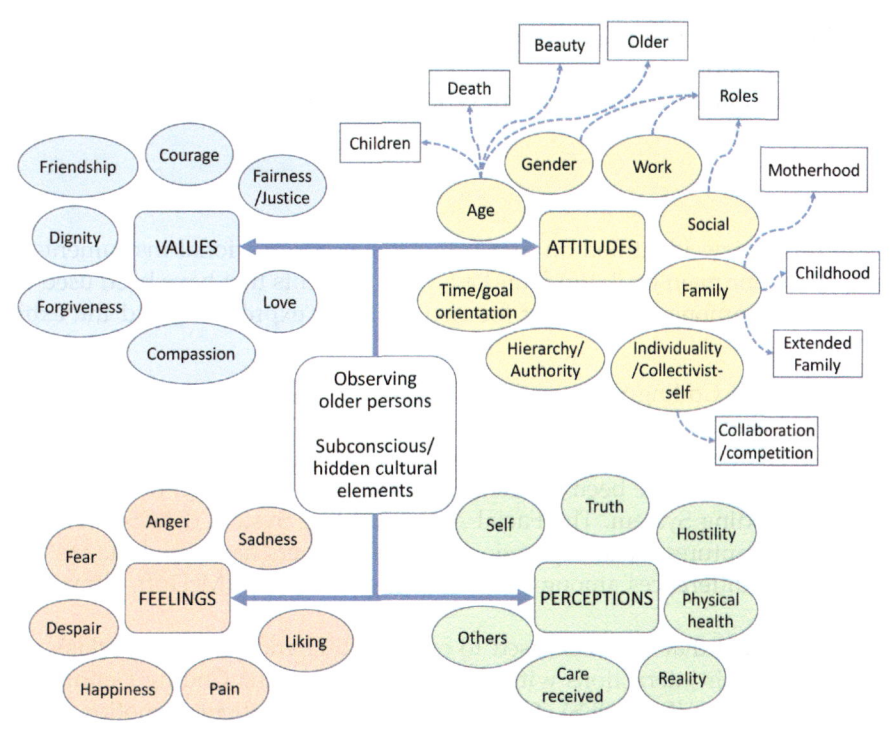

FIGURE 7.4 Subconscious cultural components and elements.

Since the cultural elements of the visible part of the iceberg can be easily described and included in the guidelines we were trying to develop, we focused our attention on the invisible subconscious elements, which we needed to find a way to capture and describe in the guidelines. In order to be transparent as well as systematic about our observations of the enactments of culture residing in the hidden parts of the iceberg, we selected to study the key elements of values, feelings, perceptions and attitudes, which we analyzed and provided some possible subelements. This work enabled us to prepare the observation tools we used to capture the influence of culture on our behaviors (see Fig. 7.4 read above).

7.3 The observation study: the processes used for the development of observation tools

In order to collect the type of data described in the previous section, we conducted an observation study which involved video and manual recordings. Both observation methods were conducted contemporaneously. The study took place in care facilities for older adults.

The following steps outline the work we undertook for the development of the two tools which we used in the observation study:

a. **Step 1**: we conducted a literature review to identify existing observational measures designed to capture observable elements of behavior (verbal and nonverbal) belonging to the visible part of the iceberg as described above.

b. **Step 2**: a literature review to identify measures that capture patient-healthcare professional communication.
c. **Step 3**: Brainstorming—development of observation templates and representation of the iceberg culture theory.

7.3.1 Step 1

The literature review identified an array of existing observational instruments but none directly related to our main goal. We found a few instruments that have been used to capture cultural differences among groups that focused on facial expressions and the exhibition of emotions such as

a. The Specific Affect Coding System (SPAFF) an observational measure designed to capture affective behavior in the context of marital conflict (Coan & Gottman, 2007). The codes of SPAFF of positive effects (affection, humor, etc.) and negative effects (anger, sadness, disgust, etc.) have been influenced by the work of Ekman & Friesen, on the Facial Action Coding System. The Facial Action Coding System (FACS; Ekmna, Friesen, & Hager, 2002) captures facial expressions and researchers have used the instrument to observe cultural differences among people around the world (McDuff, Girard, & Kalioudy, 2017).
b. Another instrument that has been used to explore differences among Turkish and Dutch patients during their interactions with their GP is the Verona Coding Definitions of Emotional Sequence (VR-CoDES). This measure captures patients' emotional cues/concerns and GP's responses to these cues (Schouten & Schinkel, 2015).

Although we did not directly make use of the above instruments, they provided useful insights for the development of the tools which we used in our observation study.

7.3.2 Step 2

Subsequently, we searched for instruments that have been used to capture and assess the nurse—patient interaction. Many such instruments exist such as the Caris-Verhallen et al. (2004) instrument which deals with nonverbal behaviors in nurse-elderly patient communication. The Rotter Interaction Analysis System (RIAS) (Roter & Hall, 1992) which was used in the care of older people captures verbal and nonverbal communication. The RIAS instrument was originally designed to code doctor—patient communication and uses verbal utterances (a small distinguishable speech segment that can be coded) as a unit of analysis. In our study, we expanded the RIAS tool and the codes for nonverbal communication as defined by Caris-Verhallen, Kerkstra, & Bensing (1999). The six nonverbal categories were (1) patient-directed gaze, (2) affirmative head nods, (3) smiling, (4) forward leaning, (5) instrumental touch, and (6) affective touch. We added the use of gestures and of personal space.

Regarding the verbal communication, we used the five categories related to socio-emotional and instrumental communication as described by Caris-Varhallen et al. (1999) which are:

a. Social communication;
b. Affective communication;
c. Communication that structures the encounter;

d. Communication about care and health;
e. Communication about lifestyle and feelings.

We added tone of voice, taking turns in conversation, silence, use of humor and laughter.

We also added the "other elements" category to enable us to capture visible elements which are related to one's culture but cannot be classified as part of communication. For example, we observed and coded the participants' use of language, their dressing and the presence or not of religious artifacts in their private environment.

7.3.3 Step 3

During this stage, we had multiple brainstorming sessions discussing ways that we could capture the hidden/subconscious part of one's cultural iceberg. We first decided to define the components of this part of the iceberg and as seen in Fig. 7.4. A diagram was created that captures the components: (1) values, (2) feelings, (3) perceptions, and (4) attitudes, each being linked to their key elements. In the case of the "attitude" component, we also added sub-elements.

Following our hypothesis that observable behaviors may surface from the invisible/subconscious part of the culture iceberg when everyday routines are disrupted, we created a table of possible triggers of such disruptions that can be positive or negative. Our goal was to observe and look for possible triggers that may occur during our observational visits and may influence a participant's behavior.

7.4 Creation of the observation tools and how to use them

7.4.1 Tool 1 (Fig. 7.5)

Tool 1 was designed to capture the visible elements of culture and some general information about the person being observed. It consists of four main columns: A. General Information, B. Verbal communication, C. Nonverbal communication and D. Other elements. Each one of these columns is subdivided into a number of smaller columns. One page is expected to be collected for every one snap shot video observation which could last from 2 to 10 min. The tool was accompanied by the following instructions:

7.4.1.1 General information

Record participant's gender, heritage, religion, medical history, and time lived in the UK. Record additional information about the encounter, for example, who were the people involved with the participant (an informal or formal caregiver), the time of the day that the observation occurred and whether the participant was involved in an individual or a group activity.

7.4.1.2 Verbal communication

A list of verbal behaviors is included in the second main column of the tool. Detailed explanation for each behavior is provided in the next section. Records were made for each behavior code: (1) the presence or absence of the behavior (in the ± column); (2) the frequency (column F), the number of times the behavior occurred during the observation, (3) qualitative elements/properties of the behavior, such as "soft" for the tone of voice (column Q) (4) the duration of the event (column D).

7.4.1.3 Nonverbal communication

A similar approach was taken for the nonverbal behaviors: coding presence/absence, frequency, and qualitative elements.

7.4.1.4 Other elements

This column is for capturing the use of language (other than English), type of dressing, and the presence of religious artifacts (e.g., statues, icons, cross, etc.). Further information about the quotes used can be found below. The table has many empty boxes in order to capture and record behaviors that had not been listed but they were observed.

7.4.1.5 Definitions of verbal communication

a. **Social communication**: *Communication* which provides information about the degree to which the carer uses social conversation that has no particular function in caring activities, such as personal statements, banter, jokes, and small talk.
b. **Affective communication**: *Communication* which provides information about the extent to which the carer shows verbal attentiveness, concern, empathy, and sympathy with the person/patient.
c. **Communication that structures the encounter**: *communication* which involves utterances that indicate guidance and direction such as orientating and instructing, requests for clarification, asking for understanding and asking for opinion.
d. **Communication about care and health**: *communication* which contains all items with respect to caring, medical or therapeutic topics.
e. **Communication about lifestyle and feeling**: *communication* which contains all verbal expressions with respect to lifestyle issues and emotional topics.
f. **Tone of voice**: *loud or soft*. Other adjectives may be used so please keep a note.
g. **Taking turns in conversation**: persons are taking turns to express themselves and discuss by listening when the other person talks and waiting to respond, as opposed to talking over each other, simultaneously overlapping conversation.
h. **Silence**: *keeping quiet.*
i. **Use of humor**: *saying a joke.*
j. **Laughter**: *Laughing out loud* in response to a joke.

7.4.1.6 Other elements

a. **Use of language other than English**: Code as T = traditional when another language is used in the interaction or NT = nontraditional when the interaction is always in English.
b. **Type of dressing**: Code as T = traditional if wearing sari/salwar or NT = nontraditional when western clothes are worn.
c. **Religious ornaments and artifacts**: Code as T when religious ornaments are worn or religious artifacts (e.g., icons, scripts from the Koran, or Hindu statues) are present and NT when none is present.

7.4.1.7 Definitions of nonverbal communication
a. **Eye Contact:** making eye contact
b. **Smiling:** an utterance of friendliness.
c. **Body posture:** a special focus on forward leaning.
d. **Affective touch:** relatively spontaneous and affective, and not necessary for the completion of a task (e.g., putting the arm around a distress patient/person)
e. **Instrumental touch:** deliberate physical contact, which is necessary in performing a caring task (e.g., dressing a wound)
f. **Head nodding:** agreement or just acknowledgment, or attentiveness to the conversation and/or reinforcing the spoken word.
g. **Use of gestures:** the use of gestures when talking (e.g., moving hands)
h. **Personal space:** the distance kept between two parties; for example do they sit closely together almost touching or in opposite chairs across the room having a conversation.

7.4.2 Tool 2 (Fig. 7.6)

Tool 2 was designed to capture the triggers and the subsequent subconscious responses. If behaviors were exhibited which could be linked to values, feelings, perceptions, and attitudes, the trigger which in the observer's view caused the behavioral response was circled. For example, if the participant was waiting for her/his food but there was a delay, that could be a trigger of a subconscious reaction, which may be manifested as anger. Or if a participant received a pleasant phone call, that was considered a trigger for a happy feeling which was expressed with words or with laughter/smiling.

7.4.2.1 Triggers

Triggers are events that can produce a response in the deep subconscious of a person which manifests as a visible behavior which is unique to the individual's cultural values, perceptions, attitudes, and feelings. In this study, we have summarized such triggers in six main domains:

1. **Health and wellbeing:** Coded negative (−) such as not feeling well, when, for example, a person is experiencing pain or stress/anxiety, and positive (+) when the person is feeling well, is pain free, and not anxious.
2. **Certainty/uncertainty:** Coded negative (−) when, for example, appointments are canceled such as family visits, or absence of news from the family/significant others, or moving location, or a change of carer. The trigger is coded as positive (+) when certainty/continuity/predictability is maintained.
3. **Routines of daily living:** This is coded as negative (−) when there is a disruption to the routine, for example, meal not on time, caregiver is running late, outside appointments changed without much warning, and coded as positive (+) when there is stability and continuity in daily routines.
4. **Formal/informal caregiver's behavior:** This trigger is coded as negative (−) when a late, unkind, rude or culturally insensitive response is given by the carer, and code as positive (+) when a timely, kind, culturally appropriate response is given.

5. **Receiving news (personal or global)**: This is coded as negative (−) when the person receives bad news about self and/or family or about global/national news, and coded as positive (+) when the person receives good news.
6. **Finances**: Coded as negative (−) when the person is experiencing financial difficulties/strain, and positive (+) when there are financial gains.

7.4.2.2 Possible observable "surfaced" behaviors of subconscious/hidden cultural elements

As described in the cultural iceberg theory, the subconscious cultural components and their associated responses are related to: 1. Values, 2. Feelings, 3. Perceptions, and 4. Attitudes. Please refer to Fig. 7.5.

Participant's ID:

Date: **Name of care home facility:**   **Start Time:**   **End Time:**

A. General Information		B. Verbal Communication				C. Non-Verbal Communication:				D. Other Elements	
		+/−	F	D	Q		+/−	F	D	Q		Q
Insert the information needed in this column below:												
1. Gender: F / M/Other
2. Age:
3. Heritage: English / Indian
4. Time lived in the UK (in years):

5. Type of encounter (routine):
a. morning
b. lunch time
c. after lunch
d. tea time
e. evening

6. Religion:

7. Carer: Formal /Informal

8. Health status

9. Activity:
a. individual
b. group | Social | | | | | Eye Contact | | | | | Language | |
| | Affective | | | | | Smiling | | | | | Dressing | |
| | Instructions | | | | | Body posture | | | | | Religious artefacts | |
| | Talking about:
a)Health/ Nursing | | | | | Affective touch | | | | | | |
	b)Lifestyle/ Feeling					Instrumental touch						
	Taking turns					Head nodding						
	Laughter					Use of gestures						
	Tone of voice					Personal space						
	Use of humour											
	Silence											

+ = present, − = absent, F = frequency (none of time/some/most of the time), D =duration Q = qualitative properties: INA = inappropriate, AP = appropriate, T = Traditional, NT = non traditional, S = soft, L = loud

FIGURE 7.5 Observing visible elements of culture.

Participant's ID:

Date: **Name of care home facility:** **Start Time:** **End Time:**

Triggers (please circle all relevant present triggers)		Response to trigger (using the table below, capture and record all relevant codes as appropriate)
Not feeling well	Feeling well	
Uncertainty	Certainty	
Disruption of routine	Predictability	
Late/unkind response	Timely/kind response	
Receive bad news	Receive good news	
Lack of Money (money troubles)	Money gains	
Codes for Behavioural Responses		

1. Values	2. Feelings	3. Perceptions about	4. Attitudes	
1.1 Fairness/justice	2.1 Sadness	3.1 Self	4.1 Age	4.5 Family
1.2 Courage	2.2 Anger	3.2 Truth	4.1.1 Children	4.5.1 Motherhood
1.3 Friendship	2.3 Fear	3.3 Hostility	4.1.2 Death	4.5.2 Childhood
1.4 Dignity	2.4 Despair	3.4 Physical health	4.1.3 Beauty	4.5.3 Extended Family
1.5 Forgiveness	2.5 Happiness	3.5 Reality	4.1.4 Older age	4.6 Individuality/ Collectivist
1.6 Compassion	2.6 Pain	3.6 Care received	4.1.5 Roles	4.6.1 Collaboration/ competition
1.7 Love	2.7 Liking	3.7 Others	4.2 Gender	4.7 Hierarchy/Authority
			4.2.1 Roles	4.8 Time/goal orientation
			4.3 Work	
			4.3.1 Roles	
			4.4 Social status	
			4.4.1 Roles	

FIGURE 7.6 Triggers and behavioral responses.

7.5 Video recordings

In order to verify the scenarios (which are described in Chapter 6) and anchor them into real life, snapshot video recordings of real older people living in care homes—and in a few cases in their own homes—were taken. These video recordings were supplemented with concurrent observations of subtle everyday behaviors, responses to triggers, and verbal and non-verbal communications, using the tools we described above.

In the following paragraphs, we provide the details regarding the video recording sessions which led to the production of a list of video clips that our recruited cultural experts viewed and analyzed using our specially designed "analysis tool." We will then explain what was expected of the cultural experts and why their help was critical.

7.5.1 Sample size and procedures for the observation study

As indicated above, the main objectives during the observations were a) to capture video snapshots from the everyday life of older adults living in assistive care facilities or their own homes, and b) contemporaneously to record supplementary "pen and paper" observation data using the tools we designed specifically for this purpose (Tool 1 & 2, described in the previous section).

A total of 12 older adults, eight women (four English heritage and four Indian heritage) and four men (two English heritage and two Indian heritage) participated in the UK arm of the CARESSES observation project.

Observations were carried out during the morning, lunch-time, dinner-time, early evening. Before the initiation of the video recordings and observations, we obtained approval from the care home facilities and written informed consent from the residents and other individuals who agreed to take part. We observed and video recorded only those older adults, their carers, and family member/s who consented.

Participants were told to do everything as they would normally do during the day. For example, during mealtime, they continued to have dinner or lunch in the same place, with the same people and the same food as was usual for them. The videotaped snapshots lasted for a minimum of 2 minutes to a maximum of 10 min. For each participant, "pen and paper" data were also recorded during the video recordings.

The recorded footage (10.7 hours) was edited to a list of 39 short video clips (20 clips for English participants and 19 clips for Indian participants).

7.5.2 Cultural experts and their role

We recruited two cultural experts with Indian heritage and two with English heritage. Cultural experts were recruited not because of their professional background but because of their cultural background. The experts needed to know and understand their culture. They needed to know what is expected, what is appropriate, what is to be avoided, why certain words are used, the type of jokes, gestures, body language and so on, and what this may indicate. We produced a training manual for the cultural experts which was issued prior to a telephone meeting with them to explain the aims of the CARESSES project and specifically the aims of the observation study, their role, as well as answer any questions they had, after reading the manual. We provided contact details to them so they could contact us any time they had a question or needed help.

When watching a small selection of video clips, we requested from them to tell us what cultural expressions they observed. These could be visible evidence of culture, for example, the type of food the participants eat or the language they speak, but they can be other cultural cues which would not be so visible. We were especially interested in the not so visible

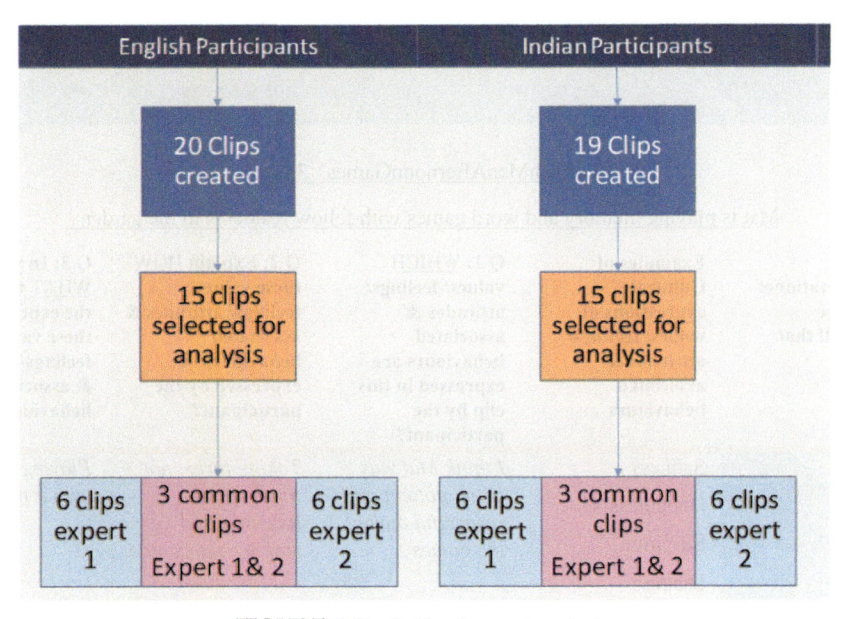

FIGURE 7.7 Cultural expert analysis.

expressions of culture that can be easily missed. For example, we may all feel frustrated when we have asked for something and we are waiting a long time for it, but we are not all expressing our feeling of frustration in the same way.

Our video footage depicted different everyday life moments. We asked the experts to observe our participants having lunch, or tea, playing games, just sitting with friends, exercising, dressing, talking, or praying. What we needed from them was to look at the video clips they were assigned with their "cultural eye," especially searching for subtle cues which could explain how deep-seated values, feelings, attitudes, and perceptions influenced the behaviors of the person/s they were observing. Their input helped us refine the preliminary (basic) guidelines we had developed for the robot by not missing critical cultural elements and without having to rely upon cultural stereotypes.

We asked the experts to watch only video clips of participants that matched their own cultural heritage, either English or Indian heritage. Each cultural expert was asked to watch a total of nine video clips (duration of 5–10 min each) and complete one analysis tool for each one of them. Three of the nine videos were given to both cultural experts of the same heritage, and the remaining six were different (see Fig. 7.7).

7.5.3 The "analysis tool"

The analysis tool we developed (Fig. 7.8) was designed to capture visible and nonvisible expressions of culture. To help the cultural experts, we provided an example of how they should use the analysis tool. In the first column, we listed different things they may see while watching a clip. This list was not exhaustive so we encouraged the experts to add to the list anything that they observed and it was specific to the English and/or Indian culture. For

ANALYSIS TOOL FOR CULTURAL EXPERTS EXAMPLE

'EnglishManAfternoonGames'_3mins.

Mat is playing memory and word games with fellow residents in the garden.'

	Visible Presentation of Culture (tick all that apply)	Examples of Cultural expressions of values/ feelings/ attitudes & associated behaviours	Q 1: WHICH values/ feelings/ attitudes & associated behaviours are expressed in this clip by the participant?	Q 2: Explain HOW these values/ feelings/ attitudes & associated behaviours are expressed by the participant?	Q 3: In your view WHAT triggered the expression of these values/ feelings/ attitudes & associated behaviours?
1	Language	Sadness	I think Mat was being patient and respectful during the games	Taking turns, not interrupting, listening and making eye contact	Playing a game with a friend
2	Dressing √	Happiness √			
3	Music	Suffering			
4	Food	Distress			
5	Drinks	Annoyance / Anger			
6	Decorations (room)	Love			
7	Activities / games √	Compassion			
8	Jewellery	Friendship √			
9	Festivals	Pain			
10	Customs	Courage			
11	Other? Please write	Dislike			
	Games and questions relevant to English way of life	Hostility			
		Trust			
		Fairness			
		Dignity			
		Self-Control			
		Contentment			
		Respect √			
		Cooperation			
		Patience √			
		Hope			
		Hopeless			
		Other:			

FIGURE 7.8   The analysis tool.

example, a picture on the wall or something that the participant was wearing may have specific cultural meaning which the experts could add to the list in the first column.

The second column included examples of different expressions of values, feelings, attitudes, and their associated behaviors. This list was also not exhaustive but provided useful examples of what the experts may expect the participants to demonstrate in the video clips. The experts were asked to read the list and think of the examples as they watched the video clip. If they thought that the participant was actually expressing any of the values, feelings, attitudes, they were asked to provide answers to the three questions which appear at the top of the third, fourth, fifth columns. We have provided an example of what we meant in the first row of the tool (the participant was Mat).

7.5.4 Profiles of cultural experts

- Expert 1 of English Heritage. A retired lecturer and researcher of nursing, who specialized in transcultural nursing. She was born in London where she has lived for most of her life. She has traveled extensively and enjoys learning about other cultures.
- Expert 2 of English Heritage. A retired lecturer of nursing with extensive experience in transcultural nursing. She continues to be involved in voluntary organizations focusing on transcultural nursing.
- Expert 1 of Indian heritage. A community Pediatrician, born and raised in India, currently living and working in the UK.
- Expert 2 of Indian Heritage. A scientist, who was born and raised in India, currently living in the UK.

7.5.5 Participants' profiles

A total of 12 older adults were recruited and observed—six of English heritage: four women (age between 83 and 93), and two men (age 79 and 83), and six of Indian heritage: four women (age between 60 and 79), and two men (both age 65).

7.5.6 Summary of the process of analysis of the data from the cultural experts

Analysis occurred within each cultural group. We first looked at the data of the common three video clips for each cultural group. We coded and compared the experts' responses. We aimed to answer the following questions:

a. Did the two experts in each of the cultural groups identified the same or similar cultural cues when they watched their three common video clips?
b. What other cultural cues did the experts identify in the non-common video clips?
c. What were the similarities and differences in the cultural explanations they provided about the cues?

We then compared the findings of the video clips from the experts, with the "pen and paper" observation data collected by the researchers. We should note at this point that neither of the researchers are of English or Indian heritage but have lived in the UK for many years and are experts in transcultural nursing and cultural competence.

We used a similar approach for the rest of the data (six different video clips per expert per group). We coded the expert responses and we compared them with the "pen and paper" observation data collected by the researchers. In this comparative analysis, we aimed to answer the following questions:

a. What cultural cues did the experts observe in the video clips that the researchers did not observe?
b. How did the cultural explanations the experts provided for the cultural cues compared with those given by the researchers?

7.6 Summary of selected example results

The following text provides some examples of the findings.

7.6.1 Common videos: Indian experts

7.6.1.1 Triggers

Overall, the two experts recorded similar answers which provided peer validation for this analysis. The most common trigger was "the recollection of past events," and it was followed by "the participation in a religious ceremony."

7.6.1.2 Behaviors

"Nodding" was a common element for the expression of cooperation and showing interest. Expressions of cooperation were captured by the use of words such as "complimenting" and "were discussing." Expressions of "happiness and contentment" were captured by clapping, engaging, responding, and smiling. "Annoyance/irritation" was noted through facial expressions.

7.6.2 Noncommon videos: Indian experts

7.6.2.1 Triggers

All the triggers were grouped in the following four main categories of triggers: a) *festival/custom* category which includes references to traditional music, or prayers or dancing and other customs such as dressing; b) *food* which includes references to meals or special dishes, c) *memories*, which includes references to events that happened in the past; and d) *environment*, which was associated with noises, unexpected interruptions, and so on.

7.6.2.2 Behaviors

Regarding the behaviors associated with feelings/values/attitudes enacted by the participants, the researchers agreed that the following were described by both the experts: "Happiness," "Pride," *and* "Patience." The behavior of "happiness" was mainly expressed by the participants' smile, while the notion of "patience" was by taking the time to answer questions and give explanations, and the expression of "pride" by the participation in a variety of customs (e.g., eating with hands, wearing saree, their family, their country, etc.).

7.6.3 Examples from the English expert

7.6.3.1 *Triggers*

The English experts captured various triggers which were grouped by the researchers in the following main categories: (a) *food* (e.g., special dishes), (b) *environment* (e.g., noise, unwanted activities), and (c) *social expectations* (e.g., etiquette*)*.

7.6.3.2 *Behaviors*

The behaviors associated with "Happiness," "Dignity," *and* "Cooperation" were the main three behaviors in the English group. Happiness was expressed through smiling, dignity by the maintenance of independence and a proper appearance. Cooperation was mainly reported through participation in social activities.

7.7 The ADORE model

To enable the robot to continue utilizing the a priori knowledge installed in its system and to produce and verify new knowledge that does not stereotype cultures and people, we developed the ADORE model to govern the culturally competent behavior of the robot.

The ADORE model enables the robot to obtain culture-specific (and base-line accurate culture generic) information about its user, thus avoiding the use of stereotypical culture-generic information. This is an important acknowledgment that our culture influences our unique identity and behaviors. To avoid damaging misunderstandings due to ignorance, this uniqueness has to be understood and must be respected by others, most importantly those who care for us or provide services to us including robots.

The genesis of the ADORE model derived from the Papadopoulos (2006) theory of transcultural nursing and cultural competence. The ADORE model (Fig. 7.9) underpins the actions, processes, and decisions made by the robot during its interactions with the user. The ADORE components **A**ssess, **D**o, **O**bserve, **R**evise, **E**valuate are dynamic and spiral in nature. Each component is applied to every action/process/decision, followed by the application of the next component and so on, until the evaluation component is applied which forms the completion of a cycle. The evaluations inform the next cycle with the components spiraling again as another decision/action/processes is considered. Cyclic models are very common in Robotics for the production of a behavior that improves over time; they are also referred to as closed-loop models. In brief, the ADORE model expects the robot to:

- **ASSESS** a topic of discussion, a goal, a norm, a qualitative behavior, and a quantitative parameter, with **Cultural Awareness, Knowledge, and Sensitivity;**
- **DO** or perform any actions required for a topic of discussion, a goal, a norm, a qualitative behavior, and a quantitative parameter, with dignity and **Culturally Competent Compassion;**
- **OBSERVE** the enactment or implementation of a topic of discussion, a goal, a norm, a qualitative behavior, and a quantitative parameter, with **Cultural Awareness** at Conscious (visible) levels; observe responses to triggers of the subconscious (invisible) level;

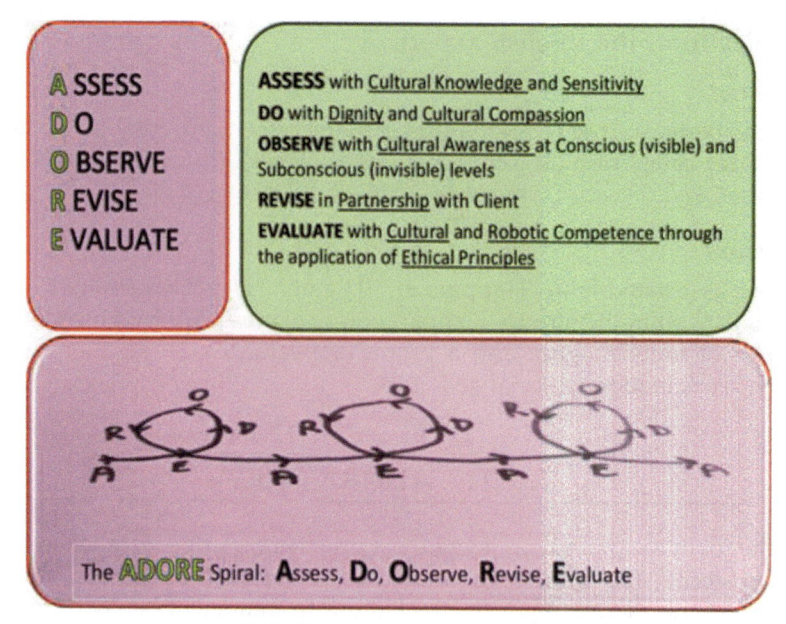

FIGURE 7.9 The ADORE model.

> **REVISE**, if needed, the action/performance of a topic of discussion, a goal, a norm, a qualitative behavior, and a quantitative parameter, in **partnership** with the client;
> **EVALUATE** the impact of the implementation of a topic of discussion, a goal, a norm, a qualitative behavior, and a quantitative parameter, with **Cultural and Robotic Competence** through the application of ethical principles.

7.8 Examples of the final guidelines produced

In this chapter, we have introduced many terms such as categories, components, elements, steps, triggers, definitions, and many more. To make sense of the following sections, we ask you to revisit Fig. 7.1 which provides a visual representation of all processes and outputs described in this chapter. Please also pay a return visit to the section titled "primary purpose of guidelines" to remind yourselves of the meaning of the key knowledge domains used in the construction of the guidelines. These are (A) Topics of conversation, (B) Goals, (C) Qualitative Behaviors, (D) Quantitative Parameters, and (E) Norms.

At the beginning of this chapter, we introduced an example of the guidelines for the knowledge domain of "topics of conversation." Here we provide a list of suggested "topics of conversation," and further down we provide a suggested list of items for the remaining domains followed by examples of guidelines for each of the domains (Tables 7.2, 7.3, 7.5–7.10).

TABLE 7.2 Suggested topics of conversation for guideline development.

Indian group	English group
Family	Family
User	User
Health	Health
Indian films	Weather
Indian festivals and religious ceremonies	Hobbies/Clubs
Marriage	English festivals and religious ceremonies
Indian cuisine/cooking	Travel and holidays
Indian music	TV and cinema
Yoga and meditation	Meal routines
Praying	British history/the empire/2nd WW
Health and ayurveda	The royal family
Indian singing group	Work related
Talk about past events	Pets

TABLE 7.3 Suggested goals for guideline development.

	Indian group	English group
Morning each day	To assist with dressing Having breakfast	To assist with dressing Having breakfast Feeding a pet
Mid-morning, everyday	Health promotion activities: Light yoga/breathing exercises Memory games Hobbies	Health promotion activities: Walk in the garden Light exercise Memory games
Mid-afternoon	Praying/meditating Calling family Reminders for health-related activity	Hobbies Reminders for health-related activity
Lunch time every day	Accompanying to and from dining room Menu options Having lunch Beverage preference Something sweet after main course Observing for safety	Accompanying to and from dining room Menu options Having lunch Beverage preference Something sweet after main course Observing for safety
Religious/Cultural festivals	Preparing for Diwali Preparing for Holi Planning for independence day Preparing for new Year's eve and day	Preparing for Christmas Preparing for new Year's eve and day
Entertainment	Choosing a movie	Choosing a movie Entertain friends with music
Evening	To ensure person has a drink	To ensure person has a drink, Hollywood movies

TABLE 7.4 Goals: The robot will encourage the user to exercise.

No.	Condition	Cultural Group	Rule	Possible Questions	Robot's actions and robot's observable cues	ADORE	Source	Likeliness
1	If mid-morning and not raining	English	To encourage and accompany user to a walk in the garden	What a beautiful day; shall we go for a walk in the garden. Would you like to hold my hand?	Follow the speed of the user. Extend hand and offer to user	Asses +Do+ Evaluate	S+O	High
2	If mid-morning	Indian	To encourage and help user perform light yoga exercises	Would you like to do some breathing and stretching exercises?	Robot gives instructions to user for example: Please close your eyes, breath in and hold your breath for a few seconds. Now breathe out slowly.	Do	S+CC	High

TABLE 7.5 Suggested qualitative behaviors for guideline development.

Explore differences on all groups on the following behaviors:	
Eye contact	Greeting
Head nodding	Enactment of distress
Hand gestures	Enactment of compassion
Body posture	Enactment of love
Touch	Enactment of suffering and pain
Time orientation	Enactment of anger
Enacting privacy	Enactment of fear
Tone of voice	Enactment of happiness
Asking for confirmation	Receiving an object
Enactment of friendship	Enactment of sadness
Enactment of respect	Enactment of pride
Silence	Enactment of dignity
Enactment of patience	Enactment of cooperation

7.8 Examples of the final guidelines produced

TABLE 7.6 Qualitative behaviors: Enactment of suffering and pain.

No	Condition	Cultural Group	Rule	Possible Questions	Robot's actions and robot's observable cues	ADORE	Source	Likeliness
1	If a person expresses that is not very well or when show signs that the person is suffering	Indian	Ask how to be helpful	I see you are not feeling very well Will I stay here close to you? Would you like me to call the family?	Use soft tone of voice and low volume Bow head to show empathy Stay in the room quietly Make a phone call to the family Help the person to pray (bring prayer book / scented stick)	Assess + Do +Observe +Revise +Evaluate	L + O	High
2	If the person expresses that is not very well or when they show signs that the person is suffering	English	Relieve pain	Would you like a tablet for the pain?	Ask the carer to bring a glass of water and pain medication Ask carer to make tea Offer to bring a blanket/pillow Put hand on shoulder to show compassion	Assess + Do +Observe +Revise +Evaluate	L + O	High

TABLE 7.7 Suggested quantitative parameters for guideline development.

	Explore differences on the following parameters:
Volume	Value in a scale from 0% to 100%
Proxemics	Distance from person during interaction = x (measured in meters)
Speed	Velocity while moving = x (meters/sec)
Frequency of jokes/use of humor	Frequency of jokes while talking = x/y sentences (e.g., 1 over 10 sentences is a joke)
Silence	Duration of silences while speaking.
Duration of pauses while talking	Duration of pauses while speaking.
Eye contact	Frequency of eye contact during interaction = eye contact seconds/interaction time (e.g., the robot keeps eye contact 1/3 of the time)

TABLE 7.8 Quantitative parameters: Volume while talking.

No	Condition	Cultural Group	Rule	Possible Questions	Robot's actions	ADORE	Source	Likeliness
1	Default value	All groups	Start at 50%	N/A	N/A	Do	CS	Certain
2	After saying hello/introduction	All groups	Ask the user whether the volume is appropriate	Can you hear me? Would you like me to speak louder? Would you like me to speak softer?	Robot responds accordingly	Assess + Do +Revise +Evaluate	CS	High
4	During prayer	Indian	Low volume	N/A	If the robot needs to say something, does so in a low voice	Do	CS	High

TABLE 7.9 Suggested norms for guideline development

Examples of norms for all cultural groups	• Asking for confirmation • Assessing before doing something • Evaluating after an action • Observing for safety • Replying to person using polite language • Raising the alarm in an emergency • Avoiding certain situations (e.g., foods, interrupting people, asking before entering a room, avoid entering bathroom, etc.)
Examples of norms for the Indian group	• Do not offer beef to Hindus • Do not greet an Indian woman with an embrace and kiss unless close member of family • Remove shoes when entering an Indian household • Do not call an older Indian woman or man by their first name • Provide a female chaperon when a male doctor is examining an Indian woman • Do not swear in front of older Indian people
Examples of norms for the English group	• Do not ask personal or intimate questions (e.g., about finances, family details, sexuality, etc.) • Older people respect the royal family • Offer older people tea rather than coffee • Older people prefer strangers to address them as Mr.... or Mrs.... • Always use "please," "thank you," and "excuse me" • Standing in line (queuing) and waiting patiently for your turn is expected • Do not speak with your mouth full of food

TABLE 7.10 Example of guidelines for Norms.

Condition	Cultural Group	Rule	Possible Questions	Robot's actions	ADORE	Source	Likeliness
Always	All groups	Asks for confirmation before doing something	Shall I walk with you to the lunch table?	Take the required action	Do	S	High
Always	All groups	Assess before doing something		Respond appropriately	Assess	CC	Certain
Always	English	Avoid asking intimate, private questions	N/A	If person shares something private about their family the robot just nods without asking any questions or commenting	Do	O +CC	High
If not a close friend of a family member or if a stranger	Indian	Avoid greeting with a hug/embrace and/or kiss	N/A	N/A	Evaluate + Do	S+O	Certain

7.9 Evaluation of the videoed encounters of robot with actor-users

Following the preparation of the guidelines we conducted an online evaluation of them to ensure that they realistically represented the cultures for which they were written. We created mock videos depicting the robot interacting with amateur actors playing the role of older users enacting scenarios which mimicked real life. It is important to clarify at this point that after the evaluation presented in this section was conducted, the guidelines were refined as needed and validated during a randomised trial (see Chapter 10) with care home residents.

7.9.1 Creating short scripts

We wrote six short dialogue scripts capturing everyday activities that could potentially occur between an older person of English and Indian heritage and the robot. We created scenarios for both men and women and our goal was for the scripts to present a culturally competent interaction between the robot and an older person based on the preliminary guidelines.

7.9.2 Online evaluation platform

The videos were uploaded on the Internet but were not publicly visible. We used Google Forms as the platform for circulating the videos for the online evaluation. All evaluation data were collected anonymously by providing participants the online link and without requiring them to provide personal sensitive information.

7.9.3 Evaluation questionnaire

A short evaluation questionnaire was included at the end of the videos to capture the opinions of older adults after viewing the "robot-actor/user interactions." Our goal was to capture whether the older adults considered the robot's interactions with the user as culturally appropriate and sensitive. The questions were scored on a visual analogue scale ranging from 1(lowest score) to 10 (highest score).

7.9.4 Data collection

We aimed to collect at least five responses for each video. We used a snowballing sampling method.

The questionnaire content is provided here (we use the Indian culture here. The questions for the English culture were the same).

1. How unique and specific is the story to the Indian culture?
   1_____10
   Not at all specific   Specific

2. Were the robot's reactions appropriate to the person's culture?
   1_____10
   Not at all appropriate   Appropriate

3. Were the robot's reactions sensitive to the person's culture?
   1_____10
   Not at all sensitive   Sensitive

4. Did the robot assess the situation in an appropriate and acceptable way for the Indian culture?
   1_____10
   No   Yes

5. Now think of the Indian lady; select from the list below all the behaviors/feelings/values that you think she displays and mark with an X.
   a. Happiness
   b. Enjoyment
   c. Disappointment
   d. Sadness
   e. Anger
   f. Frustration
   g. Patience
   h. Suffering
   i. Fear
   j. Compassion
   k. Cooperation
   l. Annoyance
   m. Other (please specify) ─────────────────────────────

6. Now tell us something about yourself. WE DO NOT NEED YOUR NAME.
   Female ☐
   Male ☐
   Other ☐

7. What is your age: ──────────────────────── (please enter the number here)

8. What is your ethnic group: ──────────────────────── (please enter here)

7.9.5 Comment on the results

The evaluation results were very encouraging. Briefly the results were:

We received 17 evaluations for the Indian-robot videos, 15 for the English-robot videos. Both men and women provided their views on the videos. Of the Indian participants 88.23% said that the story they viewed was specific enough (scores ≥ 6) to the Indian culture, whilst 73.33% of the English participants reported that the story was specific enough (scores ≥ 6) to the English culture. When rating the robot's reactions to the person's culture, 94.12% of the Indian participants said that it was appropriate enough (scores ≥ 6) to the Indian culture, and 79.97%, of the English participants reported that it was appropriate for the English culture. All Indian participants (100%) thought that the robot's reactions were sensitive enough (scores ≥ 6) to the Indian culture, whilst 53.32%, English participants considered them sensitive enough for the English culture.

The evaluators had no trouble selecting different displayed behaviors/feelings/values across all cultures.

7.10 Conclusions

7.10.1 Were our methods appropriate and effective?

Our methods were guided by a strong theoretical framework which provided a solid foundation to our investigation and the development of the tools (tool 1, tool 2, and the cultural experts' "analysis tool") used in the observation study.

Using "paper and pen" observations and engaging cultural experts to supply the analysis of the video recordings provided the necessary triangulation of data. It is well documented that the conduct of observations has inherent risk for biases. One must consider, for example, the role of the researchers. How our presence (the researchers) in the field might influence people's interactions and their reactions. In addition, we need to be aware of our own heritage and experiences and be mindful of the fact that our own cultural lenses influence our interpretations. Our methods were appropriate for addressing these risks. Firstly, multiple facilities were visited. The 12 participants were recruited from four different facilities and all participants were observed multiple times. In addition, we spent a considerable amount of time in each facility developing trusting relationships with participants and staff. We were always available to answer questions, explain our role, and use appropriate and discreet ways during observations. We kept reflective logs, debriefed after observation visits and discussed our interpretations.

Tools 1 and 2 were helpful in focusing our observations. Our eyes were looking for the participant's reactions to simple everyday events. What was difficult was the task of "counting the frequency" of verbal or nonverbal communication codes in Tool 1 during the on-site observations. On reflection, the form could be simplified. It could be easier to capture the presence or absence of the behaviors and use more qualitative codes for the frequency such as "never"/"often"/"some of the time"/"most of the time"/"always." On the other hand, using the experts' analysis form to code behaviors from a video recording is easier as the coder/evaluator can stop/start the recording.

Furthermore, the approach of capturing unstructured everyday snapshots was effective in providing long enough and rich enough video footage that led to a catalog of smaller video clips that were viewed by the experts. Our experts did not have difficulties using the analysis tool and commented positively on the number of videos that they had to watch and stated that they found the task interesting and intriguing.

7.10.2 Does what we learned enabled us to identify and make the changes to the basic guidelines in a significant way?

The numerous steps and methods described in this chapter enabled us to produce a large number of comprehensive guidelines—which of course are not exhaustive for the English or the Indian culture—which were tested in the randomized trial described in Chapter 10.

Without overstating the findings from the observation study and the subsequent on-line evaluation both of which provided enough evidence to confirm our hypothesis that cultural expressions can be small and subtle but essential components of a person's cultural identity and should not be overlooked. This is an area which demands further research.

All the processes described in this chapter enabled the development and refinement of guidelines for the programming of culturally competent socially asstivie robots.

7.10.3 Finally…

Overall, we believe that this cultural approach will definitely shape future work in this field, especially as the robot's capabilities expand. Current robots have limited capabilities to recognize and process human behaviors but we strongly believe that our work has provided an in depth understanding of the cultural influences on behavior which are critical for the work on human−robot interaction.

7.11 Reflective questions

1. What aspects of this chapter did you find useful and why?
2. Reflect on some of the largely subconscious components of your culture and record how these have influenced your behavior when you became conscious of them.
3. Using the knowledge domain of "goals" and referring to the example in Table 7.4. Please complete the columns of the table on the goal of: "choosing a movie."

References

Blanchard, E. G., & Allard, D. (2010). *Handbook of research on culturally-aware information technology: Perspectives and models* (pp. 1−665). Canada: IGI Global. https://doi.org/10.4018/978-1-61520-883-8

Bossard, J. H. S., & Boll, E. S. (1950). *Ritual in family living*. Westport, CT: Greenwood Press.

Brown, E. D., & Low, C. M. (2008). Chaotic living conditions and sleep problems associated with children's responses to academic challenge. *Journal of Family Psychology, 22*(6), 920−923.

Caris-Verhallen, W., Kerkstra, A., & Bensing, J. M. (1999). Non-verbal behavior in nurse-elderly patient communication. *Journal of Advanced Nursing, 29*(4), 808−818.

Caris-Verhallen, W., Timmermans, L., & van Dulmen, S. (2004). Observation of nurse-patient interaction in oncology: Review of assessment instruments. *Patient Education and Counseling, 54*, 307−320.

Coan, J. A., & Gottman, J. M. (2007). The specific affect coding system (SPAFF). In J. A. Coan, & J. J. B. Allen (Eds.), *Handbook of Emotion Elicitation and Assessment* (pp. 267−285). Oxford: Oxford University Press.

Ekman, P., Friesen, W. V., & Hager, J. C. (2002). *FACS investigator's guide* (p. 96). A Human Face.

Endrass, B., Hall, L., Hume, C., Tazzyman, S., & André, E. (2014). A pictorial interaction language for children to communicate with cultural virtual characters. In *International conference on human-computer interaction 2014 June 22* (pp. 532−543). Cham: Springer.

Fiese, B. H. (2006). *Family routines and rituals, Current perspectives in psychology*. New Haven, CT: Yale University Press.

Gregory, A. M., Eley, T. C., O'Connor, T. G., Rijsdijk, F. V., & Plomin, R. (2005). Family influences on the association between sleep problems and anxiety in a large sample of pre-school aged twins. *Personality and Individual Differences, 39*, 1337−1348.

Guinter, M. A., Park, Y. M., Steck, S. E., & Sandler, D. P. (2020). Day-to-day regularity in breakfast consumption is associated with weight status in a prospective cohort of women. *International Journal of Obesity, 44*(1), 186−194.

Hall, E. T. (1976). *Beyond culture*. Norwell, MA: Anchor.

Hofstede, G., Hofstede, G. J., & Minkov, M. (1991). *Cultures and organizations: Software of the mind* (Vol. 2). New York, NY: McGraw-Hill.

Koulouglioti, C., Cole, R., Moskow, M., McQuillan, B., Carno, M. A., & Grape, A. (2014). The longitudinal association of young children's everyday routines to sleep duration. *Journal of Pediatric Health Care, 28*(1), 80−87.

McDuff, D., Girard, J. M., & Kaliouby, R. (2017). Large-scale observational evidence of cross-cultural differences in facial behavior. *Journal of Nonverbal Behavior, 1*, 1−14.

O'Neill-Brown, P. (1997). Setting the stage for the culturally adaptive agent. In K. Dautenhahn (Ed.), *FS-97-02. AAAI Technical Report FS-97-02. Compilation* (pp. 93−97). Menlo Park, California: The AAAI Press.

Papadopoulos, I. (Ed.). (2006). *Transcultural health and social care: Development of culturally competent practitioners*. Edinburgh: Churchill Livingstone Elsevier.

Papadopoulos, I., & Lees, S. (2002). Developing culturally competent researchers. *Journal of Advanced Nursing, 37*(No. 3), 258−264.

Papadopoulos, I., Tilki, M., & Taylor, G. (1998). *Transcultural care. A guide for health care professionals*. Dinton: Quay Publications.

Roter, D. L., & Hall, J. A. (1992). *Doctors talking to patients/patients talking with doctors: Improving communication in medical visits*. Westport, CT: Auburn House.

Schouten, B., & Schinkel, S. (2015). Emotions in primary care: Are there cultural differences in the expression of cues and concerns? *Patient Education and Counseling, 98*, 1346–1351.

CHAPTER 8

From guidelines to culturally competent artificial intelligence

Antonio Sgorbissa

DIBRIS Department, Università degli Studi di Genova, Genova, Italy

LEARNING OBJECTIVES

- To become aware of some of the most popular knowledge representation techniques, aiming to represent knowledge in a formal language that an Artificial Intelligence (AI) program can process.

- To understand the fundamental mechanisms to store knowledge using computer ontologies and perform probabilistic reasoning about known and unknown facts using Bayesian networks.

- To understand how cultural competence can be embedded into an AI program that encodes guidelines provided by transcultural nursing experts, using the CARESSES system as a case study.

- To understand the fundamental mechanisms to make the robot interact verbally and nonverbally with people by considering cultural differences and learning personal preferences to avoid stereotyped representations.

8.1 Introduction

"Does the robot know how to do this?" "The robot knows that I am doing that." "The robot doesn't know how to do that; therefore, it is searching on the Internet for it."

Knowledge plays a crucial role in all activities of our life. We may know or not know how to do things, we may know or not know how to answer a question, we may know or not know how to deal with people. Everything that implies an intentional act relies on some sort of knowledge. According to the online Oxford Dictionary, knowledge is "the information, understanding, and skills that you gain through education or experience."

Given these premises, we start by describing two of the most popular technologies commonly used in Artificial Intelligence (AI) for knowledge representation: Ontologies (Gruber, 1995) and Bayesian Networks (Pearl, 2000). Here, we will explain the basic principles of how they work. In the following sections, we will discuss how these technologies can provide the basis to embed a social robot with the required cultural knowledge to behave culturally competently according to the guidelines presented in previous Chapters 6 and 7.

The reader may be surprised that we are not mentioning Neural Networks in this chapter, given society's great expectations for Deep Learning applications (Schmidhuber, 2015). This choice is arbitrary and follows the motivations that have been presented in the last part of Chapter 2 and the fact that the CARESSES project will be presented as a case study to clarify key concepts. Due to the limited space, we will emphasize the technological solutions adopted in CARESSES.

8.2 Representing knowledge

8.2.1 Ontologies from parmenides to artificial intelligence

We said that knowledge plays a crucial role in doing things: knowing the correct phone number is a mandatory requirement for making a phone call, but also activities such as walking, picking an object from the floor, or riding a bicycle require knowledge. The difference between "knowing phone numbers" and "knowing how to ride a bike" is that phone numbers are expressed in "symbolic form": knowledge of this kind can be easily stored and communicated by using symbols, digits in this case. Conversely, the knowledge required to ride a bike cannot be easily described using symbols. In principle, we might record the exact movements of all the joints of a person riding a bike, all the forces and momentum applied versus time, etc., and transform them in a sequence of numbers to be stored somewhere. Motion capture systems adopt this approach for creating Computer Generated Imagery (CGI) characters in movies. For instance, Gollum in "The Lord of the Rings" movie series was "created" by placing markers all over the body of the actor Andy Serkis and recording his exact movements, later processed by software for CGI animation. However, this works only with movies, since the detailed description of all the movements performed by a cyclist is not the knowledge used by the cyclist to ride his or her bicycle: nobody rides a bike by replicating prestored movements in a cyclic pattern. Not even a robot might work in that way: any minimum error or environmental change, for example, a slippery road or a sudden gust of wind, would likely produce a fall if a more robust mechanism to generate in real time the right movements that may restore the balance is absent. Finally, notice that, even in the case of motion capture for CGI animation, the sequence of numbers that we are using to describe the actors' movements is just an approximation of their actual movements in the real world. When we describe some aspect of the world using numbers or other symbols and mathematical or logical relationships between them, we say that we create a "model" of that particular aspect of the world. If the knowledge to be stored is a list of phone numbers, the situation is different: phone numbers are already composed of symbols. We might say that, in this case, the model to represent phone numbers corresponds exactly to actual phone numbers as they are in the real world.

It is not a surprise that there are not many situations as easy as modeling phone numbers. Typically, building a world model is easy when describing "codes" that humans have invented: car plates, passport IDs, people names, brands, etc., are intrinsically symbolic. However, in most situations, knowledge is not already available in symbolic form, and an effort to build a model of what we know is almost always required. The way to develop models of the world has been one of the preferred subjects of investigation in philosophy since its birth: later, it has become one of the most crucial research areas in AI and, more generally, Computer Science. Starting from the Greek philosopher Parmenides (515 BCE−450 BCE), many philosophers addressed the problem of defining "what is" (the Greek word, ὄν—being or existence, in Latin characters "on"). After that, philosophers moved to the definition of the possible categories of "being" and their attributes, a problem that the Greek philosopher Aristotle (384 BCE−322 BCE) addressed with the true spirit of a "knowledge engineer." Notice that the concept of "being" or, in Ancient Greek, "on" is at the basis of the term "Ontology," the branch of philosophy that studies reality: what exists, what are the attributes of things that exist, and the mutual relations between them. The word Ontology was first used by the German philosopher and pedagogue Jacob Lorhard (1561−1609) in his work Ogdoas Scholastica (1606), even if the interest for these studies dates back to Parmenides. More relevant for the scope of this book, the term Ontology has recently become popular in Computer Science; however, computer scientists use this term not to refer to the philosophical study of what exists and its categories but to a computer-understandable model of the world that is appropriate to describe the relevant aspects for a given application. Ontology is a countable noun for a computer scientist: you will likely hear computer scientists talking about "an Ontology," meaning some formal representation that they can use to store the knowledge required by an AI program to work.

These concepts may be better explained through an example. Think about the room in which you are now (if you are in a room, otherwise please imagine it): there may be chairs, a table or a desk, walls … or a bed if you are in a bedroom. The table can be of wood, plastic, or metal, and the same is probably true for your chair. The table has probably four legs unless you are sitting in a café in Paris, whereas the chair may have four legs or wheels, in case it is an office chair. These are just some of the things that exist in the small part of the world you are in now. The right way to describe knowledge of this kind is one of the problems that the branch of philosophy called Ontology may address; a formal description of the things around you and their mutual relationships would be called an Ontology by Computer Scientists.

But how is a computer Ontology built?

For instance, one may start by considering that the table I have in my kitchen is only one of the possible tables: other kinds of tables are office tables, café tables, séance tables, etc. All tables share some common properties related to their shape and, even more, to their functionality: however, they are also different from each other, for instance, in their dimensions and weight. Suppose I think about a "kitchen table": a different mental image appears in my mind than a "café table," and this mental image will likely impact my plans to look for a friend to help me move the table from one place to another place. An excellent way of representing this idea is to assume a general concept called "table," and then define "kitchen table," "café table," and "séance table" as particular cases, which we will also refer to as "children" or "subconcepts" of "table," Fig. 8.1. It shall be pretty straightforward to replicate this process for all objects in the room, for instance, chairs: for sure, there are different kinds of chairs, and all of them can be represented as children of the generic concept "chair." Please notice that the drawing in Fig. 8.1 is

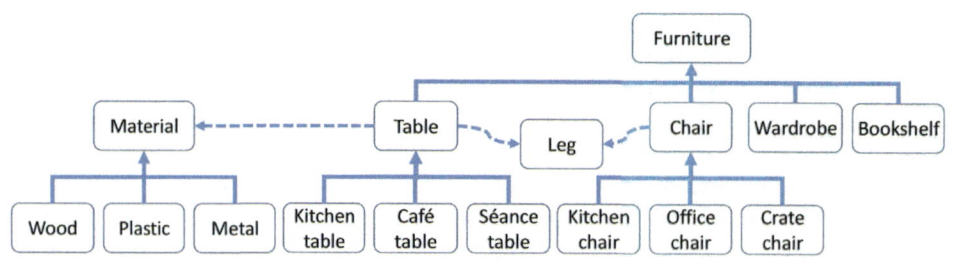

FIGURE 8.1 A computer ontology representing concepts and relationships between concepts.

not a flowchart, and therefore it is entirely different from the sketches that have been shown in Chapter 2 to represent computer programs. In Ontologies, there is no flow of execution since there is no computer program to be executed: an Ontology is a static representation showing what exists in a given domain and mutual relationships between things that exist.

We can say something more about chairs. Suppose we focus on the functionalities of chairs, that is, the fact that they afford people to sit on them, and not on the fact that chair factories produced them: then, even a crate can be a chair. Only a few guests would complain if they are asked to sit on a crate, perhaps in a postindustrial style apartment, because a crate used as a chair is definitely a chair, isn't it? There may be some discussion among philosophers and knowledge engineers regarding this claim. Assessing the most appropriate position of each concept in the taxonomy is an arduous task, and some relationships may be less intuitive than others (or be different in different cultures, thus making the whole process more complex). However, we are confident that the idea of considering a "Crate chair" as a particular kind of chair may not look that absurd. Finally, one could observe that both a "Table" and a "Chair" are nothing more than "Furniture," a characteristic they share with a "Wardrobe" or a "Bookshelf," Fig. 8.1.

Parent–child relationships (also referred to as "is-a" relationships, as they allow to express the concept "a table is-a type of furniture") are not the only possibility: for instance, one may observe that both tables and chairs have legs. This observation may lead to the idea of representing in the Ontology the concept "Leg," and then establishing a relationship between "Table" and "Chair" on the one side, and "Leg" on the other side: in this case, the relationship is not between a concept and its children, but rather it describes a property of tables and chairs, that is, the property of "having legs." Property relationships, differently from parent–child relationships, have not a unique name or meaning: the same concept may have heterogeneous properties such as, in the case of a table, the fact of having legs, the material it is made of, its dimensions, or its weight. Despite their different meaning, it is common to call all these properties using the prefix "has-N," where "N" is an arbitrary number. We will likely say that "Table" has the property "has-1-material" that relates it to the concept "Material," which may then be specialized into different kinds of materials; a property "has-4-leg" that links "Table" to the concept "Leg," and so on. In Fig. 8.1, "is-a" parent–child relationships are shown as thick arrows; "has-N" properties are shown as dashed arrows.

This is almost everything we need for now. The knowledge encoded in the Ontology might also be written using a different, nongraphic formalism. For instance, we might use a logic language called Description Logics (Baader et al., 2007), its implementation called Ontology Web Language OWL2 (Grau et al., 2008), or its equivalent language used by Protégé, a popular tool for the design of OWL2 Ontologies that we welcome you to try[1]. Sentences look different in these languages, but they convey the same meaning. Very importantly, once we have created an Ontology as the one in Fig. 8.1 or its text-based equivalent, we may claim that we have created a "vocabulary," which defines concepts based on other concepts: a description in this vocabulary might sound like "a table is a kind of furniture which has a tabletop, legs, a material, a dimension and a weight" (some of these elements are not shown in the figure). Researchers refer to this vocabulary as the Terminological Box (or TBox) of the Ontology.

Second, it is crucial to understand the implications of the taxonomy of concepts represented in Fig. 8.1. If a parent–child relationship exists in the Ontology between two concepts, it is assumed that the child concept inherits all properties of the parent concept. Think about the concepts "Table" (the parent) and "Café table" (the child): "Café table" is obviously made of some material and has legs, and this follows the fact that a "Café table" is indeed a "Table," which is characterized by having those properties. Something exciting happens when encoding knowledge using an Ontology language: the formalism does not need to explicitly replicate for the child all the properties that have been declared for the parent since it is implicitly assumed that the child will inherit all the properties. This tremendously increases the expressiveness of the Ontology.

Third, Ontologies are typically designed by hand by humans: by keeping on with the same formalism we just used for tables and chairs, we might jokingly say that the design of Ontologies requires a particular child of the "Human" concept known as "Computer scientist" or, better, "Knowledge Engineer." Recently, research has explored the possibility of automatically creating Ontologies starting from text written in natural language, for example, books, websites, or social media (Cimiano, 2006). However, knowledge learning is quite a complex task to be automated because it ideally requires a computer program to understand the meaning of the text to be extracted. As such, we will ignore automatic Ontology learning by suggesting that, in our view, humans are the ones that shall translate knowledge written in natural language, that is, the language they use to communicate, to the language used by computer Ontologies. Since, differently from natural language, Ontologies are written in a formal language without ambiguities, they can be easily processed and understood by a robot, which can use the knowledge stored therein to do valuable things. What makes this idea appealing is that the result will be easily understandable both by humans and robots.

Fourth, it is essential to remember that Ontologies, like any description made in any language, are just a model of reality and not reality. We will not venture into a debate about the "true nature of things": still, we have to admit that we feel very uncomfortable to claim that there exist things that can be unambiguously classified as chairs or tables out there in the real world. Instead, we think that such words as "chair" or "table" are required by humans as basic bricks for communication and problem solving, but they are once again the results of a "modeling" process, that is, aimed at providing a simplified description that can be used to talk about the world. Without emphasizing too much the philosophical side of it, the example of a crate used as a chair may help capture what we are saying. Assigning univocal labels to things in the real world is not always straightforward, precisely because all these labels are an invention of humans to simplify their own lives, but things in the world do not have unambiguous labels in most cases. Computer scientists and knowledge engineers

---

[1] https://protege.stanford.edu/

face this kind of problem every day when trying to encode knowledge into Ontologies, an arduous work requiring a lot of thinking to properly organize things.

8.2.2 Probabilistic knowledge from reverend Bayes to Bayesian networks

Ontologies are not the only available tool to encode knowledge in a way understandable both by humans and by computer programs (or robots). The portfolio of possible tools and languages is vast, each having its peculiarities in terms of expressiveness (i.e., what kind of knowledge can I encode?), reasoning (i.e., what kind of hidden knowledge can I infer starting from the knowledge that was explicitly encoded in the system), and ease of use (i.e., what is the process to encode knowledge, and to what extent can this process be automated?).

According to the classification above, it is a well-known characteristic of Ontologies that they do not deal with knowledge expressed in probabilistic form. Since standard Ontologies come from formal logic, they tend to be quite "Manichaean": things are either true or false[2]. Please remember that formal logic was born to make such inferences as "Socrates is a man; all men are mortal; therefore, Socrates is mortal." In standard Ontology languages, it is not possible to say something like "a crate in the living room of a post-modern apartment has an 80% chance of being a chair." Either we say crates are chairs, or we say they are not: there is no possibility for "it might be," and it is not allowed to assign a numerical probability for an assertion to be true or false. As an aside, please notice that we said "80% chance" instead of "80% probability" because probabilities are typically expressed as values in the range from 0 to 1, where one means that a fact is undoubtedly true and zero means that a fact is surely false. Values in-between zero and one represent different levels of probability: when you flip a coin, you may say you have almost a 0.5 probability that the head comes out (we say "almost" because, once again, we are making an approximate model of how things work).

As the reader can observe, due to the impossibility of talking about probabilities, Ontologies' expressivity turns out to be quite limited if you need to represent uncertain knowledge: this might look like a minor limitation, but, unfortunately, it is a major one. Experience tells us that knowledge about the world is typically uncertain; it doesn't happen very frequently that we are in the condition of making statements that are undoubtedly true under any possible situation. Somebody might argue that the physical world is uncertain and vastly unknown, but this is not a big problem when we talk about facts of everyday life: how often do you use probabilities when discussing with somebody during your day? This argument may look even stronger considering that Ontologies are used to encode our own definitions of concepts: the definition of "Table" should not require us to introduce any probabilistic information as far as we agree on its meaning. A table has legs, a top, and it is made of some material that may be wood, plastic, or even steel: do we really need to say "maybe ..." or "it has a 0.8 probability of ..."? Of course, the example we made earlier in this chapter about the crate used as a chair would benefit from a description using probabilities, but are we really capable of producing many examples like that one? Or, more reasonably, is this "crate-chair-thing" an exception to the more general case in which knowledge is well-defined and can be represented with neither ambiguity nor uncertainty? It is well known that, in the history of

---

[2] Manichaeism is an ancient religion born in the Middle East, that taught a view of the things of the universe as being either completely good or evil, with no option in the middle.

biology, the platypus put naturalists and epistemologists in a severe crisis because of the complexity of classifying it both as a mammal and an animal that lays eggs. But, come on, let's be realistic: how many "platypuses" are there in the world that we want to represent?

It turns out that there are many platypuses around us. Even worse, platypuses tend to happily prosper when we consider the fact that, in the world, there are many different cultures. For instance, "God" is understood by most people in the world, who will use other words in their own languages but would agree on this translation in English. Almost every human being can materialize a mental image of "God" when hearing this word, whether you believe or not in God's existence. But once you start asking people what "God" is, it is very likely that the properties associated with this concept will tend to vary depending on the area of the world in which you ask the question. And what about other, more pragmatic concepts such as "Marriage" and the relationships between "Marriage" and the concept of "Family," "Parent," "Child," "House," "Sex," "Wedding party"? Do all people of the world materialize the same mental image of what a "Wedding party" is? Or take something as simple and familiar as "Bread," or "Coffee," or "Tea": what does an Italian person think when hearing the word "Coffee"? What does an American person think? Suppose you ask an Italian or an American person to draw a "Coffee:" would you get the same picture?

We will come back to this discussion again. For the moment, it is sufficient to say that, when dealing with knowledge expressed in probabilistic form, a popular tool exists for representing such knowledge and reasoning about it: Bayesian Networks (Pearl, 2000), which owe their name to Thomas Bayes (1701–61), an English philosopher and mathematician who laid the foundation of modern probability theory. As Ontologies, Bayesian Networks require defining the most important concepts involved in a given domain. However, in this case, relationships between concepts do not correspond to "is-a" parent–child relationships or "has-N" property relationships but rather express causal relationships between facts.

Probably, the most famous example ever of a Bayesian Network is the one shown in Fig. 8.2, which you may likely find in many introductory handbooks or online tutorials. If

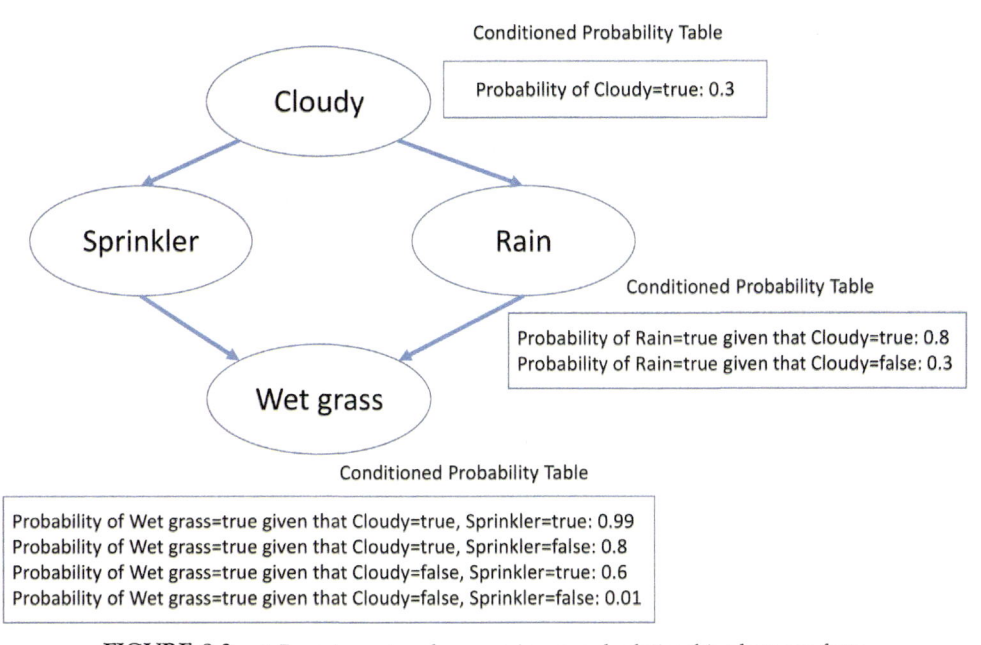

FIGURE 8.2 A Bayesian network expressing causal relationships between facts.

you want to have great fun, you may also download and try a software called Netica[3] and try this and other examples by yourself. As you can easily see from the figure, four facts are involved in this network: these facts are the basic bricks to model the knowledge we have about that portion of reality we want to model. Who decides the basic bricks? As usual, this is a task for application domain experts, who choose the facts represented in the network and their mutual relationships. In this example, we want to represent the fact that the sky can be "Cloudy" or not, which impacts the fact that it may "Rain" or not. However, since we set up a smart "Sprinkler" in our garden, the fact that the sky is cloudy may also have an impact on the fact that the smart sprinkler will be automatically turned on today or not. Finally, the fact that it rained today (or not) and the fact that the sprinkler was turned on (or not) may have an impact on having "Wet grass" or not.

Experts will likely start by representing the fact that the sky can be "Cloudy" in a given day: this is modeled as a binary possibility if we assume that, at any given time, the sky can either be cloudy or not in a given place (whatever "Cloudy" means). Representing facts as binary possibilities is not mandatory in Bayesian Networks. In theory, we might consider that there are three (or more) possible situations concerning the sky: "Clean," "Somehow cloudy," "Very cloudy." However, this does not change the following discussion and, therefore, we stick to the original description in which the sky can either be cloudy or not: we write the two possible events as "Cloudy = true" or "Cloudy = false."

Imagine now that, at a given time, we do not know if the sky is "Cloudy" or not, for example, because we are prisoned in a crate in the cellar. There are multiple usages for crates: this time, our host decided not to use it as a seat but to imprison undesired guests! Then, since we do not know the actual state of the sky because we cannot observe it, we may want to represent it with a probability value. For instance, after asking a weather expert, we might guess that the sky has a 0.3 probability for "Cloudy = true" and a 0.7 probability for "Cloudy = false." This concept can be generalized: what about using the probabilities to represent, at any given time and not only in this very moment, the a priori knowledge we have about the sky being "Cloudy" or not "Cloudy"? What is the probability that tomorrow at 3 p.m. the sky will be "Cloudy"? What about next Monday at noon? This is precisely the purpose of the rectangle close to the "Cloudy" ellipse in Fig. 8.2: it represents the probability that, at any given time, the sky will be in one of the two possible states. Please notice that the rectangle contains only "Probability of Cloudy = true: 0.3" because one of the two mutually exclusive events must necessarily be true, and, therefore, the sum of the two probabilities is always 1: either "Cloudy = true" or "Cloudy = false," which allows us to compute "Probability of Cloudy = false: 0.7". The same happens when flipping a coin, throwing dice, or doing anything else: the probability of all mutually exclusive events must always be one since they cover 100% of the possibilities.

One might argue that the probabilities above are not easy to be computed, as they depend on many factors, including the season and the area of the world in which we are. We will come back soon to the problem of computing probabilities: for the moment, this consideration is helpful to introduce a crucial concept in Bayesian Networks, that is, the idea of "conditioned probability." There is no doubt that things are related to each other and that the probabilities of some facts may depend on different facts. For instance, the probability that it rains in a given area of the world and a given season could be 0.2: however, if we

---

[3] https://www.norsys.com/netica.html

may observe in advance that today is "Cloudy = true," this probability will likely increase. More formally, we say that the probability of "Rain" is conditioned by "Cloudy," and we introduce the concept "Probability of Rain given Cloudy." The word "given" tells us that the second fact conditions the probability of the first fact.

There are a few essential concepts that the reader needs to remember.

First, and similarly to Ontologies, the Bayesian Network structure is typically designed by humans, who know the particular application domain they want to model and define the most important facts and how they relate to each other through cause–effect relationships. However, the probability values are not necessarily chosen by humans but can be automatically learned through observations. For instance, the probability that it will rain given that the sky is cloudy can be simply computed by considering a series of historical data (e.g., in the last year) and by calculating the ratio of times that it rained when the sky was cloudy: this is written as the "Probability of Rain = true given Cloudy = true."

Second, and most importantly, we can use Bayesian Network to reason about facts that a robot observes or does not observe in the real world. Indeed, since the network encodes the knowledge about how a fact is affected by other facts, it can be used to collect information as time passes and draw conclusions about the probability of an unknown fact depending on the observations that have been done up to that moment. Consider the situation that we have no a priori information about the current state of things: we have not observed yet if it is cloudy or not, it rains or not, the sprinkler is on or off, and the grass is wet or not. Even if we do not know these facts for sure, we may know a priori probabilities: as already mentioned, it is sufficient that, during the last year, we recorded how many days the sky was cloudy or not, how many days it rained or not, etc., and we use the ratio of times that an event materialized as the basis to compute probabilities. But suppose now that, at some point, we can make some observation: for instance, from within our crate (we are prisoned in a crate in the cellar, do you remember?), we might hear the sprinkler turning on. This information is no more uncertain: in Bayesian Network terminology, "Sprinkler" is no more a "hidden fact" but an "observed fact." We are now allowed to recompute all the probabilities in the network conditioned by the fact that the sprinkler is on, a piece of information that was not available before. For instance, we might expect the probability that the grass is wet to increase and the probability that the sky is cloudy to decrease, to mention two.

8.3 How to embed cultural competence into robots

8.3.1 Following guidelines to design artificial intelligence programs: knowledge representation without stereotypes

Cultural knowledge is one of the key elements at the core of cultural competence. As it has been already mentioned in Chapters 1 and 5, cultural competence requires culture-awareness (i.e., being aware of the fact that culture permeates our own and other people lives), cultural knowledge (i.e., knowing the aspects of people's lives on which culture has an impact), and cultural sensitivity (i.e., knowing how to interact with people appropriately). However, when implementing the three key elements of cultural competence into an intelligent system, keeping a clear distinction between them is pretty challenging. For the robot, culture-awareness is the direct consequence of taking culture and cultural differences into account and encoding them through a proper formalism for knowledge representation. Cultural sensitivity is the consequence of knowing how to interact with people following guidelines for culturally competent interaction that have been defined by transcultural nursing experts and are, once again, encoded through formal tools for knowledge representation. Therefore, in the following, please keep in mind that cultural knowledge will not only include such concepts as "Table," "Chair," "God," "coffee," and how these concepts might be different in different cultures: instead, it will be extended to include the notion of how such knowledge should be used to interact with people, both verbally and nonverbally, up to the point of encompassing the whole idea of cultural competence.

The key idea to encode cultural knowledge in the system is to exploit the dualism that characterizes Ontologies, typically made of two components: the so-called Terminological Box (TBox) and Assertional Box (ABox). Notice that the connection between cultures and ontologies we propose takes inspiration from the so-called ontological turn that has produced an intense debate in anthropology in the last decades, starting from the seminal work "Thinking Through Things" by Henare, Holbraad, and Wastell (Henare et al., 2006). The interested reader is welcome to have a look at the report about the motion tabled at the 2008 meeting of the group for debates in anthropological theory at the University of Manchester, revolving around the question "Ontology Is Just Another Word for Culture?" (Carrithers et al., 2010).

The TBox is nothing more than what we have described in Section 7.1: a definition of all the relevant concepts in a given domain, together with their mutual relationships. In the case of cultural knowledge, we may want to include not only tables and chairs but also concepts that are more evidently related to culture and cultural differences, such as beliefs, values, or habits. Very importantly, we will put together key concepts in all the cultures considered, possibly including side-by-side concepts that exist only in some cultures: the final vocabulary will be the union of all concepts. For example, after defining "Table," we may want to create the children "Office Table," "Kitchen Table," "Séance Table," "Café table." But also, if needed, we might add "Chinese table" as a child of "Table," or "Chinese Kitchen Table" as a child of "Kitchen Table" and so on. Or we may decide that the children of "Breakfast food" are "Scrambled egg," "Coffee," "Cappuccino," "Tea," "Miso soup," "Natto," "Ham": to this end, we will add side-by-side typical breakfast food in the English, Italian, and Japanese cultures, some of which may be almost unknown to other cultures.

The ABox has never been mentioned before and needs now to be introduced. Unlike the TBox, the ABox is not used to describe concepts but "instances of concepts," also known as "individuals" in Ontologies. To better understand the difference between the two, consider that TBox concepts are sometimes interpreted as "sets" or "classes" of things sharing the same properties: when we mention the concept "Table," we are thinking about the set of all possible tables, that is, all objects that we would be happy to categorize as belonging to the same "Table" class. Things that have the "tableness" or, to put it with ancient Greek Philosophy, concepts corresponding to the Platonic ideal of "Table." Following the same rationale, ABox instances shall be interpreted as specific elements of the set: "the table I have in my kitchen today May 24, 2021" or "the table I have in my office." For example, after defining in the ABox the individual "The mug that my wife gave me as a birthday's present," the ABox is the right place to say that this very mug is on table I have in my office at this very moment.

The dualism between TBox and ABox is very useful in our case because it allows for distinguishing between "the world" (i.e., the TBox, describing the union of all concepts of interest in different cultures) and different "views of the world" (i.e., the ABox, that uses instances to describe how concepts in the TBox are perceived in different cultures). For example, think about the concept of "Breakfast food" and its children: after being encoded as concepts in the TBox, they may be associated with a number N of different instances in the ABox that represent the different attitudes of N different cultures toward "Breakfast food." What is "Breakfast food" for an Italian person? And for a Nigerian person? These multiple "views" of the same concept may simply be encoded through multiple ABox instances of "Breakfast food," one for each different culture. Ideally, we can imagine that, for a given TBox, we will have a number N of ABoxes (we prefer to say "a number N of ABox layers since in each Ontology there should be one TBox and one ABox), one for each of the N cultures we want to represent. All instances belonging to a given ABox layer (say, the Italian ABox layer) express the view of Italian people about all concepts in the TBox. Fig. 8.3 shows this idea: green boxes represent instances corresponding to three different ABox layers, corresponding to the views of an English, Italian, or Japanese person of the same concept.

Before moving forward, we shall make two observations.

First, cultures are not countable: can we really draw the boundaries that define where a culture ends and another culture begins, allowing us to encode one culture in an ABox layer and the other in a different ABox layer? Does an "Italian culture" exist at all, or are there many different cultures whose boundaries are fuzzy? Is it true that the view of the world shared by people in one region of Italy will differ from another region, the view shared by people living in one town will differ from another town in the same region, the view of the world shared by people in one neighborhood will differ from another neighborhood in the same town? How many cultures do we need to describe in the Ontology to allow the robot to interact with people in a culturally competent way?

Second, if we push this rationale to its extreme consequences, isn't it true that everyone is different from others? Perhaps we should focus on "personalization" in Robotics, whereas the concept of "cultural competence" may not be required at all? We know all too well that every attempt to associate a person to a culture incurs the risk of stereotyping. Taking culture into account may help the robot give more appropriate suggestions and behave more appropriately, but this works only in a probabilistic sense: guessing that an Italian person may like coffee or cappuccino for breakfast has more chance to succeed than assuming that the same person likes

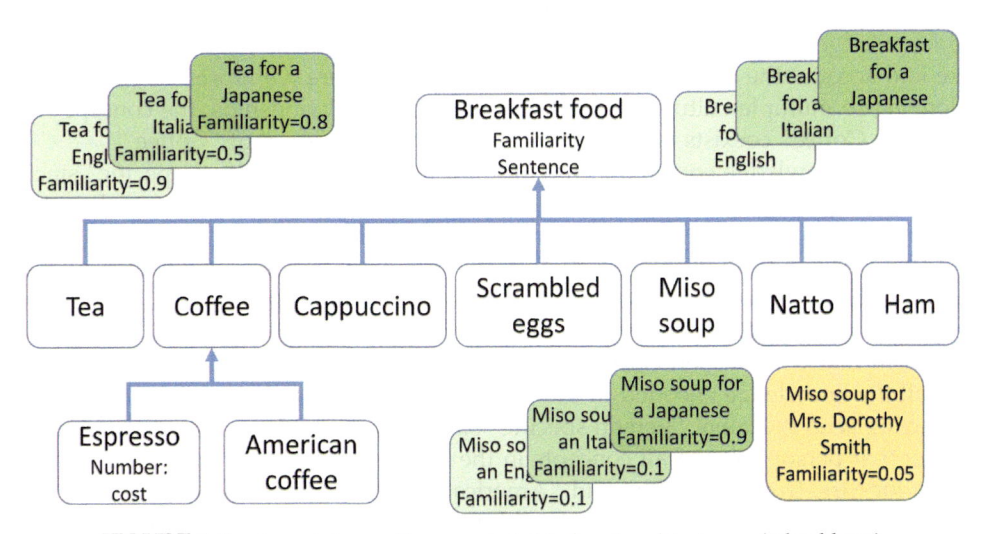

FIGURE 8.3 An ontology with concepts (*white boxes*) and instances (*colored boxes*).

having Japanese miso soup or natto, but this is not 100% safe. As discussed earlier in this chapter, associating a culture to a person corresponds to making a model of that person, which is approximate by its nature. When we make assumptions about what is most appropriate for a person depending on "how this person is expected to work," we will necessarily fail sooner or later. Of course, there are different ways of building such a model, as discussed in the previous paragraph. For instance, we can choose to model Italians "as if" they shared a common view of the world, or we can choose to model people living in Genova "as if" they shared a common view. The second representation is a "higher resolution" way of stereotyping because there are more chances that people living in Genova will have some points in common, but it is still stereotyping. The only way to avoid stereotyping would be to develop a fully personalized system that "knows" the person and is specialized in interacting in the best possible way with this very person. As an aside, this is what typically happens with humans: knowing other people's cultural background may initially help but, after we become close with somebody, knowing them becomes more relevant than knowing their cultural background. Unfortunately, adapting the robot behavior to a specific person requires a long time for learning: taking decisions based on the culture that the person identifies with, despite all limitations, provides a very efficient shortcut to start doing the right things as soon as possible.

In line with the observations above, please notice that using ABox layers to encode different "views" of the world, one is not constrained to represent cultures at the national level. The same mechanism can be used to represent the shared view of an ethnic group, people living in a region, or members of a family. There are no limitations on how this dualism between a unique TBox (the world) and multiple ABox layers (cultures) can be exploited. Then, why not using an ABox layer for each person, which might represent the particular view of the world that characterizes that person? This is precisely the solution we suggest: when a person interacts with the robot, a specific ABox shall be built that stores information about that person and only that person, coexisting with ABox layers representing different cultures. The ABox layer that encodes the individual preferences of Mrs. Dorothy Smith, an English woman, is shown in Fig. 8.3 using yellow boxes.

We summarize the whole idea introduced so far as follows (Bruno et al., 2019).

- We call the knowledge encoded in the TBox layer "culture-generic" since it represents the knowledge that is not specific to any culture but is structured in such a way as to take into account the fact that different cultures exist. Here we represent all concepts belonging to multiple cultures as well as their mutual relationships: the concept "Espresso Coffee" coexists with "American Coffee" as children of "Coffee."
- We call the knowledge encoded in the multiple ABox layers "culture-specific" since each ABox layer represents a different culture, encoding information about the attitude of that culture toward the corresponding concepts. For example, in the ABox corresponding to the Italian culture, the instances "Espresso Coffee for an Italian" and "American Coffee for an Italian" will include information about the attitude of Italian people toward "Espresso coffee" and "American coffee," respectively, using a formalism that will be soon clarified.
- We call the knowledge encoded in the ABox layer corresponding to the person that is interacting with the robot "person-specific" since it includes information about the attitude of that person toward all concepts in the TBox. For example, instances "Espresso Coffee for Mrs. Dorothy Smith" and "American Coffee for Mrs. Dorothy Smith" will include information about the attitude of Mrs. Dorothy Smith, an English woman, toward "Espresso Coffee" and "American Coffee."

But what is written precisely in the TBox and the ABox layers? What do we mean with "attitude toward a concept"? And how can we use this mechanism to avoid stereotyping, for example, to prevent the robot from postulating that all Italian people will have the same attitude toward espresso coffee (or toward miso soup, tables, chairs, God?). How can the guidelines for robotic cultural competence produced by transcultural nursing experts be implemented in the system?

Some additional information is required. Ontologies, as already mentioned, allow us to represent concepts, relationships between concepts, instances of concepts, and relationships between instances. Additionally, in the TBox, we can associate numerical properties to concepts (or even sequences of characters), and, analogously, we can assign values to these properties in the ABox. For instance, the concept "Espresso Coffee" might have numerical property expressing the fact that ordering an espresso in an Italian bar has a cost (what a surprise!) to be interpreted as a price in Euros. When we create an instance of "Espresso coffee" in the ABox, we can associate a specific number to that instance, representing the cost that espresso has in that particular bar at a given time.

In our case, we associate two main pieces of information to concepts in the culture-generic layer and then to instances of such concepts in the culture-specific layers:

- the familiarity that a given culture has with a concept (property "familiarity," discussed in this section);
- the sentences that the system can use to talk about that concept when the latter is interpreted as a possible topic of conversation with the person (property "sentence," discussed in the next section).

Please notice that, in Fig. 8.3, the data properties "familiarity" and "sentence" are only shown in the block "Breakfast food." However, as already said, they are inherited by all its children by exploiting the hierarchical structure of the Ontology.

The term "familiarity" shall be interpreted as a probability, and therefore, it can assume values in the range from 0 to 1. For example, consider the concept "Miso soup": we need to represent the fact that people identifying with different cultures have a distinct familiarity with miso soup, not just meaning that they may know or not know what miso soup is, but also in the sense that they may have tried it or not, they may have miso soup more or less frequently, it may happen more or less regularly that somebody in their circle of friends or their family have a miso soup. Familiarity has all these meanings: the number associated with the instances of "Miso soup" for a given ABox layer, say the layer representing the English culture, corresponds to the probability that an English person will have familiarity with miso soup. Please notice that the familiarity value is stored in the culture-specific layer, but the information it encodes concerns individual persons: it is a guess, which may be wrong, that a randomly picked person selfidentifying with that culture may have familiarity with that concept. The "familiarity," however, is not only stored in the culture-specific layer but also the person-specific layer of the ABox. Suppose again that the robot is interacting with Mrs. Dorothy Smith. In this case, the "familiarity" values in the person-specific layer describe whether Mrs. Dorothy Smith has or has not familiarity with having miso soup for breakfast.

The "familiarity" is the crucial element we propose to represent cultural knowledge in a nonstereotyped way, and may derive from the knowledge about different cultures provided by experts under the form of guidelines, see Chapter 7 that introduced this concept. The robot, when interacting with a person, will have all the concepts in the Ontology at its disposal: even if it may be unlikely, an English person may love to have miso soup for breakfast, something which is definitely more popular in Japan than in the UK, and we do not want to exclude this possibility. However, even if the robot has access to the entire Ontology, it will give priority to those concepts that are associated with a higher familiarity. For instance, if the robot needs to know what Mrs. Dorothy Smith usually has for breakfast, it will explore the possibility that she has tea before asking her if she has miso soup. This fact is reflected, in the figure, by "Tea" having a higher familiarity value than "Miso soup" in the culture-specific ABox Layer for the English Culture.

During the interaction, the system will acquire new information about the user. For instance, the robot may ask her if she ever tried miso soup even if it estimates that this is unlikely, and Mrs. Dorothy Smith may surprise the robot by positively replying that she indeed loves it. In this case, the information in the culture-specific layer will not change since nothing Mrs. Dorothy Smith says can modify our knowledge about the general attitude of English people toward miso soup: however, the "familiarity" value in the person-specific ABox layer of Mrs. Dorothy Smith will be updated accordingly. For example, if Mrs. Dorothy Smith declares she loves miso soup, the value will be updated to the maximum value, that is, 1. Similarly, suppose the robot poses a question about miso soup to Mrs. Dorothy Smith, and she replies that she does not know what the robot is talking about (something very likely for an older English person). In that case, the "familiarity" value will be updated to the minimum value, that is, 0. In principle, a "familiarity" value in-between 0 and one might be chosen if Mrs. Dorothy Smith declares that "well, I may know that miso thing ... but I am not that sure", but we will not consider this possibility in the following.

Fig. 8.4 shows that this concept also concerns the actions that the robot can perform. The way to perform actions or, more generally, how to behave when interacting with people and with the environment may also be different depending on the cultural context. An example is greeting somebody: even if greeting by waving a hand is nowadays popular worldwide, greeting people with a bow is popular in Japan and other Asian countries, but not everywhere. Once again, actions and different ways of performing actions, or creating sequences of actions to achieve a given objective, are encoded as concepts in the culture-generic layer of the Ontology: instances in the culture-specific layers will then be assigned different "familiarity" values. As such, the instance of the concept "Bowing" in the Japanese ABox layer will have a higher familiarity value than the instance of "Bowing" in the Italian ABox layer, which does not exclude that Italian people may greet each other with a bow, but it makes it a less viable option with respects to different kinds of greetings.

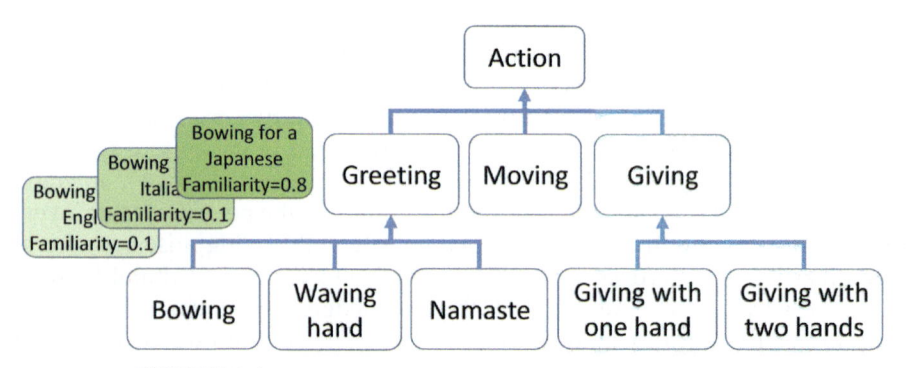

FIGURE 8.4 A section of the ontology representing robot actions.

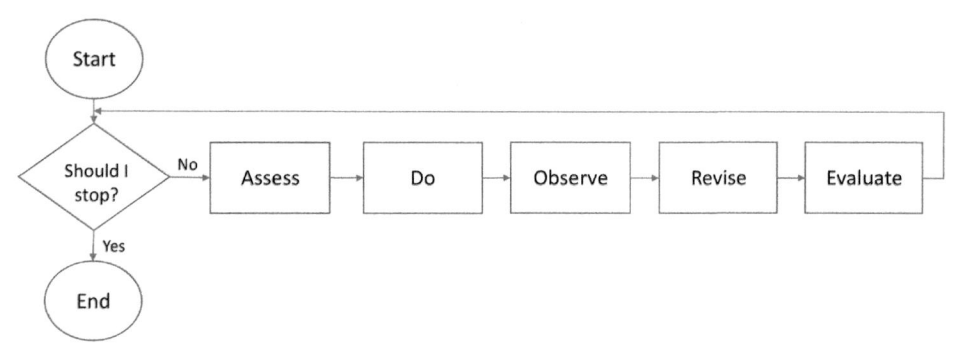

FIGURE 8.5 The flowchart of the ADORE model implemented as a computer program.

At this point, it shall be clear how the system may take advantage of cultural information and, at the same type, avoid stereotypes. Following Chapter 7, the ADORE guidelines for culturally competent behavior can be implemented as follows:

- Assess the cultural identity of the person, which means choosing the appropriate culture-specific layer, that is, all instances in the corresponding ABox and the corresponding "familiarity" values;
- Do things with cultural sensitivity, which means choosing the topic of conversation and the actions of the robot that are associated with the highest "familiarity" values for that particular culture or, in case that person-specific information is available, for that specific person;
- Observe what the person does and says during the interaction, acquiring verbal, and nonverbal inputs through robot sensors;
- Revise with cultural sensitivity the knowledge that the robot has about the person, that is, by adequately updating "familiarity" values in the person-specific layer depending on what the person said in reply to the robot and on the observed behavior of the person;
- Evaluate, together with the person, the robot's behavior, that will enable the system to improve in time.

We do not provide additional details on how the ADORE model is implemented as a computer program. Still, please remember that the Ontology is just knowledge structured in a particular way, that is, something static: to use such knowledge according to the steps required by the ADORE model, a computer program needs to be implemented that repeatedly acquires data from the environment through sensors, processes them at the light of the available cultural knowledge, perform actions in the environment in a way that is appropriate depending on the information in the culture-specific and the person-specific layers, and possibly update the knowledge in the ontology accordingly. The program to implement the ADORE guidelines will have the structure, generally speaking, of the flowcharts shown in Chapter 2: we report an example in Fig. 8.5.

8.3.2 From knowledge representation to language generation and dialog management

As mentioned in the previous section, another essential data property is associated with concepts, allowing experts to write sentences to talk about them. When interpreting concepts as something that one can speak of, we refer to them as "topics of conversation" or simply "topics." There are as many topics in the Ontology as there are concepts, and every concept is a possible topic of conversation as long as it has sentences associated with it. Topics of conversation that are more or less relevant for different cultures may, once again, be determined by experts—see Chapter 7.

Please notice that the sentences associated with topics may have different roles: they can be used by the robot to ask questions to the user, which can either be yes/no questions (e.g., "Do you ever have espresso in the morning?") or open ones (e.g., "Please tell me what you like about having a coffee with friends"), they can be positive assertions about some topic (e.g., "I think that having an espresso is the best way to taste coffee") or negative ones (e.g., "I don't like espresso, there is nothing to drink there!"). Also, the same topic may have more than one sentence of the same kind associated with it: this means that the robot will have different possibilities to choose among when asking a question or making a positive or negative assertion. Finally, the same sentence can be stored in multiple languages to allow the robot to talk with people of different nationalities.

This approach might raise some criticism: we are in the Era of neural networks: as discussed in Chapter 2, the so-called neural generative models (Wang et al., 2017) can be used to produce faked data that look realistic starting from examples and can be used to synthesize everything from pictures to music, to alter a video of a trotting horse to a trotting zebra, to switch the face of Jack Nicholson in Kubrick's Shining with Jim Carrey's[4], or more simply to change the age and gender of a person in a photograph (we suggest to try FaceApp[5] if you haven't done it yet). Given that generative models can learn how to do or say things starting from a large amount of available data, do we really need to store prewritten sentences in the Ontology to allow the robot to talk about the concepts that are encoded in it? Why not design a robot that learns how to talk about a topic by taking inspiration from discussions that can be found on the Internet, for example, in forums or social media? If this is possible, there would be no need to write or store any sentence in the Ontology manually: the robot will autonomously learn how to reply to what the user says, perhaps considering not only the last sentence of the user but the current context, that is, the history of the most recent things that the person has said. We expect the result of this process to be more natural than using prewritten sentences.

Neural generative models exist that automatically produce replies depending on what the user said. They are used by some of the most popular chatbots (Zhou et al., 2020) to make realistic discussions with users. However, the risk of generative models has already been mentioned in Chapter 2. Who has control of what such a system will say? How can we ensure that the sentences in the dataset are appropriate for the user, that is, they handle sensitive matters in the right way, do not contain offensive languages, etc.? This is known to be an open problem of generative models: developers do not have control of what the system will say, which can be very dangerous, especially in sensitive contexts. Social and health care is precisely one of such contexts, which requires handling this issue with greater attention by guaranteeing that everything the robot says is appropriate for the context in which the interaction occurs.

Having abandoned the idea of using a neural generative model, we need another solution to guarantee sufficient variability in the robot's sentences: as the reader can imagine, a whole Ontology that covers all aspects of daily life, including also the actions that the robot might

---

[4] https://www.youtube.com/watch?v=HG_NZpkttXE

[5] https://www.faceapp.com/

perform, may easily include more than 10,000 concepts. Chapter 2 extensively debated the importance of "robust" systems capable of providing a coherent reply in almost all situations. Who will manually encode all the required sentences to talk about such topics of conversation, considering that each topic will likely have multiple sentences associated with it to allow a sufficient degree of variability when the robot asks questions or makes assertions?

The key idea is to exploit the hierarchy of the Ontology: that is, the fact that knowledge is hierarchically organized into concepts (e.g., "Coffee"), children of such concepts through a parent-child "is-a" relationship (e.g., "Espresso coffee is-a Coffee") and other concepts related to them through a "has-N" property (e.g., "Coffee has-1 Brand"). Please remember that the hierarchical structure of the Ontology implies a side effect: if a concept has a property, this property is inherited by all children. In our system, inheritance turns out to be very useful for allowing children topics to inherit sentences from parent topics. Suppose that the topic "Hot drink," which is the parent of "Coffee," has been associated with the sentence "Great, I love to have a hot drink when I wake up from my bed": the sentence will be inherited by "Coffee" and "Espresso coffee," as well as by all the other children of "Hot drink" and the children of these children. Whenever the robot is talking about "Coffee," "Tea," "Espresso coffee," or any other subconcept in the hierarchy, this sentence will be available and associated with that concept.

Let's consider a possible dialogue about the robot and a person.

> User: I love Coffee in the morning.
> Robot: Great, I love to have a hot drink when I wake up from my bed.
> User: I love to have Espresso Coffee, to be more precise.
> Robot: Great, I love to have a hot drink when I wake up from my bed.

There are two evident problems in this exchange between the user and the robot.

First, we cannot use only one sentence for all the topics in the hierarchy: the final result sounds quite repetitive, doesn't it? A solution to this problem is to add more than one sentence that can be used to make positive assertions: if we have 10 sentences for "Hot drink," the chances of having a repetition are lower. But this is not the only problem.

The second problem is that the reply is not very specific. The user is talking about "Coffee" and about "Espresso coffee," not about a generic "Hot drink." The sentence contains the word "Hot drink" because the sentence was initially stored in the parent concept. However, in the second part of this short dialogue, we are not talking about "Hot drink," but about its child "Coffee": can't the robot say something more specific?

The key, once again, is to exploit the inheritance mechanism of Ontologies. We can store in the Ontology sentences that contain variable parts: a sentence will be associated with a parent concept at the higher level of the hierarchy and inherited by children, but it will not be inherited "as is." Instead, when inherited by a child topic, all variable parts of the sentences will assume a value that depends on the child inheriting it. For example, let's consider again the sentence "I love to have *a hot drink* when I wake up from my bed": the words "a hot drink" are now in Italics, which means they are a variable part of the sentence. When inherited by "Coffee," the sentence will become "I love to have *a coffee* when I wake up from my bed"; when inherited by "Espresso coffee," it will become "I love to have *an espresso* when I wake up from my bed." Suppose that the concept "Hot drink" has 50 subconcepts: by writing just one sentence, we will have added 50 sentences in the Ontology, each specifically tailored to talk about that topic.

The newly added sentences are more specific than the previous ones; however, this is not sufficient. All sentences inherited by subconcepts look very similar, and the reason is that we are only exploiting "is-a" parent–child relationships between concepts, but we are entirely ignoring "has-N" relationships relating a concept to its properties. Suppose that the concept "Food" is related to the concept "Time of the day" through a property "has-1-Time of the day," Fig. 8.6, meaning that some food may be more or less common at breakfast, lunch or dinner. "Hot drink" is a child of "Food," whereas "Breakfast time," "Lunchtime," "Dinner time" are all children of "Time of the day." Then, we might think about storing the sentence "I usually have *food sometimes*" in the concept "Food," where *food* and *sometimes* are in Italics and therefore are interpreted as parts of the sentence that may vary. As previously, the sentence will be automatically inherited by all children of "Food," which will substitute the variable part *food* with the name of the inheriting concept. Additionally, the variable part *sometimes* will be substituted as well, but this time with the name of the concepts associated with "Food" and its children through the "has-1-Time of the day" property. By adding just one sentence written by hand in "Food," this will produce a set of sentences that share a common structure but are indeed quite different from each other. Some examples are: "I usually have *cappuccino at lunchtime*"; "I usually have *cappuccino at breakfast*"; "I usually have *coffee after dinner.*" The number of automatically produced sentences can become huge when the number of children increases! Other variations of the same sentence can be produced by adding random prefixes or suffixes, such as *"Do you know?* I usually have Indian food at lunch", *"I need to tell you that* I usually have Espresso at Breakfast. *I am not the only one*", or "Yep, I usually have coffee after dinner. *You should try.*"

Finally, Fig. 8.6 shows sentences as if they are only encoded in the culture-generic TBox for ease of representation. However, it is also possible to encode sentences in culture-specific ABox, to express that different cultures are likely to have a different approach to talk about the same topic.

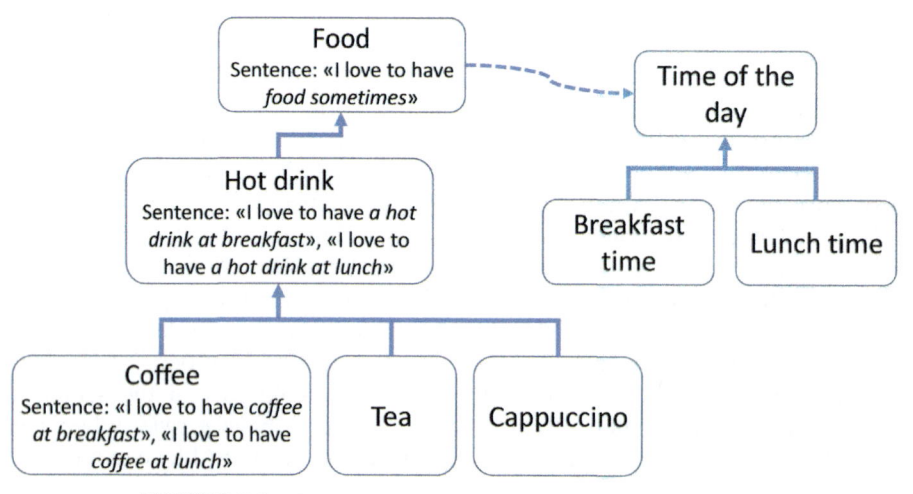

FIGURE 8.6 Concepts in the ontology with associated sentences.

8.3.3 From language generation to dialogue management

The mechanism above clarifies how sentences are automatically composed starting from sentences stored into topics of conversation, that is, concepts of the Ontology. Next, we need a procedure telling the robot when and how to talk with the user using such sentences.

If you refer to the ADORE program in Fig. 8.5, we are now focusing on the "Assess," "Do," and "Observe" blocks of the program. When focusing on actions that the robot can "physically do" to interact with the environment and the person (which are being paid lesser attention in this discussion), the blocks "Assess" and "Do" of the ADORE model refer to the physical actions that the robot is executing, and the block "Observe" refers to the observations that the robot is making through its sensors. When focusing on the verbal interaction between the robot and the person, the block "Assess" refers to choosing the correct culture-specific layer and topic of conversation, the block "Do" refers to selecting the new sentence to be pronounced among those stored in the Ontology and automatically composed, and the block "Observe" refers to the robot acquiring the reply of the person, interpreting it, and possibly using the information contained therein to select the next robot's sentences.

You may know more about the implementation of the ADORE model as an AI program in Chapter 9. Here, we will focus on the implementation of the "Assess," "Do," and "Observe" blocks for culturally competent verbal conversation. This mechanism is sometimes referred to with a name: "chit-chatting." Other researchers call this kind of verbal interaction "open conversation," meaning a conversation that is not bounded to a specific application domain (Huang et al., 2020). In the case of the robot, chit-chatting is different from a task-oriented conversation, that is, issuing verbal commands to perform tasks, such as turning on the lights or playing a song. Instead, chit-chatting refers to a conversation open to any possible topic, without any additional purpose than the conversation itself. The distinction between chit-chatting and a task-oriented conversation should be straightforward: see two examples of task-based conversation (first dialog) and chit-chatting (second dialog) below to avoid confusion.

> U: robot, tell me the weather.
> R: For sure: tell me the location you want to know the weather about.
> U: Rome.

> R: Are you a religious person?
> U: Well, I am not sure. Sometimes.
> R: Believing in something may be important for people. Please, tell me more about what you think about this.

Since we emphasize chit-chatting, it is essential to clarify that task-based conversation is crucial as well: indeed, it is the basis for giving instructions to the robot to do things. Task-based conversation will not be discussed in detail only because it is less related to cultural competence: when we want to assign a task to the robot, we are willing to learn specific commands for the robot to understand us!

Ideally, task-based conversation and chit-chatting might even be performed by two completely distinct mechanisms. The interpretation of the user's commands to assign tasks to the robot may, for instance, be based on the detection of simple keywords in the user's speech or rely on a third-party system on the Internet for Natural Language Processing (NLP). There are many commercial systems available that work very well in the case of speech processing for command understanding: given a sentence such as "Robot, tell me the weather in London," these systems have no problems in extracting the command (i.e., "tell me the weather") and additional parameters (i.e., "in London"). On the contrary, the system for culturally competent chit-chatting works on different principles and cannot be easily implemented using off-the-shelf NLP tools. For this reason, our proposal to develop such a system is described in greater detail. Finally, remark that the command interpreter for task-based conversation and the procedure for chit-chatting shall always work in parallel: at any time during chit-chatting, the person might ask the robot to do something specific such as turning on the lights; vice versa, when the person issues a command that the robot is not capable of interpreting, the robot should at least be capable to chit-chat about it. See a possible conversation interweaving task-based conversation and chit-chatting below.

> R: Are you a religious person? (chit-chatting about religion).
> U: Well, I am not sure. Sometimes. (chit-chatting about religion).
> R: Believing in something may be important for people. Please, tell me more about what you think about this. (chit-chatting about religion).
> U: Ok, but before turn-on the air conditioner, please. It's too hot! (command that the robot can execute).
> R: Ok, done. (command that the robot can understand).
> U: Bring me a glass of water, please. (command that the robot cannot execute).
> R: It's very important to drink water regularly. (chit-chatting about drinking water).

The requisites to allow successful chit-chatting with the user are different from task-based conversation. In chit-chatting, the key is not understanding what the user wants to do using advanced NLP techniques but rather managing the dialog with the user in a way that is engaging and rewarding by providing the robot with the opportunity to show its knowledge and cultural competence. Specifically, to design a system for culturally competent chit-chatting, two simple mechanisms might be implemented. Mechanism one and Mechanism two heavily rely on how we proposed to organize the knowledge in the Ontology.

Mechanism one is based on the fact that all topics in the Ontology are already related to each other through semantic relationships: parent-child "is-a" relationships between concepts encode the information that the parent concept is more general concept than the child concept, that is, "Espresso coffee is-a Coffee"; "has-N" properties relate concepts that are semantically close to each other in a given domain, that is, "Coffee has-1 Brand". So then, as far as links between concepts correspond to the notion of semantic closeness between topics of conversation, they may be used to explore the Ontology by guaranteeing a coherent conversation in which subsequent sentences will always be related to each other. Consider once again Fig. 8.6, where the links between concepts identify semantic relationships are shown. The robot might start talking about "Coffee," next move to "Espresso," and finally to the "Brand" of espresso that the user prefers (remember that all "has-N" properties are inherited from parents to children in the Ontology, even if they are not shown in the figure).

This mechanism might produce, for instance, the following conversation.

> R: Do you like coffee? (the topic is "Coffee"; Yes/no question).
> U: Yes, I definitely need coffee when I wake up. (the topic is "Coffee")
> R: Great! I think that having a coffee in the morning can improve your day. Tell me what you like the most about coffee if you want. (the topic is "Coffee"; Positive Sentence followed by an open question).
> U: Well, I like that it really wakes you up, especially if you did not sleep too well. Something which happens very often in the last weeks. (the topic is "Coffee")
> R: I understand. And do you like espresso coffee? (the topic is "Espresso coffee"; Yes/no question).
> U: Of course, when I say "coffee" I mean "espresso", I am Italian. (the topic is "Espresso coffee")
> R: Good to know. Espresso is very popular in Italy and France, but not everywhere in the world. Tell me what you like the most about Espresso Coffee if you want. (the topic is "Espresso coffee"; Positive Sentence followed by an open question).
> U: Well … Not sure … for me Espresso coffee is just … coffee. I don't like American Coffee. (the topic is "Espresso coffee")
> R: I see. Do you like Illy Coffee? (the topic is "Brand"; Yes/no question).
> U: No … it's a little too expensive. (the topic is "Brand")
> R: I see. I don't like that brand as well, it's too sour. (the topic is "Brand"; Negative Sentence).

The dialog above provides the opportunity to see Mechanism one at work. First, there are three topics of conversation in this short dialog: the abovementioned "Coffee," "Espresso coffee," and "Brand." These topics are connected in the Ontology through "is-a" or "has-N" relationships. Since, for the moment, we are only considering Mechanism one to browse the knowledge base, the sequence in which different topics of conversation are addressed may look very rigid: when a topic of conversation is considered as fully covered, the robot will pick one of the connected topics randomly, with a probability that is proportional to the "familiarity" in the culture-specific layer (i.e., the "familiarity" that the user is expected to have toward that topic depending on his or her culture). For instance, in the dialogue above, after talking about "Coffee" the robot has chosen "Espresso Coffee": this may be a consequence of the fact that the person interacting with the robot is Italian, and then "Expresso Coffee" has a very high probability of being chosen, or simply because all choices ultimately have a chance of being selected, and even a person that has a very low familiarity with "Espresso Coffee" has a nonzero probability that this topic will be chosen.

Second, every topic of conversation requires multiple exchanges between the robot and the user, with the robot using the sentences encoded in the Ontology to talk. Indeed, the dialog clarifies that the sentences stored in the Ontology may be of different kinds:

- Yes/no questions such as "Do you like coffee?", to which the user can reply with "yes," "no," but also variations such as "sure," "of course," "always," "never," etc. Yes/no questions are essential because the person's reply is easily recognizable as either a positive or negative reply. Then, such a reply can be used to update "familiarity" values in the person-specific layer corresponding to that user. For example, remember that all Italian users are initially assumed to have a very high "familiarity" with "Espresso coffee," but a specific user may not like it. User preferences can be unambiguously acquired

through a straightforward Yes/no question (and, consequently, the robot may choose to avoid that topic in the future).
- Positive sentences such as "Great! I think that having a coffee in the morning can improve your day." The robot says positive sentences following an affirmative reply to a Yes/no question.
- Negative sentences such as "I don't like that brand as well, it's too sour." The robot says negative sentences following a negative reply to a Yes/no question.
- Open questions such as "Tell me what you like the most about coffee if you want." The robot asks open questions to allow the person to talk freely about a topic, thus encouraging him or her to say things that may be helpful to jump from a topic a conversation to another one. Jumping from one topic to another is dealt with by Mechanism two, which will be soon explained.
- Suggestions for activities, such as "Do you want me to order coffee from the online grocery?" These sentences may or may not be added to some topics to trigger activities. There is no such example in the dialog above, but this and other kinds of sentences may be added to the Ontology structure to make the conversation around topics richer and more engaging.

Mechanism one may not be sufficient to guarantee a sufficiently rich and engaging interaction with the person. For this reason, Mechanism two is implemented, allowing to break this predefined dialog pattern and explore the Ontology unpredictably depending on what the user says.

Mechanism two can be as simple as a keyword-based mechanism detecting keywords in what the person says, or it can be based on more sophisticated NLP tools capable of understanding, in a general sense, the topic about which the person is talking. For instance, a simple keyword-based mechanism might extract the keywords "football" and "TV" from the sentence "On Sunday evening, I love watching the football match on TV in the common room." In contrast, a more complex service for NLP running on the Internet may be capable of understanding that this sentence is about sport, entertainment, television, and things alike. Whatever strategy is used to detect the topic of conversation (possibly both), the information is then used by Mechanism two for switching in-between topics of conversation, thus breaking the rigid pattern determined by Mechanism one.

Consider the same dialogue as before, but now assume that Mechanism two is also active: the following exchange may be produced.

> R: Do you like coffee? (the topic is "Coffee"; Yes/no question).
> U: Yes, I definitely need coffee when I wake up. ("wake up" is recognized as a keyword).
> R: Do you like waking up in the morning? (the topic is "Waking up"; Yes/no question).
> U: Yes, I like it if it is a sunny day.
> R: Great to know. Many people like to wake up early in the morning, and I think this is good for health, especially after a good sleep! Tell me more about what you like about waking up early in the morning. (the topic is "Waking up"; Positive Sentence followed by an open question).
> U: Well, most of all, I like having a cup of coffee waiting for me! ("coffee" is recognized as a keyword).
> R: Great! I think that having a coffee in the morning can improve your day. (the topic is "Coffee"; Positive Sentence followed by an open question).

It is essential to be aware that, during the conversation, the robot is not capturing all details of what the person is saying. Understanding everything is not the purpose of chit-chatting, and achieving this would be highly complex considering the vast range of topics that can be raised during a conversation. However, the robot can understand when the person wants to move from one topic to another. In the example, it promptly switches from "Coffee" to "Waking up" and then back to "Coffee," following the rationale of what the person says.

This approach is pretty simple; however, it can "almost always" pick a coherent reply. It starts from the consideration that, at the end of the day, the most frustrating response you may get from a robot during the conversation is probably "Sorry, I don't understand what you are talking about."

Isn't it?

8.3.4 Acquiring new cultural knowledge

The system described so far uses the information in the Ontology, particularly the "familiarity" data property in the culture-specific layer, to make educated guesses about what the person may like or not like depending on a priori knowledge about his or her culture. During the conversation, the person is allowed to express his or her actual preferences, which will be used to update the knowledge about that person in the person-specific layer of the Ontology. Next, person-specific knowledge may be used to drive the conversation toward topics that the person likes instead of using prestored information. This mechanism allows for avoiding stereotyped representations of people and their cultures; however, it is possible to do more.

It is reasonable to conjecture that there may be a correlation between the "familiarity" that a person has with a concept, that is, "watching tennis on TV," and his or her "familiarity" with another concept, that is, "playing tennis." Of course, a rigid causal dependence between playing tennis and watching tennis on TV cannot be inferred. However, there are reasonable elements to think that a person who likes to play tennis (or played tennis when he or she was young) is more willing to watch tennis on TV. Similarly, think about an English person that likes Japanese paintings, writes haiku poems, and loves sushi. Wouldn't you be tempted to guess that this person, even if she is not from Japan, is attracted by the Japanese culture? Maybe this person would be more willing than another one to visit Japan? Can we infer that this person would be more interested in talking about kimono manufacturing or zen gardens than a person that hates Japanese paintings, does not understand what's the point in reading a haiku, and thinks that sushi is "just" raw fish?

Our cultural preferences are related to each other, possibly because they may have a common cause: perhaps the first person has a Japanese friend or watched Japanese animated movies when a child. Causal relationships are challenging to prove; this is a general truth in scientific research. However, correlations between facts in a probabilistic sense are much easier to find, even if they may sometimes lead to wrong conclusions. Can we make inferences about the unknown preferences of a person based on what we already know about him or her? The reply is yes: this kind of inference, which is necessarily probabilistic in its nature since a cause-effect relationship may not always exist, can rely on the use of Bayesian networks that have been introduced in Section 7.2.

As usual, the familiarity associated with the concept "Zen garden" in the culture-specific layer corresponding to the English culture may be interpreted as a probability: the probability that a randomly chosen English person, if asked, will reply that he or she is familiar with zen gardens. Suppose that the "familiarity" with "Zen garden" has also been computed for the culture-specific layer corresponding to the Italian and Japanese cultures. If you consider all these "familiarity" values taken together, it is pretty straightforward to interpret them as a set of conditioned probabilities. More specifically, the three "familiarity" values associated with "Zen garden" and corresponding to the English, Italian, and Japanese culture-specific layers can be interpreted as "the conditioned probability that a person is familiar with zen gardens given that he or she is English"; "the conditioned probability that a person is familiar with zen gardens given that he or she is Italian"; "the conditioned probability that a person is familiar with zen gardens given that he or she is Japanese." After some additional considerations that would require technical details beyond the purpose of this book, it may be shown that all these conditioned probabilities may be used to build a Bayesian Network that mirrors the Ontology structure (Bruno et al., 2019).

A figure of this new Bayesian Network is not reported; however, please consider once again Fig. 8.2, where a Bayesian Network was shown containing all the required information to infer, for instance, the probability that it is raining given that the grass is wet. Analogously to what happened with that Bayesian Network, the robot may use the Bayesian Network that mirrors the Ontology structure to make inferences about hidden facts starting from observed facts. For example, suppose that, at some point, the robot acquires information about the person, that is, the fact that he or she has familiarity with Japanese painting and poetry (observed facts). Then, by using the structure of the network and all the conditioned probabilities, the robot will infer that the probability that this person is familiar with other aspects of the Japanese culture (hidden fact) has increased and will use this information during the interaction. For instance, to guess other Japanese things that the person may be interested in, for example, zen gardens, or propose related activities, for example, suggesting an online shop to buy a kimono.

In conclusion, Bayesian Networks reveals additional tools that may parallel Ontologies to enable a proper culturally competent behavior. As soon as the system "observes" more and more about the person, a complex personalized representation of the user will emerge in the person-specific layer, merging in the same person different aspects of different cultures, which is coherent with what happens with real people living in the real world.

8.4 Conclusions

Culturally competent robots need cultural knowledge to interact appropriately with people; however, this knowledge must be encoded in a formalism that a robot can process and understand. To this end, we introduced two of the most popular approaches to encode knowledge in a formalism easily understandable both by humans and robots, Ontologies and Bayesian Networks. Next, we discussed the basic principles for designing a computer program that uses such knowledge to implement the guidelines provided by transcultural nursing experts. During this process, the readers should have familiarized themselves with the mental approach that computer scientists adopt to develop complex AI and Robotic solutions and become aware of the vast amount of work required when pursuing the goal of culturally competent robotic behavior.

8.4.1 Reflective questions

- When we use an ontology to describe a part of the world that is interesting for a computer application, we say that we are building a world model. What does it mean? What are the choices that Computer Scientists need to make when building such a model?
- What is the characteristic of computer ontologies that can be exploited to represent different views of the world corresponding to multiple cultures? How can this characteristic be used to avoid a stereotyped representation of people and cultures?
- Bayesian networks allow computing the probability of a fact or event we do not know based on what we know. How can this property be exploited to have a more faithful representation of people's attitudes toward things?

References

Baader, F., Calvanese, D., McGuinness, D., Nardi, D., & Patel-Schneider, P. (Eds.). (2007). *The description logic handbook: Theory, implementation and applications* (2nd ed.). Cambridge: Cambridge University Press. https://doi.org/10.1017/CBO9780511711787

Bruno, B., Recchiuto, C. T., Papadopoulos, I., Saffiotti, A., Koulouglioti, C., Menicatti, R., Mastrogiovanni, F., Zaccaria, R., & Sgorbissa, A. (2019). Knowledge representation for culturally competent personal robots: Requirements, design principles, implementation, and assessment. *International Journal of Social Robotics, 11*(3), 515–538.

Carrithers, M., Candea, M., Sykes, K., Holbraad, M., & Venkatesan, S. (2010). Ontology is just another word for culture: Motion tabled at the 2008 meeting of the group for debates in anthropological theory, University of Manchester. *Critique of Anthropology, 30*(2), 152–200.

Cimiano, P. (2006). Ontology learning and population from text: Algorithms, evaluation and applications. *Ontology Learning and Population from Text: Algorithms, Evaluation and Applications*, 1–347.

Grau, B. C., Horrocks, I., Motik, B., Parsia, B., Patel-Schneider, P., & Sattler, U. (2008). Owl 2: The next step for OWL. *Web Semantics, 6*(4), 309–322.

Gruber, T. R. (1995). Toward principles for the design of ontologies used for knowledge sharing. *International Journal of Human-Computer Studies, 43*(5–6), 907–928.

Henare, A., Holbraad, M., & Wastell, S. (2006). Thinking through things: theorising artefacts ethnographically. *Thinking Through Things: Theorising Artefacts Ethnographically*, 1–237.

Huang, M., Zhu, X., & Gao, J. (2020). Challenges in building intelligent open-domain dialog systems. *ACM Transactions on Information Systems, 38*(3).

Pearl, Judea (2000). *Causality: Models, reasoning, and inference*. Cambridge University Press, ISBN 978-0-521-77362-1.

Schmidhuber, J. (2015). Deep learning in neural networks: An overview. *Neural Networks, 61*, 85–117.

Wang, K., Gou, C., Duan, Y., Lin, Y., Zheng, X., & Wang, F.-Y. (2017). Generative adversarial networks: Introduction and outlook. *IEEE/CAA Journal of Automatica Sinica, 4*(4), 588–598, 8039016.

Zhou, L., Gao, J., Li, D., & Shum, H.-Y. (2020). The design and implementation of xiaoice, an empathetic social chatbot. *Computational Linguistics, 46*(1), 53–93.

CHAPTER 9

Development of a fully autonomous culturally competent robot companion

Carmine Tommaso Recchiuto and Antonio Sgorbissa
DIBRIS Department, Università degli Studi di Genova, Genova, Italy

LEARNING OBJECTIVES

- To become aware of some of the challenges that intelligent robots need to address when operating autonomously 24/7 in social environments.
- To learn a portfolio of smart solutions helping researchers to develop robots that convincingly "look" autonomous.
- To understand the general structure of a computer program required to make a robot operate autonomously and with cultural competence.
- To become aware of opportunities offered by the so-called Cloud systems to manage multiple users interacting with a community of culturally competent robots and devices.

9.1 Introduction: autonomous robots revisited from Shakey to Boston dynamics legged robots

A video on the Internet shows a four-legged robot climbing in the woods, keeping its balance when kicked and slipping on ice, traveling through snow and mud, and climbing rubble[1]. A CNBC journalist interviews an android looking like a real woman that has been

---

[1] https://www.youtube.com/watch?v=cNZPRsrwumQ.

granted Saudi citizenship[2]. Social media show a biped humanoid robot capable of climbing stairs, jump and even doing a somersault by landing on its feet[3]. Wow! A "baby robot" is invited to the Italia's Got Talent competition[4]. A dog-looking robot with an arm in the place of its head can open doors: it looks exactly the same as the creepy killer robot of a popular sci-fi TV serial[5].

We are getting used to seeing robots everywhere: at the cinema, on the Internet, on TV. All these robots are amazing. They are characterized by outstanding mechanical design and control capabilities, making them capable of doing things that most humans cannot. For instance, the authors of this book are not capable of somersaulting (believe us), whereas the biped robot Atlas designed by Boston Dynamics is. A long time has passed since good-old Shakey (Nilsson, 1984) moved its first steps back in 1966 (see Chapter 2). Things have visibly changed since then. Have they?

We are getting used to seeing robots at the cinema, on the Internet, on TV: the only place where it is hard to see robots is the "real world." Yes, there are robots in factories that repeatedly perform heavy, boring, and dangerous tasks in place of humans, for instance, assembling or painting cars. There may be a cleaning robot in your house or a lawn mowing robot in your garden. You may have encountered a humanoid robot welcoming visitors in commercial centers, airports, or cruise ships. However, we are not too far from the truth by saying that this is almost the maximum you can expect. In the last decade, movies, the Internet, and TV news periodically show robots that look very intelligent and, apparently, capable of executing tasks in complete autonomy: that is, capable of autonomously perceiving the world around them, making decisions, and acting appropriately. However, when looking around you, you will soon realize that there are not many robots capable of autonomously performing complex tasks for people.

"Wait a minute, the robots we see in the media are not autonomous? Can you repeat that?"

It may not surprise you that robots in movies are mostly produced with computer-generated imagery (CGI) and other special effects. But let's focus on the "real robots" that we can see on the Internet and TV. Are they a fraud? Are they not intelligent? Are they not capable of executing tasks autonomously by perceiving the environment, making decisions, and finally acting accordingly?

It is out of doubt that robotic researchers are interested in fully autonomous behavior, and therefore, they aim to design robots that operate autonomously. However, this mostly happens during short and controlled experiments in their laboratories. On the opposite, almost everything you see in the media is always carefully planned or even remotely controlled: robots act following a script, with no space for autonomy. And this is not a surprise, considering how challenging it is to develop a fully autonomous robot. Can you imagine an important university or a big company participating in a TV show with the risk that their biped robot hits a person and falls on its face? Is it acceptable that an android closely

---

[2] https://www.youtube.com/watch?v=S5t6K9iwcdw.

[3] https://www.youtube.com/watch?v=uhND7Mvp3f4.

[4] https://www.youtube.com/watch?v=5-1VcTmJkOk.

[5] https://www.youtube.com/watch?v=wXxrmussq4E.

resembling humans does not reply properly to the interviewer's questions? By giving an offensive answer or, worse, staying silent while tens of millions of people are watching it (including "evil" journalists)? Can somebody design autonomous robots that will not risk an epic failure in front of the world?

It is time to make a revelation.

Concerning mechanical design and control, things have notably changed in the last decades. Shakey had wheels, could not jump, and its movements did not look as "natural" as the robots' movements you can see today. Up to a few years ago, there were no robots capable of somersaulting and landing in a stable position on their feet. When RoboCup (Kitano et al., 1997), a football competition between wheeled robots, started in 1997 with the ambitious goal of creating a team of robots "capable of winning against the human soccer World Cup champions by 2050[6]," several robotic scientists raised their eyebrows. How can you expect robots running on the football field as fast as human players? Ah ah ah. We don't laugh about it anymore. Nowadays, companies such as Boston Dynamics are so good in the mechanical design and control of legged robots and so ahead of their competitors that it is hard to imagine what research may say more than that. And what about the mechanical design and control of other kinds of robots, such as flying or surgery robots? Is there still space for smaller research groups, for example, universities, to investigate innovative solutions, given that big companies have become interested in robotics and are developing these fantastic technologies at such a pace? Or is it reasonable to conjecture that, after the "far west" of robotics when there were unexplored opportunities for everybody to come out with new technological solutions, robots' mechanical design and control will become the exclusive prerogative of a small number of industry leaders? What will become the main objective of scientific research, in this case? What is left?

Autonomy.

We now need these fantastic pieces of technology to become intelligent: capable of perceiving the world around them, making decisions in autonomy, and acting appropriately. We need robots capable of fully autonomous behavior. You may object that, also concerning intelligence, things have changed since good old Shakey made its first steps, which is true, but not so visibly. Can you name any big company capable of producing robots with superior capabilities in intelligent interaction with people? Do you know any commercially available robots capable of moving in a chaotic domestic environment without getting lost, reliably recognizing objects and picking them up, sustaining a long-term conversation with humans? Can I buy a robot like the ones we can see in movies, a robot companion helping me do chores and other everyday activities?

The answer is negative, and this is not a surprise[7]. Achieving a genuine autonomous behavior is complex, perhaps one of the most complicated things in robotics. We already

---

[6] https://www.robocup.org/objective.

[7] Perhaps somebody might mention "autonomous cars," which, however, are not fully autonomous yet. You cannot trust them in urban streets crowded with vehicles and people, for example. Still, even if autonomous cars were to become a reality soon, they are not the kind of companion robots you expect from movies, are they?

discussed in Chapters 2 and 5 that this is due to the real world's unpredictability, which requires the robot to adapt its decisions and behavior to continuously changing environmental conditions. Still, we need autonomous robots, given that we want to address the problem raised by aging populations worldwide. Only autonomous robots can assist human caregivers, thus helping to reduce the pressure in hospitals and care homes and improve care delivery at home, as suggested in Chapters 2 and 3. What can we do to make robots meeting people's expectations?

In Chapter 5, we already suggested that adopting simple but smart solutions is the key, with the objective to create robots that can do only a limited subset of the things we would like but can do them autonomously 24/7 in social environments. Here, we restate our position: making simpler robots that work reliably in the real world is more important than mimicking complex human behaviors in robotic laboratories. You may conjecture that big robotic companies, which up to now have focused on mechanical design and control, might start exploring autonomous behavior soon, breaking down all barriers to the development and widespread deployment of amazingly intelligent robots in the future (whatever "intelligent" means). However, the real challenge is to make robots capable of operating in the real world today, not tomorrow, since society needs robots now.

Therefore, while we are waiting for autonomous robots with unique superpowers capable of doing the same things humans do (or better), this chapter will investigate the tools and the strategies we have today to make autonomous robots capable of assisting people a reality.

9.2 Yet some more words about 24/7 autonomy and robustness

9.2.1 Programming autonomy: things that "good robots" should never do

An autonomous robot shall never get lost. Never being lost: based on our experience, this is probably the most crucial feature that an autonomous robot shall have. But, please, notice that being lost can mean different things.

For instance, you can think about a robot lost in a house, that is, a robot that can move between different locations in a house but, at some point, does not know the place where it is. "In which room am I?" "Is this the bathroom or the kitchen?" Maybe the robot is aware of the room where it is, but not the exact position within the room. "Am I close to the toilet?" "Is this thing the fridge?" For a robot operating in a house, knowing its current position is crucial. Indeed, if it needs to reach a goal, for example, the entrance door, how could it plan the proper movement sequence without knowing where it starts?

Robotic researchers refer to the problem of moving from a start to a goal location as "navigation" (Hoy et al., 2015). In Chapter 2, we hypothesized a robot that needs to navigate from the entrance to the desk of a hotel, finding its way among obstacles. We explained that researchers address navigation in different ways, for example, following a Sense Plan Model Act (Nilsson, 1984), a Behavior-based (Brooks, 1991), or a hybrid approach (Gat, 1997). Whatever the approach adopted, the same crucial information is needed to reach the goal: the robot needs to be constantly aware of the goal position compared to its own current position. Or, in other words, the robot must know its current position and the goal position in the same coordinate frame. You may be familiar with Cartesian coordinates and use them to describe the robot and the goal's position along the X and the Y axes in meters or feet. Or you may be more familiar with latitude and longitude, typically used for describing the robot and goal position in wider outdoor regions.

By hearing of latitude and longitude, one may be tempted to equip the robot with a Global Positioning System (GPS). After all, this is what a GPS does: it returns the latitude and longitude of your car's current position in world coordinates. When asking a GPS navigator to find a route to a destination whose latitude and longitude are known, the navigator computes the shortest path from the car's current position. Or the cheapest path if the driver wants to avoid paying tolls. The problem faced by robots looks the same: unfortunately, the solution cannot be the same, at least with socially assistive robots, since the GPS works only outdoors. Even if the robot operates in your garden, the information provided by GPS satellites might not have the required accuracy for distinguishing between two neighboring places, for example, "in front of the barbecue" and "to the left of the inflatable pool." An assistive robot helping with the barbecue would risk putting the pork ribs in the water among swimming children.

So, how can we ensure the robot will not be lost while moving between places of a person's house, from the bathtub to the fridge, from the bedroom to the balcony?

Robotics researchers refer to the problem of understanding one's position in the environment as "self-localization," which is known to be a hard one in robotics. At the dawn of robotics, researchers have addressed this problem by replicating the principles of ship navigation, using visible landmarks along the coast. They used markers with color or bar codes attached to walls: the robot could then use cameras for marker detection and then compute its position using well-known navigation techniques known as triangulation or trilateration (Borenstein et al., 1996). Other researchers have applied the same ideas but using special transmitting devices distributed in the environment, sometimes called "beacons," to emulate an indoor GPS. More recently, several robotics researchers rejected the idea of purposely modifying the environment by sticking markers or beacons to walls. Instead, they suggest designing robots capable of autonomously creating a map of the environment using their onboard sensors, for example, sonars, laser sensors, or particular "depth" cameras capable of returning the distance from walls and obstacles. According to the Simultaneously Localization And Mapping (SLAM) paradigm, robots shall be able to draw a map incrementally and, at the same time, compute their position in the map they are making (Cadena et al., 2016).

As the reader can observe, several approaches to self-localization exist. However, as it often happens with robots, solutions work well during lab experiments or in specific environments but are less reliable in others. The capability to unambiguously recognize almost any place, shared at different degrees by all biological beings, reveals to be a philosopher's stone for robots. Indeed, robots moving in human-inhabited environments have a craze for periodically getting stuck somewhere, with no idea what to do next. Probably, the only examples of robots successfully moving around people's houses are cleaning robots, some of which can build maps of the house but still have the chance of moving almost randomly to cover the floor if they do not know their position. The fact that everybody tends to be incredibly tolerant toward cleaning robots is not a surprise: even if a cleaning robot takes the entire day to clean my house, it is still better than if I have to do the job!

Being lost in the environment is not the only way of "being lost." There are other possible acceptations of the term, most of which are metaphorical. For example, the robot may be lost because it cannot understand what is happening around it or does not know how to behave in a given context. Suppose a person is brushing their teeth and, at some point, hands the toothpaste to the robot. Are the robot's sensorimotor and cognitive capabilities appropriated to recognize what the person intends to do? Is the robot capable of identifying the object the person is holding out, planning an appropriate sequence of actions, and executing them?

Let us focus on object recognition. As we clarified in Chapter 2, recognizing objects characterized by well-defined colors and shapes is easy. However, identifying complex objects such as a toothpaste tube (or a human activity) in the presence of changing lighting conditions and occlusions due to other objects (or people) may be a nightmare. Robotic researchers can make object recognition simpler by integrating a third-party program into the robot's program (Redmon et al., 2016) or a service provided by Internet colossuses such as Amazon[8], Google[9], or Microsoft[10]. However, all state-of-the-art tools incur the risk of failing when processing a snapshot taken with robot cameras, which may be blurry, have low resolution, contrast, and lighting, or feature several objects occluding or projecting shadows on each other. To make things worse, the performance in understanding if an object belongs or not to a given category ("is this a toothpaste tube?") heavily depends on the number of different object categories between which you want to distinguish. In Chapter 2, we made the example of a Neural Network for face recognition using only two categories, "this is a face" and "this is not a face." Suppose now you have 100 object categories (including "toothpaste tube," but also "mayonnaise tube," "condensed milk tube," "cream for pimples tube," plus 96 more), and you want to classify objects as belonging to one of the 100 categories. With 100 categories instead of 2, we will require many more pictures to train the Neural Network: each picture shall contain one or more objects labeled with their corresponding categories by varying their scale, perspective, color, lighting, contrast, etc. When training ends and the robot starts working, the possibility of confusing similar objects during the robot's operations unavoidably increases as the number of categories increases.

When object recognition fails, similarly to navigation, the robot will be lost, that is, incapable of appropriately understanding the current context. And what if the robot correctly recognizes the toothpaste but does not understand what the person wants? Maybe the robot shall grab it? What if the robot understands the person's intentions but does not have the physical capability to do what it must do?

Several other examples of robots "lost somewhere," either metaphorically or not, could be provided, all leading to people's frustration and annoyance: "What is the robot waiting for?" "Why is it not acting properly?" "Maybe should I do something?" "Is it my fault?" "DID I BREAK IT?"

As the concluding example, we will mention verbal conversation with humans, one of the most crucial capabilities that a socially assistive robot shall exhibit. The reader may easily figure out a robot that does not reply appropriately to people. Please recall the short story at the end of Chapter 2. (...) *It is Thursday afternoon. We are ready to test our new robot in a*

---

[8] https://aws.amazon.com/rekognition/.

[9] https://cloud.google.com/vision.

[10] https://azure.microsoft.com/en-us/services/cognitive-services/computer-vision/.

care home starting from Monday. (…) To make our audience more familiar with it, we invite nurses and caregivers to have a conversation with the robot (…) A young nurse makes a step forward. We invite him to say something to the robot, and he says: "Do you know Harry Potter?". The robot, very frustratingly, replies: "There are many things I can do for you. Do you want to talk with me about your daily routines?" The story ended like this, with the robot lost in the conversation since it does not recognize the person's intention to talk about Harry Potter. We could imagine an even more dramatic ending, with the robot replying: "I don't understand what you say. Can you repeat, please?" Whatever the robot's answer is, the nurse who posed the question is frustrated and annoyed. The trust of medical staff and caregivers in the robots' capabilities collapses. Somebody in the audience, who was worried about losing their job, is relieved. Somebody else starts to laugh under their whiskers.

Game, set, match. We are lost, too.

Up to now, we have not mentioned the word "robustness" in this chapter. However, the reader may object that they have already heard a similar discussion in Chapter 2. In all three examples above, for example, self-localization, object recognition, and conversation, the robot gets lost because its sensorimotor and cognitive capabilities are not robust enough in the presence of unpredictable and highly dynamic environmental conditions. Whether literally or metaphorically, getting lost is one of the consequences of a robot not being capable of robust behavior. A robot programmed to work robustly in almost all real-world situations and not only in a minimal subset of cases will exhibit an autonomous behavior without ever getting lost. But we repeatedly said that the current technology does not allow robotic researchers to provide robots with the sensorimotor and cognitive capabilities to operate 24/7 in the real world with the same robustness humans do! So then, once again, what strategy shall we follow if we want to deploy assistive robots today?

We know that a robot that "gets lost" frequently, that is, incapable of understanding and responding appropriately to the current situation, induces frustration and distrust in people. Perhaps the key is to ensure that a robot never "looks lost" and can always do something appropriate, even if it is not as robust as we would like and it sometimes fails? A robot having something meaningful to say even when it has not a real clue about what's going on? Should we use our intelligence as designers to make robots that can convincingly "look autonomous?" even if they are not as "robust" as we would like?

After all, when the robot interacts with humans, it is not very far from an actor improvising in front of an audience, and all professional actors know that all the "magic" of theater boils down to a set of well-thought-out tricks.

Hold on to your robotic researcher's hat. We are going to open our bag of tricks.

9.2.2 Tricks and cheats revealed

Please, keep in mind that the problems introduced in the previous sections are general and acknowledged as fundamental problems by most robotic researchers. The solutions we present in the following, on the opposite, derive from our experience in the CARESSES project, which shall be considered a case study and, as such, taken "cum grano salis." We do not claim to have the ultimate solution for making robots (look) autonomous. We just want to share with the reader the lessons we learned while designing fully autonomous robots interacting with older care home residents, hoping to inspire other researchers.

From a broader perspective, ensuring the overall behavior of the robot requires designing a complex computer program like the ones presented in Chapter 2, Fig. 2.2. We will present and discuss the main program controlling our robot and its flowchart later. For the moment, we focus on the basic sensorimotor and cognitive capabilities that, taken together, contribute to determining the robot's overall autonomous behavior. The reader may think of basic capabilities if they were a portfolio of smaller, dedicated programs, each capable of doing something specific: navigation between two places, self-localization, recognizing objects, chitchatting with the person, etc. Each of these basic capabilities is a brick that will contribute to the general structure of the main program: the main program may choose to execute one of the smaller programs to do something specific depending on requests by the users or environmental conditions. For example, the user may ask the robot to play the "Yesterday" song, activating the specific program for playing music; or the robot may detect a marker purposely attached to a wall, activating the program for self-localization. For the main program to be robust, it is necessary (even if not sufficient) that all smaller programs are robust. The good news is that new capabilities can be incrementally added as soon as they are available: we start from a robot with minimal functionalities that may later become a robot with superpowers as research progresses. On the other side, if we discover that one of the smaller programs is not robust enough to ensure the performance we want to achieve, researchers can easily remove it from the main program. We weigh it down with a concrete block and throw it in the ocean forever.

And now, let us move on with our tricks. Some of the strategies we propose are known to robotic researchers. Some are our proposals.

> *Trick number 1: "The frugal researcher"* (difficulty of execution: medium).
>
> Execution: choose and program on the robot only the basic capabilities that, based on the literature, previous experience, and a discussion among all parts involved (including end-users), are expected to be sufficiently robust and have the highest impact on the user's experience.
>
> Challenges: convince robotic researchers that they have to give up trying fancy new solutions that may look amazingly cool but will have a 50% of success in the real world out of their labs. Similarly, convince non-robotic researchers that things that may look simple for humans can be highly complex for robots, such as taking clothes from the wardrobe and handing them to a person. Everybody should stick to simple, robust programs that maximize the chances of success and make people happy. Academic researchers shall keep in mind that the objective is to produce a long-lasting impact on society, not only publishing scientific articles.

Trick number 1 is probably the most important one. In CARESSES, robotic researchers, transcultural nursing researchers, care home managers, and psychologists used this trick during several lengthy discussions to write realistic scenarios (see Chapter 6), and they came out with a list of high-priority capabilities for the robot Pepper, which included: searching for people in the room; greeting people in culturally appropriate ways;

navigating between different locations in the environment; following people holding their hand; operating environmental devices such as a smart lamp; making Skype or phone calls; playing music and videos, including instructions on how to do light physical exercises and other things; reading audiobooks; playing memory games; reading the menu for lunch or dinner; showing weather information, providing privacy; reminding things such as taking pills. And, last but not least, conversing with the person about many different topics with cultural knowledge by acquiring new information from the person during the interaction (see Chapter 8). Other capabilities were developed, including recognizing people's activity and habits using different sensors distributed in the house or smartwatches worn by people: however, "frugal researchers" agreed not to include them in the final prototype because they were judged not robust enough for experiments with care home residents. Perhaps we might include this capability in the future by adding a new "brick" to the structure?

> *Trick number 2: "Prickett's cow" (difficulty of execution: medium-low).*
>
> Execution: address the navigation problem by avoiding to use SLAM, that is, the idea that the robot shall autonomously build a map and understand its position on the map. Good self-localization is mandatory for navigation, and SLAM may not always be as reliable as we would like, especially if robots are not equipped with sensors especially designed for this. A safer solution for self-localization is to use visual landmarks attached to walls, whose position in the environment is known to the robot, and let the robot move only within areas where landmarks are always visible. If the robot has a recharging station, as is the case of cleaning robots, use the charging station for self-localization whenever the robot goes back to the station for recharging. When the robot docks to the station, you know with 100% accuracy it is there!
>
> Challenges: The trick works only if landmarks or the charging stations are always visible (e.g., within the same room), which may not be a significant limitation because social robots available today have limited capabilities to interact with the environment. Indeed, if a robot can't get you a glass of water, it may be useless to send it far away to the kitchen. Landmarks attached to walls are more versatile than the charging station, but recognizing such markers may still be challenging in a chaotic domestic environment. A challenge of different nature is that SLAM has been a gold mine for academic researchers to publish scientific articles in the last 2 decades. We may insist on using SLAM because it is a more honorable solution (with more chances of publishing our results!).

Trick number 2 takes its name after Lee Master's poem "Roger Heston" within Spoon River Anthology: "My favorite metaphor was Prickett's cow Roped out to grass, and free you know as far As the length of the rope." The idea is to give the robot autonomy, but only within certain boundaries to ensure safe motion in the environment. Providing the robot with a sort of "conditional free will" is a good idea also because if you let a robot wander too much, the risk of being blocked by a chair or a pair of shoes lying on the floor becomes incredibly high. Should this happen, a related trick is programming the robot to verbally ask people to move it (or take it by hand) to a known place. Much better than being stuck somewhere forever! Since the recharging station can typically be detected only within a given distance, you may also think of putting more than one charging station in different rooms in the person's house.

> *Trick number 3: "The wise nurse" (difficulty of execution: low).*
>
> Execution: Be aware that when people talk to the robot, there will be many situations where the robot will not understand what they mean. However, you shall always prevent the robot from replying using such expressions as "I don't understand what you say. Can you repeat, please?" Even when the robot does not understand what the person is saying, it should always give a reply to make the conversation move on.
>
> Challenges: To implement this trick, you may need not only the experience of robotic and healthcare experts but also creative writers. Writing the proper sentences for the robot to "look like" it understands what the person is saying may require experience, sensitivity, and a pinch of cunning. A related challenge is that a robot purposely hiding its limitations may raise ethical issues and undermine trust. Finally, some robotic researchers may not understand why this trick is needed at all. Researchers may prioritize understanding a precanned set of commands to do useful things like playing music or turning off the light. Even worse, they will think their approach works because, during experiments, they are biased to test it with sentences that always produce an appropriate reply from the robot. Don't listen to us! Having a proper answer to the sentence *"Do you know Harry Potter?"* may be extremely important for a socially assistive robot, even if robotic researchers may not understand why! On the other side, robotic researchers are right when they claim that adding a specific answer for every possible sentence is an approach doomed to fail, as discussed in Chapter 2. Here is where "The wise nurse" comes into play.

When talking with home assistants such as Alexa or Google Home, people are happy to give specific commands to execute specific activities. However, this is not sufficient in socially assistive scenarios since we want to allow the person to talk about any topic with the robot. Luckily, experience shows that people find it more engaging to tell their own experiences to a robot that "looks like" is paying attention to them, rather than paying attention to a robot saying very clever things. This is particularly true for older people who like to talk with the robot about their memories, family, and feelings. The trick is called "the wise nurse" since it was suggested by nursing experts interviewed during CARESSES. Experts confirmed that, unfortunately, they sometimes do not understand what older people want to communicate. In these cases, a generic, positive reply to show empathy may be very effective, such as "I understand," "Please, tell me more," "I see, and how do you feel now?"

9.2.3 One more trick: choosing a robot not resident in the "Uncanny Valley."

Until now, we have discussed how social robots might look "autonomous" and "intelligent" by emphasizing their characteristics in terms of sensorimotor and cognitive capabilities. But what about their physical appearance?

Probably, you are picturing a robot with some *humanoid* characteristics (two eyes, a mouth, two arms) but different from a human being. For example, if you check how the Pepper robot looks in Fig. 9.1, you may imagine that the robot does not have legs but a base with wheels, which significantly reduces the robot's chances of falling. Or, more generically, you may be imagining a robot that, even if it possesses some human physical characteristics, is more stylized: big round eyes, a body composed of geometrical shapes, metallic or plastic arms and hands that only partially resemble human ones, a different way of moving.

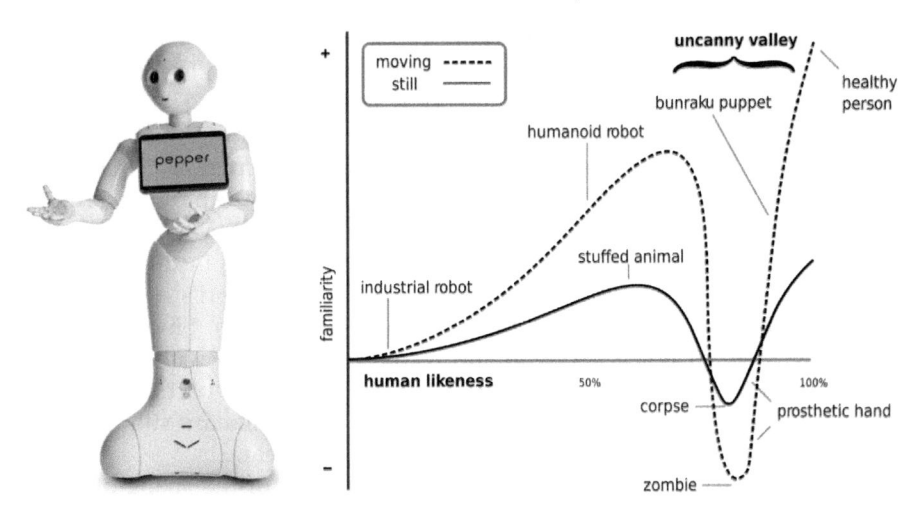

FIGURE 9.1 *Left*: SoftBank Robotics Pepper. *Right*: The Uncanny Valley is the steep descent in how familiar we find a robot or a character when it gets too close to appearing human, without being human. *Courtesy: Wikipedia*.

How did we guess? Of course, you may have been influenced by the examples provided at the beginning of this chapter (if you watched the videos). We already debated in Chapter 5 that our expectations about robots highly depend on how the media represent them. But this brings up other questions: Why do we not build robots that look exactly like humans? Why do we usually have robots with only some typical human traits? Why do we not have social robots with augmented capabilities (e.g., more than two eyes or arms) or a non-humanoid appearance?

Perhaps choosing the proper physical appearance may reveal an additional trick to achieve our objective, that is, having a robot that "looks like" it is autonomous and intelligent?

You may have heard of the Uncanny Valley theory before. It is an attempt to describe the sense of concern and anxiety you may feel when encountering a slightly too-lifelike robot (see the Sophia robot, footnote 2 of this chapter). Or the feeling of uncomfortableness that you may experience when you see a very creepy doll. More specifically, the Uncanny Valley is the steep descent in how familiar and likable we find a robot or a character when it gets slightly too close to appearing human without being human (Fig. 9.1). Even if we do not fully understand this phenomenon and its causes, the idea is quite old. It was first proposed in an essay written in 1970 by the Japanese roboticist Masahiro Mori (Mori et al., 2012), who hypothesized that people's sense of familiarity with a robot would increase as the robot becomes more and more human-like. But, at a certain point, quite abruptly, this familiarity would drop off, replaced by repulsion. The figure shows that Mori plotted human likeness (on the horizontal axis) versus familiarity (on the vertical axis) by considering both robots and puppets to enforce this hypothesis. He came up with a graph with a sharp dip: that's the Uncanny Valley. Even more interesting, Mori suggested that the capability to make movements might steepen the slopes of the plot. If we consider animated characters such as robots, zombies, and puppets, the sensation of eeriness in case they are too much similar to humans is amplified compared to stuffed animals.

This whole idea was not even new in 1970. About 50 years earlier in 1919, the Austrian psychologist Sigmund Freud had identified uncanny as "that class of frightening which leads back to what is known of old and long familiar" (Freud, 1953). But the Uncanny Valley theory has not received much attention until the last 20 years and was introduced in pop culture in the early 2000s, thanks to a popular animation movie: Robert Zemeckis's Polar Express, starring Tom Hanks animating different characters through motion capture techniques. If you watched that movie, you might also know that it was not a hit for everyone, mainly because of its hyper-realistic style, a great example of characters "residing in the Uncanny Valley": critics described them as zombie-like and dead-eyed. In 2005, Mori's essay was translated into English, and psychologists started to study the phenomenon. Since then, researchers have explored whether or not it is possible to recreate Mori's plot with experimental data. Recently, an Uncanny Valley plot resulted from a study with 342 participants and 80 real-life robot faces (Mathur & Reichling, 2016). However, the results are still controversial, as other studies have shown that the effect does not always appear.

Researchers have tried to understand what are the causes of the shape of Mori's curve. Why this sensation of eeriness? For example, the "pathogen avoidance hypothesis of conservatism" suggests that the uncanny feeling is rooted in the primary emotion of disgust as a defensive strategy to avoid someone who might be carrying a transmissible disease (Moosa & Ud-Dean, 2010). The "mortality salience hypothesis" has proposed that uncanny faces, like clowns, dolls, wax figures, corpses, and zombies, might remind us of death, triggering defense mechanisms correlated to the rooted anxiety for mortality (MacDorman, 2005). The "violation of expectation hypothesis" suggests that human-like robots might lead us to think that they will behave in a human-like way but then create a sense of disorientation by violating this expectation (Mitchell et al., 2011). The "categorical uncertainty hypothesis" tries to make sense of how our brains are processing uncanny faces, arguing that the main problem is the uncertainty in the category boundary (Wang & Rochat, 2017). And, finally, "the mind perception hypothesis" suggests that we find robots uncanny when we feel that these non-human things might be capable of human behaviors (Gray & Wegner, 2012). In other words, you can make a robot creepy by telling users that they will interact with the robot that it is capable of human thinking and feeling. Brrr.

At least some evidence supports all of these hypotheses, but we do not have sure answers. Still, we now have some answers to the questions we have posed at the beginning of this Section: we know why social robots should have some human-like characteristics but not resemble humans too closely.

This discussion about the robot's physical appearance paves the way to a very important trick.

Trick number 4: "The smart-looking guy" (difficulty of execution: medium).

Execution: Choose accurately the robotic platform you want to use. If you are working on intelligent, autonomous behavior and not on mechanical design, building your robot from scratch is probably not a good idea, however exciting it can be. Many robotic companies produce amazing robots with a carefully studied design: the physical appearance of the robot, the basic movements of the head and the body that are already part of the robot as it comes out of the factory, may play a key role in making it look "intelligent," do not underestimate this aspect! On the other side, avoid baby dolls and other robots that closely resemble humans. Horror movies have already proved that a baby doll following you with its head and eyes can make you shiver with fear.

Challenges: robotic researchers may be tempted to choose a robotic platform because of its functionalities rather than its appearance, including the number of motors, the type and number of sensors, and how easy it is to write a software program to control it. A good compromise between functionalities and appearance is crucial. An additional challenge is that the cost of the robotic platform may increase depending on the quality of the design, and low cost may be vital if you want to impact society.

In the CARESSES project, we chose as a robotic platform the robot Pepper produced by SoftBank robotics, Fig. 9.1, which proved to be a good compromise between functionalities, appearance, and cost. To our spite, we had to admit that, during exhibitions, people appreciated the robot because of its cute appearance and smooth movements, even when the AI program we developed to make it autonomous was not running at all! When this happened, we needed to explain to people that Pepper could not do useful things without our software and that the credit for the intelligent behavior they were observing was due to our work.

This is not surprising. People saw a robot that was "sooo cute!" that it could not but be very intelligent. Do you think we should consider this as a failure or the result of good strategic decisions?

9.3 A seemingly autonomous robot: the CARESSES case study

9.3.1 Sensing, knowledge, planning, and acting

It has been a long trip, but you should now have at least an idea of the general approach adopted in the CARESSES project. You have learned the basics of programming in Chapter 2; what people expect from socially assistive robots in Chapter 3; how to deal with ethic issues in Chapter 4; how to write scenarios as the basis for developing social robots assisting humans in Chapter 6; how to write guidelines for culturally competent behavior in Chapter 7; how culturally competent dialogue works in Chapter 8; and, finally, some strategies adopted to make the robot (look) autonomous in this chapter, including the rationale for its physical appearance. It is time to provide a detailed picture of the structure of the main program that determines the interaction with the robot.

The program in Fig. 9.2 may look a little more complex than the flowcharts that you have seen in the previous chapters. The first thing to notice is that the program has a "Start" block (on the top left) but not an "End" block. Indeed, we have designed this program to be constantly running, ideally 24/7. From the "Start" block, an arrow immediately leads to the "Rest" block, corresponding to the robot waiting for the person to call it. Thus, we have something similar to what vocal assistants such as Alexa and Google Home do: when you switch them on, they wait for being activated with a "magic word" and then process the user's requests. We might say vocal assistants are always in a "waiting state" (you rarely unplug your home assistant), waiting for the user to get their attention. The same

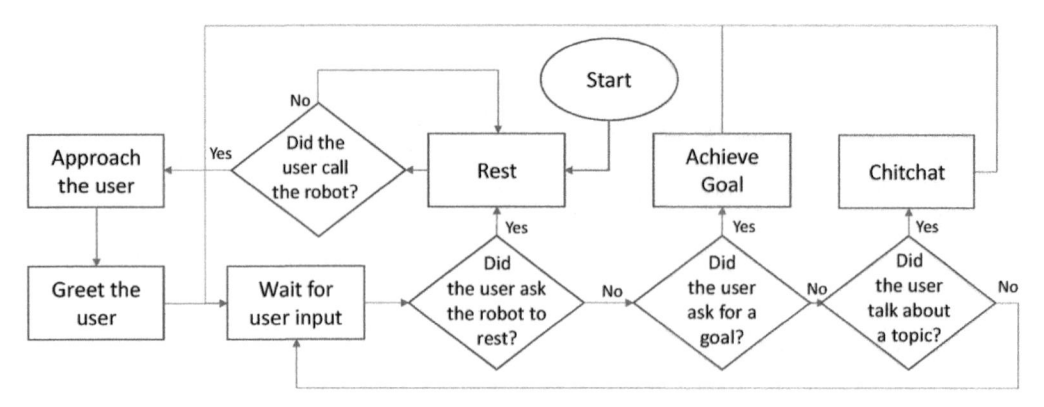

FIGURE 9.2 Flowchart of the main program used in CARESSES.

happens with our "Rest" block. Like a vocal assistant, the robot is waiting to be called by the user to come back to life, a condition checked by the block labeled "Did the user call the robot?" If the answer is "No," that is, the user is not calling the robot, an arrow leads back to the "Rest" block, and nothing happens.

Suppose that the robot has been interacting with the person for some time. You can notice another arrow leading back to the "Rest" block, which means that the program will enter the "waiting state" again when the user asks the robot to stop the interaction or has not interacted with the robot for a while. When the robot enters the "waiting state" after the interaction, it autonomously moves to the charging station. Do you remember the *Pricket's cow* trick? Besides being a way for letting the robot recharge, this is also a trick for the robot's self-localization. Pepper may find and reach the charging station since the latter is equipped with bright blue lights easily detectable by cameras in its head; at the same time, the position of the charging station is well-known and fixed in the environment. Result: each time the robot reaches the charging station, it resets its current position, reducing the possibility of getting lost—two birds with one stone.

When in the "Rest" block, if the user calls the robot, the arrow leads to three blocks in sequence: "Approach the user," "Greet the user," and "Wait for user input." Their meaning is relatively straightforward: the robot searches for the user in the environment, approaches and greets them, and starts the interaction. These blocks of the flowcharts use some of the basic capabilities mentioned in the previous Sections, such as searching for people, navigation, greeting, conversation. As usual, we try to keep things simple, avoiding complex strategies for robot navigation. For example, to approach the user, the robot attempts to detect a person in the environment using cameras: then, it moves toward the detected person relying on its sensors to avoid obstacles without creating a global environment's map, in a Behavior-based spirit (see Chapter 2). In the final trial with care home residents, we used an even simpler approach since their bedrooms were usually small, cluttered with obstacles, and had bad lighting conditions. We commanded the robot to move to specific coordinates in space, for example, in front of the armchair where the user was usually sitting. In this way, the robot knew in advance the positions it needed to move to without requiring vision processing to search for people—the *Frugal researcher* at its best.

After approaching and greeting the person, the program enters the block "Wait for user input." Here the person may ask for a specific goal, that is, playing some music or turning on a light. If this happens, the arrows lead to the "Achieve Goal" block that activates all required capabilities and, when the goal has been achieved, goes back to the "Wait for user input" block. Over and over again, 24/7.

Fig. 9.3 describes the internal structure of the "Achieve Goal" block: always remember that a block in a flowchart can hide a complex program that corresponds, in its turn, to a flowchart. As the first step, the flowchart in Fig. 9.3 takes the selected goal as input. The user may trigger goals during the conversation by giving a command to the robot (as already mentioned) or by positively replying to a robot's suggestion. For example, imagine that you are talking with the robot about clothes you like to wear: the robot might, at a certain point, ask you if you need help to get dressed. In case of a positive answer, the program moves to the "Achieve Goal" block to fulfill your request by achieving the goal "Help the person get dressed." The program itself can automatically trigger goals due to external events, as in the unpredictable occurrence of a person falling to the floor. However, this possibility is not shown in the figure.

Given the goal as input, a program named "Planner" makes a plan by selecting the most appropriate capabilities to achieve it. Some goals, such as "Play some music" or "Turn on a light," may require only one capability. Still, other goals may be more complex and require multiple steps automatically arranged in the proper sequence by the Planner. For example, in the case of "Help person get dressed," the robot makes a plan to first move to the wardrobe along with the user and then show on its screen a video clip about the person's favorite clothes. In this case, the goal requires combining two capabilities, one involving robot navigation and the other involving playing videos on the robot's tablet. When the first capability has achieved its part of the goal, the program activates the second capability. Ideally, this process may require repeatedly making plans and using the required capabilities until the goal has been finally achieved (see the loop in Fig. 9.3, where an arrow leads back to the question "Was the goal achieved?").

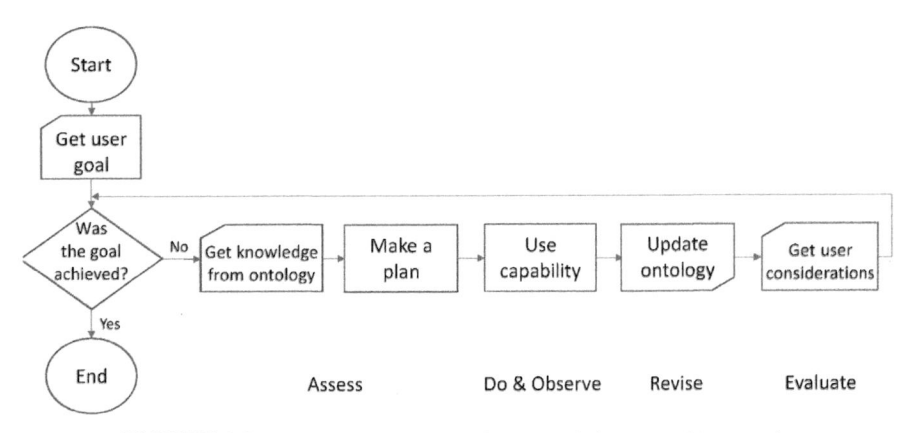

FIGURE 9.3 Flowchart for using robot's capabilities to achieve goals.

The reader may have noticed a problem here: how does the robot know the person's favorite clothes? As for the verbal interaction described in Chapter 8, the cultural knowledge base, implemented as an Ontology, plays a fundamental role. As you may recall, the Ontology stores cultural (and, if any, personal) information. So, besides ensuring a culturally competent verbal interaction, it also informs the Planner about everything needed to operate in a culturally competent way. For example, it may tell the Planner that approaching the person should be done by staying at a specific distance, following a given culture's proxemics rules. Or that the robot should greet the person with a bow, waving its hands, or joining the hands in the Namaste greeting. Even better, if the robot has specific knowledge about the person, such knowledge may be used to feed the Planner with the most suitable information. For example, suppose I have previously chitchatted with the robot about how much I like wearing hats. In that case, the "Help person get dressed" goal will probably show me a video clip about the most fashionable hats.

This strategy directly comes from the ADORE guidelines described in Chapters 7 and 8. The robot uses the person's cultural identity to make educated guesses about what the users may like. But it also continuously revises its knowledge about the person by acquiring new information and using it for future interactions. This process, already described in Chapter 8 concerning conversation, is also implemented in the "AchieveGoal" block. Fig. 9.3, mimicking Fig. 8.5, shows that: the Planner considers the person's culture in the Ontology to select the most appropriate capabilities with cultural competence (Assess); the robot uses its capability to operate and observe the person's reaction, or even ask for feedback (Do and Observe); the Ontology is updated based on the robot's observation (Revise); the robot asks the person for comments and report them to healthcare and technical staff (Evaluate). Concerning the last two points, we do not continually update the Ontology and ask people for their considerations to avoid making the interaction too repetitive and cumbersome. But consider again the "Help person get dressed" goal: the robot may guess the person is interested in fashionable hats but then realizes that the person does not watch the full video clip about hats from start to end, and, once the process is over, the person may confirm they did not enjoy watching the video. In this case, using the acquired information to revise the knowledge encoded in the Ontology may be crucial.

If the person has not commanded the robot to achieve a specific goal, maybe the robot shall interpret what the person says as the intention to talk about some topic; see the arrow leading to the "Chitchat" block in Fig. 9.2. We extensively described the culturally competent conversation mechanism in Chapter 8: here, we only show the internal structure of the "Chitchat" block represented as a flowchart according to the ADORE guidelines, Fig. 9.4. The reader may observe how the mechanism for culturally competent verbal interaction has been integrated into the main program, allowing the robot to converse with the person 24/7 while constantly assessing and revising its knowledge. During chitchatting, the "wise nurse" trick reveals to be crucial, allowing the robot to give appropriate yet generic replies to make the conversation move on even when it cannot find anything specific in its cultural Ontology. Notice also that the evaluation phase of ADORE is missing during chitchatting, as it would be boring and confusing to ask people for considerations about the conversation!

We have almost finished. A few more words about the "Wait for user input" block. In that block, the robot mainly waits for the person to say something, which may directly trigger some goal ("Pepper, help me to get dressed!"), start a conversation ("I feel really happy

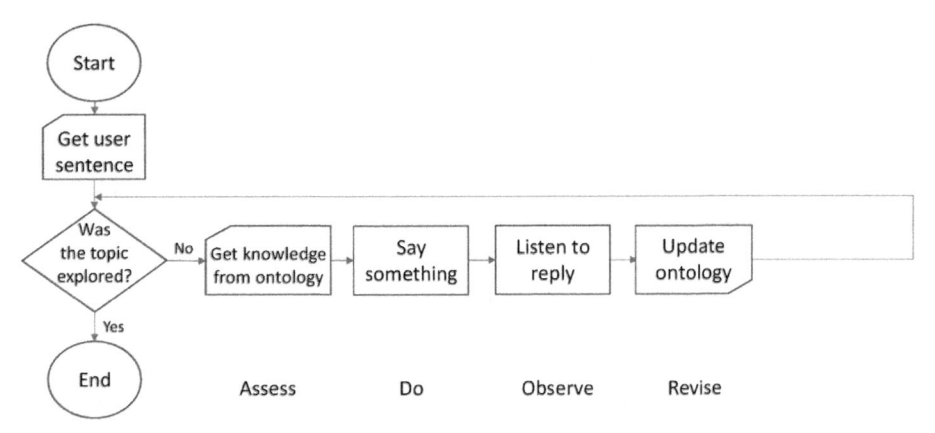

FIGURE 9.4 Flowchart for using robot's capabilities to chitchat with the person.

today!"), or instruct the robot to rest ("Goodbye, my friend"). Cultural competence plays a role also in this block since the robot here may propose some activities or topics of conversation to the user.

You may guess how it chooses these activities: using the cultural and personal information stored in the Ontology!

9.3.2 The long and winding road to experiments with people

So here we are again, after 2 years of hard work, after a significant effort for making all pieces of software work together to make the general structure emerge, after having struggled to find the best way to let researchers cooperate most fruitfully. We shared ideas, defined clear objectives, developed our Artificial Intelligence (AI).

We are ready to test the robot.

Two years ago, we learned a very important lesson when the young nurse asked the robot about Harry Potter. Today, we know very well when and why robots tend to get lost, either literally or metaphorically. We have also learned a few tricks to make the robot "look more intelligent" than it really is. And we used them!

And now here we are again, ready to test the robot. However, this time, we have decided to perform some preliminary tests to avoid another epic failure in the presence of care home staff. Very smart of us! We ask some colleagues, students, and young researchers working in different computer science fields, to come to our lab and interact with the robot. How long? Let's say for 20 min, after a brief explanation on how to do it.

What can go wrong?

Thanks to our tricks, we may think we have finally developed an excellent program with a supposedly "natural" User Interface (UI) (Perzanowski et al., 2001). We might be tempted to conjecture that interacting with our system will be easy for everybody. However, this comes out, once again, to be only a hope. After a few seconds of the first experiment, it immediately becomes evident that problems are not only related to "what" the person does to interact with the robot but also to "when" and "how" the person does it. Things that may be obvious for researchers that developed the robot, such as knowing the exact moment the microphone is listening or how and when to use the touch screen on the robot's chest instead of speaking, are not evident to everybody. Participants talk when the robot is talking. They wait indefinitely for something to happen while the robot is also waiting for them to speak (a deadlock!). They do not clearly understand when the robot is just chitchatting or needs crucial information, without which it cannot achieve a goal. We soon have to realize that our colleagues, students, and young researchers may not be able to interact with the robot without our help. And, if such a situation may occur in a laboratory crowded with computer scientists, we start figuring out with horror how many problems may arise when we bring the robot to a public exhibition. An area crowded with people. The robot cannot understand a word of what the person is saying because of the environmental noise. The robot is subject to a burst of contemporary commands, with many mouths talking at the same time and many fingers touching the tablet simultaneously. Did someone say "kids"?

The scientific literature has deeply investigated problems related to UI development, and opinions may be controversial (Norman, 2010). Although robotic researchers have the long-term objective of developing robots with a "natural" UI, allowing people to interact with robots the same way they interact with other people, this is likely not to happen tomorrow. At the same time, we don't want to ask people to learn tens of rules to interact with the robot: no one in the world is used to read a manual to operate a piece of technological equipment anymore. The "one-button" approach to the UI, which has become popular thanks to smartphones, taught people that things must be simple.

Even if we don't discuss all problems related to developing a good UI, we want to remind the reader that these problems exist, need addressing, and are different from the problems addressed so far.

Wait a moment: what about a couple of tricks to make the UI "look" natural?

> *Trick 5. "One method fits all"* (*difficulty of execution: medium*)
> Execution: People are not used to interacting with robots: make their lives as easy as possible. Ideally, the long-term objective of robotics is natural interaction, but no robotic researcher thinks that this may happen today. So then, given that following some basic instructions is required for interaction, keep instructions the fewest and most coherent as possible. The way to interact with the robot should always be the same, even when doing different things.
> Challenges: Ensuring a coherent UI may be harder with robots than with vocal assistants because a robot will have many different capabilities (playing music, moving between different places, making a phone call, following the person by the hand), and the conversation with the person may follow a different flow depending on what the robot is currently doing (asking the person what songs they want to listen to is different from asking the person to tell their memories). Convincing robotic researchers to focus on UI design before developing intelligent behaviors may be hard but fundamental to avoid the number of interaction possibilities explode.

In CARESSES, if the person can use the tablet on Pepper's chest to choose among different options, this should indifferently happen when choosing the song to play, the place to go, or the phone number to call. If tapping the robot's head stops an activity, this should work both when the robot is reading the lunch menu and following the person by the hand. If "yes/no" questions can be answered interpreting "of course," "correct," "sure" as synonyms, the same should work both when the robot asks a person if they are an atheist and when the person asks the robot to show instructions to cook cinnamon rolls.

> *Trick 6. "The honest-looking guy" (difficulty of execution: low)*
>
> Execution: Make evident to the person what the robot is currently doing or waiting for, always. However is structured the program controlling it, the robot will likely execute different "blocks" of the flowchart when doing different things, for example, "Rest," "Wait for User Input," "Achieve Goal," "ChitChat" in Fig. 9.2. Different blocks run different programs and may require the person to do and say things differently (despite our efforts to keep interaction the most coherent as possible). Then, it may help to use visual and auditory signs (e.g., lights, sounds, images, head, and body posture, etc.) to make the user aware of what the robot is doing or expecting from the person at any instant.
>
> Challenges: Using this strategy requires that the robot has the physical possibility to produce easily interpretable visual and auditory signals. For example, Pepper has a tablet on its chest useable for this purpose and lights on its shoulder and eyes, but other robots may offer other possibilities. Also, if we ask the person to interpret too many signals, we risk increasing the cognitive burden and the confusion instead of reducing it.

The "honest-looking" is somehow related to the concept of Explainable AI (Adadi & Berrada, 2018), the idea that AI programs should always make clear to the people the rationale of their reasoning processes to help them make better decisions (and trust AI more). In CARESSES, simple drawings on Pepper's screen help the person understand what the robot is doing or expecting. For instance, when the robot has finished talking, a microphone is shown on the screen to signal that the person can speak. The microphone disappears again as soon as the robot is ready to reply. This is not very different from what people do with head nods, eye gazes, etc., which play a key role during the conversation (Rich et al., 2010)!

The long story of the CARESSES prototype ends here. After preliminary tests in our lab and a pretrial with one care home resident, we decided to completely redesign the UI according to the two simple strategies above. As a result, we observed a notable improvement in predictability, ease of use, and facility to learn (and remember!) how to interact with the robot.

We are finally ready to go "into the wild," Chapter 10 is waiting for you.

But first, after revealing what we learned in the past, let's conclude with a few words about the future.

9.4 Cultural competence everywhere and the cloud hypothesis

"Ciao Carmine, welcome back." Thanks to its sensors, the new-generation vocal assistant I recently purchased has just recognized that I am back from work. It warmly greets me.

"Hi, thanks a lot,"—I answer absently. "Can you read me the sports news?" "Sure, I will do that."

The vocal assistant reads the headlines of the Italian newspaper that I prefer and asks me if I want to listen to the whole article. I choose a piece of news about my favorite football team.

The championship just started, and I have plenty of expectations this year. I thank the vocal assistant while moving to my kitchen, where I keep my robotic pill dispenser. A lasting sound indicates that the dispenser is searching for me since it is time for my daily vitamins. I get closer to the dispenser, which recognizes my face and dispenses my pill.

"Thank you. I don't know what I would do without you!" I really believe this; it is actually a very friendly robot.

"Thanks, Carmine," replies the pill dispenser. "I know that you like football. Please, tell me more about the last match you watched." Such a lovely thought! We chitchat for a while about my favorite sport, and the reasons why we both like it. Did I already mention that I love this robot? The pill dispenser finally reminds me that I need to call my parents. It asks me if I want to do it now.

"Sure, let's do it now!" is my prompt answer. I wait for some seconds before I realize that this robot, although being so lovely, cannot make phone or video calls. Instead, it kindly tells me that my phone will make the call, which already knows the number. I take out my smartphone from my pocket, and I talk for a few minutes with my parents, who are fond of knowing about my latest travel. When I hang up, I realize that I can finally have some rest in my bedroom. As I lie down on the bed, another vocal assistant placed on my night table suggests that I might call my parents again next week, and following its suggestion, I set a reminder. It also observes that family is an essential aspect of the Italian culture and looks interested in learning more about it. It may be right about Italians and family, but I politely decline the conversation without answering and ask the assistant to put on some music. It already knows my musical tastes, so I just lay down and relax. Zzz ….

This is not an imaginative vision of a far future. Instead, it is a possible interaction that may ideally occur tomorrow in an ordinary house filled with smart devices. These devices already exist; they only need an Internet connection to interact with a program for culturally competent knowledge storing, action planning, and conversation. Do you have any guesses about the system that I had in mind when describing the example? Correct. The same approach described so far, adapted to handle multiple devices and users, Fig. 9.5.

You may have noticed in the example that all devices share the same knowledge about the person. The pill dispenser knows that I just asked the vocal assistant to hear the sports news, and therefore, it offers to talk with me about football; the second vocal assistant in my bedroom knows that I just called my parents and keeps on talking about that. How can we obtain this cooperative behavior? You might be familiar with the concept of a Cloud system: several computers located worldwide and accessible through the Internet making their services available to users. In our daily life, we use Cloud systems mainly for storing data. For instance, on your phone, you have tools to save all photos and videos "in the Cloud" to spare your device's memory and visualize them at any time. This approach has a lot of advantages: you may retrieve your photos and documents even if you do not have your phone with you, since you only need to remember your password to access Cloud storage services, and in the unlucky event that you lose your phone, you will not lose all your data. Everything is safe on the Cloud! Of course, this comes with some privacy issues that need to be handled. We will talk about this.

In robotics, programs running in the Cloud may help not only to store information but also to do things. In our case, to control robots and devices to make decisions better and faster by using "Cloud computing" and "collective robot learning" (Vojić, 2018). Imagine having a complex program that controls a robot, such as the one presented earlier in this chapter. This program

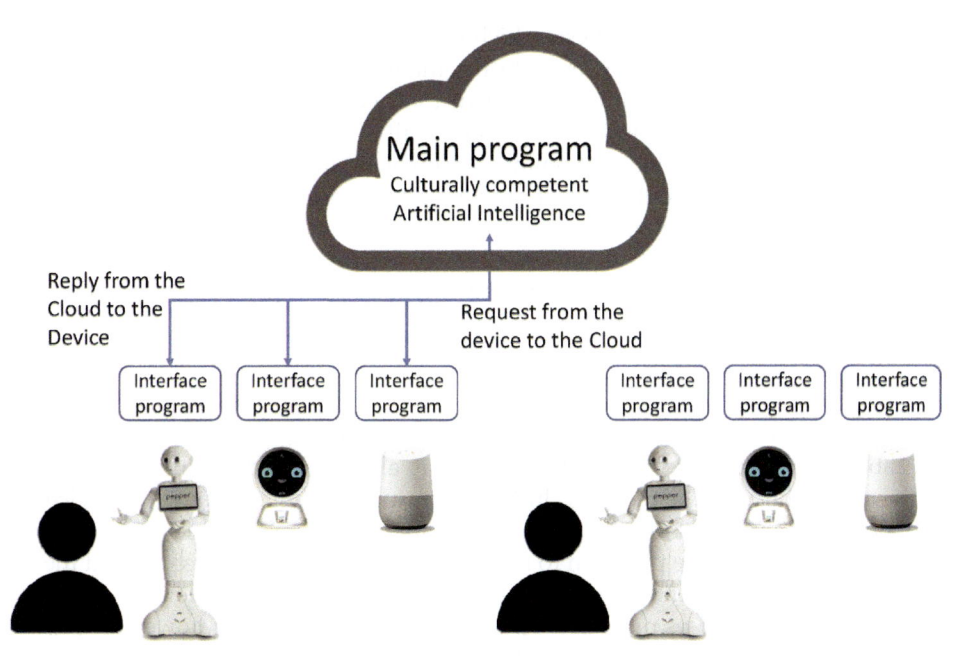

FIGURE 9.5 Two users interacting with different devices: Pepper, Pillo the dispenser, Google Home assistant. Devices access the program in the Cloud to receive instructions for culturally competent interaction.

might require many computational resources to run on a standard computer, which may slow down the robot's reactions to user requests and other events, causing delays and frustration. Of course, one can think about running the same program on a more powerful computer, highly reducing the time required to perform computations. But having a dedicated "high-performance computer" controlling each robot is very expensive and a waste of resources because the robot will not continuously use it. You may have already guessed the problem's solution: multiple robots may rely on the same high-performance computer using an Internet connection, sharing computational resources and cost. Or, more in detail, robots will send data to programs running on high-performance computers managed by big computer companies such as Google, Amazon, and Microsoft (without even knowing where these computers physically are) and receive the outputs in a blink. Roughly speaking, this is the meaning of Cloud computing. Concerning collective robot learning, the name speaks for itself. Different cooperating robots may learn how to solve a problem by acquiring data from their surrounding environment and sending these data to a remote, powerful computer (in the Cloud!) that will process them and use results to increase the knowledge of each participating robot. In both cases, the robots themselves do not require to do that much: they only handle the interaction with the person and the environment to acquire information on the one side, and with the Cloud to send the collected data and receive the response on the other side.

It is now easier to imagine how to make the scenario at the beginning of this Section come true. The original system described in this chapter heavily relied on the Pepper robot chosen as a platform for the interaction. For instance, we developed basic capabilities to show videos because Pepper has a tablet on its chest, which is not true for all robots. Also, so far, we have supposed a dedicated computer to execute the main program in Fig. 9.2. A winning idea might be to rewrite that program to implement the two concepts above: Cloud computing and collective robot learning. The main program shall not run anymore on a dedicated computer physically close to the robot but online, somewhere "in the Cloud." Multiple robots will be allowed to connect to our culturally competent program in the Cloud by sending the data collected from the environment (among them, the sentences that the person says) and receiving the information from the Cloud about what to do next. For every connecting robot, the program in the Cloud will plan the proper capabilities to achieve the current goal and how to reply to the person's sentences.

Let's point out the most exciting aspects of this new approach.

First, we can now connect multiple robots and devices, Fig. 9.5. The main program does not care about which device made the request: it always provides the most appropriate output based on the input it receives. In the minimum configuration, each device needs a microphone to record what the person says, a speaker to pronounce the reply received from the Cloud, and a simple program to manage microphones and speakers and the Internet connection to the Cloud. Nothing more. Thanks to this approach, even devices such as a vocal assistant may use the services provided by the Cloud. No "incredibly powerful" hardware is needed, where "incredibly powerful" hardware usually means "incredibly expensive" hardware. Thus, low-cost systems can also benefit from this solution (the ones we like the most). Of course, if you want your device to dispense pills automatically, make a phone call or somersault while keeping a glass full of water and a rubber duck on its head, a microphone and a speaker will not be sufficient. However, the key idea remains the same: each device requires only a program to implement sensorimotor capabilities. Decisions are taken in the Cloud.

Second, the Cloud may handle not only multiple devices but also multiple users. We explained that the results returned by the Cloud only depend on the information received by the devices and the person's profile. But what does this information include? The last sentence pronounced by the person is undoubtedly part of it. But please, recall the scenario at the beginning of the chapter. The vocal assistant on my night table guessed I might want to talk about my family because I am Italian. The first vocal assistant and the pill dispenser knew about my specific sport preferences (football). All devices remembered the interaction flow as if they were a single device: the pill dispenser chitchatted with me about football after I asked the vocal assistant to read the sports news; the second vocal assistant asked me to set a reminder to call my parents after I phoned them. To interact appropriately with each person and avoid confusion when multiple users are using the system, the program running in the Cloud needs additional information from the device; what the user says is insufficient. This information includes the person's cultural background and specific preference, the state of the conversation, and, we will see, a unique user identifier (ID).

Importantly, sensitive information required to interact with each person shall not be permanently stored in the Cloud but safely on the devices. Privacy is important. People may reasonably be concerned about storing personal data in a distant, unknown place, even if this information is typically encrypted to make it extremely hard for somebody to steal it, as it happens with credit card numbers. Luckily, the Cloud does not need to know sensitive information about the user. Translated from machine to natural language, the information exchange between the program in the Cloud and the interface programs on the devices might sound like this.

> Pill dispenser. "Hey CARESSES, I am a pill dispenser. I am now talking with the user ID 70043, Italian, who likes sport, football, Japanese food, ..., and action movies. He just told me this: << Thank you. I really don't know what I would do without you! >>. The last time he talked with us, he asked the vocal assistant to read out loud the sports news."
> Cloud: "Ho Ho Ho, good to know, pill dispenser. Tell him this: << Thanks, __*username*__, I know that you like football. If you want, please tell me more about the last match you have seen. >>"

You can verify that the program in the Cloud does not know the person's name since the latter is only stored locally on the program running on the pill dispenser, which will replace the placeholder __*username*__ with the person's actual name "Carmine" only when required. The program in the Cloud needs only to be informed about the state of the interaction and the user's preferences so that it can propose a proper sentence to keep talking with him.

But why the user ID 70043 is needed? In our scenario, the pill dispenser uses the ID to know that a person corresponding to ID 70043 asked the vocal assistant about football. Similarly, the vocal assistant on my night table uses the ID to know that the same person used the smartphone to call their family. Each time the person interacts with a specific device connected to the Cloud, all other devices associated with the ID 70043 (i.e., all my devices) can access the Cloud to retrieve information about what has happened so far. And, again, nothing needs to be stored permanently in the Cloud: information associated with ID 70043 flows encrypted from one device to the other "through the Cloud," hopefully leaving no sign of its passage. Please, notice that many Cloud systems actually store some information in the Cloud to make things easier. However, the example above shows that this is not mandatory, which may help reassure people who keep privacy in the greatest concern.

Finally, robots and other devices connected to the Cloud are typically able to do things like reading the news, making a phone call, or playing music. The program in the Cloud manages the goals requested by the person by planning the appropriate sequence of capabilities in the same spirit already explained earlier in this chapter. If the person wants to achieve a goal, the reply from the Cloud will include a list of things to do. Then, it will be up to the program running on the device to check if it has the required capabilities to do what is needed next. Of course, not all devices have all capabilities! For example, the two vocal assistants in our scenario could read the news and play music, but the pill dispenser was not able to place the phone call as suggested by the Cloud, and it notified me about that. Once again, since all my devices share the same user ID, they can periodically ask the Cloud if there is some job to do, and my smartphone finally volunteered to start a call. My parents' phone number is not stored on the Cloud, but only in my phone's contact list and retrieved when necessary.

These are just ideas, and several researchers are already working toward them, even if the fundamental aspect of cultural competence is mostly ignored. Thus, while research in this field progresses, opening new research avenues, we hope that our experience may play a key role in inspiring future researchers in the industry and academia.

We hope that our experience may pave the way to a new generation of Cloud-connected, culturally competent robots and devices.

9.5 Conclusion

Developing autonomous robots is challenging for several different reasons, most of them related to the complexity and unpredictability of the world. Interacting with people appropriately under all environmental conditions is extremely hard. Consequently, big robotic companies tend to invest more in mechanics and control than in autonomy, whereas academic researchers explore amazingly innovative solutions that, however, may not be ready for deployment in the real world "today."

This chapter argued that making robots capable of 24/7 autonomy "today" is crucial to address the problem raised by aging populations, thus helping to reduce the pressure in hospitals and care homes and improve care delivery at home. Following this rationale, we proposed a portfolio of strategies that may help researchers during robot development and showed an example of how a program to produce fully autonomous, culturally competent behavior might look. Finally, we discussed how Cloud-based solutions might help control robots and devices to make decisions better and faster.

9.5.1 Reflective questions

- When robots cannot manage unpredictable situations, we say that they are not robust and may "get lost," literally or metaphorically. In what situations a social robot interacting with people in a home may be lost? What about a robot operating in a hospital or a care home?
- We suggested that it may be convenient to plan smart strategies to deal with problems that may emerge when robots interact with people, and we call these strategies "tricks." Can you figure our other tricks, in addition to the one we proposed? Can you suggest a specific case in which a trick may be used to simplify problems?
- The main program controlling the robot has limitations since the goals can only be selected by the person, not by the robot. How shall we modify the program to consider the possibility that the robot itself can start a goal immediately after chitchatting with the person?

References

Adadi, A., & Berrada, M. (2018). *Peeking inside the black-box: A survey on explainable artificial intelligence (XAI)* (Vol. 6, pp. 52138–52160). IEEE Access.

Borenstein, J., Everett, H. R., & Feng, L. (1996). *Where am I?—systems and methods for mobile robot positioning*. Tech. Report. University of Michigan.

Brooks, R. A. (1991). Intelligence without representation. *Artificial Intelligence, 47*(1–3), 139–159.

Cadena, C., Carlone, L., Carrillo, H., Latif, Y., Scaramuzza, D., Neira, J., Reid, I., & Leonard, J. J. (2016). Past, present, and future of simultaneous localization and mapping: Toward the robust-perception age. *IEEE Transactions on Robotics, 32*(6), 1309–1332.

Freud, S. (1953). The Uncanny. In J. Strachey (Ed.), *17. The standard edition of the complete psychological works of Sigmund Freud, 17* (pp. 219–254). London: Hogarth.

Gat, E. (1997). On three-layer architectures. In D. Kortenkamp, R. P. Bonnasso, & R. Murphy (Eds.), *Artificial intelligence and mobile robots*.

Gray, K., & Wegner, D. M. (2012). Feeling robots and human zombies: Mind perception and the uncanny valley. *Cognition, 125*(1), 125–130.

Hoy, M., Matveev, A. S., & Savkin, A. V. (2015). Algorithms for collision-free navigation of mobile robots in complex cluttered environments: A survey. *Robotica, 33*(3), 463–497.

Kitano, H., Asada, M., Kuniyoshi, Y., Noda, I., & Osawa, E. (1997). RoboCup: The robot world cup initiative. *Proceedings of the International Conference on Autonomous Agents*, 340–347.

MacDorman, K. F. (December 2005). Mortality salience and the uncanny valley. In *5th IEEE-RAS international conference on humanoid robots* (pp. 399–405). IEEE.

Mathur, M. B., & Reichling, D. B. (2016). Navigating a social world with robot partners: A quantitative cartography of the uncanny valley. *Cognition, 146*, 22–32.

Mitchell, W. J., Szerszen Sr, K. A., Lu, A. S., Schermerhorn, P. W., Scheutz, M., & MacDorman, K. F. (2011). A mismatch in the human realism of face and voice produces an uncanny valley. *i-Perception, 2*(1), 10–12.

Moosa, M. M., & Ud-Dean, S. M. (2010). Danger avoidance: An evolutionary explanation of uncanny valley. *Biological Theory, 5*(1), 12–14.

Mori, M., MacDorman, K. F., & Kageki, N. (2012). The uncanny valley. *IEEE Robotics & Automation Magazine, 19*(2), 98–100. https://doi.org/10.1109/MRA.2012.2192811

Nilsson, N. J. (1984). *Shakey the robot*. Sri International Menlo Park CA.

Norman, D. A. (2010). The way I see it: Natural user interfaces are not natural. *Interactions, 17*(3), 6–10.

Perzanowski, D., Schultz, A. C., Adams, W., Marsh, E., & Bugajska, M. (2001). Building a multimodal human-robot interface. *IEEE Intelligent Systems and Their Applications, 16*(1), 16–21.

Redmon, J., Divvala, S., Girshick, R., & Farhadi, A. (2016). You only look once: Unified, real-time object detection. In *Proceedings of the IEEE computer society conference on computer vision and pattern recognition, 2016-December* (pp. 779–788).

Rich, C., Ponsleur, B., Holroyd, A., & Sidner, C. L. (2010). Recognizing engagement in human-robot interaction. In *5th ACM/IEEE international conference on human-robot interaction, HRI 2010* (pp. 375–382).

Vojić, S. (June 2018). Cloud robotics. In *International conference "new technologies, development and applications"* (pp. 191–195). Cham: Springer.

Wang, S., & Rochat, P. (2017). Human perception of animacy in light of the uncanny valley phenomenon. *Perception, 46*(12), 1386–1411.

CHAPTER 10

The CARESSES trial and results

Chris Papadopoulos
Institute for Health Research, University of Bedfordshire, Luton, United Kingdom

> **LEARNING OBJECTIVES**
>
> - To become aware of the aims of the CARESSES trial including what existing research evidence it was attempting to build upon.
> - To learn about the trial design and methodological choices made to reduce bias, maximize feasibility, and explore effectiveness
> - To understand the range of ethical considerations made during the trial
> - To understand the key findings related to the feasibility of the trial, and the impact the intervention produced in relation to participants' physical and mental health, user satisfaction and attitudes, and user perceptions of robotic cultural competence
> - To understand the study limitations and their implications

10.1 Introduction

The final phase of the 2017–20 CARESSES project (the theoretical and technical development of which is discussed in previous chapters) was to conduct an experimental trial of the technology among older adults residing in long-stay care homes. The trial represented one of the largest attempts to explore the level and type of impact that autonomous social robots may produce in relation to the health and wellbeing of older adults, particularly in nonlaboratory real-life settings.

The trial builds on previous evidence that has indicated that Socially Assistive Robots (SARs) could play a role in improving the health and well-being of older adults. For example, Abdi et al.'s (2018) scoping review of 33 robotics studies ($n = 1574$ participants) found that 28 of the included studies reported positive outcomes linked with the robotic assistance of cognitive training, companionship, social facilitation, and physiological therapy among the older adults they interacted with. Similar conclusions were produced by a systematic review that collated evidence from 11 randomized controlled trials of interventions involving SARs for older adults (Pu et al., 2018). The review highlighted that anxiety and agitation could be reduced by SARS, and health-related quality of life increased. They also found evidence for social robots improving older adults' quality of social interaction and engagement, as well as loneliness being reduced. However, both aforementioned authors concluded that despite the positive results and thus clear potential for social robots to support older adults' health and well-being, further research was required.

Therefore, the CARESSES trial described in this chapter aimed to address the call for further evidence pertaining to the potential impact of SARs in improving the health and well-being of older adults. The trial also aligns with the growing need for safe and effective solutions for supporting aging populations across the world, particularly within the care home settings which as a result is under increasing pressure and being stretched further due to employee turnover and shortages. It also represents an attempt to explore the effectiveness of a system that has clear relevance and potential to support isolated and clinically vulnerable individuals during pandemics such as Covid-19.

The principal aim of the trial was to explore the extent to which a Pepper robot embedded with CARESSES culturally competent artificial intelligence (the "Experimental Robot") was able to improve the health and well-being of older adults residing in long stay care homes compared to a control robot with an alternative culturally competent artificial intelligence (the "Control Robot"), and participants who do not receive a robot and instead continue to receive care as usual. In line with this, a number of specific study analytical objectives were set. Those objectives relevant to this chapter were as follows:

1. To evaluate whether and to what degree participants supported by a CARESSES Experimental Robot perceived this robot to be more culturally competent than participants who were supported by a CARESSES Control Robot.
2. To evaluate whether and to what degree the Experimental Robot improved health-related quality of life and reduced loneliness among care home residents compared to the Control Robot and care as usual.
3. To evaluate whether and to what degree the Experimental Robot improved participants' attitudes toward robots, and whether any improvements were larger than those among participants who were supported by the Control Robot.
4. To evaluate whether and to what degree participants experienced greater user satisfaction with using an Experimental Robot compared to the participants who used a Control Robot.
5. To assess the feasibility of the trial procedures including the screening and recruitment strategy, the data collection protocols and the implementation of the robotic interventions.

10.2 Trial design

The design of the study was a mixed-method, parallel group, randomized controlled trial that took place within long-term older adult care homes in England and Japan during 2019.

The trial took place after an initial pretrial pilot which was conducted in late 2018 in one UK-based older adult care homes. This pretrial enabled the research team to test the feasibility and acceptability of our planned study protocols, the results of which proved successful. Both the pretrial and the main study also involved range of complex ethical issues that were carefully considered and addressed (see Chapter 4 and Section 10.2.7). Ethics approval in the UK was granted from the University of Bedfordshire's Research Ethics Committee (Ref: UREC130), whereas in Japan approval was provided by the Human Subject Research Ethics Review Technical Subcommittee of the Japan Advanced Institute of Science and Technology Life Science Committee (Ref: 30−001). The University of Bedfordshire and Advinia Health Care jointly led the trial. The other research partners involved were University of Genova, Middlesex University, Orebro University, Nagoya University, Chubu University, Japan Advanced Institute for Science and Technology and Softbank Robotics.

10.2.1 Participants

Selecting and recruiting enough participants appropriate for the trial was a complex and key aspect of the trial. Ultimately, all study participants were recruited from UK-based care homes (predominantly through Advinia Health Care, a full research partner in the project), whereas the Japanese participants were recruited from an assisted living facility in Japan. After careful consideration of which types of participants would be best to test the intervention in a safe way aligned to our study objectives, the selected participant inclusion criteria were selected:

- Aged ≥65 years
- Reside in a single occupancy bedroom/bedroom area within their care home
- Participants assessed as reasonably unlikely to express aggression toward themselves, the robot, and/or the researcher
- Participants assessed to possess sufficient cognitive competence and sufficient physical health
- Participants able to verbally communicate in English (UK) or Japanese (Japan)
- Residents selfidentify as primarily identifying with the English or Indian culture (UK) or the Japanese culture (Japan)

The first step toward determining potential eligibility was to invite care home staff to nominate residents (in an anonymized way) who they, based on their experience of working with their residents, believed were reasonably likely to meet the above inclusion criteria. After receiving these nominations, the research team began with brief screening interviews with the staff who made nominations. These interviews with staff employed the use of the inter-RAI-Long Term Care Facility "Cognitive Performance Scale" and "Aggressive Behavior Scale" subscales (Carpenter & Hirdes, 2013), as well as and the FRAIL-NH scale (Kaehr et al., 2015). Together, these tools enabled a valid and reliable identification of the nominated older adult's cognitive competence, aggressiveness, and frailty levels (a proxy to physical health). The nominated older adult residents who passed this initial level of screening were then introduced to a member of the research team by a familiar care home staff member (at a convenient time and in an appropriate environment), who proceeded to introduce themselves and invite the resident to participate in a way that followed our informed consent recruitment process.

10.2.2 Allocation and blinding

The residents who agreed to participate in the study were then allocated to one of following three groups using random allocation (stratified by gender to maximize gender balance across groups):

1. Experimental Group (utilizing a CARESSES experimental robot)
2. Control Group 1 (utilizing a CARESSES control robot)
3. Control Group 2 (Care as Usual only)

To help prevent differences in responses and bias, participants who received a robot were "blinded" to which type of robot they received (the experimental or control robot). Care home staff were also blinded.

10.2.3 Trial preparation

Prior to the trial commencing, all research staff were subject to Disclosure and Barring Service checks (in the UK) and criminal record checks (in Japan). Researchers also completed a series of ethics and methods training, had weekly supervisory meetings and team support on an on-going basis to support them further.

A brief presentation was prepared for care home staff to inform them on what to expect during testing procedures and to answer any questions. This included a request that they continue their jobs as usual (so not to bias any outcomes) and to not rely upon the robot for any caring roles (for ethical reasons). The presentation also clarified that the project was about exploring the use of social robots in conjunction with current care rather than replacing care. This was explicitly stated so to help protect staff morale and concerns surrounding the possible implications of technological interventions. This information was also disseminated via leaflets which were also made available for all staff.

The study also involved significant technical preparation involving the project's technical team. These set-up procedures took approximately 1 h and took place within each participant's bedroom prior to the commencing of any testing. They took place either with the resident present or without their presence if they preferred and provided consent for.

Finally, a brief preparatory meeting with each participant allocated to receive a robot (i.e., those allocated to the Experimental Group or Control Group 1) was conducted with a member of the research team. This was to answer any remaining questions the participant may have had, provide them with another opportunity to withdraw from the project should they wish to, and to collect some personal information required to customize the robot (e.g., name, age and the contact information of close family members the robot could use to contact if the resident wished).

10.2.4 The interventions

Only participants that were allocated to the Experimental Group or Control Group 1 received a robot for testing (i.e., "the intervention"). The robotic hardware that was used throughout the trial was the "Pepper" robot manufactured by SoftBank Robotics (a study partner). This is a 4 ft tall, 63 lb robot which, due to its artificial robotic appearance, is not disadvantaged by the "Uncanny Valley" effect (Gee et al., 2005).

Two culturally competent artificial intelligence versions were used to underpin how the robot interacted, responded and behaved with the participants. One of these versions represented our best effort at producing robotic cultural competence and this version was embedded into the Pepper robots used in the Experimental Group (i.e., the "CARESSES Experimental Robot"). This version of the software involved the following:

(a) the robot being made aware of the particular participants' cultural background prior to the commencement of testing and retaining such knowledge throughout
(b) preloading and employing the appropriate Cultural Knowledge Base (CKB) during testing (for which three such databases were developed for the English, Indian, and Japanese cultures)
(c) initially tailoring its interactions to a "culture-specific level" and then, during week two of testing only, shifting toward more personalized cultural interactions after learning more about the participants' individual preferences and values
(d) proliferating its learning of the participant in one particular area, automatically to other related areas

A different culturally competent artificial intelligence version was embedded into the Pepper robots used in Control Group 1 (i.e., the "CARESSES Control Robot"). This version of the software was an attempt to ensure clinical equipoise through producing a robotic artificial intelligence that, while likely to be less culturally competent, would not be culturally incompetent (where it might be reasonably likely to expect harm). Unlike the CARESSES Experimental Robot, this robot was therefore not preaware of the participant's cultural background prior to testing, it did not propagate its learning and it was preloaded with a generic and more limited CKB that was not tailored for any particular cultural profile. However, the robot was able to tailor its interactions to become more personalized over time. To provide a practical illustration of the differences between these two software versions, the following example can be made. Participant A is someone who primarily identifies with the English culture. The Experimental Robot knows this and prepares the English CKB upon first meeting the individual, initiating a greeting that is likely to be valued (e.g., a handshake), and conversing in topics of conversation likely to be valued (e.g., talking about rugby, old Hollywood movies, World War 2). Conversations could then lead to the robot asking whether the participant might like to watch videos, listen to music, or play a memory game associated with such interests. However, for the Control Robot, upon initially meeting Participant A, it guesses what might be appropriate initial greeting gesture (e.g., a bow) and is also likely to make less accurate conjectures about the kinds of conversational topic likely to be valued (e.g., Sumo Wrestling or Bollywood movies), and enquiring whether the participant might wish to watch, listen, or play a game associated with these topics.

During the second week of the residents using the robots, both versions were programmed to adapt to the particular responses obtained when in conversation (e.g., if a participant were to state that he/she does not like Japanese food, then regardless of which version of the robot they were using (i.e., the Experimental Robot or Control Robot), their robot would remember this and explore other foods which he/she may instead like). If the participant agrees that he/she likes Indian food, the Experimental robot propagates this learning to also guess that he/she might also value other aspects of Indian culture, whereas the Control Robot does not form such connections. A full explanation on how the artificial intelligence for the experimental and control robots was developed for the purpose of testing and evaluation, has been previously described by Recchiuto et al. (2019).

10.2.5 The testing procedures

The study participants allocated to the Experimental Group or Control Group 1 received a robot which they could have access to in six different sessions spread across 2 weeks at convenient times. The six sessions lasted for up to 3 h each during which participants were free to use the robot as much or as little as they wished in their private room. In the first of the six sessions, a researcher spent time with the participant to train him/her on how to use the robot and access the various functionalities. This included training on how to communicate with the robot, how to request assistance, and how to ask for privacy. It also provided participants an opportunity to ask questions.

For the remaining five sessions, participants used the robot independently and privately (although for safety reasons, sessions were audio—video monitored by researchers nearby which participants were aware of). At the outset of each session, the robot was placed near to the resident (within 3 ft) who could then specify how close or far away they wished the robot to remain positioned. The robot would then remain in this specified position and not move around to follow the resident, although it would swivel to face the resident as necessary. Thereafter, the participants could use the robot to engage in conversation, listen to music, watch videos, play games, and to contact friends and relatives via text, video messages, video or audio calls (see Table 10.1 for a full list of functionalities). After the six testing sessions were completed, the research team spent additional time to support participants in case any

TABLE 10.1 Robot functions developed specifically for the CARESSES study.

Type of functions	Specific function
Communication	❖ The robot initiates conversations with the person by asking yes/no questions or an open-ended question to encourage them to talk about something. ❖ Encourages the person to make requests, by suggesting possible activities (e.g., based on their every-day schedules). • If a request is detected, the robot starts a specific activity. • If a keyword is detected which does not correspond to a request, the robot starts to chat about the corresponding topic.
Entertainment	❖ Plays a YouTube video/music (using a YouTube search). ❖ Plays simple games. ❖ Reads out an audiobook through YouTube (using a YouTube search). ❖ Plays karaoke (using a YouTube search). ❖ Reads out the news/weather forecast/newspapers. ❖ Displays the local weather forecast and verbally comments it. ❖ Shows pictures and photographs of family/friends/relatives.
Provision of help/recommendations	❖ Dials the care home manager's mobile phone if a person needs help and requests it. ❖ Sets a reminder for something and reminds the person about something at a given time. ❖ Provides recommendations regarding the menu, clothes, physical exercises, localisation of favorite belongings. ❖ Switches the lights on/off using a smart plug.
Connection	❖ Places a Skype video or phone call to the recipient. ❖ Sends a predefined Telegram message corresponding to a topic to the recipient. ❖ Send a dictated by the user Telegram message to the recipient.

confusion, sadness or distress from missing the robot were suspected or expressed. The participants allocated to Control Group 2 (Care As Usual) did not receive a robot and therefore were not involved in any tests and instead continued to receive their usual level and type of care.

10.2.6 Data collection tools

It was necessary to ensure that the appropriate type of data was being collected throughout the trial in order to address our study objectives. This involved collecting data within the context of one to one structured interviews with residents at baseline (i.e., just prior to testing commencement) and postintervention (i.e., within several days of testing completion), and in some instances after the mid-way point (i.e., just after 1 week of testing). These were:

(1) Short Form (36) Health Survey version (SF-36) (Ware & Sherbourne, 1992). The SF-36 is a widely used, reliable and validated multipurpose, short-form health survey with 36 questions. It measures the following eight dimensions of health: general health, bodily pain, emotional role limitation, physical role limitation, mental health, vitality, physical functioning, and social functioning
(2) Short Form UCLA Loneliness Scale (ULS-8) (Hays & DiMatteo, 1987). The scale measures internal perceptions of loneliness and is comprised of eight items using a four-point Likert scale with values ranging from "never" to "always"
(3) The Cultural Competence Assessment Tool—Robotics (CCATool-Robotics) (Papadopoulos et al., 2004). The tool measures older adults' perceptions of the robot's cultural awareness, cultural knowledge, cultural sensitivity, and cultural competence
(4) Negative Attitudes toward Robots Scale (NARS) (Nomura et al., 2004). This scale, which assesses participants' attitudes toward robots NARS, is comprised of 14 items scored on a five-point agreement Likert Scale which measure three attitudinal domains: "Situations of interaction with robots," "Social influence of robots," and "Emotions in interaction with robots"
(5) Questionnaire for User Interface Satisfaction (QUIS) (Chin et al., 1988). The QUIS instrument uses a nine-point scale to measure users' overall satisfaction of a technological system and its interface. Some of the original statements were amended to assess the ease of usability of a robot.

10.2.7 Ethical issues and considerations

To identify and address the range and complexity of the ethical issues associated with this project, both an internal and external ethics advisor were appointed whose expertise was leveraged across the entire study (including during the trial).

The Ethical Guidelines of Alzheimer Europe for older adults with mild cognitive impairment was selected as the basis of assessment and managing the key ethical issues inherent to the trial. A thematic analysis of the guidelines led to the identification of nine broad ethical themes which were addressed (Battistuzzi et al., 2018). These were as follows:

- <u>Attachment, authentic interaction, and reciprocity</u>: It was deemed reasonable to expect that participants may feel upset or distressed from no longer having access to the robot after their testing period has ended. Similarly, they may miss the researcher's attention and time given to them during the testing period. Therefore, an attachment reduction procedure was designed and implemented. This involved providing participants with a photo journal, clips of videos of their time, and phone calls to check in on them (1 week and 3 weeks after the completion of testing)

- <u>Substitution for social contact</u>: The possibility of participants using the robot in place of other social contacts was another concern. Therefore, it was made clear to participants that they should be free to use the robot as little or as much as they wish, and they should not feel obliged or pressured to spend time with the robot if their preference was to spend time with other people. The participant could also ignore the requests for conversation, and/or put the robot into sleep mode.
- <u>Autonomy</u>: It was ethically important to ensure that interactions with the robot did not reduce participants' sense of autonomy. The research team therefore made it clear to participants during training (and with reminders throughout the 2 weeks) that the participants should feel free to reject suggestions for assistance as they wish, and that they should contact care staff as they normally would do if they required any care-related support.
- <u>Culturally determined values and preferences</u>: The Ethical Guidelines of Alzheimer Europe recognize the importance of respecting and valuing culturally determined priorities and preferences. Thus, the use of the robot should respect and correspond with the cultural traditions of the resident.
- <u>Dignity and personhood</u>: Another concern was that it was possible that the intervention may serve as unwanted reminders of diminished competencies and independence. Therefore, the software was programmed to ensure that the direction of interactions and conversations are ultimately led and determined by the resident, rather than the robot. The robot was also programmed to express politeness, praise, and respect during its interactions which we hoped would enhance feelings of dignity and selfworth.
- <u>Privacy</u>: Sleep and privacy modes were made available, and the participant could also request full privacy, meaning testing and surveillance are paused, and robot removed. This is all explained during training and stated in guidebook. Skype calls were not recorded, no conversations generated between the participant and robot were stored, and photos and videos sent via the robot to friends/family were also not stored.
- <u>Informed consent</u>: Voluntarily and freely participating with no pressure or coercion was key. Therefore, it was made clear in the information and consent forms, and during recruitment, there were no penalties for not participating, that participation was completely voluntary, and that they could drop-out at any time without giving any reason. The informed consent process was sensitive, not rushed, and residents encouraged to take time to make a decision over whether to participate or not by talking with their informal caregivers.
- <u>Preventing harm</u>: Due to robot's design, the software being used, and the live surveillance, it was viewed as very unlikely that any direct physical harm might take place. The data collection tools used were validated, reliable and proven to be acceptable and sensitive. The pretrial pilot also showed no issues. Researchers and technicians were trained to interact sensitively and appropriately and were provided supervision and encouraged to produce a reflective diary (for personal use).

- <u>Stigma</u>: Negative labeling of participants by others (social stigma) or through themselves (selfstigma) was viewed as potentially resulting in harm. Therefore, the study team treated and interacted with participants with dignity, respect, and sensitivity. The researchers and technicians were also trained on these issues to ensure they do not stigmatize (now or in the future). Findings were anonymized and identities protected during dissemination, with the population addressed with respect and in a nonstigmatizing way.

Protocols for the management of participant distress, incidental findings (i.e., observations or findings that may have occurred during the trial but were unrelated to the specific goals of the trial) and reportable events (i.e., an adverse event or incident that was assessed as being reasonably likely to pose a significant risk to participants or others) that were also produced.

Protocol modifications were discussed, recorded, justified, and communicated with the Research Ethics Committees if deemed necessary. Throughout the project and trial, a commitment to the maintenance of participants' anonymity and confidentiality during all procedures was made, including during screening, recruitment, testing, evaluation, and dissemination procedures. Data collection, usage, and storage procedures complied with national laws and the EU's General Data Protection Regulation (GDPR) including the commitment of participants' the right to access, right to be informed, right to withdraw, and right to data erasure. Data collection complied with the principle of data minimization, that is, that the collection of personal information from study participants is limited to what is directly relevant and necessary to accomplish the specific goals of the testing and evaluation work packages. No data related to a third party was stored. This included any audio, video, or sensory data collected upon a person, not part of the study, such as a visitor or a staff member, who entered a bedroom during testing. All screening data were deleted upon completion of the project. During the testing procedures, all visual, auditory, and sensory data that the robot collected and processed in order to function as planned were also destroyed after the procedures had been completed. The exception to this was the collection of the number of interactions that the robot logged with each participant. However, these interactions were anonymous. Research data were entered, stored, and managed online through an encrypted and secure Google Drive project account with only project team members having access.

10.3 Trial feasibility

Recruitment spanned a 10-month period between February and November 2019 across eight UK and one Japanese site. Thirty participants ($n = 15$ Indian, $n = 15$ English) successfully completed the trial in the UK, and three participants completed in Japan (see Table 10.2 for a full breakdown of participant sociodemographic background, cultural identity, and trial allocation).

During the first 2 months of the trial, it became apparent that recruiting our targeted sample size ($n = 15$ per cultural group; $n = 45$ in total) would be more difficult to achieve than previously believed. Therefore, to mitigate for this, the trial period was extended by an additional 2 months. This enabled UK researchers to approach a range of additional sites and revisit others in order to continue recruitment, ensuring the target of 15 participants per cultural group was

TABLE 10.2 Sociodemographic background, cultural identity, and group allocation of trial participants.

N	ID	Age[a]	Sex	Highest education	Marital status	Religion	Cultural identity	Group allocation	Completed or withdrew?
1	R1	65–70	M	College	Single	Atheist	English	Control group 1	Completed
2	R2	80–85	F	Secondary school	Widower	Church of England	English	Experimental	Completed
3	R3	80–85	F	Primary school	Widower	Hindu	Indian	Control group 1	Completed
4	R4	65–70	M	Secondary school	Married	Hindu	Indian	Experimental	Completed
5	R6	80–85	F	Primary school	Married	Hindu	Indian	Care as usual	Completed
6	R7	80–85	M	Secondary school	Widower	Christian	English	Experimental	Completed
7	R8	75–80	F	No recall	Single	Christian	English	Experimental	Completed
8	R9_2	80–85	F	Primary school	Married	Hindu	Indian	Care as usual	Completed
9	R9	65–70	M	Secondary school	Divorced	Church of England	English	Experimental	Completed
10	R10	90–95	M	Secondary school	Widowed	Hindu	Indian	Control group 1	Completed
11	R11	65–70	F	Degree	Divorced	Hindu	Indian	Experimental	Completed
12	R12	65–70	M	Secondary school	Single	Hindu	Indian	Control group 1	Completed
13	R13	85–90	F	Secondary school	Widowed	Hindu	Indian	Care as usual	Completed
14	R14	70–75	M	Secondary school	Widowed	Church of England	English	Care as usual	Completed
15	R15	80–85	F	Primary school	Widower	Catholic	English	Control group 1	Completed
16	R16	80–85	F	Primary school	Widower	Church of England	English	Control group 1	Completed
17	R17	90–95	M	College level	Widower	Church of England	English	Control group 1	Completed
18	R18	95–100	F	Primary school	Widower	Atheist	English	Care as usual	Completed
19	R19	95–100	F	Secondary school	Widower	Scottish presbyterian	English	Experimental	Completed
20	R20	90–95	M	College level	Widower	Hindu	Indian	Experimental	Completed

TABLE 10.2 Sociodemographic background, cultural identity, and group allocation of trial participants.—cont'd

N	ID	Age[a]	Sex	Highest education	Marital status	Religion	Cultural identity	Group allocation	Completed or withdrew?
21	R21	80–85	F	Degree	Widow	Hindu	Indian	Experimental	Completed
22	R22	80–85	F	Primary school	Widow	Hindu	Indian	Control group 1	Withdrew
23	R23	95–100	F	Degree	Widower	Hindu	Indian	Care as usual	Completed
24	R24	80–85	F	Primary school	Divorced	Hindu	Indian	Care as usual	Withdrew
25	R25	75–80	M	Primary school	Widowed	Hindu	Indian	Experimental	Completed
26	R26	75–80	F	Secondary school	Widowed	Christian	English	Control group 1	Completed
27	R27	85–90	F	Secondary school	Widowed	Christian	English	Control group 1	Completed
28	R28	90–95	F	Primary school	Widowed	Christian	English	Care as usual	Completed
29	R29	75–80	F	Secondary school	Widowed	Hindu	Indian	Control group 1	Completed
30	R30	95–100	F	Secondary school	Widowed	No religion	English	Care as usual	Completed
31	R31	80–85	M	Primary school	Single	Christian	English	Care as usual	Completed
32	R32	65–70	F	Secondary school	Widow	Hindu	Indian	Care as usual	Completed
33	R1_J	75–80	F	Primary school	Widow	No religion	Japanese	Experimental	Completed
34	R2_J	75–80	F	Secondary school	Widow	No religion	Japanese	Experimental	Completed
35	R3_J	85–90	F	Secondary school	Widow	No religion	Japanese	Control group 1	Withdrew
36	R4_J	90–95	F	Primary school	Married	No religion	Japanese	Control group 1	Completed

[a]Age range provided to protect participant identity.

achieved. Having multiple sites recruited in the UK arm of the study was a key factor in achieving recruitment for each cultural group as it increased the likelihood of identifying eligible older adults, as was conducting the trials in and around a large city. It was also viewed necessary to recruit participants from residential care settings, which was another change to the original protocol. This significantly boosted our recruitment of participants and led to no discernible bias or negative influence on outcomes. The CARESSES trial started later in Japan in July 2019 and was limited to one care home, reducing opportunities to recruit sufficient numbers. Efforts were made to identify additional care homes within driving distance of this care home in Japan, but none were found in what was predominantly a rural area.

Negotiating access to care homes, the screening of residents and seeking informed consent entailed a complex, multistage process. Older adults who passed screening were approached and invited to participate in the CARESSES study. A significant proportion declined at this stage, giving a range of reasons as summarized in Table 10.3. The most common was being

TABLE 10.3 Number and types of reasons given by eligible and approached residents for declining participation per care home.

Reason	Care home 1	Care home 2	Care home 3	Care home 4	Care home 5	Care home 6	Care home 7	Care home 8	Japan care home	Total tally count of reasons
Too tired/old age	3	2	1	1	0	3	3	1	0	14
No clear reason	0	2	2	3	0	0	2	2	0	11
No interest in project	0	0	0	0	0	0	5	0	0	5
Against idea of robots and prefers human interaction	1	1	0	1	0	0	0	0	0	3
Not enough time/busy with other preferred activities	0	2	0	1	0	0	0	0	0	3
Family refused to consent	0	0	0	0	0	0	0	0	3	3
No interest in trying something new/different	0	2	0	0	0	0	0	0	0	2
Felt too depressed	0	0	0	2	0	0	0	0	0	2
Felt too anxious/stressed	0	0	0	0	0	2	0	0	0	2
Bereavement	0	0	0	0	0	1	0	0	0	1
Against idea of cultural competence	0	0	1	0	0	0	0	0	0	1
Put off by length of information and consent form	0	0	0	0	0	1	0	0	0	1
Felt English was not good enough	0	0	0	1	0	0	0	0	0	1
Preferred to do tests in group format, not alone	0	0	0	1	0	0	0	0	0	1
Concerned about safety of robot	0	0	0	0	0	0	1	0	0	1

too tired/old age, followed by refusal with no clear explanation, and having no interest in the project. As older adults in receipt of care, many were vulnerable and felt unsure and anxious about trying something novel and unknown.

A considerable number of residents were nominated in order to reach the relatively modest final total of trial participants. Of the 134 older adults nominated, less than a quarter (33 participants) successfully completed the trial. The process of screening and recruitment was complex and comprised a number of stages which resulted in the majority of nominated residents either being excluded, declining or withdrawing from the study. While 111 passed initial screening, a further 12 were excluded based on observation during recruitment where concerns were raised about cognitive function, degree of dementia, and therefore capacity to consent to participate. When approached, more than half ($n = 51$) declined to participate. Of the 45 participants who gave consent, a further 10 withdrew prior to starting or after one or more trial sessions (see Table 10.4).

Ultimately, the target of 15 participants per cultural group was met for English and Indian groups but not for Japanese ($n = 3$) mainly due to a delay in the trial start date in Japan and recruitment restricted to one care home only.

Postintervention qualitative interviews with the participants highlighted a range of issues related to how study design interfered with interactions between older adult participants and the robot. Participants were video and audio recorded during sessions, with at least two researchers sitting outside a participant's bedroom at all times to monitor equipment and the sessions themselves, plus to provide assistance with the robot whenever needed. Consequently, participants were aware of being observed during sessions, a factor which affected some more than others:

> I don't let out and always in the back of your mind knowing that there is someone sitting outside the door and whether they are listening to it or not, it is being recorded and it's your personal life and you don't ... divulge that to just anybody. But that's as I say me rather than anything to do with the robot. *R9 (English, male, Experimental Group)*

TABLE 10.4 Number and types of reasons given by participants for withdrawing or dropping out of the study.

Reason	Care home 1	Care home 2	Care home 3	Care home 4	Care home 5	Care home 6	Care home 7	Care home 8	Japan care home	Total tally count of reasons
Became too tired/old age	0	1	0	0	0	1	1	0	0	3
No clear reason	0	1	0	0	1	0	0	0	1	3
Health deteriorated/physical pain	0	1	1	0	0	0	0	0	0	2
Became too busy	0	0	0	2	0	0	0	0	0	2
Became anxious/overwhelmed	0	1	0	0	0	0	0	0	0	1

As well as being careful about what he disclosed, R9 was aware of the activities he was choosing, distinguishing between those perceived as more valuable to be observed doing for research purposes and what he might do in his spare time to relax:

> I was thinking for your research for me to just sit there and watch a two- and half-hour film. I can't see what you can get from that? If I could sit there and watch a two- and half-hour film or I play music for the whole 3 hours what do you get out of that? I just felt it would have been a waste for me to do that. .... And I can't put any input in after them 3 hours other than I enjoyed that film. *R9 (English, male, Experimental Group)*

Sessions were scheduled for 3 hours duration; however, participants were free to take a break or finish a session at any time and were reminded of this regularly. As older adults, participants tended to tire easily, and sometimes experienced some form of pain and/or discomfort as a result of ill health the symptoms of which could fluctuate from session to session. However, when subsequently interviewed at the end of the trial period, a couple of participants commented on the lengthy sessions and how they would have preferred them to be shorter.

While sessions themselves were viewed by some as too long, comments were also made that participants could have got more out of the experience had they used the robot over a period of time longer than six sessions over 2 weeks, *"Time is not enough for me to touching all the topics"* R11 (Indian, female, Experimental Group); *"I only had it for that short amount of time and it wasn't long enough and toward the end it did probably get easier talking to it"* R9 (English, male, Experimental Group).

Overall, the trial design was found to be feasible and acceptable. However, there were several aspects related to feasibility that could have been improved further. These were the participant recruitment which required more time than anticipated, the involvement of more care homes than anticipated and the inclusion of a wider range of residential accommodation for older adults than initially expected. Such additional measures implemented in the UK resulted in the successful recruitment of the planned number of English and Indian participants. The later start and limited care home sites available in Japan meant that the number of participants recruited fell significantly short of the target set for the Japanese cultural group. For those older adults approached, a major barrier to recruitment was their concern about trying something new. Low mood and isolation prevented many from participating, resulting in many participants declining at this stage. The qualitative interviews suggested that some participants experienced a degree of selfconsciousness, knowing that they were being observed while interacting with the robot. Some participants also described feeling tired, that the sessions could be too long, but also that the trial period overall was too brief to experience all the robot had to offer.

10.4 Quantitative results and interpretations

10.4.1 Data characteristics

As previously stated, 45 residents provided initial consent to participate although 10 residents subsequently withdrew prior to the testing phase commencing, leaving 35 residents who commenced testing. Two residents then withdrew during the first week of testing. Therefore, a total of 33 participants fully participated in the trial and completed all testing procedures. A breakdown of these participants' characteristics can be found in Table 10.5.

10.4 Quantitative results and interpretations

TABLE 10.5 Sociodemographic frequencies—allocation and robot grouping.

	Age		Sex		Educational level				Marital status			Religiousness		
	Mean (SD)	Median	F N (%)	M N (%)	Primary or less N (%)	Secondary/ high school N (%)	Professional/ college N (%)		Widow N (%)	Not widow N (%)	Not religious N (%)	Slightly/ moderately religious N (%)	Very/ extremely religious N (%)
All robots N = 23	80.65 (9.48)	81	14 (60.9%)	9 (39.1%)	5 (15.2%)	9 (27.3%)	9 (27.3%)		16 (48.5%)	7 (21.2%)	5 (15.2%)	13 (39.4%)	5 (15.2%)
Exp robot N = 12	79.50 (9.03)	79	7 (21.2%)	5 (15.2%)	1 (3.0%)	5 (15.2%)	6 (18.2%)		8 (24.2%)	4 (12.2%)	3 (9.1%)	8 (24.2%)	1 (3.0%)
Control robot N = 11	81.91 (10.23)	83	7 (21.2%)	4 (12.1%)	4 (12.1%)	4 (12.1%)	3 (9.1%)		8 (24.2%)	3 (9.1%)	2 (6.1%)	5 (15.2%)	4 (12.1%)
No robot N = 10	84.90 (10.44)	84	8 (24.2%)	2 (6.1%)	6 (18.2%)	3 (9.1%)	1 (3.0%)		7 (21.2%)	3 (9.1%)	2 (6.1%)	3 (9.1%)	5 (15.2%)

231

10.4.2 Physical and mental health

Participant health and well-being were quantitatively assessed through the SF-36 and ULS-8 tools which measured a range of different health-related quality of life domains and loneliness, respectively.

In terms in physical health, the intervention was not able to produce any discernible improvement for participants in either the Experimental Group or Control Group 1 (i.e., those participants who used a robot) compared to Control Group 2. When looking at the overall aggregated physical health scores in Table 10.6, all three robot groups (i.e., "any robot," "experimental robot group," and "control robot group") produced slight decreases in physical health whereas Control Group 2's overall physical remained stable (61.69—62.56). This picture is reflected in each of the physical health SF-36 subscales including "physical function" (which measures the degree to which people are limited in performing physical activities such as bathing or dressing), "role limitations—physical" (the degree to which people are not able to perform their daily activities due to physical health problems), "pain" (the degree to which people experience bodily pain), and "general health" (the degree to which personal physical health feels poor or excellent).

However, for mental health, some discernible improvements for the participants using a robot were observed. Firstly, as can be seen in Table 10.6, fairly large positive score changes in the "emotional well-being" subscale can be observed in both the "any robot" group and the Experimental Group, whereas no change in score is observed for Control Group 1 and a large decrease in score is observed for Control Group 2 (Control Group 2). Some of these differences were observed to be statistically significant; specifically (a) the difference between improved scores in the "any robot" group as compared to Control Group 2 (see Table 10.7) and (b) the difference between improved scores in the Experimental Group compared to Control Group 2 (see Table 10.8). The difference in score improvement between the Experimental Group and Control Group 1 was also large but these were not found to be statistically significant (see Table 10.9). The implication of this finding is that using a CARESSES robot (ideally the experimental robot) compared to not using any robot is likely to improve older adults' mental health and emotional well-being, even only after a period of 2 weeks.

A broader, arguably less precise way of measuring mental health via the SF-36 is to group the "emotional wellbeing," "energy and fatigue," "role limitations—emotional," and "social functioning" subscales together and produce one overall measure ("mental health total"). Using this measure, the differences are just outside of the statistical significance threshold (Experimental Group vs. Control Group 2: $F[1] = 4.249$, $sig = 0.054$; Experimental Group vs. Control Group 1: $F[1] = 3.836$, $sig = 0.065$). As can be seen in Table 10.6, the "mental health total" scores for Control Group 2 significantly reduced over the 2 weeks, from 76.22 (T0, i.e., baseline) to 63.30 (T2, i.e., postintervention) ($Z = -1.988$; $sig = 0.047$), whereas the scores for the Experimental Group remained stable, from 77.59 (T0) to 78.39 (T2). Again, for Control Group 1, the scores did not improve, although they did not decrease as extensively as Control Group 2. Overall, these findings substantiate the notion that using a version of the system over 2 weeks is likely to protect one's mental health compared to not using the system, and that the experimental robot is likely to be particularly effective at this.

10.4 Quantitative results and interpretations

TABLE 10.6 Mean SF-36 subscale scores per time point by robot grouping.

	SF 36 subscales—physical												SF 36 subscales—mental							
	Physical function		Role limitations—physical		Pain		General health		Role limitations—emotional		Energy and fatigue		Emotional well-being		Social functioning	
	T0 mean (SD)	T2 mean (SD)	T0 mean (SD)	T2 mean (SD)	T0 mean (SD)	T2 mean (SD)	T0 mean (SD)	T2 mean (SD)	T0 mean (SD)	T2 mean (SD)	T1 mean (SD)	T2 mean (SD)	T0 mean (SD)	T2 mean (SD)	T0 mean (SD)	T2 mean (SD)
Any robot N = 23	34.32 (27.06)	32.83 (27.87)	63.32 (41.13)	60.60 (42.45)	69.57 (23.94)	65.43 (28.17)	65.22 (19.57)	59.13 (20.43)	86.96 (31.36)	76.09 (39.19)	56.30 (24.13)	58.48 (22.69)	78.78 (17.16)	82.43 (16.66)	80.43 (23.18)	76.63 (21.75)
Exp group N = 12	32.45 (28.46)	26.25 (23.66)	58.85 (43.00)	61.98 (39.03)	67.08 (25.56)	68.33 (31.39)	70.42 (13.22)	59.17 (19.87)	86.11 (33.21)	90.28 (28.83)	57.92 (23.82)	60.00 (24.31)	83.00 (11.83)	89.33 (7.69)	83.33 (23.44)	73.96 (21.62)
Control group 1 N = 11	36.36 (26.65)	40.00 (31.38)	68.18 (40.45)	59.09 (47.79)	72.27 (22.95)	62.27 (25.31)	59.55 (24.23)	59.09 (22.00)	87.88* (30.81)	60.60* (44.27)	54.55 (28.82)	56.82 (21.83)	74.18 (21.19)	74.91 (20.64)	77.27 (23.60)	79.55 (22.55)
Control group 2 N = 10	46.00 (30.62)	47.50 (37.21)	57.50 (47.21)	60.00 (44.41)	71.25 (35.46)	72.75 (32.13)	72.00 (22.63)	70.00 (24.94)	73.33 (37.84)	53.33 (47.66)	62.50 (18.60)	56.00 (22.46)	82.80 (12.66)	67.60 (29.96)	86.25 (17.13)	76.25 (25.99)

Table notes: *$P < .05$ (Wilcoxon Signed Ranks Test); SF36 scores range from 0 to 100 with 100 representing perfect health.
T0, Baseline; *T2*, Postintervention.

TABLE 10.7 ANCOVA results for outcome scores for participants in 'Any Robot' group versus 'Care as usual' group.

Outcome variable	F	df	Sig.	Partial eta squared
SF36 physical function	0.512	1	0.480	0.017
SF36 role limitations physical	0.057	1	0.813	0.002
SF36 role limitations emotional	1.203	1	0.281	0.039
SF36 energy and fatigue	0.848	1	0.364	0.027
SF36 emotional well-being	**5.128**	**1**	**0.031**	**0.146**
SF36 social functioning	0.024	1	0.878	0.001
SF36 pain	0.665	1	0.421	0.022
SF36 general health	0.928	1	0.343	0.030
SF36 health change	0.778	1	0.385	0.025
SF36 physical total	0.903	1	0.349	0.029
SF36 mental total	2.251	1	0.144	0.070
ULS-8 total scores[+]	1.163	1	0.290	0.041
NARS subscale 1	**6.304**	**1**	**0.018**	**0.174**
NARS subscale 2	**9.292**	**1**	**0.005**	**0.236**
NARS subscale 3	3.815	1	0.060	0.113
NARS total T2	**5.986**	**1**	**0.020**	**0.166**

Table notes: [+] = Japanese ULS-8 data excluded; "Partial Eta Square" statistic measures overall effect size (0 = no effectiveness; 1 = 100% effective) and may be used to assist future trials to statistically power their required sample sizes.

The experimental robot also produced better scores over the two-week intervention period on the "role limitation–emotional" SF-36 subscale compared to both Control Group 1 and Control Group 2. This scale measures how limited individuals are in conducting their usual activities because of emotional problems. As can be observed in Table 10.6, the Experimental Group scores slightly increased from a mean score of 86.11 (T0) to 90.28 (T2), whereas Control Group 1 scores dropped from 87.88 to 60.6 (which was a statistically significant change: $Z = -2.041$; sig $= 0.041$) and Control Group 2 dropped from 73.33 to 53.33. As can be seen in Tables 8 and 9, these between-group differences are close to significance (Experimental Group vs. Control Group 2: $F[1] = 3.993$, sig $= 0.06$; Experimental Group vs. Control Group 1: $F[1] = 3.792$, sig $= 0.066$). Overall, however, as assessed by this particular subscale, these findings provide further evidence of the notion that using a culturally competent robot is reasonably likely to protect against mental health problems, including impacting upon one's everyday activities.

Another quality of health domain in which the experimental robot performed reasonably well in comparison with Control Group 2 was "energy and fatigue" (also referred to as the "vitality" scale). Control Group 1 also performed well when compared to Control Group 2

10.4 Quantitative results and interpretations

TABLE 10.8 ANCOVA results for outcome scores for participants in 'Experimental robot' group versus 'Care as usual' group.

Outcome variable	F	df	Sig.	Partial eta squared
SF36 physical function	1.352	1	0.259	0.066
SF36 role limitations physical	0.007	1	0.934	0.000
SF36 role limitations emotional	3.993	1	0.060	0.174
SF36 energy and fatigue	1.612	1	0.220	0.078
SF36 emotional well-being	**6.614**	**1**	**0.019**	**0.258**
SF36 social functioning	0.031	1	0.861	0.002
SF36 pain	0.009	1	0.924	0.000
SF36 general health	2.095	1	0.164	0.099
SF36 health change	0.940	1	0.345	0.047
SF36 physical total	0.660	1	0.427	0.034
SF36 mental total	3.836	1	0.065	0.168
ULS-8 total scores[+]	1.250	1	0.280	0.072
NARS subscale 1	**6.992**	**1**	**0.016**	**0.269**
NARS subscale 2	**5.203**	**1**	**0.034**	**0.215**
NARS subscale 3	1.654	1	0.214	0.080
NARS total	4.184	1	0.055	0.180

Table notes: [+] = Japanese ULS-8 data excluded; "Partial Eta Square" statistic measures overall effect size (0 = no effectiveness; 1 = 100% effective) and may be used to assist future trials to statistically power their required sample sizes.

and equally to the experimental robot. Specifically, both robot groups showed a slight increase in scores over time (Experimental Group: M = 57.92 at T0 and M = 60 at T2; Control Group 1: 54.55 to 56.83), whereas Control Group 2 had a large numerical decrease (62.50—56.00). Why it should be the case that the intervention should increase energy may relate to the associated finding of improved feelings of mental health and emotional well-being, that in turn boost energy (indeed, a significant correlation between emotional well-being and energy/fatigue was found: rho = 0.499; sig = 0.003). Another explanation is that their use of the system built up their energy and stamina over time, in the same way that physically exercising may be tiring but over time stamina and energy increases.

Another SF-36 subscale is "social functioning" which measures the extent to which physical and emotional problems interfere with normal social activities. For this measure, participants in both the Experimental Group and Control Group 2 saw considerable score decreases over time (83.33—73.96; 86.25—76.25, respectively). However, Control Group 2 participants' scores slightly increased (77.27—79.55). Therefore, overall, when comparing the "any robot" group against Control Group 2, the relative score decreases in the robot group were smaller than Control Group 2. This may suggest that using a robot is reasonably unlikely to have a

TABLE 10.9 ANCOVA results for outcome scores for participants in 'Experimental robot' group versus 'Control robot' group.

Outcome variable	F	df	Sig.	Partial eta squared
SF36 physical function	1.603	1	0.220	0.074
SF36 role limitations physical	0.211	1	0.651	0.010
SF36 role limitations emotional	3.792	1	0.066	0.159
SF36 energy and fatigue	0.027	1	0.872	0.001
SF36 emotional well-being	3.336	1	0.083	0.143
SF36 social functioning	0.460	1	0.505	0.023
SF36 pain	1.288	1	0.270	0.060
SF36 general health	1.014	1	0.326	0.048
SF36 health change	0.123	1	0.729	0.006
SF36 physical total	0.001	1	0.977	0.000
SF36 mental total	1.385	1	0.253	0.065
ULS-8 total scores[+]	0.007	1	0.934	0.000
NARS subscale 1	0.063	1	0.805	0.003
NARS subscale 2	0.362	1	0.554	0.018
NARS subscale 3	0.704	1	0.411	0.034
NARS total	0.039	1	0.845	0.002
CCATool A	0.358	1	0.556	0.018
CCATool B	0.378	1	0.546	0.019
CCATool C	0.352	1	0.560	0.017
CCATool D	1.930	1	0.180	0.088
CCATool total	0.230	1	0.637	0.011

Table notes: [+] = Japanese ULS-8 data excluded; "Partial Eta Square" statistic measures overall effect size (0 = no effectiveness; 1 = 100% effective) and may be used to assist future trials to statistically power their required sample sizes.

greater detrimental effect upon social functioning than not using a robot (indeed, it may be slightly protective given the overall smaller relative decrease observed in the "any robot" group compared care as usual). However, given that the intervention did not produce better scores on this subscale may not be considered surprising given the intervention was not designed with a strong focus on improving the social circumstances of the individual. It is also worth noting that this measure consists of items that assess the impact of both emotional and physical health upon social activities, the latter of which, as highlighted earlier, was not found to be improved and therefore makes any significant increases in social functioning more difficult to observe.

Loneliness was measured by the ULS-8 loneliness scale. The total ULS-8 scores for the "Any Robot" group, Experimental Group and Control Group 1 groups showed a slight reduction in loneliness severity between baseline and postintervention whereas the Control Group 2 participants saw an increase in loneliness scores (see Table 10.10).

These findings can be interpreted in several ways. First, they indicate that using a culturally competent robot is reasonably unlikely to increase loneliness compared to care as usual. Second, they indicate that, even over a short period of time (2 weeks), a slight reduction in loneliness can be reasonably expected to be observed. Third, they indicate that if both of these trends were to continue over time, these differences may become more meaningful. Fourth, the experimental robot was not observed to be more effective at reducing the severity of loneliness compared to the robot used in Control Group 1. Finally, these results indicate that more work to improve the depth and impact of the intervention to drive down loneliness is required. Such improvements may tie-in with enhancements to the "social functioning" drive of the system, so that future systems can have a stronger focus on improving the social capital and circumstances of the individual.

10.4.3 User satisfaction and attitudes

Table 10.11 describes the QUIS total and subscale mean scores at T2 (only). Overall, both the Experimental Group and Control Group 1 total QUIS scores were found to be fairly high (M = 134.42 and M = 144.78, respectively). The highest scoring QUIS subscale was "Terminology and System Information" (M = 12.42 and M = 14.81 for Experimental Group and Control Group 1, respectively; highest possible score = 18). This subscale refers to the clarity and consistency of the "position of messages on tablet" and the "messages on tablet which prompt user for input." The "Overall reactions to the robot" subscale also scored well. This scale measures participants' views regarding how wonderful, satisfying, stimulating, easy and flexible such reactions were (M = 31.17 and M = 34 for the Experimental Group and Control Group 1, respectively; highest possible score = 45).

The least positively rated subscale was the "Learning" scale which measured how easy it was for participants to learn how to use the robot, explore its features, and remember various commands (M = 34.25 and M = 35.27 for the Experimental Group and Control Group 1, respectively; highest possible score = 54). Overall, however, it can be concluded that the intervention was received positively, and participants were satisfied with the overall use of the system, in particular those participants in the UK trial arm.

Table 10.12 describes the results of the NARS measure which measured participants' attitudes toward robots. At baseline, attitudes toward robots were observed to be mostly negative in all groups (particularly in terms of the "social influence of robots" and "emotions in interacting with robots" subscales). However, mean scores consistently reduced between time points with the exception of subscale 3 ("emotions in interacting with robots") which experienced little change, implying that participants' attitudes grew more positive as they continued to use the robots. This is reflected by a statistically significant difference in NARS total scores between time-points was observed for the "any robot" group (Z = −2.297, sig = 0.022). Further, a similar significant difference in subscale 2 ("social influence of robots") was observed for Control Group 1 (Z = −2.298, sig = 0.022) and almost for the Experimental Group (Z = −1.841, sig = 0.066).

TABLE 10.10 Mean outcome scores per time point by robot grouping.

| | SF36 totals ||||| ULS-8 totals[+] ||
| | Physical health totals || Mental health totals |||||
	T0 mean (SD)	T2 mean (SD)	T0 mean (SD)	T2 mean (SD)	T0 mean (SD)	T2 mean (SD)
Any robot N = 23	58.11 (20.79)	54.50 (18.28)	75.62 (16.81)	73.41 (18.99)	16.80 (5.13)	15.75 (5.28)
Experimental group N = 12	57.20 (20.36)	53.93 (15.21)	77.59 (16.40)	78.39 (12.15)	14.9 (4.98)	14.3 (3.53)
Control group 1 N = 11	59.09 (22.20)	55.12 (21.91)	73.47 (17.79)	67.97 (23.84)	18.8 (4.73)	17.2 (6.46)
Control group 2 N = 10	61.69 (27.92)	62.56 (30.41)	**76.22* (16.51)**	**63.30* (25.30)**	15.70 (4.73)	16.50 (5.40)

Table notes: *$P < .05$ (Wilcoxon Signed Ranks Test).
SF36 scores range from 0 to 100 with 100 representing perfect health; ULS-8 scores range from 8 to 32 with 32 representing severe loneliness; NARS scores range from 14 to 70 with 70 representing highly negative attitudes; CCATool scores range from 0 to 28 with 28 representing highest perceived cultural competence; QUIS scores range from 0 to 198 with 198 representing perfect satisfaction.
T0, Baseline; T2, Postintervention.
[+] = Japanese ULS-8 data excluded.

TABLE 10.11 QUIS totals and subscale scores per time point by allocation.

	QUIS total	QUIS overall reactions to the robot	QUIS tablet on the robot	QUIS terminology and system information	QUIS learning	QUIS robots capabilities
	T2 mean (SD)	T2 mean (SD)	T2 mean (SD)	T2 mean (SD)	T2 mean (SD)	T2 mean (SD)
Any robot N = 23	139.35 (27.87)	32.52 (8.39)	27.83 (5.85)	13.57 (3.93)	34.74 (10.57)	30.65 (5.38)
Experimental group N = 12	134.42 (28.62)	31.17 (7.25)	25.50 (5.87)	12.42 (4.58)	34.25 (10.86)	31.08 (5.50)
Control group 1 N = 11	144.73 (27.32)	34.00 (9.62)	30.36 (4.88)	14.82 (2.75)	35.27 (10.73)	30.18 (5.47)

Table notes: QUIS total scores range from 0−198 with 198 representing perfect satisfaction; Overall reactions scores range from 0 to 45 with 45 with 45 representing perfect satisfaction; Tablet on the robot scores range from 0 to 36 with 36 representing perfect satisfaction; Terminology and system information scores range from 0 to 18 with 18 representing perfect satisfaction; Learning scores range from 0 to 54 with 54 representing perfect satisfaction; Robot capabilities scores range from 0 to 45 with 45 representing perfect satisfaction.
T0, Baseline; *T2*, Postintervention.

TABLE 10.12 NARS Total and subtotals scores per time point by robot grouping.

	NARS totals		NARS S1: situations and interactions toward robots		NARS S2: social influence of robots		NARS S3: emotions in interacting with robots	
	T0 mean (SD)	T2 mean (SD)	T0 mean (SD)	T2 mean (SD)	T0 mean (SD)	T2 mean (SD)	T0 mean (SD)	T2 mean (SD)
Any robot N = 23	**42.46*** **(7.65)**	**38.70*** **(8.80)**	17.46 (5.86)	16.97 (6.53)	16.27 (3.94)	14.15 (4.22)	10.00 (2.83)	10.18 (3.59)
Experimental group N = 12	41.47 (7.83)	38.25 (10.10)	15.58 (5.05)	14.75 (5.40)	15.50 (3.68)	13.00 (3.67)	10.33 (2.53)	10.50 (3.34)
Control group 1 N = 11	43.54 (7.66)	39.18 (7.60)	17.64 (5.78)	15.27 (7.25)	**15.00*** **(3.55)**	**12.00*** **(3.13)**	10.91 (2.77)	11.91 (3.78)
Control group 2 N = 10	46.70 (9.30)	47.30 (5.33)	19.50 (6.67)	21.50 (4.95)	18.60 (3.98)	17.90 (3.60)	8.60 (2.95)	7.90 (2.60)

Table notes: *$P < .05$ (Wilcoxon Signed Ranks Test); **$P < .01$ (Wilcoxon Signed Ranks Test).
NARS total scores range from 14 to 70 with 70 representing highly negative attitudes; NARS subscale one scores range from 7 to 35 with 35 representing highly negative attitudes; NARS subscale two scores range from 5 to 25 with 25 representing highly negative attitudes; NARS subscale three scores range from 3 to 15 with 15 representing highly negative attitudes.
T0, Baseline; *T2*, Postintervention.

As can be seen in Table 10.7, the NARS total score differences between the "Any Robot" group and Control Group 1 were also found to be statistically significant (F[1] = 5.986, sig = 0.020), and just outside of statistical significance when comparing the Experimental Group against Control Group 1 (F[1] = 4.184, sig = 0.055). The NARS subscales one and 2 (i.e., "situations and interactions with robots" and "social influence of robots," respectively) produced the largest changes, with score improvements in both of these subscales found to be statistically significant in the "any robot" versus "Control Group 1" comparison (Subscale 1: F[1] = 6.304, sig = 0.018; Subscale 2: F[1] = 9.292, sig = 0.005) and also Experimental Group versus Control Group 1 comparison (Subscale 1: F[1] = 6.992, sig = 0.016; Subscale 2: F[1] = 5.203, sig = 0.034; see Table 10.9). NARS subscale 3 (i.e., "emotions in interaction with robots") was close to being significant in the Any Robot versus Control Group 2 comparison (F[1] = 3.815, sig = 0.06).

Therefore, it can be concluded with reasonable confidence that using the system produced a significant positive impact upon participants' attitudes toward robots. This was one of the most consistent and clear findings of the trial. This positive experience was also reflected by the high QUIS satisfaction scores.

10.4.4 Perceptions of cultural competence

A key study objective was the assessment of participants' perceptions of the robot's ability to demonstrate cultural competence. Table 10.13 describes the CCATool total and subscale mean score differences between T1 (after 1 week of intervention) and T2 (postintervention). The subscales are "cultural awareness" (subscale A), "cultural knowledge" (subscale B), "cultural sensitivity" (subscale C), and cultural competence (subscale D). The results show that after 1 week of use and 2 weeks of use, both the experimental robot (used in the Experimental Group) and control robot (used in Control Group 1) were, overall, perceived to be reasonably

TABLE 10.13 CCATool total and subscales scores by robot grouping.

	CCATool totals T1 mean (SD)	CCATool totals T2 mean (SD)	CCATool subscale A T1 mean (SD)	CCATool subscale A T2 mean (SD)	CCATool subscale B T1 mean (SD)	CCATool subscale B T2 mean (SD)	CCATool subscale C T1 mean (SD)	CCATool subscale C T2 mean (SD)	CCATool subscale D T1 mean (SD)	CCATool subscale D T2 mean (SD)
Any robot N = 23	20.17 (4.60)	21.87 (3.44)	5.13 (1.49)	5.91 (1.16)	4.48 (1.73)	5.22 (1.51)	5.52 (1.47)	5.96 (0.98)	4.83 (1.44)	4.78 (1.20)
Experimental group N = 12	20.83 (4.84)	22.42 (2.91)	5.25 (1.54)	6.08 (1.08)	4.92 (1.73)	5.17 (1.19)	5.58 (1.88)	6.08 (0.90)	4.75 (1.42)	5.08 (0.79)
Control group 1 N = 11	19.45 (4.44)	21.27 (4.00)	5.00 (1.48)	5.73 (1.27)	4.00 (1.67)	5.27 (1.85)	5.45 (0.93)	5.82 (1.08)	4.91 (1.51)	4.45 (1.51)

Table notes: CCATool total scores range from 0 to 28 with 28 representing highest perceived cultural competence; CCATool subscale scores range from 0 to 7 with 7 representing highest perceived cultural competence; *T1*, After 1 week of intervention; *T2*, Postintervention.

culturally competent. This is demonstrated by overall T1 mean total scores of 20.83 and 19.45 for the Experimental Group and Control Group 1, respectively, and T2 mean total scores of 22.42 and 21.27, respectively (0 = lowest possible score, 28 = highest possible score). However, both at T1 and T2, it was observed that the experimental robot produced higher CCATool scores than the control robot on most of the measures.

Both the experimental robot and control robot were perceived to be more culturally competent at T2 than compared to T1, although the experimental group showed greater improvement in scores overall, despite such differences in improvement not being statistically significant (see Table 10.9). This implies that the changes made to the system after week 1, to increase cultural competence of the system (e.g., by enabling personalization toward individual cultural values), did have a positive impact upon perceptions of cultural competence and, as expected, a greater level of impact upon the experimental robot. An alternative possible explanation is that the scores increased over time because of the participants' growing understanding of how to use the system more as time passed. It may of course also be that both explanations contributed to these differences.

Given that cultural competence was, overall successfully perceived by both the Experimental Group and Control Group 1 participants at T1, the theory that robotic cultural competence can indeed be experienced without user personalization is substantiated while the theory that cultural competence and user personalization are identical concepts is rejected. However, as cultural competence was perceived at a slightly greater level at T2, after personalization had been implemented for a week, it can be concluded that personalization to individual values and preferences improves the experience even further. Thus, overall, it can be said that the concepts of cultural competence and user personalization are not homogeneous but rather they complement each other. It is also likely that had the experimental robot utilized the CARESSES software during T2 from the outset of testing, that perceptions of cultural competence at both T1 and T2 may have been scored even higher than observed in the study.

10.5 Study limitations

Interpreting the results of the trial should be considered in relation to the study limitations, for which there were several. Firstly, although the trial was one of the most rigorous, complex, and largest of its kind to date, the sample sizes were not statistically powered and fairly small. This reduces the reliability and depth of the analysis. Consequently, wide standard deviations, inconsistent homogeneity of group differences and generally nonnormal data distributions were observed, although the latter was partially managed through the utilization of nonparametric inferential tests. Furthermore, although every attempt to control key potential confounding variables was made, and that stratified random group allocation (by gender) was employed, it is likely that some confounding variables were present. For these reasons alone, any interpretations of the statistical results, including making wider generalizations, should be treated cautiously.

Several other potential biases were highlighted by participants during the qualitative interviews. This includes reference to participants in the experimental and control group that feeling aware that they were being audio and video monitored by researchers, may have inhibited some of their conversations and interactions with the robot. This was a bias that had been previously considered during the trial design but one that could not be avoided given that it was critical to monitor participants to ensure their safety and to intervene when technical problems occurred.

The observed technical problems were another potential bias. However, after an analysis of the recorded problems as measured by the development of the "Technical Problems Scale" that was used in the study, no evidence was found that technical problems biased the trial outcomes. It is recommended that future similar trials should employ the Technical Problems Scale produced in the current study, to measure the degree and severity of technical problems, their intervention(s) encountered in order to assess the overall statistical impact technical problems produce on outcomes.

Another potential bias was the possible effect of the trial participants in the Experimental Group and Control Group 1 having additional human contact by the research team during the training and supporting of the system during the 2 weeks of testing. This potential confounding variable was controlled between the groups (since this additional level and type contact was similar in both groups), but meant that the participants in Control Group 2 had less contact. This was also previously considered and managed as much as possible (e.g., through ensuring that no unnecessary additional contact was provided) but the differences between the robotic groups and Control Group 2 could not be avoided.

Another constraint was the limitation in the speech recognition. This was a limitation referenced many times by the participants during the qualitative interviews and had a clear negative impact upon the overall effectiveness of the intervention. Unfortunately, this was not solvable during the course of the trial; Pepper's on-board microphone is positioned on the top area of the head was found not to be an effective position for the participants given that the frail older adults would often be sitting or lying down when attempting to converse with Pepper. The microphone's sensitivity was also unable to be boosted which meant that older adults with fragmented, lower voice volumes were often not effectively comprehended by the robot.

It could be viewed that 2 weeks as an intervention duration is brief and that more time would be required to produce meaningful effects. This may indeed have been desirable but doing so would have reduced the overall sample size which were a priority for between- and within-group analyses. To yield an even richer dataset, it would also have been advantageous to run more tests with more participants. However, to do this would have yielded significant cost and resource implications with more time, robots, research staff, and more care homes to recruit from, both in the UK and Japan. Further, it would have likely been beneficial for the robot to be able to converse in Indian languages. However, this too required additional expense and resource, and given that Indian participants were based in the UK it was reasonable to expect that the requirement of conversing with the robot in English was not a significant constraint (indeed, a required eligibility criteria was the ability to speak English).

Finally, it should be reminded that the results of this trial are based on a particular type of population, namely, older adults residing in care settings without severe dementia, severe mental health problems, or severe frailty (that would require hospitalization). The participants were all cognitively and physically able to understand and interact with the robot across the 2 weeks. Therefore, inferences made on the potential impact of the intervention on other populations based upon the current system should be treated with caution, particularly older adults with more severe levels of dementia and frailty.

10.6 Reflective questions

- What are your views regarding the study design? For example, do you believe there may have been a more effective approach toward identifying and recruiting participants? What other outcome measures do you believe would have provided useful data?
- Which findings stand out to you as particularly interesting or important? What findings were surprising to you?
- What do you believe may have increased the feasibility of the trial further?
- What implications for policy and practice do you believe these results might have?

References

Abdi, J., Al-Hindawi, A., Ng, T., & Vizcaychipi, M. P. (2018). Scoping review on the use of socially assistive robot technology in elderly care. *BMJ Open, 1:8*(2), e018815.

Battistuzzi, L., Papadopoulos, C., Papadopoulos, I., Koulouglioti, C., & Sgorbissa, A. (2018). Embedding ethics in the design of culturally competent socially assistive robots. *IEEE/RSJ Intelligent Robots and Systems,* 1996−2001. https://doi.org/10.1109/IROS.2018.8594361

Carpenter, I., & Hirdes, J. P. (2013). Using interRAI assessment systems to measure and maintain quality of long-term care. *Good Life Old Age, 17,* 93−139.

Chin, J. P., Diehl, V. A., & Norman, K. L. (1988). Development of an instrument measuring user satisfaction of the human-computer interface. In *Proceedings of the SIGCHI conference on human factors in computing systems* (pp. 213−218).

Gee, F. C., Browne, W., & Kawamura, K. (2005). Uncanny valley revisited. In *IEEE international workshop on robot and human interactive communication.* https://doi.org/10.1109/ROMAN.2005.1513772

Hays, R. D., & DiMatteo, M. R. (1987). A short-form measure of loneliness. *Journal of Personality Assessment, 51*(1), 69−81. https://doi.org/10.1207/s15327752jpa5101_6

Kaehr, E., Visvanathan, R., Malmstrom, T. K., & Morley, J. E. (2015). Frailty in nursing homes: The FRAIL-NH scale. *Journal of the American Medical Directors Association, 16*(2), 87−89.

Nomura, T., Kanda, T., Suzuki, T., & Kato, K. (2004). Psychology in human-robot communication: An attempt through investigation of negative attitudes and anxiety toward robots. In *13th IEEE international workshop on robot and human interactive communication* (pp. 35−40).

Papadopoulos, I., Tilki, M., & Lees, S. (2004). Promoting cultural competence in health care through a research based intervention in the UK. *Diversity in Health and Social Care, 1*(2), 107−115.

Pu, L., Moyle, W., Jones, C., & Todorovic, M. (2018). The effectiveness of social robots for older adults: A systematic review and meta-analysis of randomized controlled studies. *The Gerontologist, 12;59*(1), e37−51.

Recchiuto, C. T., Papadopoulos, C., Hill, T., Castro, N., Bruno, B., Papadopoulos, I., & Sgorbissa, A. (2019). Designing an experimental and a reference robot to test and evaluate the impact of cultural competence in socially assistive robotics. In *IEEE international conference on robot and human interactive communication.* https://doi.org/10.1109/ROMAN46459.2019.8956440

Ware, J. E., Jr., & Sherbourne, C. D. (1992). The MOS 36-item short-form health survey (SF-36). Conceptual framework and item selection. *Medical Care, 30*(6), 473−483.

CHAPTER 11

The role of culturally competent robots in major health disasters

Irena Papadopoulos and Runa Lazzarino

Research Centre for Transcultural Studies in Health, Middlesex University, London, United Kingdom

> **LEARNING OBJECTIVES**
>
> - To raise awareness of the importance of preparedness for major health disasters (MHDs)
> - To explore the role which artificially intelligent devices, such as socially assistive robots, can have during MHDs
> - To raise awareness of the robotic devices currently being used in MHDs
> - To discuss the need for an MHD strategy which includes socially assistive robots and other devices
> - To provide a brief discussion related to the training of health and social care (HSC) professionals to prepare them for effective and efficient actions during MHDs.

11.1 Introduction

The United Nations (UN) defined major disaster as "a serious disruption of the functioning of a community or a society involving widespread human, material, economic or environmental losses and impacts, which exceeds the ability of the affected community or society to cope using its own resources" (UNISDR, 2009). Disasters of any kind have a tremendous impact on public health and the health systems of affected populations: this can be seen in the destruction of health facilities, with a drastic reduction of essential medicines and medical equipment, as well as of healthcare workers (Noji, 2000; Shoaf & Rottman, 2000; Waters et al., 2015); other detrimental side effects can be the outbreak of communicable diseases

(Waring & Brown, 2005) and malnutrition, along with mental health and psychosocial problems (Murthy & Lakshminarayana, 2006). From its inception, during the 1960s, up to the development of the most recent framework (now called the UN Office for Disaster Risk Reduction—DRR), the UN has worked to prevent and reduce the detrimental consequences of major disasters onto affected populations. Up to the beginning of the 21st century, disaster management had focused on preparedness and response, while paying little attention to the importance of risk reduction and postdisaster recovery (Olu et al., 2016). The Hyogo Framework for Action (HFA) 2005—15 (ISDR, 2007) produced an international paradigm shift from limited emergency actions, to more comprehensive approaches, to disaster management (Olu et al., 2016). The current Sendai Framework for DRR (SFDRR) 2015—30 (UN, 2015) further reinforced the necessity to adopt a broad approach to disaster risk management and to strengthen DRR in relation to health: for this, it postulated the reinforcement of national health systems (Olu et al., 2016). Furthermore drawing from previous responses arising from the HFA guidelines, the World Health Organization (WHO) acknowledged the importance of an all-hazard and whole-of-health approach for health sector disaster management (Olu et al., 2016) in two World Health Assembly Resolutions (WHO, 2012, 2011).

Building upon the key messages stemming from the previous chapters, we will now discuss the use of culturally competent robots during major health disasters (MHDs). The utility of robots is magnified in health emergencies which see a massive, and often sudden, demand for health and social care (HSC). In MHDs, robots may have the capacity to provide unimaginable and precious help in saving human lives. As we will see, different types of robots can serve different functions, and most of those can prove key in MHDs—from connecting people to surgery, from sanitization and cleaning the clinical environment to information giving and transportation.

The growing number of MHDs worldwide urges the design of robots that are user-friendly, safe, culturally appropriate, and ethical. The design of such robots, in particular artificially intelligent (AI) socially assistive ones, demands the multidisciplinary collaboration of social and healthcare professionals, roboticists, patients, public health experts, politicians, as well as experts in culture, transcultural health, transcultural ethics, and healthcare systems. We will also discuss, in addition to several important non-social functions, how socially assistive robots could fulfill the important task of delivering quality holistic care, which is culturally competent and compassionate, in moments where the human workforce is under extreme pressure.

We will discuss the above issues, and others related to COVID-19 pandemic, which we will use as a living laboratory case study. We present some of the pandemic multiple purposes of SARs and other AI devices in order to:

1. Show the actual use and usefulness of SARs and other robotic devices in HSC sectors during the COVID-19 pandemic.
2. Discuss the great potential that culturally competent SARs and other AI devices can have in many fields of HSC applications, such as acute hospital environments and care homes for elderly, with a focus on their potential contribution in the reduction of harm to HSC staff from the transmissibility of COVID-19.
3. Consider the need for companions, offering holistic and spiritual care, with whom hospital patients and older people can connect with, since robots are not affected by social distancing.
4. Identify and consider the limits of AI technologies, and how these impact on and how they are dealt with by governments facing MHDs.

The chapter will examine the MHDs preparedness of HSC systems focusing on the incorporation of robots in their strategic plans. This will be followed by a discussion about the training and preparedness of HSC workforce in the use of SARs and other robotic devices. The discussion is based on the findings of a transnational online survey and on an interview-based qualitative study with HSC professionals on SARs (Papadopoulos et al., 2021). A proposal of a workforce basic training curriculum for MHDs using transcultural SARs will conclude the chapter.

11.2 The need for transcultural AI robotics in major health disasters

Some readers may remember the iconic image of the robot *WALL-E* on top of mountains of waste, surrounded by abandoned skyscrapers. *WALL-E* is the only robot of a legion of similar robots which had the purpose of cleaning the planet. Humanity has long ago left the Earth after this was turned into an unlivable wasteland, due to environmental neglect and aggressive consumerism. Planet Earth, in the film, is hit by an irreversible and global disaster, and *WALL-E* represents, in this image, the epitome of a disaster robot.

11.2.1 Disaster robots: a quick glance

Those readers who have watched the Pixar movie will know that *WALL-E* is a pretty clever robot, which, after 700 years, developed some discernment, curiosity, and emotional engagement. Instead of blindly creating one trash cube after the other, it starts wondering, selecting, and collecting in his home some of the items that it finds around. We all know that robotic sciences are still a bit far away from the development of such clever machines. In fact, the most widespread disaster robots are still remotely controlled to fly, dig, and swim to the rescue: they have cameras and sensors to offer overviews of the affected areas, and they can help look for victims. In other words, like WALL-E they may have some capabilities to identify and reach human victims in hard to reach conditions. Unlike WALL-E, once they have reached people needing help, their provision of comfort, including interaction and medical/caring skills, is still rudimentary. We will now superficially glance through disaster robotics to start building the case for the necessity of having transculturally competent and compassionate robots to the rescue.

Natural and human-made disasters are dramatically increasing. According to the United Nations, cataclysmic events worldwide have quadrupled since the 1970s (Gossett, 2020). This trend has seen a parallel development of disaster robots that could be sent instead of human first responders when the conditions are too dangerous or logistically challenging. We will look at some disaster robots by anchoring the discussion to a few of the biggest and most renown disasters of the last 20 years.

Let us start from what has been described as "the largest maritime salvage operation ever" (Lorenzi, 2014), the one about the shipwreck of the huge Italian cruise ship Costa Concordia in 2012. Remotely Operated Vehicles (ROVs) were successfully used to aid the complex raising and refloating of the wreck. ROVs are mobile robots that have been more and more used for patrolling and monitoring in underwater interventions for disaster recovery, at least since 2004 (Murphy et al., 2011). ROVs are becoming increasingly sophisticated, both in relation to their hardware and software (Allotta et al., 2017). In the Concordia cruise ship disaster, a specific type of marine ROVs, the *VideoRay Pro 4*, was massively used to survey and inspect the entire wreck. These agile diving cameras ensured that it was safe and sensible for a human submarine to search for victims, as well as proceeded with the wreck removal. The video footage recorded was impressive, making this among the most intensive deployment of underwater ROVs in the history of rescue (Lorenzi, 2014).

Mobile remotely operated robots, in particular various small ROVs, as well as autonomous underwater vehicles and unmanned surface vehicles (USVs), vary in terms of "depth resistance, propulsion system, navigation sensors, localization equipment and integrated payload" (Allotta et al., 2017).[1] Other examples of their use, or of similar and ad hoc developed machines, can be found by looking at other disasters, such as earthquakes, tsunamis (Murphy et al., 2011), avalanches, fires, and hurricanes. Several catastrophes involve both sea and land, and therefore the necessity to implement a coordinated use of aerial, land, and marine machines. A notable example of this was the deployment of an unmanned water surface vehicle, *AEOS-1*, to survey damage on an island hit by the disastrous Hurricane Wilma in 2005 (Murphy et al., 2008). This was the first known use of USV in an emergency context, and served to "established their suitability for the recovery phase of disaster management by detecting damage to seawalls and piers, locating submerged debris (moorings and handrails), and determining safe lanes for sea navigation" (Murphy et al., 2008, p. 164). The use of different disaster robots during Hurricane Wilma pointed to the need to improve cooperative strategies in the use of USVs together with unmanned aerial vehicle and microaerial vehicle and disclosed issues for autonomous operations near structures (Murphy et al., 2008).

Another important example of use of disaster robots is the case of contaminated areas, by radiation, fuel, or mines. The largest earthquake in the history of Japan that occurred in 2011 caused a very destructive tsunami, which in turn severely damaged a few reactors of the Fukushima Daiichi Nuclear Power Plant. The resulting explosions dispersed radioactive materials and made it impossible for nuclear workers to access the site. This situation called for the development of "remote-controlled/autonomous machines for radiation measurement, investigation, and debris removal from both inside and outside the reactor buildings" (Ohno et al., 2011, p. 38). A few remote-controlled robots were developed, such as *PackBot*, *TALOCN*, and *Quince*, and were located on a robotic control truck which could approach the reactor buildings and the debris through the roads used for fire engines (Ohno et al., 2011). Several lessons were learnt from the use of robots in the emergency response to the Fukushima-Daiichi accident, and in other disasters involving both land and sea operations, such as the Great Thailand flood in 2011. Two of these lessons were:

1. the necessity of improving the organization and operations' systematization (Kawatsuma et al., 2012);
2. the necessity of quickly collecting understandable images for researchers and other technical and logistic personnel (Srivaree-Ratana, 2012).

---

[1] Mobile, remotely operated, disaster robots have been commercially available for some years and demonstrated in several disasters to be a valuable support to perform inspections. Examples of commercially available underwater mobile robots can be found for example at https://gnomrov.com/(Accessed: 15.10.2021).

11.2.2 Robots to the rescue

In addition to the mentioned functions of monitoring, inspecting and assessing hard-to-reach areas affected by disasters via cameras and other sensors, there is another important skill of disaster robots. This is the active search for, handling of, and increasingly also caring for human bodies. Disaster robots with this specific function are known as rescue robots. Rescue robots, which were first discussed during the 1980s (Murphy, 2012), have been developed in the 1990s (Tadokoro et al., 1997), and they were first deployed during the urban disaster of the 9/11 World Trade Center (WTC) attack in 2001 (Murphy et al., 2016). On the day of the attack, the Center for Robot-Assisted Search and Rescue (CRASAR) was immediately involved in deploying robots and documenting the first known urban search and rescue operation. Robots were used on site for "searching for victims, identifying ways through the rubble, conducting structural inspection, and identifying dangerous materials" (Murphy, 2004). Of note is the employment of small tactical mobile robots which could go deeper into the very dense rubble and access voids too small for a human or search dog, in addition to being able to enter places at risk of collapsing and on fire. The models used in the WTC disaster were the *micro-Tracs*, the *Inuktun micro-VGTV*, and the *Solem*: all were teleoperated (Murphy, 2004).

Murphy and Burke listed some key lessons based on three major disasters (World Trade Center, Hurricane Charley, and La Conchita mudslide) and overall highlighted the fundamental aspect of human–robot interaction (HRI) in victims' search and rescue (Murphy & Burke, 2005). HRI is to be intended at 360 degrees, that is including operators, researchers, healthcare professionals, and the victims themselves. The WTC rescue operation in particular emphasized the need for improving HRI in order to better enable the teleoperator to perceive the environment, and identify and communicate with victims. Furthermore, Murphy (2004) suggested that advances in the civil and biomedical engineering disciplines, combined with telemedicine, should lead to robots that can care for unconscious and trapped victims. Other key lessons listed by Murphy and Burke (2005) from the use of disaster robots in previous responses could be encapsulated into two broad areas:

1. the necessity of teamwork and team coordination to exploit the robot as an active information source in order to increase the chances to find a victim;
2. the importance of both the cognitive and social features of the robots. Murphy and Burke (2005) stated that on the one hand, the major bottleneck in robot autonomy appears to be the ability to build situation awareness; on the other hand, all humans interfacing with the robot, respond to it "socially."

Before exploring the implications of these lessons, in particular the social response to disaster robots and their healthcare functions, let us briefly summarise the key points made so far (Box 11.1). We will then have a quick look at where rescue robots meet the medical ones.

11.2.3 Emergency carers

In the 10 years following the biggest man-made, war-related calamity in the dawn of the 21st century (i.e., the WTC attack), rescue robots have been used in nearly 30 disasters across the world (Murphy, 2012), including other war-related applications (Yoo et al., 2011). Rescue

> **BOX 11.1**
>
> **Robots in major health disasters—summary points**
>
> **Key points:**
>
> - MHDs are on the rise worldwide and the advancement of disaster robots to help save human lives is at the top of robotic sciences agenda
> - Disaster and rescue robots deployed in past MHDs are remotely controlled to fly, dig, and swim, with the function of monitoring, inspecting and assessing hard-to-reach areas via cameras and other sensors
> - Rescue robots are being developed toward increasing machine autonomy, AI, and deep learning skills in order to advance their medical and caring skills
> - Robot-Assisted Medical Reachback (RAMR) incorporates psycho-social support for victims, and user-friendly, safe, culturally appropriate, and ethical robots are increasingly needed

robots are still being refined and further developed (Baldemïr et al., 2020) for actual victims rescue operations (Nallathambi, 2018). Land, sea, and aerial robots have been deployed in the different phases of disasters (i.e., prevention, response, and recovery), as well as in different types of disasters from fires, to urban calamities, and sea and mountain catastrophes. To cater for all these different environments and specific purposes, new robot designs (e.g., snakes, humanoid) and concepts (e.g., sensor networks) have been developed.[2] Increasing machine autonomy (Murphy et al., 2016), AI, and deep learning techniques (Niroui et al., 2019), as well as designs with more sophisticated medical skills, is also under development. As mentioned, the care for victims once they are found is an important and equally challenging function of rescue robots.

Within the whole medical mission, victim management (i.e., keeping victims alive until extrication) can prove as key as victim localization and general conditions' assessment (Murphy et al., 2004). As Murphy and colleagues highlight (Murphy et al., 2004), one of the elements turning these medical missions challenging is that they occur in "area denial conditions." This refers to situations where healthcare professionals are denied physical access to and contact with the victims, who are in danger and often in critical conditions. The findings of a survey with healthcare professionals, who operated rescue robots during a simulation, revealed that medical staff wanted to teleoperate the robot, but also keep the robot available for support. Therefore, respondents declared that the robot operator should have medical training and should be able to collect some initial data, as well as provide some psychological

---

[2] Several examples of rescue robots that can fly, swim, crawl through rubble, douse fires or otherwise help first responders tackle trouble can be found in websites, such as these ones: https://builtin.com/robotics/rescue-robots (Accessed: 15.10.2021).

comfort to the victims (Murphy et al., 2004). In another study, a novel snake-like search and rescue robot assisting with victim management was tested; one of the findings, that the authors described as surprising, was that victims were concerned about the robot appearance (Murphy et al., 2009). Other literature has shown that in search and rescue scenarios, the victim will respond to the robot socially (Bethel et al., 2009; Fincannon et al., 2004) "raising the possibility that people become distrustful as well as cognitively confused" (Murphy et al., 2010, p. 127) by a robot which does not have a consistent verbal and nonverbal communication strategy. This was one of the findings of the Survivor Buddy project, which aimed to explore how trapped victims would use a web-enabled robot to interact with the outside world. That study suggested that disaster robots involved in actual victim rescuing should maintain "a consistent affective presence and that presence is a social medium, an identity between a social actor and a pure medium" (Henkel et al., 2011, p. 387). This is also why the Survivor Buddy was designed so to be able to switch to different affective expressions.

The mention of psychological comfort in the area of robot-assisted medical reachback (RAMR) is obviously pertinent within the broader aspects of this book. We now introduce our case study, which is the recent, unprecedented global MHD, the COVID-19 pandemic. The role, importance, and future introduction of intelligent SARs in HSC, which can offer culturally competent support, have been explored in previous chapters of this book (i.e., see Chapter 1 & 3). In Chapter 3, we learnt about the types of robots utilized in healthcare settings, from *DaVinci*, the surgical assistant, to *Shiva*, the multiarmed robotic nurse which draws blood, checks vital signs, and monitors patients' condition. We also learnt about the main case study of this book which is the development of the CARESSES robot, the first culturally competent socially assistive humanoid robot (see Chapters 5 to 10). The quick overview above on disaster and rescue robots aimed to offer a sense of the types of robots utilized in this field, their level of development, some lessons learnt and challenges ahead. Specifically, the key learnings revolve around:

- mobility and other technical capabilities, for example, images and videos;
- coordination within teams, and among different robots and teams;
- HRI between operators, medical staff, and victims, including factors related to usability and acceptance;
- autonomy, AI, and learning;
- social affective functions, which encompass the robot's appearance, affective expressions, delivery of psychological comfort, etc.—in other words, the whole spectrum of verbal and non-verbal communication.

All these factors should be kept in mind during the following overview of the use of AI technologies and other robotic devices during the COVID-19 pandemic, and even more when we will narrow the focus onto the realm of spiritual support during the outbreak.

11.2.4 AI devices and robots during the COVID-19 pandemic

11.2.4.1 Before COVID: the Ebola outbreak

The COVID-19 pandemic has turned the entire inhabited world in area denial conditions. The sense of desolation that we can see in the movie *WALL-E* is not too far from that of some deserted scenarios captured during the early phases of the pandemic, in some cities, airports, and ports. The levels of emergency which urge for very quick responses to save lives, the high rates of contagiousness which impose physical distance and prohibit human-to-human contact—unless when extremely necessary for healthcare reasons—and the sense of an epochal catastrophe—which ultimately speaks to an intrinsic entanglement between humans and their planet, and of the anthropocenic, disastrous environmental consequences of human neglect of nature: these factors highlight the extent to which COVID-19 pandemic shares and dramatizes the most important features of hazards and disasters, as we have covered above. Not to mention the fact that, despite COVID-19 being more strictly a health disaster caused by an infectious disease, human victims, and health-related consequences are part of almost every kind of disaster, as seen above, where rescue robots can be deployed as first-aid carers.

The pandemic caused by a virus belonging to the coronavirus family (i.e., coronavirus 2) and causing Severe Acute Respiratory Syndrome (SARS)[3] is only the last of a long series of virus-related outbreak affecting humans. One of these severe respiratory diseases outbreaks was caused, for example, by another strain of coronavirus (SARS-CoV-1) and struck in 2002–04. However, what came to be known as SARS was relatively rare, with relatively low incidence and case fatality rate—11% at the end of the epidemic in June 2003 (Chan-Yeung & Xu, 2003). As it is known, epidemics consist in the quick spreading of a disease across a given population within a short period of time; pandemics instead affect the entire globe. The disease may have been there before, and it will linger after the outbreak, either under control due to vaccinations, or resurging due to several factors, such as a new variant, or other retriggering elements. This is the case of the numerous forms of plagues, influenza, cholera, and smallpox, or of tuberculosis and HIV/AIDS—these latter considered ongoing pandemics (National Academies of Sciences et al., 2017). There have been other pandemics in history; renown is, for example, the Spanish flu which killed 50 million people between 1918 and 1920. However, the world was not as tightly interconnected 100 years ago as it is now. It is also obvious that information and communication technology (ICT), AI and other robotic devices were not that advanced at the time, and their role has become relevant only more recently.

The real testing laboratory for the use of robots in an MHD was the 2014–16 Ebola outbreak in West Africa (Yang, Nelson, et al., 2020). This was the largest outbreak of the virus since it was discovered in 1976 (Kalra et al., 2014). Similar to corona viruses, the viruses causing the Ebola disease have as hosts wild animals, such fruit bats which, via other mammals and nonhuman primates, transmit the virus to humans. In the case of the Ebola virus, transmission occurs via blood and other body fluids (WHO, 2021). In the case of COVID-19, transmission is primarily transmitted between people through respiratory particles (droplet and aerosol) and indirect contact through contact with contaminated surfaces. When someone with COVID-19 breathes, speaks, coughs or sneezes, they release droplet or aerosol particles containing the virus SARS-CoV-2. People are likely to be infected when they are closer than 1 meter to each other, as they inhale the virus or it comes in direct contact with the eyes, nose, or mouth (WHO, 2020a). During the last Ebola outbreak, several roboticists' teams worked at deploying Ebola fighting robots, and discussed possible interventions and specific tasks for robots to help during a highly contagious and fatal disease. Even if robots used during that outbreak did not get very close to providing human-like health care, as mentioned, the Ebola epidemic

---

[3] This acronym is the same used in this volume to refer to Socially Assistive Robots; hence, in the context of the pandemic, we will refer to it in terms of COVID-19 only, in order to avoid confusion in our readers.

constituted an important impetus for infectious disease disaster robots research and development (R&D). Some robotic devices were designed and tested targeting routine yet equally lifesaving tasks (PBS, 2015). This is the case, for example, of the robots *Neil* and *Saul* developed by Xenex, which are devices carrying UV lights on a wheeled cart connected to a timer and used to destroy deadly pathogens and decontaminate hospital rooms (Charu, 2014). Other Ebola virus-fighting robots included mobile telepresence robots, such as *Vita*, whereby healthcare professionals can remotely consult with patients and outreach affected or at-risk communities (TelepresenceRobots, 2020). However, telepresence robots do not have human dexterity, and the physical care of healthcare professionals is still required (Halperin, 2014). Yet, in the longer term, robots will be able to carry out some clinical tasks in direct contact with patients; for example, they would insert intravenous catheters for drawing blood or providing hydration (Leipheimer et al., 2019). Furthermore, robots would be able to help in the lab and run routine experiments in the research about the Ebola virus (Myers, 2014). Other robots were tested for transporting patients infected with Ebola, to limit health care workers' exposure to the virus, and for administering food and medicine to patients (PBS, 2015).

The case of the Ebola virus outbreak forced roboticists to consider logistic and environmental factors of the context of deployment, such as the difficulties posed by the muddy rainy season to robots' transportation, easiness to use for local staff, as well as maintenance (Ackerman, 2014). Similar limitations apply also to humanoid robots whose potential was not translated into action during the Ebola outbreak. In fact, it has been argued (Ackerman, 2014) that robots' limitations in a highly infectious disease, like Ebola, could be pinned down to the same general problem faced with the Fukushima radioactivity disaster (Guizzo, 2011, also above): robots are neither ready nor prepared, even though they "would be immensely valuable in this situation" (Ackerman, 2014). However, robotics R&D was highly stimulated by the Ebola virus epidemics as a new area for disaster robots to be applied to. CRASAR—the same center which was involved in the WTC attack—identified a list of areas where available robots could be useful. In addition to the mortuary robots, robots for disinfection and contamination detection, telepresence, and those helping in labs and field hospitals, robots for humanitarian relief, also robots providing physical security for the workers and handling waste, especially biowaste, all these were also conceived during the Ebola outbreak. Furthermore, happening in a non-Western context, the Ebola epidemic was an important test field pointing to several non-technical difficulties too. One of these is the role of culturally competent social robots. In fact, as it was noticed (Ackerman, 2014), mortuary robots, for example, should not be limited to being able to transport and bury the dead. They should also be designed to do this in a culturally appropriate way, and for this, consultations should be carried out with the people who are going to use the robots. Another example of this kind are telepresence robots, which should serve as "rolling interpreters" for the different languages and dialects in the context of deployment (Ackerman, 2014). Clearly, when it comes to act as interpreters within the realm of health, health care, and death, a culturally competent, holistic, and compassionate approach is highly desirable. In conclusion, while the Ebola virus outbreak in 2014 crucially paved the way for the conception, design, and deployment of robots in major heath disasters, it is with COVID-19 that we have seen an unprecedented advancement in this realm.

11.2.4.2 COVID-19 as turning point in MHDs robotics

When the COVID-19 outbreak started at the beginning of the second decade of the 21st century, the need to look at technology to contain the infection and death rates, while also "keeping the world going," became clear. The pandemic forced, to an extent, a digital transformation, in the run to swift progress in digitalization and automation in several fields (Zemtsov, 2020). The global MHD had no escaping from accelerating and overcoming several pre-2020 barriers, such as economic, political, legal, and social resistances and fears. In fact, it has been argued, the pandemic has modified the way robots in HSC are perceived (Price, 2021). This holds true both in a frontline and direct way—that is mainly in the HSC sector—as well as in a more indirect way—that is, for example, by counterbalancing the restrictions imposed by social distancing, which have had unprecedented socioeconomic and existential consequences onto everyone's life in this planet.

Advanced technologies, robots, and AI devices have been looked at for the management of the immediate response to the disease, but also to fight it and manage public health and well-being. An investigation of the literature covering the use of robotic technologies during COVID-19 reviewed and discussed in several categories the main robotic research contributions (Wang & Wang, 2021). This study found that during infectious diseases and epidemics, since the year 2000, the most important application has been robotic surgery; whereas during pandemics—and in this case the reference is COVID-19—research during 2020, AI and machine learning (ML), telemedicine, ICT, and Big Data are mentioned frequently to improve the performance of robotic applications (Wang & Wang, 2021). A report of the American Association for the Advancement of Science (AAAS, 2021) explored AI application during COVID, and assessed its actual or potential impact in several healthcare fields, such as diagnostics, monitoring, treatment, and management of diseases. Addressing also the ethical and human rights concerns (see Chapter 4), particularly in the areas of surveillance and triaging, the report aimed to offer a responsibility framework for future AI-based medical applications during crisis which can be just and ethical. AI also appears among the 10 key technologies in the fight against the coronavirus that were identified by the European Parliamentary Service (Kritikos, 2020). The COVID-19 pandemic furthermore highlighted the need of robots which can be culturally competent, especially when isolation is imposed upon victims or potential victims. Although some robotic devices are currently being used, the development of effective socially assistive autonomous robots is very complex. SARs require high levels of accuracy and sophistication in order to function within HSC environments, which are increasingly multicultural.

Systems with different levels of technological readiness, ranging from established commercial products, to prototypes and new systems, have been designed—or are still under design. These have been converted, upgraded, and deployed in disparate areas of reconnaissance, logistics, clinical care, and maintenance of socioeconomic functions. As mentioned already, in the HSC sector, robotic devices found applications, for instance, in disease prevention and detection, telesurgery and telerehabilitation, as well as telehealth, telemedicine, and bio-sample collection and disposal. More broadly, it has been reported that robots in this sector are utilized in roles as diverse as receptionists, food providers, ambulance attendants, and as nurses (Khan et al., 2020). But it is important to remember that robots are used in numerous other industries and settings other than hospitals, such as airports, transportations, hotels, attractions, and restaurants (Zeng et al., 2020). Education, entertainment, tourism, religion, e-commerce, supply chains, and production of personal protective equipment (PPE) and other useful materials are realms where advanced technologies have been of immense help. In this chapter, however, the focus is restricted on the HSC sector.

Below, we are briefly presenting five categories of robotic devices and their applications in an order of growing complexity: prevention, testing, examination, health informatics, and social interaction. We will devote more attention to the last category as we consider the potential of SARs in HSC.

11.2.4.2.1 Prevention

As for the Ebola epidemic, also during the COVID-19 pandemic crisis, robots helped to reduce the chances of spreading the infection by disinfecting and cleaning hospital rooms, but also other settings and public places; they have also assisted and speeded-up the provision of food and medical supplies (Bogue, 2020). Coronaviruses can persist on surfaces—including metal, glass, or plastic—and can infect people, other than being passed from person to person via respiratory droplets in the air. Autonomous or remote-controlled sterilizing robots, using UltraViolet-C (UVC) light, are cost-effective and efficient devices. Recent improvements focused on intelligent navigation and detection of areas at higher risk of virus spreading, such as high-touch surfaces (Yang, Nelson, et al., 2020). *GermFalcon* robot, originally developed for aeroplane hygiene, uses such technology (Moore, 2020), as well as the mobile *i-Robot*. This latter carries 10 UVC lamps and integrates different types of sensors to avoid obstacles and to measure temperature and humidity of working environments (Guettari et al., 2020). Despite their effectiveness, UVC-based technologies have also been evaluated as inadequate for the complexity of settings during pandemics. More advanced and intelligent robots are being designed, such as a wall-following robot using fuzzy logic (Muthugala et al., 2020), and others based on deep-learning methods and AI which can identify and reach potentially contaminated areas (Ramalingam et al., 2020). On the other hand, more basic designs were also converted and improved. For example, drones designed for the agriculture sector to spread fertilizers have been repurposed to disinfect public spaces, deliver supplies, testing equipment and samples, monitor public spaces, enforce the regulations, and broadcast public service messages (Murphy et al., 2020).

Still in the realm of prevention, but beyond disinfection, robots can speed up the production of PPE and other protective products, like, for example, 3D-printed face shields, isolation wards, and ventilator valves (Wainwright, 2020). Robots can also continually work to monitor temperature, in ports of entry, public places, hospitals, as well as to provide important information. In relation to the latter, researchers are working at the incorporation of vision algorithms, automated camera systems and thermal sensors, to render screening more effective and precise and link the data collected to information systems (see below, Health informatics category) (Khaleghi et al., 2020). Another example of a prevention device is the smart helmet equipped with infrared temperature detector, an augmented-reality visor, a camera that can read QR codes, plus Wi-Fi, Bluetooth, and 5G so it can beam data to the nearest hospital. This helmet has also a facial recognition technology to retrieve the medical history of 100 people in 2 min (Wainwright, 2020). In delivery and logistics too, robots could offer a great support by enabling the maintenance of social distance while also delivering food and medicine, including for disabled people and patients affected by the virus (Niamat Ullah Akhund et al., 2020). The *Little Peanut* robot delivers food to patients and people who are shielding in China (Cuthbertson, 2020).

11.2.4.2.2 Testing and examination

In most countries, nasopharyngeal and oropharyngeal swabs had to be collected, handled, transferred, and tested for a COVID-19 diagnosis. During a MHD, lack of qualified staff to swab patients and process test samples becomes a key challenge. Automated or robot-assisted swabbing has been designed (Aitken et al., 2020) in order to speed up and render testing safer, while also reducing risks for infection and freeing up the workforce. As mentioned above in relation to the Ebola virus outbreak, blood testing was also needed, as in the case of COVID-19 outbreak. In fact, the disease could be asymptomatic and only an antibody or serology test can detect previous infection. Again, to reduce risk of exposure and infection, and free up healthcare professionals, researchers are studying robotic systems based on ultrasound imaging identification of peripheral forearm veins for automated venepuncture (Leipheimer et al., 2019). Other types of robot-supported testing have also been developed, removing the patients' need to travel to a health clinic, thus reducing the risks of contamination. For example, in China, a remote robotic ultrasound system has been developed to conduct lung sonograms to assess the possible consequences of COVID-19 on the lung tissues (Evans et al., 2020). In Canada, telerobotic ultrasound systems were used to perform remote obstetric examinations in COVID-19-affected remote communities (Adams et al., 2020). Other researchers have integrated the teleultrasound device with the 5G network and were able to examine isolating patients in different hospitals and cities. This method is feasible for the lungs, but also for other organs (Yu et al., 2020). Looking ahead, AI will assist in better remote diagnosis, integrating current haptic control, for instance (Wang & Wang, 2021).

As already mentioned, AI has indeed great potential in the different fields of a MHD, from planning to reporting, and from diagnosis to treatment (Vaishya et al., 2020). AI and deep learning approaches can drive multiple analyses of data from ultrasound systems and other medical imaging methods, such as X-rays, CT, and MRI, to detect infected cases (Apostolopoulos & Mpesiana, 2020). A neural network-based mechanism was developed to classify at a large scale the respiratory patterns of COVID-19 patients (Wang, Hu, et al., 2020).

Robotic devices are also enabling the analysis of blood and other samples and the development and fast production of relevant drugs. Sample tests are complex and sensitive processes, entailing RNA extraction and amplification, and robotic workstations to this end have been worked at for over 2 decades (Cavanagh, 2001). These were perfected during the 2002-2004 coronavirus outbreak toward identifying drug targets (Ranadhir et al., 2007). Several advancements have been made during the COVID-19 pandemic in relation to robotic applications in microbiological investigations and related nanotechnologies (Marais et al., 2020). Time is a life-saving factor when it comes to finding a vaccine during a MHD based on an infectious disease. Both in the repurposing of existing clinically approved drugs and in the designing of new ones, frameworks based on AI and ML are being used (Randhawa et al., 2020). An important example of these innovations is the *AlphaFold*, a deep learning system developed by Google's DeepMind which is able to generate protein and genomic information. *AlphaFold* has been deployed for COVID-19 and helped in the vaccine preparation (Senior et al., 2020). Outside the hospital, in the community scenario, a non-contact community robot was proposed to allow citizens to perform self-diagnosis and initiate remote diagnosis when necessary. The robot can recognize speech, detect keywords, classify coughs, and convert the user's coughing audio into structured data for future processing. The audio and video results can be potentially processed and diagnosed by the AI network (Wei et al., 2020).

11.2.4.2.3 Health care and telemedicine

The application of AI and other robotic devices and advanced technologies in telemedicine is vast and keeps growing. Clinical trials showed that video consultations resulted in high satisfaction among healthcare providers and patients, independent of disease progression, with lower costs and reduced carbon footprint compared to traditional visits (Abimbola et al., 2019). Telehealth can also help for disease diagnosis through video consultations with experts (Greenhalgh et al., 2020), whereas physical HRI becomes key in bedside care and interventional procedures too (Su et al., 2021). The COVID-19 crisis has been a huge catalyst for an exponential growth in this realm, and people in many parts of the world have become more and more accustomed to virtual interactions and e-presence. HSC providers have been severely challenged in the delivery of care and other medical services, due to the persistent restrictions and preventive measures. During the outbreak, clinicians, HSC professionals, as well as service users have had to familiarize themselves with medical digital tools. These tools reveal their great usefulness during biological and environmental hazards, such as COVID-19, since they can grant regular care when physical presence is prohibitive. As highlighted already, in this way, the pandemic has contributed to accelerating the dismantling of several barriers, in both acceptance and use of robotic devices.

In Singapore and USA, chatbots have been used to allow remote triaging and the collection of patients' information (Hollander & Carr, 2020; Priya, 2020). Again, in the USA, more than 50 health systems have relied on telehealth to offer care and follow-up of patients with the disease (Hollander & Carr, 2020). In the UK, the National Health Service (NHS) has switched to online consultations in specific health areas, sometimes supported by a robot at the patient's home, to reduce physical visits to medical practices and hospitals, and free up hospital beds (NHS, 2020). "Coronavirus SUS" application is a telemedicine Brazilian tool, which integrates prevention, triage, and information by identifying possible infected cases, referring them to the nearest emergency department, and providing evidence-based insights and appropriate health advice (de Oliveira Andrade et al., 2021). In Australia, healthcare professionals have been equipped to offer services through telemedicine (Fisk et al., 2020). An information system for healthcare was designed with the potential of linking medical specialists to other applications (e.g., telemedicine, smartphones, and wearable sensors) and of incorporating a smart robot to conduct lab test, read results, and other remote supports at home, such as taking blood pressure, dispensing tablets, and releasing sterilizing gas (Wang et al., 2021). Another notable example of telepresence has been the robot with the virtual platform that allows the visual interaction between nurses and patients adopted at a hospital in Brazil (Ono et al., 2020). Similar frameworks of teleoperated robots, such as *ABBYuMi* and fully humanoid ones, were used in isolation wards to deliver medical services, ranging from auscultation, daily consultation, and UV disinfection (Brunda et al., 2020).

In a conceptual system of HRI, Pepper robot (see Chapter 2 & 5) is equipped with sensors, actuators, and integrated with cloud computing services, which are capable of human identification, visual identification, and audio-based interlocution. These are all very useful features in telemedicine and could be greatly perfected by the 5G network (Podpora et al., 2020). Personalized care and assistance are the aims, for example, of the mobile robot platform *Lio*. *Lio* has a multifunctional arm and was adjusted to perform COVID-related functions, such as body temperature and disinfection (Mišeikis et al., 2020). In 2017, with promising results, a Tele-Robotic Intelligent Nursing Assistant was also utilized to provide remote care-giving in quarantine areas, and its applicability during MHDs, such as a pandemic, is evident (Li et al., 2017). Another smart medical care project developed during COVID-19 was based on a beliefs-desires-intentions agent architecture partly devised to be deployed in a robot to offer remote human-like service, to monitor and serve patients with their needs (Lanza et al., 2020). Currently, as clarified already, remote servicing robots have limited mobility and functionality and can only provide basic communication and interactions with patients (see Chapter 2 & 5, this volume).

In light of current limitations, robots and AI devices currently have limited use in the field of mental health. The pandemic revealed that due to the rapid increase in numbers of infected cases and deaths, both healthcare personnel and the public suffered from psychological problems, including stress, anxiety, obsessive-compulsive traits, and depression (Vindegaard & Benros, 2020). These issues are likely to persist after social isolation ended (Scassellati & Vázquez, 2020). Although robotic interventions have been scarce, online mental health education through communication programs and social media have been widely promoted and used during the outbreak, in the UK, US, China, and other countries (Wright & Caudill, 2020). Additionally, online psychological consultation services were also delivered by mental health professionals (Murphy et al., 2020).

11.2.4.2.4 Health informatics

The fourth area of application of robots and advanced technologies that we are considering is that of public health. Appropriate and timely decision-making during the different stages of the outbreak requires reliable data, not only about infected patients, but also about their behavior, such as mobility and physical interactions with other people. Again, AI and Deep Learning, but also Big Data, Mathematical Modeling, Internet of Things, and Geographic Information Systems (GIS) have proven their usefulness in managing and planning to control the disease on a global scale (Chamola et al., 2020). According to Khaleghi et al. (2020), the application of AI, robotics, and advanced technologies include

- the fast gathering of multisource Big Data;
- visualization of epidemic information;
- online tracking of infected cases;
- forecasting spatial transmission;
- regional segmentation of the infection risk and prevention level;
- counterbalancing and administration of the supply and demand of resources; and,
- social education and stress management.

In fact, to summarize, these advanced technologies in health informatics have helped in detecting symptoms of COVID-19, in ensuring social distancing and maintaining patients records (e.g., with Blockchain technology), as well as in disease diffusion assessment and prediction (Ahir et al., 2020).

Applications are numerous, both in medical actions, as seen, but also in public health decision making and policies, which are not strictly of medical nature, despite being crucial in saving lives and improving people's well-being. The literature reports the development of a high precision ML-based prognostic model to predict the survival of critically ill COVID-19 patients with three main clinical data (Yan et al., 2020). Mathematical modelling was used to investigate and predict the effect of control strategies on outcomes of the epidemic (Debnath & Bardhan, 2020). In China, an analysis platform through GIS and

Big Data technologies assessed the spatial representations of the patients, material resources, population, and social media behavioral data were used to create epidemic maps; these maps identify problems in the main risk regions and spatial inconsistency of medical resources together with public attitude to better guide governments (Zhou et al., 2020). Others used cell phone data for modelling the geographical dissemination of epidemics in relation to human mobility (Oliver et al., 2020), and several European governments collaborated with researchers as well as mobile network operators to estimate the efficacy of the restrictions against the spread of the COVID-19 virus (Pepe et al., 2020). In the USA, location data were collected from nearly 200 applications to develop a contact network to estimate contact patterns using epidemiological models and the impact of policies (Martín-Calvo et al., 2020). In countries where the virus was well contained, such as South Korea and Taiwan, information technology-based tracing strategies were used by aggregating data from a number of sources (e.g., cell phones, medical records, immigration and travel records, card transaction data, public transportation records, and closed-circuit television scenes). The information is categorized through Big Data analytics and made available to implement containment strategies accordingly (Wang, Ng, et al., 2020). In China, an intelligent automated platform recognizes cases of infection and can be helpful in follow-up of patients in the long run (Bai et al., 2020). The future cities were also discussed in light of AI urban robotics and automation in a new era of urban bio-(in)security (Chen et al., 2020) (Box 11.2).

BOX 11.2

COVID-19, AI technologies and the need for preparedness

Key points:

- Ebola virus outbreak in 2014 stimulated R&D of robots in MHDs, highlighting limits as well as new areas for deployment, including cultural competence
- COVID-19 pandemic accelerated the Fourth Industrial Revolution (Chapter 1), in the run to swift progress in digitalization and automation in several human activities
- During COVID-19, progress in AI devices in health care occurred in the realms of prevention, testing and examination, telemedicine, and health informatics
- COVID-19 has unveiled the potential of culturally competent SARs in the provision of meaningful companionship and holistic care in MHD mass isolation and social distance
- Governmental strategies which consider the use of SARs are needed and must include training and preparing HSC workers

11.2.4.2.5 Socially assistive robots

Our overview of robotic and advanced technological AI devices during the COVID-19 pandemic has, by no means, been exhaustive and there was no over-celebratory intent of boosting robots and their software and hardware advancements. In fact, while we have highlighted areas of potential and actual applicability, there are many limitations too in this technological field (see Chapters 2, 5, 8 to 10). In particular, robotic applications in patient care are still limited, despite the promising potentials of their implementations in the fight against COVID-19. It is worth bearing in mind the limitations in robots' social skills in particular.

Let us look back at *WALL-E,* the clever, curious, and emotional waste lifter robot in the Pixar movie that we have introduced above in this chapter. One aspect of *WALL-E* we failed to flag up is that the items it collects, in what has become its home, represent each an emotional realm, or a feeling, and, in this sense, they can be seen as replacements of relationships and communication with others. In sum, *WALL-E* is not only isolated and alone on planet Earth, but it also *feels lonely*. *WALL-E* is in a state similar to the one in which billions of people were during the COVID-19 crisis. Until one day, *EVE*, a probe droid which can fly and shoot, lands on our abandoned Earth, sent to scan the planet for human-sustainable life. After a while, *WALL-E* and *EVE* establish a bond and they become good friends.

Is there any current autonomous robot able to befriend a human? This is one way to formulate the question on the status of the advancements in the technology of SARs in HSC. Thinking of friendship is indeed a good way of grasping the spectrum of social interactions SARs are meant to perform, something which was explored in other chapters of this book (see Chapters from 5 to 9). As we have seen for rescue robots, their ability to be autonomous learners and have social affective functions—which encompass robot's appearance, affective expressions, delivery of psychological comfort, and other skills related to verbal and non-verbal communication—are all prerequisites to the delivery of holistic care. As for numerous other technologies, also in relation to SARs, the pandemic constituted an important cornerstone, functioning as a catalyst in the research, development, and deployment of this technology, the use of which greatly grew during the crisis (Aymerich-Franch, 2020).

AI and robotics technologies are progressing in developing autonomous robots which can have more sophisticated and "fulfilling" social interactions and communications. Despite a lack of consensus on a unique definition for social robots (Henschel et al., 2021), SARs are expected to use gestures, speech, facial recognition, movements and, in general, social interaction to assist their users (Feil-Seifer & Mataric, 2005). As mentioned in Chapter 3 of this book, the goal of these robots is to create effective interaction with the human user for the purpose of giving assistance and achieving measurable progress in convalescence, rehabilitation, learning, and well-being (Papadopoulos et al., 2020). Typically, they are being developed to be applied as companions, educators, assistants for older adults and children with disabilities (Tavakoli et al., 2020). It is to this advanced technology that we are now switching the focus, to make the case for their potential usefulness during a MHD, like the pandemic.

Prolonged social isolation and the impossibility of close physical presence with dying loved ones during the pandemic have been issues of major public mental health concerns (Banerjee & Rai, 2020). On the one hand, the detrimental effects of loneliness, both social and emotional (Russell et al., 1984), onto humans' well-being and health have been ascertained (Hawkley & Cacioppo, 2010). Conversely, the positive impact of social support in mitigating a sense of loneliness and its negative effects were also demonstrated (Courtet et al., 2020). In fighting the "loneliness virus" of what has been described as a "behavioral epidemic" (Jeste et al., 2020), SARs as companions and holistic carers can play a very valuable role (Henkel et al., 2020; Odekerken-Schröder et al., 2020). SARs might be deployed to offer ongoing social interactions, in–home methods for monitoring the mental and emotional state of users, identifying those who show depressive symptoms, and connecting those users with professional help (Rabbitt et al., 2015). SARs can also support mental health treatment adherence and activities, by reinforcing psychological strategies suggested by health experts for users to cope with negative mental states and stress. Interestingly, a study identified three potential roles of companion robots to alleviate different types of loneliness (Odekerken-Schröder et al., 2020); these are

1. personal assistant (to help when social interactions are diminished);
2. relational peer (to compensate for reduced relationships);
3. intimate buddy (when a bond is established with the robot).

These are very useful insights to lead future research and development. Currently, the potential of SARs to be well-being coaches during the pandemic remains underdeveloped. Robotic companions are still away to come, obviously none could have been used during COVID-19, and indeed instances of autonomous SARs during the pandemic are scarce. The already mentioned *Pepper*, *Nao*, and *Paro* (see Chapter 3, this volume), but also others such as *Jibo*, *Zora*, and *Buddy*, are all existing examples of companion robots, or according to some, they are potential examples (Meskó, 2019). However, the prospective functions of a well-being buddy of these robots, some of them still comparable to robotic toys, have rarely been specifically adapted or enhanced to the conditions caused by the pandemic (Aymerich-Franch & Ferrer, 2020), and several barriers need to be overcome, not least, the robots' cost.

Despite several barriers, as companions in the future, SARs could offer more refined verbal interaction to provide basic and motivational conversation, while also expressing emotions and having physical contact with the patient. An example of this is the use of the zoomorphic *Paro* in Texas to help patients reduce the feeling of loneliness (Knibbs, 2020). *Paro* (modeled after a baby harp seal and weighing as a human infant) was precisely conceived to offer comfort to people. This pet robot has been tested with older adults suffering from Alzheimer and dementia. Promising pre-post differences were found in several physiological measures, in addition to a very positive interactional effect (see Chapter 3). During the pandemic, the use of *Paro*, as a therapeutic tool in elderly with memory challenges, increased, but also new uses were found. At a call center in Tokyo dealing with calls for coronavirus tests, workers were given a *Paro* to release stress, and, in Atlanta, Intensive Care Unit nurses started using *Paro* to better cope with the isolation and distance from their family and living pets (Knibbs, 2020). Another example is *ElliQ*, an AI device also designed to provide proactive companionship and entertainment to older adults, while serving as a healthcare assistant (Intuition Robotics, 2021). For over 2 years and throughout the pandemic, the Israeli start-up behind *ElliQ* carried a user acceptance testing with older adults across the USA and Canada. Results relative to the early pandemic peak (April and May 2020) showed, for example, that users became very likely to agree to or asked *ElliQ* for conversational topics or mindfulness exercises (Intuition Robotics Team, 2020).

To summarize this section, the COVID-19 pandemic has highlighted the need for culturally competent SARs during MHDs. Although some robotic devices are currently being used, the development of effective socially assistive autonomous robots is very complex and requires high levels of accuracy and sophistication in order to function within HSC environments, which are increasingly multicultural (see Chapters 2 & 5 to 9). This is a challenging area of robotic development because social interactions require building and maintaining complex models of people, including their knowledge, emotions, and cultural beliefs and habits, as well as the context and environment of the interaction (Yang, Lv, et al., 2020). To be effective, SARs will need to perceive emotional states, calculate when it is appropriate to intervene, and develop long-term models of behavior, mood, and affect (Scassellati & Vázquez, 2020). It is not only a matter of transcultural competence, but a technological problem that comes first. There are many issues to be solved yet, concerning perception, action, verbal interaction, and so on. These issues have been explored in Chapter 2, and Chapters 5 to 9, which describe the development of CARESSES *Pepper*, the first culturally competent SAR. Chapter 1 clarifies why making robots is very complex.

HSC robotics are inevitable additions to the existing tools which caring services and their workforce are already using. The demand for these services continues to increase while both human carers and other resources are struggling to cope. There is a growing interest among care providers in using robotics to improve quality of care and ease the pressure on the caring systems. In addition to the technical and scientific challenges that need to be addressed, and as mentioned in previous chapters, there is a need for stimulating dialog with the public as well as with the HSC professionals. This is necessary in order to identify and address the challenges and concerns they have, such as the numerous ethical questions (see Chapter 4) and the impact that these AI autonomous robots will have on them and the multicultural societies at large. Technological R&D, together with workforce education and training, and appropriate policies and strategies, will enable humanity to create their *EVE* robot ready to go through the next MHD.

11.2.4.3 *The potential of transcultural robots in an existential disaster: Gamila's story*

The COVID-19 pandemic has changed our world and impacted multiple layers of our society. We have seen, in this and other chapters of this book, how culturally competent social robots can potentially fulfill the important task of providing quality holistic and compassionate care, in moments where human healthcare workforce is under extreme pressure, when social distance is required and the number of deaths is very high. We have also ascertained that the time still has to come for this technology to constitute a significant tangible contribution in the delivery of holistic HSC, including the mitigation of negative feelings, in particular loneliness, and the support in existential issues, particularly in the face of death. To conclude this long section around the COVID-19 crisis, we are presenting the story of Gamila, which serves to amplify the potential and usefulness of culturally competent SARs during a MHD through contributing to the provision of holistic, quality care, which includes spiritual support (Box 11.3).

Spiritual care is recognized as a key element of the growing model of holistic care pivoting around compassion and cultural competence (Papadopoulos, 2018). The WHO includes the evaluation of and care for the spiritual needs of the patients with life-threatening illness in the definition of palliative care (WHO, 2020b). The International Council of Nurses, in its code of ethics, stresses the importance of respecting the spiritual beliefs of patients, their families

BOX 11.3

The potential of SARs in holistic and spiritual care: Gamila's story[4]

Gamila is a Muslim British citizen of Pakistani origin residing in Manchester in North West England. Gamila had recently turned 66 and decided to retire from her job as administrative officer at one of the city's colleges. Her husband passed away several years back, and Gamila is leaving alone, after her youngest daughter moved to London for her studies, joining her older sister. Gamila's son is living and working in the Netherlands; he has two children in primary school.

Toward the end of April 2020, after a few weeks of self-isolation due to the COVID-19 restrictions imposed by the UK government, Gamila went to the grocery store as she needed some mangoes for her lassi, as a heatwave made her feel very thirsty. A couple of days later, while watching some TV, her head started spinning and her stomach felt unsettled: by the next day she realized that she had a fever and called the emergency number 111, and a little later an ambulance came to take her to the nearest NHS hospital. There she was tested for COVID-19 which proved to be positive. Gamila was transferred to the COVID ward and the following day a nurse offered her a tablet device so that Gamila could video-call her daughters and her son. Gamila's conditions worsened slightly and she began to feel the need to connect with her religion; however, no Muslim chaplain was onsite and spiritual leaders from her mosque were prohibited accessing the hospital. Nonetheless, Gamila managed to have a couple of e-conversations with the Buddhist chaplain using a tablet, during which she expressed the need to have readings from the Quran. After liaising with the large Muslim faith community in Manchester, a donation of a Quran cube was made to the hospital. These small cubes offer Quranic readings, recitals and singing, in 12 different languages from a variety of different readers. These small devices made also possible to listen to Hadiths, Nasheeds, the Call to Prayer, and the Names of Allah, which provided great comfort and spiritual strength to Gamila. Luckily, Gamila's blood oxygen saturation normalized, and after 10 days in hospital, she was able to return home.

However, despite the immense luck of having survived COVID, Gamila's troubles did not end: she developed long-COVID symptoms and she was alone, self-isolating again from relatives and friends. This situation was particularly painful for Gamila, especially during the Muslim holy month of Ramadan that was still ongoing when she went home. Her son purchased a smartphone for her, so that Gamila could video-call her children and her Imam. Her daughters provided her with a virtual assistant, equipped with a smart speaker and a touch screen display. Gamila enjoyed these devices, listening to music, connecting with live-streamed Jumuah, the Islamic Friday prayer, and setting reminders for her medicines and so on. However, days felt long, and her sense of solitude and low mood were growing, along with worrying about her health conditions. One day, after watching a video on her TV regarding an intelligent

Continued

> **BOX 11.3** *(cont'd)*
>
> humanoid robot which was also culturally competent and had been deployed in some care homes in the country for a trial period, Gamila started dreaming of having one in her house. She wished for a robot which, not only combined all the tasks of her smart devices in one, but which could be both intelligent, sensitive and a skillful companion. This robot could have conversations with her, not only in English, but in Urdu too, her mother tongue, about topics that were of interest to her, more and more as it was learning about Gamila's culture, life story, and personality. The robot could express emotions and empathy, and would sense when to talk or not, and would know how to offer spiritual and religious support. It would also be an excellent assistant, capable to monitor Gamila's health, offer reminders, connect with her medical doctor if necessary, help with mobility, cleaning and shopping. In other words, Gamila wished for a presence who could always be there, particularly when no one else could. A presence that could complement that of her human beloved ones and of human professional carers, and making her feel always connected with them, as well as with her spirituality.
>
> [4] The story of Gamila is a reconstructed collage of true stories yielded during a study conducted in 2020 by the Research Center for Transcultural Studies in Health at Middlesex University London aimed at investigating spiritual support during the pandemic.

and communities (ICN, 2012). Policy documents and institutional guidelines included spiritual care as key to quality healthcare. Spirituality and religion are crucial elements of an individual's cultural values and beliefs, including health beliefs; and spiritual needs vary across cultural and ethnic groups (Busolo & Woodgate, 2015). Compassion is associated with several major religions and philosophies, and their virtues (Papadopoulos, 2018; Papadopoulos et al., 2016). During the first peak of the COVID-19 pandemic, the media reported that, due to safety regulations, many of the thousands of dying patients were deprived of the last act of compassion—spiritual support—in the absence of family members, friends, and spiritual leaders. Indeed, in line with the WHO interim guidance (WHO, 2020c), religious leaders, including chaplains, were unable to perform regular services and provide the same bedside spiritual support as pre-pandemic (Cockell, 2020; Papadopoulos et al., 2021). During a MHD, such as COVID-19, where human-to-human physical presence is difficult or altogether prohibited, the possibility to have an autonomous and culturally competent SAR able to offer quality care and companionship could not only eventually improve, but also save the lives of millions of people.

11.3 Developing a transcultural AI robotics strategy for major health disasters

The pandemic was considered as an extreme, unprecedented existential crisis, which caught health providers and governments unprepared in terms of national strategies which were adequately resourced, had been well rehearsed, and could be immediately initiated. The pandemic also created new societal systems and conditions of living, working, and behaving, including how individuals care for themselves and others, when death is imminent (Bland, 2020). The increased use of robots and AI devices during COVID-19 was very helpful, while the absence of effective SARs was regrettable. But while storing caches of hospital supplies is sensible, storing a reserve of specialized robots for use in a future emergency can be more problematic (Murphy et al., 2020). This was the strategy of the Japanese nuclear power industry, but it failed during the Fukushima Daiichi nuclear accident because even the non-SARs robots that had been stored were outdated and nonfunctional when needed (Murphy et al., 2020). Instead, the Tokyo Electric Power Company acquired and deployed commercial bomb squad robots, which were commonly used throughout the world. While the commercial robots were not perfect in dealing with a radiological emergency, they were convenient and effective enough to be used throughout the facility (Murphy et al., 2020).

In light of the COVID pandemic, the greatest disaster of recent times, it is indeed necessary that governments design strategies to pave the way for a strong preparation of the HSC systems which pivots around quality and holistic care. For this, transcultural SARs will be increasingly needed. This becomes even more pressing when considering two important sociodemographic factors:

1. an increasingly multicultural and interconnected society, which goes hand-in-hand with the necessity of having robots ready to be deployed in many different countries and cultures;
2. the growth of the aging population on the one hand, and the reduction of birth rates on the other, resulting in a number of negative global, social, caring, and economic concerns and implications for future MHDs (UN, 2020), such as the shortage of nurses and social care staff (The King's Fund, 2021).

Increasingly, automation is changing the nature of work and will continue to do so in the future. One proposed solution to the problem of increased caring needs and shortages of care workers is to introduce robotics in HSC. Despite this, current strategies for MHDs are generally insufficient and do not include the development of SARs that can be culturally competent and able of doing real things in the real world.

11.4 Training and preparing for transcultural AI robotics in major health disasters

11.4.1 The importance of being prepared

Developing strategic guidelines and meeting the nurses' (and other health workers) training needs becomes urgent in light of disasters and emergencies being on the rise worldwide (International Federation of Red Cross and Red Crescent Societies, 2018). Preparation for transcultural SARs should become an indispensable part of MHD strategies and preparedness given its growing, undisputable potential during emergencies, as argued throughout this chapter. This has been recognized by international institutes, which urge governments to strengthen strategies for disaster reduction with concrete management plans (ISDR, 2007; WHO, 2019). These plans must include disaster preparedness training of all healthcare professionals (Achora & Kamanyire, 2016). Nurses represent an indispensable workforce during disasters, and preparedness for adequate response is crucial (ICN & WHO, 2011; Papadopoulos et al., forthcoming). In mass casualty situations, nurses bear one of the greatest burdens of care, including that of patients' spiritual well-being.

Let us reflect again on the COVID-19 pandemic: the WHO declared the outbreak on the March 11, 2020, and less than 2 weeks later, in the UK for example, the Prime Minister announced the implementation of several restrictions advertised by the slogan "Stay home, Protect the NHS, Save Lives". The infection and death rates increased rapidly, and during the early weeks of the COVID-19, the UK government and the NHS were not fully aware on how to best approach its treatment and prevention and were unprepared for this health emergency (The Guardian, 2020). It is also fair to say that no country in the world was adequately prepared for this major health catastrophe which resulted in the death of millions of people. It is also fair to assume that a comprehensive global strategy, as well as national strategic plans for MHDs that were piloted and well resourced, would have saved many lives.

11.4.2 General considerations about training

As discussed in Chapter 12, a key component in any strategy for MHD preparedness is the training of HSC workers, including training on how to deploy and use SARs during a MHD. Although currently SARs are limited in what they can do, rapid progress is evident by the growing levels of investment in SARs developments by governments and commercial companies across the world. Any training in the use of robots should also include SARs and have a strong focus on patient safety, privacy of patient's information, and obtaining consent in line with the key values of person-centered and compassionate care (see Chapter 4). These recommendations were made by two recent studies—an international surveys and an interview-based study conducted by the Research Center for Transcultural Studies in Health (RCTSH, 2021). These studies explored the training needs of nurses and other HSC workers in terms of their preparation to work with SARs. Although the two studies were not MHD related, their recommendations can also be applied during MHDs. Research participants prioritized the welfare and safety of care home residents and patients, and wanted to ensure that a SAR would benefit them without increasing the risk or harm to them (Papadopoulos et al., 2021). Examples of risk or harm given by the interviewees are incidents of robot malfunctions, the accidental collision and injury of users with the robots, or the inappropriate use of data which the robot routinely collects. The research participants also indicated their desire to achieve proficiency in digital skills and competency in using the robots. Indeed, an essential part of any successful strategy for digital transformation in HSC is planning, which includes reviewing the skillsets, resources, and infrastructure that will be needed and ensures that organizations are equipped for the upcoming change (Maguire et al., 2018; Papadopoulos et al., forthcoming). This type of planning, combined with ongoing evaluation and adaptation, can also help to achieve quality person-centered care and maximize efficiency of resource utilization.

It should be noted that training needs may vary by culture, and that cultural variables such as individualism/collectivism, uncertainty avoidance, and long-term orientation may need to be taken into account. The needs identified by the RCTSH studies resonate with the training needs for the future HSC workforce which were identified by stakeholders in a report by the Consilium Research & Consultancy (2018). The report listed a number of potential areas that could be covered when training the HSC workforce, including a general introduction to robots with examples of how they can be used; skills training in how to use robots and how to interpret data collected by robots (digital skills competency); training about benefits and challenges of using robots; health and safety training; guidance about regulation; and training on how to introduce robots to service users. Share and Pender (2018) have suggested a number of pedagogical approaches for teaching HSC professionals about social robotics. The suggested learning activities included research and theoretical tasks (e.g., discussion of case studies and hypothetical scenarios), debating ethical issues, conducting literature reviews, but also more applied teaching activities, such as role-playing, simulation or real-life interactions with robots and programming of robots.

11.4.3 A proposal for a training curriculum for MHD using transcultural AI

In this section, we briefly outline three topics that may be covered in both a fast track short course and in longer undergraduate and postgraduate modules to prepare the human HSC workforce to make the most of SARs, particularly when massively deployed in the case of MHDs and emergencies. It is reasonable to assume that currently the majority of HSC workers do not have any previous experience with using robots, and therefore training should start at an introductory level, based on a number of MHD scenarios. The three topics below originate from recommendations found in the literature and our own research; we have adapted them to be more relevant to MHDs. They are offered here as stimuli for future research and further development.

11.4.3.1 Topic 1—knowledge about the robot's purpose, functionality, and capabilities

Learning should start by exploring the purpose of the SAR (and any other type of robots) that may be deployed in HSC workplaces. Being able to answer the question of "why" the robots will be, or are being, used is important and relates to knowing about the motivation of using the robots, their meaningfulness and added value, and how they could be useful, advantageous, or beneficial. Nurses and HSC professionals need to become aware of what the SARs may be able to do in the future and what they can actually do at present. For example, during a future viral or bacterial pandemic, SARs could be deployed in places and situations where human nurses or other health workers could not be present due to the high risk to their health. Future SARs could provide information and instructions to health staff and visitors.

Learning about a robot's capabilities is important for HSC providers with regard to setting and managing their expectations of the robot. Knowing about the robot's functionality will enable HSC professionals to use the robot appropriately and efficiently, to maximize its potential effectiveness and efficiency. These are important considerations because, arguably, the move toward using more technology, and specifically the introduction of robots in general, and SARs in particular, is a significant change to current ways of working within HSC systems. Therefore, as key stakeholders in this type of change, HSC workers should be very clear about the reasons for the use of SARs and other robots and be assured that, during non-MHD times, these intelligent machines will not replace them, but they will either complement, or supplement what they are already providing. During a MHD, the robots will indeed take over some of their functions in order to protect them and the public.

11.4.3.2 Topic 2—how to operate the robot

A second important training topic should focus on how to operate and use the robot. This type of training is needed irrespective of MHDs. Based on research recommendations, prioritizing practical training needs, such as knowing how to use the basic functions of the robot and other technical competences, in order to provide the best care for the patient, is essential. Related to this, a key priority of the training is patient safety. During MHDs, SARs can also promote the safety of staff and the public. This topic should also include scenarios and instructions on how to deal with potential problems of the robot such as malfunctions, in MHDs and non-MHDs situations.

11.4.3.3 Topic 3—legal and ethical issues

Learning about the ethical codes, the relevant legislation and implications of using a robot with patients is of key importance in both MHDs and non-MHDs times. Informed consent is one key consideration, especially during MHDs where the health landscape is changing by the minute and the priority in the early stages is saving lives. Nurses and other caring professionals must receive training on how to use AI devices and SARs in giving information to patients and relatives, how to obtain urgent, legally acceptable informed consent when needed, in order to protect themselves, and to be able to proceed providing the best patient care, often in difficult and uncertain situations. During MHDs, nurses are involved in a huge number of ethical decisions regarding the provision of new and experimental treatments, often involving technologies which were hastily made available, as well as withdrawing technological treatments which may end the life of a person. Such dilemmas should be part of the training in order to discover the future impact of AI and SARs technologies and the future role which such technologies may or may not have.

11.5 Conclusion

Global MHDs could kill a huge number of people while also leaving a large number to suffer the chronic consequences of ill health. Major health pandemics are not a new phenomenon; what is new is the increasing realization that these will continue to happen at a more frequent pace. Humanity must not only learn to manage these, it must also address their underlying causes. The growing corpus of scientific evidence suggests that chief causes of MHDs are linked to the long-term destructive human activities that affected the ecological balance of our planet in the anthropocenic era we are living in. If we do not find solutions, planet Earth may become an unlivable rubbish dump where only robots like *WALL-E* would be able to survive.

While humanity must urgently undertake a massive existential contemplation, in the short term, it must find ways to respond and manage these global events. This chapter has provided much food for thought and for action. It has provided a realistic picture of what AI and robotic technologies were able to offer in past MHSs, the solutions they provided during the COVID-19 pandemic, as well as making suggestions for the future, in particular by looking at the promising technology of SARs.

Most people will agree that AI and robotic technologies have the potential to benefit humanity during such stressful and unprecedented times, but many people will also agree that such technologies are currently in their early stages of development. Governments must strategize and heavily invest resources in order to convert the potential into real products and effective solutions. R&D needs to be nurtured in order for scientific breakthroughs and innovations to happen. This chapter has, in this sense, discussed the importance of developing and resourcing a national MHD strategy, the implementation of which is regularly rehearsed. A major component of such a strategy is the provision of training to all HSC workers in order to become equipped with a skillset that will enable them to use the AI robotic devices effectively, as they become available in their workplace and during MHDs.

11.6 Reflective questions

1. Reflect on your professional experiences during the COVD-19 pandemic. What AI robotic devices did you, or your colleagues, used to help them communicate with COVID patients and their families? Which one was most useful and why?
2. It is commonly known that during the early stages of the COVID-19 pandemic governments and hospitals did not know how best to manage the acute and uncertain conditions resulting from the pandemic and most of them did not have a MHD strategy. If you were asked to contribute to the development of such a strategy, what would you recommend in terms of resources, processes, and training, and what role would AI and robotic technologies have in this strategy?

References

AAAS. (2021). *Artificial intelligence and COVID-19: Applications and impact assessment, (report prepared by Ilana Harrus and Jessica Wyndham under the auspices of the AAAS scientific responsibility, human rights and law program)*. Washington (DC): American Association for the Advancement of Science.

Abimbola, S., Keelan, S., Everett, M., Casburn, K., Mitchell, M., Burchfield, K., & Martiniuk, A. (2019). The medium, the message and the measure: A theory-driven review on the value of telehealth as a patient-facing digital health innovation. *Health Economics Review, 9*, 21. https://doi.org/10.1186/s13561-019-0239-5

Achora, S., & Kamanyire, J. K. (2016). Disaster preparedness. *Sultan Qaboos University Medical Journal, 16*, e15–e19. https://doi.org/10.18295/squmj.2016.16.01.004

Ackerman, E. (2014). Real robots to help fight Ebola. *IEEE Spectrum: Technology, Engineering, and Science News*.

Adams, S. J., Burbridge, B., Chatterson, L., McKinney, V., Babyn, P., & Mendez, I. (2020). Telerobotic ultrasound to provide obstetrical ultrasound services remotely during the COVID-19 pandemic. *Journal of Telemedicine Telecare*. https://doi.org/10.1177/1357633X20965422, 1357633X20965422.

Ahir, S., Telavane, D., & Thomas, R. (2020). The impact of artificial intelligence, Blockchain, Big data and evolving technologies in coronavirus disease - 2019 (COVID-19) curtailment. In, *Presented at the 2020 international conference on smart electronics and communication (ICOSEC)2020 international conference on smart electronics and communication (ICOSEC)* (pp. 113–120). https://doi.org/10.1109/ICOSEC49089.2020.9215294

Aitken, J., Ambrose, K., Barrell, S., Beale, R., Bineva-Todd, G., Biswas, D., Byrne, R., Caidan, S., Cherepanov, P., Churchward, L., Clark, G., Crawford, M., Cubitt, L., Dearing, V., Earl, C., Edwards, A., Ekin, C., Fidanis, E., Gaiba, A., ... Wu, M. (2020). Scalable and robust SARS-CoV-2 testing in an academic center. *Nature Biotechnology, 38*, 927–931. https://doi.org/10.1038/s41587-020-0588-y

Allotta, B., Brandani, L., Casagli, N., Costanzi, R., Mugnai, F., Monni, N., Natalini, M., & Ridolfi, A. (2017). Development of Nemo remotely operated underwater vehicle for the inspection of the Costa Concordia wreck. *Proceedings of the Institution of Mechanical Engineers - Part M: Journal of Engineering for the Maritime Environment, 231,* 3–18. https://doi.org/10.1177/1475090215605133

Apostolopoulos, I. D., & Mpesiana, T. A. (2020). COVID-19: Automatic detection from X-ray images utilizing transfer learning with convolutional neural networks. *Physical and Engineering Sciences in Medicine,* 1–6. https://doi.org/10.1007/s13246-020-00865-4

Aymerich-Franch, L. (2020). Why it is time to stop ostracizing social robots. *Nature Machine Intelligence, 2.* https://doi.org/10.1038/s42256-020-0202-5, 364–364.

Aymerich-Franch, L., & Ferrer, I. (2020). The implementation of social robots during the COVID-19 pandemic, 2007.03941 [cs] *arXiv.*

Bai, L., Yang, D., Wang, Xun, Tong, L., Zhu, X., Zhong, N., Bai, C., Powell, C. A., Chen, R., Zhou, J., Song, Y., Zhou, X., Zhu, H., Han, B., Li, Q., Shi, G., Li, S., Wang, C., Qiu, Z., ... Tan, F. (2020). Chinese experts' consensus on the Internet of Things-aided diagnosis and treatment of coronavirus disease 2019 (COVID-19). *Clinical eHealth, 3,* 7–15. https://doi.org/10.1016/j.ceh.2020.03.001

Baldemïr, Y., İyïgün, S., Musayev, O., & Ulu, C. (2020). Design and development of a mobile robot for search and rescue operations in debris. *International Journal of Applied Mathematics Electronics and Computers, 8,* 133–137. https://doi.org/10.18100/ijamec.800840

Banerjee, D., & Rai, M. (2020). Social isolation in COVID-19: The impact of loneliness. *International Journal of Social Psychiatry, 66,* 525–527. https://doi.org/10.1177/0020764020922269

Bethel, C. L., Bringes, C., & Murphy, R. R. (2009). Non-facial and non-verbal affective expression in appearance-constrained robots for use in victim management: Robots to the rescue. In *Proceedings of the 4th ACM/IEEE international conference on human robot interaction, HRI '09* (pp. 191–192). New York, NY, USA: Association for Computing Machinery. https://doi.org/10.1145/1514095.1514130

Bland, A. M. (2020). Existential givens in the COVID-19 crisis. *Journal of Humanistic Psychology, 60,* 710–724. https://doi.org/10.1177/0022167820940186

Bogue, R. (2020). Robots in a contagious world. *Industrial Robot: The International Journal of Robotics Research and Application, 47.* https://doi.org/10.1108/IR-05-2020-0101

Brunda, R. L., Keri, V. C., Sinha, T. P., & Bhoi, S. (2020). Re-purposing humanoid robots for patient care in COVID-19 pandemic. *The International Journal of Health Planning and Management, 35,* 1629–1631. https://doi.org/10.1002/hpm.3052

Busolo, D., & Woodgate, R. (2015). Palliative care experiences of adult cancer patients from ethnocultural groups: A qualitative systematic review protocol. *JBI Database System Review Implement Rep, 13,* 99–111. https://doi.org/10.11124/jbisrir-2015-1809

Cavanagh, D. (2001). Innovation and discovery: The application of nucleic acid-based technology to avian virus detection and characterization. *Avian Pathology, 30,* 581–598. https://doi.org/10.1080/03079450120092071

Chamola, V., Hassija, V., Gupta, V., & Guizani, M. (2020). A comprehensive review of the COVID-19 pandemic and the role of IoT, drones, AI, Blockchain, and 5G in managing its impact. *IEEE Access, 8,* 90225–90265. https://doi.org/10.1109/ACCESS.2020.2992341

Chan-Yeung, M., & Xu, R.-H. (2003). Sars: Epidemiology. *Respirology, 8,* S9–S14. https://doi.org/10.1046/j.1440-1843.2003.00518.x

Charu. (2014). *Saul robot will help fight Ebola.* Technotification. URL https://www.technotification.com/2014/12/saul-robot-will-help-fight-ebola.html (accessed 6.23.21).

Chen, B., Marvin, S., & While, A. (2020). Containing COVID-19 in China: AI and the robotic restructuring of future cities. *Dialogues in Human Geography, 10,* 238–241. https://doi.org/10.1177/2043820620934267

Cockell, N. (2020). COVID-19 and grief : A chaplain's reflection on the experience of supporting bereaved parents and widows in lockdown. *Health and Social Care Chaplaincy, 8.*

Consilium Research & Consultancy. (2018). Scoping study on the emerging use of Artificial Intelligence (AI) and robotics in social care. *Skills for Care, Leeds, No. WP2.1a6-CON-17001.*

Courtet, P., Olié, E., Debien, C., & Vaiva, G. (2020). Keep socially (but not physically) connected and carry on: Preventing suicide in the age of COVID-19. *Journal of Clinical Psychiatry, 81*(0–0). https://doi.org/10.4088/JCP.20com13370

Cuthbertson, A. (2020). Robot serves food to people in coronavirus quarantine. *The Independent.*

Debnath, R., & Bardhan, R. (2020). India nudges to contain COVID-19 pandemic: A reactive public policy analysis using machine-learning based topic modelling. *PLoS One, 15*, e0238972. https://doi.org/10.1371/journal.pone.0238972

Evans, K. D., Yang, Q., Liu, Y., Ye, R., & Peng, C. (2020). Sonography of the lungs: Diagnosis and surveillance of patients with COVID-19. *Journal of Diagnostic Medical Sonography, 36*, 370−376. https://doi.org/10.1177/8756479320917107

Feil-Seifer, D., & Mataric, M. J. (2005). Defining socially assistive robotics. In *9th international conference on rehabilitation robotics, 2005. ICORR 2005. Presented at the 9th international conference on rehabilitation robotics, 2005. ICORR 2005* (pp. 465−468). https://doi.org/10.1109/ICORR.2005.1501143

Fincannon, T., Barnes, L. E., Murphy, R. R., & Riddle, D. L. (2004). Evidence of the need for social intelligence in rescue robots. In, *Presented at the 2004 IEEE/RSJ international conference on intelligent robots and systems (IROS) (IEEE cat. No.04CH37566): Vol. 2. 2004 IEEE/RSJ international conference on intelligent robots and systems (IROS) (IEEE cat. No.04CH37566)* (pp. 1089−1095). https://doi.org/10.1109/IROS.2004.1389542

Fisk, M., Livingstone, A., & Pit, S. W. (2020). Telehealth in the context of COVID-19: Changing perspectives in Australia, the United Kingdom, and the United States. *Journal of Medical Internet Research, 22*, e19264. https://doi.org/10.2196/19264

Gossett, S. (2020). *12 examples of rescue robots*. Built In.

Greenhalgh, T., Wherton, J., Shaw, S., & Morrison, C. (2020). Video consultations for COVID-19. *BMJ, 368*, m998. https://doi.org/10.1136/bmj.m998

Guettari, M., Gharbi, I., & Hamza, S. (2020). UVC disinfection robot. *Environmental Science & Pollution Research, 28*, 40394−40399. https://doi.org/10.1007/s11356-020-11184-2

Guizzo, E. (2011). Fukushima robot operator writes tell-all blog. *IEEE Spectrum: Technology, Engineering, and Science News*.

Halperin, C. (2014). Robots that may help fight Ebola. *New YorkTimes*.

Hawkley, L. C., & Cacioppo, J. T. (2010). Loneliness matters: A theoretical and empirical review of consequences and mechanisms. *Annals of Behavioral Medicine, 40*. https://doi.org/10.1007/s12160-010-9210-8

Henkel, A. P., Čaić, M., Blaurock, M., & Okan, M. (2020). Robotic transformative service research: Deploying social robots for consumer well-being during COVID-19 and beyond. *Journal of Service Management, 31*, 1131−1148. https://doi.org/10.1108/JOSM-05-2020-0145

Henkel, Z., Rashidi, N., Rice, A., & Murphy, R. (2011). *Survivor buddy: A social medium robot*. https://doi.org/10.1145/1957656.1957795

Henschel, A., Laban, G., & Cross, E. S. (2021). What makes a robot social? A review of social robots from science fiction to a home or hospital near you. *Current Robotics Reports, 2*, 9−19. https://doi.org/10.1007/s43154-020-00035-0

Hollander, J. E., & Carr, B. G. (2020). Virtually perfect? Telemedicine for COVID-19. *New England Journal of Medicine, 382*, 1679−1681. https://doi.org/10.1056/NEJMp2003539

ICN. (2012). *The ICN code of ethics for nurses*. Geneva, Switzerland: International Council of Nurses.

ICN, WHO. (2011). *ICN framework of disaster nursing competencies*. Geneva Switzerland: International Council of Nurses and World Health Organisation.

International Federation of Red Cross, & Red Crescent Societies. (2018). *World disasters report 2018: Leaving no one behind*. Geneva, Switzerland: International Federation of Red Cross and Red Crescent Societies.

Intuition Robotics. (2021). *ElliQ, the sidekick for happier aging [WWW Document]*. Intuition Robotics. URL https://elliq.com/ (accessed 6.23.21).

Intuition Robotics Team. (2020). Helping seniors cope with loneliness: ElliQ's usage data takeaways. *Intuition Robotics*. https://blog.elliq.com/helping-seniors-cope-with-loneliness-elliqs-usage-data-takeaways (accessed 6.23.21).

ISDR. (2007). *Hyogo Framework for Action 2005-2015: Building the resilience of nations and communities to disasters*. Geneva, Switzerland: United Nations International Strategy for Disaster Reduction.

Jeste, D. V., Lee, E. E., & Cacioppo, S. (2020). Battling the modern behavioral epidemic of loneliness: Suggestions for research and interventions. *JAMA Psychiatry, 77*, 553−554. https://doi.org/10.1001/jamapsychiatry.2020.0027

Kalra, S., Kelkar, D., Galwankar, S. C., Papadimos, T. J., Stawicki, S. P., Arquilla, B., Hoey, B. A., Sharpe, R. P., Sabol, D., & Jahre, J. A. (2014). The emergence of Ebola as a global health security threat: From 'lessons learned' to coordinated multilateral containment efforts. *Journal of Global Infectious Diseases, 6*, 164−177. https://doi.org/10.4103/0974-777X.145247

Kawatsuma, S., Fukushima, M., & Okada, T. (2012). Emergency response by robots to fukushima-daiichi accident: Summary and lessons learned. *Industrial Robot: International Journal, 39*, 428–435. https://doi.org/10.1108/01439911211249715

Khaleghi, A., Mohammadi, M. R., Pirzad Jahromi, G., & Zarafshan, H. (2020). New ways to manage pandemics: Using technologies in the era of COVID-19: A narrative review. *Iranian Journal of Psychiatry, 15*, 236–242. https://doi.org/10.18502/ijps.v15i3.3816

Khan, Z. H., Siddique, A., & Lee, C. W. (2020). Robotics utilization for healthcare digitization in global COVID-19 management. *International Journal of Environmental Research and Public Health, 17*, 3819. https://doi.org/10.3390/ijerph17113819

Knibbs, K. (2020). *There's No cure for COVID-19 loneliness, but robots can help*. Wired.

Kritikos, M., 2020. Ten technologies to fight coronavirus: in-depth analysis (No. PE641.543). EPRS | European Parliamentary Research Service - Scientific Foresight Unit (STOA), Brussel.

Lanza, F., Seidita, V., & Chella, A. (2020). Agents and robots for collaborating and supporting physicians in healthcare scenarios. *Journal of Biomedical Informatics, 108*, 103483. https://doi.org/10.1016/j.jbi.2020.103483

Leipheimer, J. M., Balter, M. L., Chen, A. I., Pantin, E. J., Davidovich, A. E., Labazzo, K. S., & Yarmush, M. L. (2019). First-in-human evaluation of a hand-held automated venipuncture device for rapid venous blood draws. *Technology, 07*, 98–107. https://doi.org/10.1142/S2339547819500067

Li, Z., Moran, P., Dong, Q., Shaw, R. J., & Hauser, K. (2017). Development of a tele-nursing mobile manipulator for remote care-giving in quarantine areas. In , *Presented at the 2017 IEEE international conference on robotics and automation (ICRA)2017 IEEE international conference on robotics and automation (ICRA)* (pp. 3581–3586). https://doi.org/10.1109/ICRA.2017.7989411

Lorenzi, R. (2014). *Mini robot subs help guide Concordia salvage*. Seeker.

Maguire, D., Honeyman, M., Omojomolo, D., & Evans, H. (2018). *Digital change in health and social care*. The King's Fund.

Marais, G., Naidoo, M., Hsiao, N., Valley-Omar, Z., Smuts, H., & Hardie, D. (2020). The implementation of a rapid sample preparation method for the detection of SARS-CoV-2 in a diagnostic laboratory in South Africa. *PLoS One, 15*, e0241029. https://doi.org/10.1371/journal.pone.0241029

Martín-Calvo, D., Aleta, A., Pentland, A., Moreno, Y., & Esteban, Moro (2020). *Effectiveness of social distancing strategies for protecting a community from a pandemic with a data-driven contact network based on census and real-world mobility data [WWW Document]*. URL https://www.semanticscholar.org/paper/Effectiveness-of-social-distancing-strategies-for-a-Mart%C3%ADn-Calvo-Aleta/797d7a4bc0279cc02a2d6e6d19acd8aa89a1c7a0 (accessed 6.23.21).

Meskó, B. (2019). *Benefits of robotics in healthcare: Tasks medical robots will undertake*. The Medical Futurist.

Mišeikis, J., Caroni, P., Duchamp, P., Gasser, A., Marko, R., Mišeikienė, N., Zwilling, F., de Castelbajac, C., Eicher, L., Früh, M., & Früh, H. (2020). Lio-A personal robot assistant for human-robot interaction and care applications. *IEEE Robotics and Automation Letters, 5*, 5339–5346. https://doi.org/10.1109/LRA.2020.3007462

Moore, S. K. (2020). Flight of the GermFalcon: How a potential coronavirus-killing airplane sterilizer was born. *IEEE Spectrum: Technology, Engineering, and Science News*.

Murphy, R. (2004). Trial by fire [rescue robots]. *IEEE Robotics and Automation Magazine, 11*, 50–61. https://doi.org/10.1109/MRA.2004.1337826

Murphy, R. (2012). A decade of rescue robots. In, *Presented at the 2012 IEEE/RSJ international conference on intelligent robots and systems2012 IEEE/RSJ international conference on intelligent robots and systems* (pp. 5448–5449). https://doi.org/10.1109/IROS.2012.6386301

Murphy, Robin, Adams, J., & Gandudi, V. B. M. (2020). *Robots are playing many roles in the coronavirus crisis — and offering lessons for future disasters [WWW Document]*. The Conversation. URL http://theconversation.com/robots-are-playing-many-roles-in-the-coronavirus-crisis-and-offering-lessons-for-future-disasters-135527 (accessed 4.7.21).

Murphy, R., & Burke, J. L. (2005). Up from the rubble: Lessons learned about HRI from search and rescue. *Proceedings of the Human Factors and Ergonomics Society - Annual Meeting, 49*, 437–441. https://doi.org/10.1177/154193120504900347

Murphy, R., Calugi, S., Cooper, Z., & Grave, R. D. (2020). Challenges and opportunities for enhanced cognitive behaviour therapy (CBT-E) in light of COVID-19. *The Cognitive Behaviour Therapist, 13*. https://doi.org/10.1017/S1754470X20000161

Murphy, R., Dreger, K. L., Newsome, S., Rodocker, J., Steimle, E., Kimura, T., Makabe, K., Matsuno, F., Tadokoro, S., & Kon, K. (2011). Use of remotely operated marine vehicles at Minamisanriku and Rikuzentakata Japan for disaster recovery. In, *Presented at the 2011 IEEE international symposium on safety, security, and rescue robotics2011 IEEE international symposium on safety, security, and rescue robotics* (pp. 19–25). https://doi.org/10.1109/SSRR.2011.6106798

Murphy, R., Konyo, M., Davalas, P., Knezek, G., Tadokoro, S., Sawata, K., & Van Zomeren, M. (2009). Preliminary observation of HRI in robot-assisted medical response. In *Proceedings of the 4th ACM/IEEE international conference on human robot interaction, HRI '09* (pp. 201–202). New York, NY, USA: Association for Computing Machinery. https://doi.org/10.1145/1514095.1514135

Murphy, R., Riddle, D., & Rasmussen, E. (2004). Robot-assisted medical reachback: A survey of how medical personnel expect to interact with rescue robots. In , *Presented at the RO-MAN 2004. 13th IEEE international workshop on robot and human interactive communication (IEEE catalog No.04TH8759)RO-MAN 2004. 13th IEEE international workshop on robot and human interactive communication (IEEE catalog No.04TH8759)* (pp. 301–306). https://doi.org/10.1109/ROMAN.2004.1374777

Murphy, R., Srinivasan, V., Rashidi, N., Duncan, B., Rice, A., Henkel, Z., Garza, M., Nass, C., Groom, V., Zourntos, T., Daneshwar, R., & Prasad, S. (2010). Survivor buddy and SciGirls: Affect, outreach, and questions. In , *Presented at the 2010 5th ACM/IEEE international conference on human-robot interaction (HRI)2010 5th ACM/IEEE international conference on human-robot interaction (HRI)* (pp. 127–128). https://doi.org/10.1109/HRI.2010.5453233

Murphy, R. R., Steimle, E., Griffin, C., Cullins, C., Hall, M., & Pratt, K. (2008). Cooperative use of unmanned sea surface and micro aerial vehicles at Hurricane Wilma. *Journal of Field Robotics, 25*, 164–180. https://doi.org/10.1002/rob.20235

Murphy, R. R., Tadokoro, S., & Kleiner, A. (2016). Disaster robotics. In B. Siciliano, & O. Khatib (Eds.), *Springer handbook of robotics* (pp. 1577–1604). Cham: Springer Handbooks. Springer International Publishing. https://doi.org/10.1007/978-3-319-32552-1_60

Murthy, R. S., & Lakshminarayana, R. (2006). Mental health consequences of war: A brief review of research findings. *World Psychiatry, 5*, 25–30.

Muthugala, M. A. V. J., Samarakoon, S. M. B. P., Mohan Rayguru, M., Ramalingam, B., & Elara, M. R. (2020). Wall-following behavior for a disinfection robot using type 1 and type 2 fuzzy logic systems. *Sensors, 20*, 4445. https://doi.org/10.3390/s20164445

Myers, M. (2014). *How robots could be used to fight Ebola*. CNET.

Nallathambi, D. J. (2018). Comprehensive evaluation of the performance of rescue robots using victim robots. In , *Presented at the 2018 4th international conference on control, automation and robotics (ICCAR)2018 4th international conference on control, automation and robotics (ICCAR)* (pp. 60–64). https://doi.org/10.1109/ICCAR.2018.8384645

National Academies of Sciences, E., Division, H., Health, B. on G., States, C. on G. H., & the, F. of the U. (2017). *Addressing continuous threats: HIV/AIDS, tuberculosis, and malaria, global health and the future role of the United States*. National Academies Press (US).

NHS. (2020). *Online consultations - NHS App help and support [WWW Document]*. nhs.uk. URL https://www.nhs.uk/nhs-services/online-services/nhs-app/nhs-app-help-and-support/online-consultations/ (accessed 5.19.21).

Niamat Ullah Akhund, T. Md, Jyoty, W. B., Siddik, MdA. B., Newaz, N. T., Al Wahid, S. K. A., & Sarker, M. M. (2020). IoT based low-cost robotic agent design for disabled and COVID-19 virus affected people. In , *Presented at the 2020 fourth world conference on smart trends in systems, security and sustainability (WorldS4)2020 fourth world conference on smart trends in systems, security and sustainability (WorldS4)* (pp. 23–26). https://doi.org/10.1109/WorldS450073.2020.9210389

Niroui, F., Zhang, K., Kashino, Z., & Nejat, G. (2019). Deep reinforcement learning robot for search and rescue applications: Exploration in unknown cluttered environments. *IEEE Robotics and Automation Letters, 4*, 610–617. https://doi.org/10.1109/LRA.2019.2891991

Noji, E. K. (2000). The public health consequences of disasters. *Prehospital and Disaster Medicine, 15*, 21–31. https://doi.org/10.1017/S1049023X00025255

Odekerken-Schröder, G., Mele, C., Russo-Spena, T., Mahr, D., & Ruggiero, A. (2020). Mitigating loneliness with companion robots in the COVID-19 pandemic and beyond: An integrative framework and research agenda. *Journal of Service Management, 31*, 1149–1162. https://doi.org/10.1108/JOSM-05-2020-0148

Ohno, K., Kawatsuma, S., Okada, T., Takeuchi, E., Higashi, K., & Tadokoro, S. (2011). Robotic control vehicle for measuring radiation in Fukushima Daiichi nuclear power plant. In , *Presented at the 2011 IEEE international symposium on safety, security, and rescue robotics2011 IEEE international symposium on safety, security, and rescue robotics* (pp. 38–43). https://doi.org/10.1109/SSRR.2011.6106792

de Oliveira Andrade, A., Soares, A. B., de Andrade Palis, A., Cabral, A. M., Barreto, C. G. L., de Souza, D. B., de Paula Silva, F., Santos, F. P., Silva, G. L., Guimarães, J. F. V., de Araújo, L. A. S., Nóbrega, L. R., Mendes, L. C., Luiz, L. M. D., Brandão, M. R., Milagre, S. T., de Lima Gonçalves, V., de Freitas Morales, V. H., da Conceição Lima, V., & Pereira, A. A. (2021). On the use of telemedicine in the context of COVID-19: Legal aspects and a systematic review of technology. *Research on Biomedical Engineering*, 1–19. https://doi.org/10.1007/s42600-021-00133-8

Oliver, N., Letouzé, E., Sterly, H., Delataille, S., De Nadai, M., Lepri, B., Lambiotte, R., Benjamins, R., Cattuto, C., Colizza, V., de Cordes, N., Fraiberger, S. P., Koebe, T., Lehmann, S., Murillo, J., Pentland, A., Pham, P. N., Pivetta, F., Salah, A. A., … Vinck, P. (2020). Mobile phone data and COVID-19: Missing an opportunity?, 2003.12347 [cs] *arXiv*.

Olu, O., Usman, A., Manga, L., Anyangwe, S., Kalambay, K., Nsenga, N., Woldetsadik, S., Hampton, C., Nguessan, F., & Benson, A. (2016). Strengthening health disaster risk management in Africa: Multi-sectoral and people-centred approaches are required in the post-hyogo framework of action era. *BMC Public Health, 16*, 691. https://doi.org/10.1186/s12889-016-3390-5

Ono, S. K., Andraus, W., Terrabuio, D. R. B., Cobello-Júnior, V., Arai, L., Ducatti, L., Haddad, L. B. de P., D'Albuquerque, L. A. C., & Carrilho, F. J. (2020). Technological innovation in outpatient Assistance for chronic liver disease and liver transplant patients during the coronavirus disease outbreak: A method to minimize transmission. *Clinics, 75*. https://doi.org/10.6061/clinics/2020/e1946

Papadopoulos, I. (2018). *Culturally competent compassion*. Oxon: Routledge.

Papadopoulos, I., Ali, S., Papadopoulos, C., Castro, N., Faulkes, N., & Koulouglioti, C. (2021). A qualitative exploration of care homes workers' views and training needs on the use of socially assistive humanoid robots in their workplace. *International Journal of Older People Nursing, 00*, e12432. https://doi.org/10.1111/opn.12432

Papadopoulos, I., Koulouglioti, C., Ali, S., Lazzarino, R., Wright, S., Martín-García, Á., Oter-Quintana, C., Kouta, C., Rousou, E., Papp, K., Krepinska, R., Tothova, V., Malliarou, M., Apostolara, P., Lesińska-Sawicka, M., Nagórska, M., Liskova, M., Nortvedt, Alpers, L.-M., … Nissim, S. (2021). Under review, Training needs of health and social care professionals in relation to socially assistive robots: an international online survey. *Contemporary Nurse*.

Papadopoulos, I., Koulouglioti, C., Lazzarino, R., & Ali, S. (2020). Enablers and barriers to the implementation of socially assistive humanoid robots in health and social care: A systematic review. *BMJ Open, 10*, e033096. https://doi.org/10.1136/bmjopen-2019-033096

Papadopoulos, Irena, Lazzarino, Runa, Koulouglioti, Christina, Ali, Sheila, & Wright, Steve (forthcoming). Towards a national strategy for the provision of spiritual care during major health disasters: a qualitative study. *International Journal of Health Planning and Management*.

Papadopoulos, I., Lazzarino, R., Wright, S., Ellis Logan, P., & Koulouglioti, C. (2021). Spiritual support during COVID-19 in England: A scoping study of online sources. *Journal of Religion & Health, 60*(4), 2209–2230. https://doi.org/10.1007/s10943-021-01254-1

Papadopoulos, I., Shea, S., Taylor, G., Pezzella, A., & Foley, L. (2016). Developing tools to promote culturally competent compassion, courage, and intercultural communication in healthcare. *Journal of Compassionate Health Care, 3*, 2. https://doi.org/10.1186/s40639-016-0019-6

PBS. (2015). *Scientists develop Ebola-fighting robots*. PBS NewsHour Extra. URL https://www.pbs.org/newshour/extra/daily-videos/scientists-develop-ebola-fighting-robots/ (accessed 5.13.21).

Pepe, E., Bajardi, P., Gauvin, L., Privitera, F., Lake, B., Cattuto, C., & Tizzoni, M. (2020). COVID-19 outbreak response, a dataset to assess mobility changes in Italy following national lockdown. *Scientific Data, 7*, 230. https://doi.org/10.1038/s41597-020-00575-2

Podpora, M., Gardecki, A., Beniak, R., Klin, B., Vicario, J. L., & Kawala-Sterniuk, A. (2020). Human interaction smart subsystem—extending speech-based human-robot interaction systems with an implementation of external smart sensors. *Sensors, 20*, 2376. https://doi.org/10.3390/s20082376

Price, S. (2021). *The future of robotics in healthcare*. Health Europa. URL https://www.healtheuropa.eu/robotics-in-healthcare/106671/ (accessed 5.6.21).

Priya, S. (2020). *Singapore government launches COVID-19 chatbot*. OpenGov Asia. URL https://opengovasia.com/singapore-government-launches-COVID-19-chatbot/ (accessed 5.19.21).

Rabbitt, S. M., Kazdin, A. E., & Scassellati, B. (2015). Integrating socially assistive robotics into mental healthcare interventions: Applications and recommendations for expanded use. *Clinical Psychology Review, 35*, 35–46. https://doi.org/10.1016/j.cpr.2014.07.001

Ramalingam, B., Yin, J., Rajesh Elara, M., Tamilselvam, Y. K., Mohan Rayguru, M., Muthugala, M. A. V. J., & Félix Gómez, B. (2020). A human support robot for the cleaning and maintenance of door handles using a deep-learning framework. *Sensors, 20*, 3543. https://doi.org/10.3390/s20123543

Ranadhir, D., Srijit, K., & Bhaskar, S. (2007). A novel functional approach toward identifying definitive drug targets. *Current Medicinal Chemistry, 14*, 2380–2392.

Randhawa, G. S., Soltysiak, M. P. M., El Roz, H., de Souza, C. P. E., Hill, K. A., & Kari, L. (2020). Machine learning using intrinsic genomic signatures for rapid classification of novel pathogens: COVID-19 case study. *PLoS One, 15*, e0232391. https://doi.org/10.1371/journal.pone.0232391

Research centre for transcultural studies in health [WWW document].(2021). URL https://cultureandcompassion.com/ (accessed 6.23.21).

Russell, D., Cutrona, C. E., Rose, J., & Yurko, K. (1984). Social and emotional loneliness: An examination of weiss's typology of loneliness. *Journal of Personality and Social Psychology, 46*, 1313–1321. https://doi.org/10.1037//0022-3514.46.6.1313

Scassellati, B., & Vázquez, M. (2020). The potential of socially assistive robots during infectious disease outbreaks. *Science Robotics, 5*. https://doi.org/10.1126/scirobotics.abc9014

Senior, A. W., Evans, R., Jumper, J., Kirkpatrick, J., Sifre, L., Green, T., Qin, C., Žídek, A., Nelson, A. W. R., Bridgland, A., Penedones, H., Petersen, S., Simonyan, K., Crossan, S., Kohli, P., Jones, D. T., Silver, D., Kavukcuoglu, K., & Hassabis, D. (2020). Improved protein structure prediction using potentials from deep learning. *Nature, 577*, 706–710. https://doi.org/10.1038/s41586-019-1923-7

Share, P., & Pender, J. (2018). Preparing for a robot future? Social professions, social robotics and the challenges ahead. *Irish Journal of Applied Social Studies, 18*. https://doi.org/10.21427/D7472M

Shoaf, K., & Rottman, S. J. (2000). Public health impact of disasters. *Australian Journal of Emergency Management, 15*, 58–63.

Srivaree-Ratana, P. (n.d). Lessons learned from the great Thailand flood 2011, HOW uav help scientists with emergency response, *Disaster Aversion 3*.

Su, H., Di Lallo, A., Murphy, R. R., Taylor, R. H., Garibaldi, B. T., & Krieger, A. (2021). Physical human–robot interaction for clinical care in infectious environments. *Nature Machine Intelligence, 3*, 184–186. https://doi.org/10.1038/s42256-021-00324-z

Tadokoro, S., Takamori, T., Tsurutani, S., & Osuka, K. (1997). On robotic rescue facilities for disastrous earthquakes -from the great hanshin-awaji (kobe) earthquake. *Journal of Robotics and Mechatronics, 6*, 46–56. https://doi.org/10.20965/jrm.1997.p0046

Tavakoli, M., Carriere, J., & Torabi, A. (2020). Robotics, smart wearable technologies, and autonomous intelligent systems for healthcare during the COVID-19 pandemic: An analysis of the state of the art and future vision. *Advanced Intelligent Systems, 2*, 2000071. https://doi.org/10.1002/aisy.202000071

TelepresenceRobots. (2020). *Vita telepresence robot*. URL https://telepresencerobots.com/robots/intouch-health-rp-vita (accessed 6.23.21).

The King's Fund. (2021). *NHS workforce: Our position*.

The Guardian. (2020). "Chaos and panic": Lancet editor says NHS was left unprepared for COVID-19. *The Guardian*.

UN. (2015). *Sendai framework for disaster risk reduction 2015-2030*.

UN. (2020). *World population ageing 2019*. New York: United Nations Department of Economic and Social Affairs Population Division.

UNISDR. (2009). *UNISDR terminology on disaster risk reduction*.

Vaishya, R., Javaid, M., Khan, I. H., & Haleem, A. (2020). Artificial Intelligence (AI) applications for COVID-19 pandemic. *Diabetes Metabolic Syndrome, 14*, 337–339. https://doi.org/10.1016/j.dsx.2020.04.012

Vindegaard, N., & Benros, M. E. (2020). COVID-19 pandemic and mental health consequences: Systematic review of the current evidence. *Brain, Behavior, and Immunity, 89*, 531. https://doi.org/10.1016/j.bbi.2020.05.048

Wainwright, O. (2020). 10 covid-busting designs: Spray drones, fever helmets, anti-virus snoods. *The Guardian*.

Wang, Y., Hu, M., Zhou, Y., Li, Q., Yao, N., Zhai, G., Zhang, X.-P., & Yang, X. (2020). Unobtrusive and automatic classification of multiple people's abnormal respiratory patterns in real time using deep neural network and depth camera. *IEEE Internet of Things Journal, 7*, 8559–8571. https://doi.org/10.1109/JIOT.2020.2991456

Wang, C. J., Ng, C. Y., & Brook, R. H. (2020). Response to COVID-19 in taiwan: Big data analytics, new technology, and proactive testing. *JAMA, 323*, 1341–1342. https://doi.org/10.1001/jama.2020.3151

Wang, J., Peng, C., Zhao, Y., Ye, R., Hong, J., Huang, H., & Chen, L. (2021). Application of a robotic tele-echography system for COVID-19 pneumonia. *Journal of Ultrasound in Medicine, 40*, 385–390. https://doi.org/10.1002/jum.15406

Wang, X. V., & Wang, L. (2021). A literature survey of the robotic technologies during the COVID-19 pandemic. *Journal of Manufacturing Systems, 60,* 823–836. https://doi.org/10.1016/j.jmsy.2021.02.005

Waring, S. C., & Brown, B. J. (2005). The threat of communicable diseases following natural disasters: A public health response. *Disaster Management & Response, 3,* 41–47. https://doi.org/10.1016/j.dmr.2005.02.003

Waters, H., Burnham, G., & Garrett, B. (2015). *Rehabilitating health systems in post-conflict situations.*

Wei, W., Wang, J., Cheng, N., Chen, Y., Zhou, B., & Xiao, J. (2020). Epidemic guard: A COVID-19 detection system for elderly people. In X. Wang, R. Zhang, Y.-K. Lee, L. Sun, & Y.-S. Moon (Eds.), *Web and Big data, lecture notes in computer science* (pp. 545–550). Cham: Springer International Publishing. https://doi.org/10.1007/978-3-030-60290-1_44

WHO. (2011). *Strengthening national health emergency and disaster management capacities and resilience of health systems (No. WHA64.10).* WHO - Emergencies Preparedness.

WHO. (2012). WHO's response, and role as the health cluster lead. In *Meeting the growing demands of health in humanitarian emergencies (No. EB130.R14).* WHO.

WHO. (2019). *Health emergency and disaster risk management framework.* Geneva, Switzerland: World Health Organization.

WHO. (2020a). *Coronavirus disease (COVID-19): How is it transmitted? [WWW document].* URL https://www.who.int/news-room/q-a-detail/coronavirus-disease-COVID-19-how-is-it-transmitted (accessed 6.23.21).

WHO. (2020b). *Palliative care [WWW document].* World Health Organization. URL https://www.who.int/news-room/fact-sheets/detail/palliative-care (accessed 3.8.21).

WHO. (2020c). *Practical considerations and recommendations for religious leaders and faith-based communities in the context of COVID-19.*

WHO. (2021). *Ebola virus disease [WWW Document].* URL https://www.who.int/news-room/fact-sheets/detail/ebola-virus-disease (accessed 6.23.21).

Wright, J. H., & Caudill, R. (2020). Remote treatment delivery in response to the COVID-19 pandemic. *PPS, 89,* 130–132. https://doi.org/10.1159/000507376

Yang, G., Lv, H., Zhang, Z., Yang, L., Deng, J., You, S., Du, J., & Yang, H. (2020). Keep healthcare workers safe: Application of teleoperated robot in isolation ward for COVID-19 prevention and control. *Chinese Journal of Mechanical Engineering, 33,* 47. https://doi.org/10.1186/s10033-020-00464-0

Yang, G.-Z., Nelson, B. J., Murphy, R. R., Choset, H., Christensen, H., Collins, S. H., Dario, P., Goldberg, K., Ikuta, K., Jacobstein, N., Kragic, D., Taylor, R. H., & McNutt, M. (2020). Combating COVID-19—the role of robotics in managing public health and infectious diseases. *Science Robotics, 5.* https://doi.org/10.1126/scirobotics.abb5589

Yan, L., Zhang, H.-T., Xiao, Yang, Wang, M., Sun, C., Liang, J., Li, S., Zhang, M., Guo, Y., Xiao, Ying, Tang, X., Cao, H., Tan, X., Huang, N., Jiao, B., Luo, A., Cao, Z., Xu, H., & Yuan, Y. (2020). Prediction of survival for severe COVID-19 patients with three clinical features: Development of a machine learning-based prognostic model with clinical data in wuhan. *medRxiv.* https://doi.org/10.1101/2020.02.27.20028027

Yoo, A. C., Gilbert, G. R., & Broderick, T. J. (2011). Military robotic combat casualty extraction and care. In J. Rosen, B. Hannaford, & R. M. Satava (Eds.), *Surgical robotics: Systems applications and visions* (pp. 13–32). Boston, MA: Springer US. https://doi.org/10.1007/978-1-4419-1126-1_2

Yu, R.-Z., Li, Y.-Q., Peng, C.-Z., Ye, R.-Z., & He, Q. (2020). Role of 5G-powered remote robotic ultrasound during the COVID-19 outbreak: Insights from two cases. *European Review for Medical and Pharmacological Sciences, 24,* 7796–7800. https://doi.org/10.26355/eurrev_202007_22283

Zemtsov, S. (2020). New technologies, potential unemployment and 'nescience economy' during and after the 2020 economic crisis. *Regional Science Policy & Practice, 12,* 723–743. https://doi.org/10.1111/rsp3.12286

Zeng, Z., Chen, P.-J., & Lew, A. A. (2020). From high-touch to high-tech: COVID-19 drives robotics adoption. *Tourism Geographies, 22,* 724–734. https://doi.org/10.1080/14616688.2020.1762118

Zhou, C., Su, F., Pei, T., Zhang, A., Du, Y., Luo, B., Cao, Z., Wang, J., Yuan, W., Zhu, Y., Song, C., Chen, J., Xu, J., Li, F., Ma, T., Jiang, L., Yan, F., Yi, J., Hu, Y., Liao, Y., & Xiao, H. (2020). COVID-19: Challenges to GIS with Big data. *Geography and Sustainability, 1,* 77–87. https://doi.org/10.1016/j.geosus.2020.03.005

CHAPTER 12

Future gazing

Irena Papadopoulos[1] and Antonio Sgorbissa[2]

[1]Research Centre for Transcultural Studies in Health, Middlesex University, London, United Kingdom; [2]DIBRIS Department, Università degli Studi di Genova, Genova, Italy

LEARNING OBJECTIVES

- To become aware of what market reports say about the future of robotics in the next 5 years, with a special emphasis on household robots, assistive robots, smart robots, educational robots, autonomous vehicles, service robots.
- To understand the key elements that, according to experts, can make tomorrow's robots more acceptable to people and robust, that is, capable of working properly in different conditions.
- To have a glimpse of a futuristic scenarios, in health and social care.
- To become aware of the need to prepare and train health and social care workers on how to work with socially assistive robots in the near future.

12.1 Introduction

What's next?

Chapter 1 of this book introduced the reader to the fourth Industrial Revolution, exploring its impact on human societies and how health and social care services may respond to the potential offered by artificially intelligent (AI) robotics and other AI devices. After a long trip, we have finally reached the last chapter: the reader may expect predictions about what will happen in the future.

The media love scientists making predictions. They never miss an opportunity to ask researchers: "what can we expect in the future?," "how many years shall we wait to have this in our homes?" and so on. This is not a surprise: making guesses about the future allow people to take flight from a reality that may not be very exciting and soar toward scenarios where everything is full of mystery, expectations, hope, and fears. Of course, fears are what the media like the most: we all love to be scared a bit and feel that shiver down the spine that makes us feel alive, and journalists learned all too well that robots and artificial intelligence (AI) offer many opportunities for scaring people, both because people think that robots will impact their jobs and because movies, books, and comics have shaped our collective imagination. The hypothesis of a very intelligent yet evil AI or robot taking control of humankind is a literary topos deeply ingrained in our minds. HAL 9000 from Kubrick's "2001: a Space Odyssey" or Wachowski's "Matrix" are two of the most famous examples, but we could mention more.

If you need confirmation that the media love to trigger people's deepest fears, please have a look at the website "Will a robot take your job?" BBC published that in 2015. You may still be able to find it[1]. After loading the webpage, a form asks you to fill a text field with the name of your job. Then, the system tells you the probability that robots will be able to do that job in the near future. Let's try. The authors of this chapter are both university teachers, and then we fall in the category "Higher education teaching professional" on the website. We insert our job in the form, and … Phew! We are classified as "quite unlikely" to be substituted by robots: we can sleep peacefully. Nurses can peacefully sleep as well, with a 1% chance that their job will be automated in the near future. But care workers and home carers are supposed to have a much higher chance to be substituted by robots, equal to 40% (if we trust this website). Even more worrying, bar workers seem to have a 77% chance, whereas bank and post office clerks apparently have a 97% chance! The website explains the rationale for these percentages and clarifies that certain aspects of a job are more straightforward to automate than others. We cannot but agree that some kinds of intelligent behavior are hard to emulate by a robot. We repeatedly state this concept throughout this book, even if it is hard to say how these percentages are computed.

Of course, the discussion about robots replacing humans in jobs or creating new job opportunities is more complex than this. Reports produced by the International Federation of Robotics[2], which might be biased in favor of robots, reach the conclusion that automation has a long history of positive impact on job quality and remuneration. There is no historical evidence that automation will destroy more jobs than it creates. According to the report, human labor will remain competitive, and experts in the healthcare industry predict a future in which humans and machines will work together, with robots making work safer and less physically demanding. Since different skills will be required, a tight collaboration between industry, government, and educational institutions will be needed to prepare workers. This is the same old story: adopting new technology may positively impact society if policy makers adequately control the process.

And then, what are our predictions for the future? In Chapter 1, we introduced the fourth Industrial Revolution, and there is no doubt that something is happening and determining a new relationship between humans and technology. But what will the robot of the future look like? Will robots be able to take care of older people in 5 years? Will social robots provide physical assistance and support, such as helping a person rise from bed or bringing a glass

---

[1] In 2022, it is still available here: https://www.bbc.com/news/technology-34066941

[2] In 2022, the report Robots and the Workplace of the Future is available here: https://ifr.org/papers

of water? Will a robot be capable of establishing a genuine, affective relationship with humans? Will robots deeply understand the subtle differences between people's cultures and behave accordingly? Chapter 9 mentioned that big robotic companies made significant investments in robot design in the last years, producing remarkable pieces of technology that, however, are not capable of operating autonomously. The dog-like robots produced by Boston Dynamics capable of moving on different terrains or the humanoid robot capable of somersaulting and landing on its feet are two examples; human-looking androids like Sophia from Hanson Robotics are another. Will these companies, in the near future, be capable of making these machines completely autonomous? Will they make a step further to develop robust robots capable of effectively coping with the real world's unpredictability? Is there any company that, at this very time, is exploring nursing robots (or, even better, culturally competent nursing robots) in a similar spirit as we suggested in this book? Will there be culturally competent, fully autonomous, socially assistive robots in people's houses and care homes within the next 5 years?

We do not know.

The reader may suggest that worldwide producers like Waymo (Google), Cruise LLC, Baidu, AutoX, and Tesla already invest in fully autonomous selfdriving cars. So, can we expect that the next big thing will be autonomous social robots?

Actually, it turns out that fully autonomous vehicles, for which there was a big hype a few years ago, might not travel on our roads soon. In 2014, the Society of Automotive Engineers suggested classifying selfdriving cars into six levels of autonomy, ranging from level 0, corresponding to complete driver control, to level 5, representing complete autonomy in any environment. At the state of the art, the only level achieved in commercial cars for private use is level 3, defined as "Conditional Automation": the system addresses all aspects of driving with the expectation that the human driver will respond appropriately to a request to intervene. That is, the human driver still needs to be there, ready to take control when something terrible is likely to happen! To the best of our knowledge, there is no car for private use that offers a higher level of autonomy. One may argue that this is more due to legal reasons than technological ones, and indeed there may be some truth in this. In the last years, there have been accidents that attracted negative attention from the media and the public, putting pressure on companies to revise their plans. However, please notice that when talking about robots—and autonomous cars share many similarities with robots—legal and technological aspects are tightly related. Prototypes of selfdriving cars have been developed and tested over long distances in cities and other environments and are currently used in special situations. See, for example, robotaxi services available in some areas. But can companies feel confident that, when billions of such cars will run on our roads, they will be safe enough to prevent thousands of accidents from happening, and they will not be held responsible for these accidents?

You may object to our pessimistic approach to autonomous behavior being very conservative and cautious. Throughout the book, we have repeated: "wait a moment, this is very hard!" and "Oh no, this cannot be done," rather than daydreaming of a bright future where robots will happily populate our world. However, after the initial big hype of recent years, the revision of expectations about autonomous cars seems once again to confirm our view.

Experts now agree that vehicles with level 5 autonomy will not be on the market soon. Instead, they will be more likely to become a reality when 5G broadband communication is available to provide cars with additional information to safely cope in real time with the different situations they can encounter. In its turn, the broad diffusion of 5G has been delayed and is expected not earlier than 2030. If this is the situation with autonomous cars, about which people have been talking for a decade, how can we make reasonable predictions about the future of socially assistive robots?

The rest of this concluding chapter will include two sections. First, we will make some guesses based on what is already happening in the industry and the market today, rather than making predictions for the long term. Our guesses will be supported by market reports published since 2019 (which may fail over a five-year horizon, let alone over more extended periods[3]). This section will also discuss what is happening concerning regulations: we will mention the recent effort made at the EU level, which explores all the problems that national laws shall address to be prepared for the forthcoming intelligent systems. Second, we will dare to look farther into the future, and we will discuss a more futuristic scenario that may change healthcare in the medium-long term.

This will allow us to conclude this chapter with a key issue, which is the ultimate reason why we wrote this book: preparing health and social care professionals and end users for the advent of the next generation of assistive robots.

12.2 My time-machine is parked in 2025: how technology will develop in the near future

Our quest for robots of the future starts from a search on the websites of MarketsAndMarkets, one of the largest market research firms, periodically publishing market research reports to identify new revenue opportunities. The methodology adopted to estimate the robot market in the next 5 years is reported on the MarketsAndMarkets website, and it involves different steps and experts in the robotics sector. When making guesses about the future, we think that the opinion of people that are ready to bet their money on it deserves attention. The search was performed in September 2021 using only one keyword: robot. In the following, we consider the online free summary of reports published from 2019 onward, which proves to be sufficient for this purpose. Among the inclusion criteria, we keep only reports focusing on robots with at least some degree of autonomy and interaction with humans or human-populated environments. All reports, unless otherwise specified, make forecasts for 5 years.

From 2019 to 2024, the Household Robots Market[4] was expected to have a 22.4% compound annual growth rate (CAGR): a market of 3.3 billion dollars was reported in 2019,

---

[3] Among the other reasons to fail a prediction, "Nobody expects Covid!", to paraphrase Monty Python's "Nobody expects Spanish Inquisition!".

[4] Household Robots Market by Offering (Products, Services), Type (Domestic, Entertainment & Leisure), Application (Vacuuming, Lawn Mowing, Companionship, Elderly and Handicap Assistance, Robot Toys and Hobby Systems), and Geography - Global Forecast to 2024. In 2022 it is still available here: https://www.marketsandmarkets.com/Market-Reports/household-robot-market-253781130.html

expected to grow to 9.1 billion dollars in 2024. This market sector includes domestic robots for vacuuming, lawn mowing, companionship, elderly assistance, entertainment, and hobby (plus pioneering work in robotic kitchens and laundry robots). Key companies include iRobot (producing the Roomba vacuum cleaner), Neato (owned by Vorwerk, a worldwide leader in vacuum cleaning thanks to the famous Kobold), Husqvarna (producing the Automower robot), but also LEGO, and others. The report summary mentions all the key technologies discussed in this book as the prerequisite for robot autonomy in social environments. Companies' investment ranges from autonomous navigation and localization, crucial for vacuuming and lawn mowing, to verbal interaction and identity recognition required for medicine dispensers.

From the report, it emerges that the integration of different technological solutions will become more and more fundamental in the next few years. Robot producers emphasize integrating their robots with home assistants produced by Google and Amazon, paying increased attention to social aspects. According to this vision, household chores, assistance, and companionship shall not be provided by a humanoid robot capable of doing everything but a team of very specialized household robots, which producers plan to make more interconnected, smarter, and social. As expected, the report's summary ignores cultural competence to adapt technology to different markets worldwide. What about making all these robots and devices culturally competent through the strategies described in Chapters 6 and 7?

In a report published in the same year, the Assistive Robotics Market[5] was expected to have a 22.3% CAGR from 2019 (4.1 billion dollars) to 2024 (11.2 billion dollars). Notice that the report partially overlaps with the previous one as they both cover socially assistive robots. However, in this second report, physically assistive robots receive greater attention: consequently, the report's summary mostly mentions companies working in the surgical, assistive, and rehabilitation sectors, which are far from the scope of our survey. On the other hand, among the companies developing social robots, the report mentions SoftBank Robotics (producer of the Pepper robot used in the CARESSES project), Double Robotics (producer of the telepresence robot Double), and finally Hanson Robotics (producers of the android Sophia and low-cost robots for entertainment and education). Notably, elderly assistance is emphasized as one of the relevant applications of the following 5 years: still, 2024 is getting closer, but we have not seen any robot capable of assisting older people on the market yet, let alone culturally competent robots. Once again, we need to acknowledge that making predictions is risky and subject to unpredictable factors, especially when robots need to interact with people: autonomous behavior is the philosopher's stone that no "robotic alchemist" has been able to create yet.

Wait a moment: what if, as somebody suggested concerning autonomous cars, higher autonomy and safety will be achievable only by distributing intelligence over more sensors and other devices in the environment, perhaps with the support of the forthcoming 5G communication technology, each device taking care of a particular aspect of autonomy? Sensors

---

[5] The Assistive Robotics Market by Mobility, Type (Physically, Socially, Mixed Assistive), Application (Elderly Assistance, Companionship, Handicap Assistance, Surgery Assistance, Industrial, Defense, Public Relations), and Geography - Global Forecast to 2024. In 2022 it is still available here: https://www.marketsandmarkets.com/Market-Reports/assistive-robotics-market-37247851.html

attached to the ceiling to detect the position of robots and people ... sensors embedded in people's clothes and accessories to detect their gestures, posture, intentions, and speech to make interaction with robots simpler .... A coherent picture is starting to emerge from these first two reports. In the future, AI may not be any more in the "brain" of a super-robot mimicking human capabilities but in the "collective brain" emerging from an ecosystem of low-cost, specialized devices communicating with each other. The idea is not new: some researchers have been working toward collective intelligence (Brambilla et al., 2013) and Ubiquitous Robotics (Sanfeliu et al., 2008) for at least 2 decades. Have a look at the last section of Chapter 9, where a scenario showing this possibility is described.

The Smart Robots Market[6] report, which includes some areas already covered by the two reports above, was expected to grow at a 30.5% CAGR from 2020 (6.1 billion dollars) to 2025 (23.0 billion dollars). Please notice that this report was published after the beginning of the COVID-19 pandemic and consequently emphasizes the key role of public funding in increasing robotic investments in the last years. In times of social distancing, governments have undertaken initiatives to deploy robots for the disinfection of buildings, delivery of food and objects such as medication and samples around hospitals, quarantined patient mobilization and entertainment, to mention a few (read more in Chapter 11). It is questionable as to whether the robot functionality specially designed to contrast COVID-19 will still play a prominent role once the emergency ends. Still, there is no doubt that the pandemic boosted automation technologies in a way that may impact the whole robotics sector. Once again, integrating robots and smart devices, referred to in this report with the popular term "Internet of Things—IoT" (Bahrin et al., 2016), is deemed critical for improving performance and maintenance, such as forecasting potential issues before they happen. In line with previous reports, the unpredictability of the real world is still considered the main challenge to make automation succeed. In addition, however, new elements are emerging.

Ethical and legal issues are expected to play an increasing role in the near future, such as the ownership of data acquired by robots (including what the user says) and safety (see also Chapter 4). An illuminating discussion about liability aspects may be found in the document "Liability for Artificial Intelligence and other emerging technologies" by European Commission, published in November 2019[7]. The document starts from the premise that, in the EU, product safety regulations try to minimize the risk of harm that smart technologies may cause. However, safety regulations cannot exclude the risk of damage, and, in this case, the victims will likely seek compensation. Unfortunately, only regulation to determine the so-called strict liability is harmonized at the EU level: strict liability covers all cases in which damages are caused by a defective product, which turns out to be insufficient in the case of intelligent systems and robots in particular. For example, a "robot" may not be defective when it exits from the factory, but it may learn and adapt its behavior as it acquires new information during usage. After all, this is what we expect from an intelligent system. To which

---

[6] Smart Robots Market with COVID-19 Impact Analysis by Component (Sensors, Actuators, Control Systems), Type, Operating Environment, Mobility, Application (Domestic, Field/Agricultural, Public Relations, Industrial), and Region - 2020 to 2025, 30.5%. In 2022 it is still available here: https://www.marketsandmarkets.com/Market-Reports/smart-robots-market-48470534.html

[7] Report produced by the Expert Group on Liability and New Technologies. In 2022 it is still available here: https://t.co/Dps7ij9ysC

extent will the producer (or a third-party operator that uses the robot) be liable, in this case? Other factors make the situation very complex. For instance, as the document reminds us, "One of the most essential requirements for establishing liability is a causal link between the victim's harm and the defendant's sphere. As a rule, it is the victim who must prove that their damage originated from some conduct or risk attributable to the defendant." Finding a causal link may be more straightforward in the presence of a hardware defect, that is, an electrical component that has deteriorated due to wear and has not received the necessary maintenance. However, finding a causal link between the damage and the "wrong behavior" of an AI program looks extremely complex, therefore making it almost impossible for the victim to prove that such a link exists. Maybe an obligatory insurance scheme for AI programs and robots could be a possible solution? These are only a few aspects considered: the report written by the EU Expert Group is worth reading in its entirety. The lesson learned is that we need to be ready since technological solutions and limitations are not the only elements that will play a key role in the future of AI and Robotics.

The Educational Robot Market[8] was expected to have a 16.1% CAGR from 2021 (1.3 billion dollars) to 2025 (2.6 billion dollars). First, the report's online summary outlines that the COVID-19 pandemic negatively impacted the educational robot market due to the temporary closure of schools, universities, and centers offering robotics education. Then, it acknowledges the high potential of humanoid robots in this sector by mentioning key companies such as SoftBank Robotics and PAL Robotics: humanoid robots may become pivotal to implement inclusive practices for students with disabilities such as autism and emotional and behavioral disorders, as they have been proven to improve social skills, confidence, and self-esteem.

Very notably, and in line with the objectives of this book, the report confirms the importance that the public, and especially future generations, be more aware of how robots work—knowing what robots can and cannot do is the key for controlling and not being overwhelmed by them. To this end, in the future, we can expect robots that can be programmed with simple languages or even by showing them what to do, without any programming skill. Also, the report observes that one of the barriers to the widespread adoption of educational robots is their cost. Then, the availability of cheaper robots with limited motion capabilities (sometimes referred to as "table-top robots") may be the key to paving new avenues to their diffusion in the future. When combined together, the need to keep the cost low and the need for advanced social-interaction skills (including verbal integration with children) suggests outsourcing capabilities to third-party services residing on the Cloud. This strategy has already been adopted by home assistants produced by big companies such as Google or Amazon: they provide their services at a cost oscillating between 20$ and 30$ in their basic versions. However, social robots may need more advanced capabilities than just replying to a user request, for example, for the weather forecast. For example, they may need to plan complex sequences of actions to move in the environment or access a vast knowledge base for culturally competent interaction with the person. To ensure this, researchers acknowledge

---

[8] Educational Robot Market with COVID-19 Impact Analysis by Type (Humanoid Robots, Collaborative Industrial Robots), Component (Sensors, End Effectors, Actuators), Education Level (Higher Education, Special Education), and Region - Global Forecast to 2026. In 2022 it is still available here: https://www.marketsandmarkets.com/Market-Reports/educational-robot-market-28174634.html

two aspects as key in the so-called Cloud Robotics (Vojić, 2018): Cloud Computing and Collaborative Learning, see Chapter 9. Cloud Computing refers to the idea that robots of the future may use the computational resources of servers remotely located somewhere; Collaborative Learning refers to the idea that robots may share the data collected and the experience they have acquired. Both elements provide an excellent strategy to address the presumed unsolvable question of increasing performance while reducing costs. Moreover, even if this discussion started from the educational robot market, it is likely that outsourcing intelligence to the Cloud will reveal to be appropriate for any personal robot since the cost is a barrier in different application scenarios. Future social robots will need to be autonomous, integrated with an ecosystem of devices, safe … but also cheap!

The Cleaning Robot Market[9] has already been discussed as part of the household robot market, and therefore we do not discuss the new report published in 2021. It is only worth observing that the report again emphasizes integration and efficiency as key elements for this market sector to grow. Concerning integration, the report notices that early cleaning robots were only designed for cleaning: however, new models will come with new functionalities, such as guarding homes through a live-streaming video acquired by a robot camera. Concerning efficiency, the report confirms that, in addition to the limited suction capability (less than traditional vacuum cleaners), the lack of performance is due to the unpredictability of unstructured human environments. Analogous problems are mentioned, as we expected, concerning the Robotaxi Market[10], which makes predictions from 2021 to 2030. Very wisely, the report refrains from making predictions for the short term and reiterates the barriers that make the deployment of fully autonomous cars complex: technological aspects, due to the complexity of collecting and processing huge amounts of data in the proper way to cope with several different environmental conditions (heavy traffic, crowded areas, rain, fog), and regulatory aspects, due to the lack of appropriate and shared regulations (De Chiara et al., 2021). Crowded areas, the report says, pose the most serious problems. Therefore, most robotaxis may be initially designed to function on roads with marked lanes and vehicles moving in the same direction. This looks like one of the tricks and cheats we presented in Chapter 9.

To conclude, the whole Service Robotics Market[11] is covered in a new report published in 2021, addressing different applications ranging from logistics and inspection to education and personal assistance (therefore partially overlapping with previous reports). The market is projected to have a 23.3% CAGR from 2021 (36.2 billion dollars) to 2026 (103.3 billion

---

[9] Cleaning Robot Market with COVID-19 Impact by Type (Professional, Personal), Product (Floor Cleaning, Lawn Cleaning, Pool Cleaning, Window Cleaning), Application (Residential, Commercial, Industrial, Healthcare), and Geography - Global Forecast to 2026. In 2022 it is still available here: https://www.marketsandmarkets.com/Market-Reports/cleaning-robot-market-22726569.html

[10] Robotaxi Market by Application (Goods and Passenger), Level of Autonomy (L4 and L5), Vehicle (Car and Shuttle/Van), Service (Rental and Station Based), Propulsion (Electric and Fuel Cell), Component and Region - Global Forecast to 2030. In 2022 it is still available here: https://www.marketsandmarkets.com/Market-Reports/robo-taxi-market-132098403.html

[11] Service Robotics Market with COVID-19 Impact Analysis, by Environment, Type (Professional, Personal & Domestic), Component, Application (Logistics, Inspection & Maintenance, Public Relations, Education, Personal), and Geography - Global Forecast to 2026. In 2022 it is still available here: https://www.marketsandmarkets.com/Market-Reports/service-robotics-market-681.html

dollars). As reported again in 2021, the main problem is still that robots are hardly capable of coping with all unpredictable situations that may emerge, that is, the lack of robustness. So then, this last report is an excellent opportunity to help us summarize all the elements that may be key to determining the success of robotics in the next few years.

- First, the integration of robots with smart sensors and devices in the environment to improve performance and predict possible malfunctions.
- Second, the use of Cloud-based solutions to outsource computations and increase robot's capabilities at a low cost.
- Third, new regulations that are appropriate to deal with new legal concerns originated by smart technology.
- Fourth, interfaces to make robots customizable by everyone without requiring complex programming skills.
- And finally, cultural competence to make people of different cultures accept robots as companions in their lives.

Remember the list above: if robots populate our world soon, they will have these characteristics. We are ready to bet all the money we will make from this book!

The reader shall now have an idea of what we expect to happen in the next 5 years. As for the farther future, the reader can make their own suppositions. Or they may take inspiration from the next section, where the impact of robotics on social and healthcare staff is discussed.

12.3 Let us now gaze a little further into the future

This section will indeed try to gaze in the world we may have in 20 years from now. As this book focuses on health and social care, we have prepared a futuristic scenario involving these domains and the AI technology which may be commonplace in the not so far future of the year 2040.

> It is a morning in the year 2040. Mr. Andreas, a 95-year-old first-generation Greek immigrant to the UK, is ready to get out of bed.
>
> He lives alone in his very comfortable bungalow which is fitted with cutting edge technology such as sensors that can open and close the lights, the curtains, the doors, the TV, and more. He has a few age-related memory issues, and some mobility issues which have resulted in a few falls recently. Nevertheless he is enjoying his life and looks forward to every day that comes. Almost everyday, one or more of his children, grandchildren or great grandchildren, many of whom live in his area, will pay him a visit. He is very proud of them and takes a lot of interest in what is happening in their lives, their jobs, their travels and so on.
>
> When he is alone, he likes to watch his large-sized TV (best for his failing eyesight), or socialises with his culturally competent socially assistive robot called Athena. He has interesting conversations with Athena who seems to know everything! Athena is his permanent 24 hour link with the outside world. She can organise online meetings with his family who live far away or in another country, she can order the shopping, make appointments with the doctor, read him his book or help him to stay healthy through exercise and good nutrition. She also remotely checks his vital signs everyday (body temperature, pulse, blood pressure), blood glucose levels and even his state of mood, and stores all data in his cloud file. These are remotely checked daily by his nurse in case any of them are abnormal and some action is needed, and of course they are important for future use and comparisons. 'Never a dull moment' Mr. Andreas is often heard to say.

Unfortunately, this morning, while trying to get out of bed Mr. Andreas had another fall which rendered him unable to get off the floor. He called Athena and asked her to call the emergency medical services. Based on the data provided by Athena, the emergency team made the provisional diagnosis of 'fractured femur', requiring surgery. The emergency team of three humans (a surgeon, an anaesthetist, and a nurse) and an AI surgical robot, arrived less than 5 minutes later and lifted Mr. Andreas on their medical trolley. The medical team provide pain control medications via a needleless device and conduct a comprehensive assessment which included vital signs, an electrocardiogram, several blood tests, and body and head scans using their small mobile hand-held devices. The team decided that Mr. Andreas needed to have a hip replacement, so a pop-up theatre was set up quickly in the living room. Mr. Andreas signed the consent form for surgery after being given all the information about his trauma, the options available to him and the surgical procedure. His next of kin was also informed of the situation.

The team had everything they needed, lights, surgical instruments, antiseptics, medicines for local anaesthesia, blood for transfusion if this was needed, monitors to be used during surgery etc. The surgical robot was programmed and after doing a small incision it managed to successfully complete the required surgery whilst Mr. Andreas was listening to his favourite Greek music using his smart ergonomic headphones without being distracted or worried about external noises. By the time his next of kin (his youngest daughter) arrived, Mr. Andreas was sitting in his armchair enjoying a cup of Greek coffee made by Athena.

The above scenario provides an indication of how health care may be provided in the future. Some of the technology used in the scenario is already available while others are currently being trialed for imminent use. Despite the fact that society, healthcare providers, researchers, and the AI/robotics industry are confident that the use of technology will increase exponentially in the next 5–10 years, those responsible for educating healthcare workers appear to be lagging behind. Ronquillo et al. (2021) stated that the dynamics between AI and nursing have yet to be critically interrogated. This is despite nurses being the largest group of healthcare professionals internationally; the International Council of Nurses reports that it represents more than 20 million nurses worldwide. The sheer volume of the nursing workforce means that nurses will likely be the healthcare professionals who are most exposed to new AI technologies.

12.4 The urgent need for training and engagement of health and social care staff

Ronquillo et al. (2017) also note that nursing education continues to struggle with incorporating basic nursing informatics competencies as part of basic nursing education, while addressing AI remains, largely, absent. A report from the WHO/ICN/Nursing Now (2020) titled "State of the World's Nursing 2020," states that digital technologies, AI, augmented reality, and the use of robots are already transforming nursing and patient care. It recommends that nurses should be equipped with the digital determinants of health which include digital literacy, access to technological equipment and internet infrastructure in order to implement the AI technologies in ways that minimize the challenges that health workers may experience.

In Chapter 1, you were introduced to the Topol (2019) report titled *"Preparing the healthcare workforce to deliver the digital future."* The report strongly recommends that the NHS staff will need to acquire, as soon as possible, digital skills and digital literacy in order to be able to deal with the changes brought about by the fourth industrial revolution. In particular, the report recommends that education providers should both offer opportunities for healthcare students to intercalate in areas such as engineering or computer science, and equally attract graduates in these areas to begin a career in health, to create and implement technological solutions that improve care and productivity in the NHS. A professor of medical education and member of the Topol review board stated that "Educating the current and future NHS workforce is key to enabling the implementation of the revolutionary changes to healthcare practice and delivery that technological advancement will bring for the benefit of patients, carers and citizens."

It is worth reminding the reader that the European Commission's report titled "AI Watch, National strategies on artificial intelligence: A European perspective in 2019" authored by Vincent Van Roy, was published in 2020. It too emphasized the key relevance of policies on formal education and training, reskilling and upskilling opportunities, and networking between academia, industry, and the public sector.

The Research Center for Transcultural Studies in Health conducted three systematic reviews (reported in Chapter 3); one online international survey, one interview study and an educational study, all investigating the need for nurses and other health professional to embrace the AI and robotic technologies which are increasingly being developed, and in some cases are being deployed in health care. In Chapter 11, the need for training nurses and other healthcare staff in the use of AI devices during MHDs is articulated, and a proposal for a training curriculum using transcultural AI is provided. Here a number of recurrent training needs which were reported in our studies are summarized.

- Raising awareness about existing societal views, values, beliefs, misconceptions, and stereotypes about AI and robotic technologies;
- Types of uses in health and social care, capabilities of AI and robotic technologies;
- Ethical and legal issues;
- Practical skills needed to operate the technologies;
- Patient and staff safety.

The list can be unpicked by educators to identify more specific issues which can be addressed in the nursing/health/social care curricula. The list also provides topics for much needed research which should ideally involve the health and social care users of the new technologies, as well as the public. When unpicking the key domains listed, educators can identify the most urgent issues, those which are for beginners and those which are for the more advanced learners, and create learning units, modules, or more substantive innovative courses. The need for training is huge and urgent for both undergraduate and postgraduate learners. Practice and education establishments should embrace and nurture this new field of learning and create environments which will inspire the collaboration between AI/robotics scientists with health/social care scientists. This kind of cross-fertilization of learning and sharing new ideas about research and teaching will produce new and exciting knowledge, practical health, and social care solutions and new methods of learning that will equip the students—the future new practitioners—with the needed skills for successful implementation of the new AI/robotics devices which will benefit the patients and society as a whole.

It is when all the above are achieved that robots, robotic researchers, health professionals, and end users may achieve the harmony and well being saught by all.

12.5 Conclusion

This chapter examined available evidence regarding the next phase in the development and use of robots and AI technologies. It is clear that considerable progress in the field of AI and robotics has been made in the last 10 years. However, the evidence we presented in this chapter suggests that fully autonomous socially assistive robots are not currently ready to enter the marketplace and consequently the health and social care domains. The main problem for this is that robots continue to be challenged by unpredictable situations that could occur in the environment where they are placed, or by the complexities presented by groups of humans and so on. We have summarized above the elements that may be key to determining the success of robotics in the next few years. These include the need to integrate smart sensors and devices in the environment, the use of cloud-based solutions, new regulations which deal with the legal concerns created by smart technologies, and customizable interfaces, which will reduce the need for complex programming.

For many reasons, which were analyzed and discussed in the chapters of this book, humans need AI technologies now and in the future. Health and social care has already begun to integrate such technologies, although it does not yet include autonomous socially assistive robots. It is imperative that world leaders embrace the future of AI with wisdom and values which benefit humanity. Aristotle taught us that virtues lie between two vices. For example, world leaders could be either very enthusiastic about AI or fearful of it. Neither position is desirable. Too much enthusiasm could lead us to act before thinking through the issues and it is likely that the hasty decisions we may take, will have the opposite effects of those we enthusiastically supported or wished for. On the other hand, too much fear and hesitation can paralyze us, delaying making decisions or making decisions which may negatively affect humanity. So, our message to world leaders is: "find the golden mean" which will enable you to make measured, positive, and well-thought through decisions. Educate yourselves and promote the education and upskilling or rereskilling the population to be prepared for the changes that are coming and be able to live with, work with and benefit from the AI revolution.

12.6 Reflective questions

- What do you expect from robots in the next 5 years? How will they look like? What will they be capable of doing? What about the next 20 or 50 years?
- What are the key technologies that can make robots of the future reach a higher level of autonomy? What are the barriers?
- What is your view about training the health and social care workforce in AI and robotics related issues? When should this begin? What would you include in the training curriculum? Should there be some international guidelines about the training of the health and social care workforce?

References

Bahrin, M. A. K., Othman, M. F., Azli, N. H. N., & Talib, M. F. (2016). Industry 4.0: A review on industrial automation and robotic. *Jurnal Teknologi, 78*(6–13), 137–143.

Brambilla, M., Ferrante, E., Birattari, M., & Dorigo, M. (2013). Swarm robotics: A review from the swarm engineering perspective. *Swarm Intelligence, 7*(1), 1–41.

De Chiara, A., Elizalde, I., Manna, E., & Segura-Moreiras, A. (2021). Car accidents in the age of robots (2021). *International Review of Law and Economics, 68*, 1–14. https://doi.org/10.1016/j.irle.2021.106022

Ronquillo, C. E., Peltonen, L.-M., Pruinelli, L., Chu, C. H., Bakken, S., Beduschi, A., Cato, K. H., Hardiker, N., Junger, A., Michalowski, M., Nyrup, R., Rahimi, S., Reed, D. N., Salakoski, T., Salanterä, S., Walton, N., Weber, P., Wiegand, T., & Topaz, M. (2021). Artificial intelligence in nursing: Priorities and opportunities from an international invitational think-tank of the nursing and artificial intelligence leadership collaborative. *Journal of Advanced Nursing, 77*, 3707–3717. https://doi.org/10.1111/jan.14855

Ronquillo, C., Topaz, M., Pruinelli, L., Peltonen, L. M., & Nibber, R. (2017). Competency recommendations for advancing nursing informatics in the next decade: International survey results. *Studies in Health Technology and Informatics, 232*, 119–129.

Sanfeliu, A., Hagita, N., & Saffiotti, A. (2008). Network robot systems. *Robotics and Autonomous Systems, 56*(10), 793–797.

Topol, E. (2019). *The Topol report. Preparing the healthcare workforce to deliver the digital future*. London: NHS. https://www.hee.nhs.uk/our-work/topol-review.

Van Roy, V. (2020). *AI watch - National strategies on Artificial Intelligence: A European perspective in 2019, EUR 30102 EN*. Luxembourg: Publications Office of the European Union, ISBN 978-92-76-16409-8. https://doi.org/10.2760/602843,JRC119974. https://publications.jrc.ec.europa.eu/repository/handle/JRC119974

Vojić, S. (June 2018). Cloud robotics. In *International conference "new technologies, development and applications"* (pp. 191–195). Cham: Springer.

WHO/ICN/Nursing Now. (2020). *'State of the World's Nursing 2020'. Investing in education, jobs and leadership*. Geneva: WHO. https://www.who.int/publications/i/item/9789240003279.

Index

'Note: Page numbers followed by "f" indicate figures, "t" indicate tables and "b" indicate boxes.'

A
ADORE model, 147f, 153–154, 179, 179f, 206
Alzheimer's disease, 110–113
Amazon, 37–38, 196
Animal-like socially assistive robots, 42–44
Appraisal theory, 85
Artificial intelligence (AI), 1–2, 83, 102–103, 134, 166–170
Assertional Box (ABox), 174–175, 177
Attitudes, 235t, 237–240
Autonomous robots, 63
  ADORE guidelines, 206
  cloud hypothesis, 209–214
  cultural competence, 209–214
  global positioning system (GPS), 195
  human-inhabited environments, 195
  Planner, 205
  programming, 194–197
  self-localization, 195
  sensing, knowledge, planning, and acting, 203–207, 204f
  simultaneously localization and mapping (SLAM) paradigm, 195
  User Interface (UI), 207–208
  writing computer programs for, 31–32
Avoidance of harm, 68–69

B
Bayesian networks, 170–173, 171f
Beginner's guide, robots work
  autonomous robots, writing computer programs for, 31–32
  conditional blocks, 25
  explainable AI (XAI), 38
  flow charts, 24–25
  neural networks, 35–39, 36f
  real world, complexity of, 26–31
    behaviour-based robotics, 28, 30
    robotic beings, 30
    robots autonomous, 26–28, 26f
    Sense, Model, Plan, Act (SMPA), 26–28, 26f
  robotic researchers, 21–22
  writing computer programs, 22–25, 24f
Behaviour-based robotics, 28–30
Beliefs, 111f
Boston Dynamics, 192

C
Caregivers, 63–72
Care recipients, 63–72
CARESSES project, 47, 62–63
  ADORE model, 147f, 153–154
  analysis tool, 149–151
  appraisal theory, 85
  artificial intelligence (AI), 83, 102–103, 134
  consciousness, 139–140
  conversations topics, 136
  cultural competence perceptions, 238t, 240–241
  cultural experts, 148–149
  cultural iceberg theory, 139
  cultural iceberg trigger theory, 140–141, 140f
  daily routines, 139–140
  data characteristics, 230
  data collection, 160–161
  dissemination, 98–101
  end-user evaluation, 102–103
  ethics, 101
  goals, 136, 156t
  ground laying, 89–90
  guidelines, 135, 135f–136f, 154, 155t–157t, 159t, 162
  knowledge domains, 136–137
  methods, 161–162
  milestones, 103f
  national/individual culture, 139
  Natural Language Processing (NLP), 85
  nonverbal communication, 144
  norms, 137
  observation tools, 141–146
  online evaluation platform, 160
  physical and mental health, 232–237
  procedures, 148
  profiles of cultural experts, 151

CARESSES project (*Continued*)
  project management, 101
  qualitative behaviors, 137
  quantitative parameters, 137
  reflective questions, 243
  robot grouping, 233t
  robot videoed encounters, 159–161
  Rotter Interaction Analysis System (RIAS), 142
  sample size, 148
  scientific objectives, 90–92
  short scripts, 160
  social robots, 85–88
  sociodemographic frequencies, 231t
  Specific Affect Coding System (SPAFF), 142
  study limitations, 241–243
  subconscious/hidden cultural elements, 146
  technological objectives, 92–97
  theoretical underpinnings, 137–141
  Theory of Mind (ToM), 86
  tool 1, 143–145
  trial design, 218–225
    allocation and blinding, 220
    data collection tools, 223
    ethical issues and considerations, 223–225
    interventions, 220–221
    participants, 219
    testing procedures, 222–223
    trial preparation, 220
  trial feasibility, 225–230, 226t–228t
  user satisfaction and attitudes, 235t, 237–240
  validation objectives, 97–98
  verbal communication, 143–144
  Verona Coding Definitions of Emotional Sequence (VR-CoDES), 142
  work packages (WPs), 103f
Caring/nursing, 11
Cleaning Robot Market, 284
Cloud Computing, 283–284
Common good approach, 61
Common videos, Indian experts
  behaviors, 152
  triggers, 152
Compound annual growth rate (CAGR), 280–281
Computer-generated imagery (CGI), 192
Conditional Automation, 279
Conditional blocks, 25
Confidentiality, 11
Consciousness, 139–140
Consequentialism, 61
Content construction, 113–122
Conversations topics, 136
COVID-19 pandemic, 246

Cultural competence, 6–10, 209–214
  CARESSES project, 9–10
  components of, 8–9
  cultural awareness, 8
  cultural knowledge, 8
  culturally competent socially assistive robots, 9–10
  cultural sensitivity, 9
  health, social, and robotic care, 6–8
Cultural dimensions, 10–13
Cultural factors, 112f
Cultural groups, writing stories for, 109–113
Cultural iceberg theory, 139–141, 140f
Cultural identity, 10
Culturally Aware Robots and Environmental Sensor Systems for Elderly Support (CARESSES)
  beliefs, 111f
  content construction, 113–122
  cultural factors, 112f
  cultural groups, writing stories for, 109–113
  humanoid socially assistive robots, 108
  human section, 122
  quality of life, 111f
  robot section, 122
  scenarios, 113–122
  use of stories, 109
  values, 111f
Culturally competent robots, 10–13
Culture-Aware Robots and Environmental Sensor Systems (CARESSES), 2

D
Daily routines, 139–140
Data collection, 160–161
Data protection and privacy, 65–66
Deception, 66–67
Deontology, 61
Digital literacy, 5
Digital skills, 5
Dignity, 64
Disaster robots, 247–248
Dissemination, 98–101
Diversity, 11
Double Robotics, 281

E
Ebola virus outbreak, 253
Educational Robot Market, 283
Embed cultural competence into robots, 173–188
End-user evaluation, technological development to, 102–103
Espresso Coffee, 185
Ethics of care, 61
European Commission, 5

Explainable AI (XAI), 38
Exploitation objectives, 98—101

F
Fairness approach, 61
False expectations, 67
Flow Chart, 23—25
Flow control, 24—25
Fourth industrial revolution (4IR)
   artificially intelligent (AI) robotics, 1—2
   autonomy, 11
   caring/nursing, 11
   case studies, 13—14
   components, 13
   confidentiality, 11
   cultural competence, 6—10
      CARESSES project, 9—10
      components of, 8—9
      cultural awareness, 8
      cultural knowledge, 8
      cultural sensitivity, 9
      health, social, and robotic care, 6—8
      socially assistive robots, 9—10
   cultural dimensions, 10—13
   culturally competent robots, 10—13
   Culture-Aware Robots and Environmental Sensor Systems (CARESSES), 2
   definitions, 13
   digital literacy, 5
   digital skills, 5
   dimensions, 13
   diversity, 11
   European Commission, 5
   health care, 3—6
   health/well-being, 11
   Hofstede's cultural dimensions, 12—13
   human societies, 3
   human values, 10—11
   illness, 11
   individualism *vs.* collectivism, 12
   indulgence/restraint, 13
   justice, 11
   long-term orientation *vs.* short-term orientation, 13
   masculinity *vs.* femininity, 12
   nursing, 3—6
   power distance, 12
   principles, 13
   Royal College of Nursing (RCN), 4
   socially assistive robots (SARs), 2
   transcultural ethical principles, 11—12
   transcultural ethics, 10—13
   transcultural health and nursing, 11
   uncertainty avoidance, 12
   underpinning values, 10—13
   values, 13

G
Geographic information systems (GIS), 258
Global positioning system (GPS), 195
Google, 37—38, 196
Governance, 72—74
Ground laying, 89—90
Guidelines, 135, 135f—136f, 154, 155t—157t, 159t, 162

H
Hanson Robotics, 281
Health and social care (HSC), 246
Health care, 3—6
Health inequalities, 67—68
Health informatics, 258—259
Health professionals, 48—49
Health/well-being, 11
High complexity, 42
Hofstede's cultural dimensions, 12—13
Honest-looking, 209, 209b
Human-inhabited environments, 195
Humanoid socially assistive robots, 42—44, 108
Human—robot interaction (HRI), 45—47, 249
Human societies, 3
Human values, 10—11
Hyogo Framework for Action (HFA), 245—246

I
Individualism
   collectivism, 110
   collectivism *vs.*, 12
Indulgence/restraint, 13
Information and communication technology (ICT), 252
Informed consent, 64—65
Inner setting, 51
Internet of Things (IoT), 282

J
Justice, 11

K
Knowledge, 267—268
   ADORE guidelines, 179, 179f
   artificial intelligence, 166—170
   Assertional Box (ABox), 174—175, 177
   Bayesian networks, reverend Bayes to, 170—173, 171f
   Café table, 169
   design artificial intelligence programs, 173—179
   dialogue management, 179—187
   domains, 136—137
   embed cultural competence into robots, 173—188
   engineer, 169
   familiarity, 177—178

Knowledge (*Continued*)
  knowledge engineer, 169
  language generation, 179–187
  learning, 169
  ontologies, 169–170, 177
  parent–child relationships, 168
  stereotypes, 173–179
  Terminological Box (TBox), 174–175, 177
  vocabulary, 168–169

L

Labor replacement, 71–72
Language generation, 179–187
Legislation, 72–74
Long- and short-term orientation, 110
Long-term orientation *vs.* short-term orientation, 13
Low complexity, 42

M

Major health disasters (MHDs), 246
  COVID-19 pandemic, 246
  health and social care (HSC), 246
  Hyogo Framework for Action (HFA), 245–246
  transcultural AI robotics, 247–264
    AI devices and robots, 251–264
    developing, 264–265
    disaster robots, 247–248
    ebola virus outbreak, 251–253
    emergency carers, 249–251
    existential disaster, transcultural robots in, 262–264
    geographic information systems (GIS), 258
    health informatics, 258–259
    human–robot interaction (HRI), 249
    information and communication technology (ICT), 252
    knowledge, 267–268
    legal and ethical issues, 268
    MHDs robotics, 253–262
    MHD training curriculum for, 267–268
    National Health Service (NHS), 257
    operation, 268
    personal protective equipment (PPE), 254–255
    preparing, 265–268
    prevention, 255
    RAMR, 251
    remote-controlled/autonomous machines, 248
    remotely operated vehicles (ROVs), 247–248
    research and development (R&D), 252–253
    Robots to rescue, 249
    socially assistive robots, 260–262
    spiritual care, 262–264
    training, 265–268
    ultraviolet-C (UVC) light, 255
    unmanned surface vehicles (USVs), 248
    9/11World Trade Center (WTC), 249
    World Health Organization (WHO), 245–246
Masculinity
  femininity, 110
  femininity *vs.*, 12
Matrix, 277–278
Microsoft, 37–38, 196
Middle complexity, 42

N

National Health Service (NHS), 257
National/individual culture, 139
Natural Language Processing (NLP), 85, 183–184
Neural generative models, 180
Neural networks, 35–39, 36f
Noncommon videos, Indian experts
  behaviors, 152
  triggers, 152
Nonverbal communication, 144
  affective touch, 145
  body posture, 145
  eye contact, 145
  head nodding, 145
  instrumental touch, 145
  personal space, 145
  smiling, 145
  use of gestures, 145
Nursing, 3–6, 48–49

O

Online evaluation platform, 160
Ontologies, 169–170, 177

P

Parent–child relationships, 168
Participants profiles, 151
Patient Reported Outcome Measurement (PROM data), 43
Personal protective equipment (PPE), 254–255
Person-centered approach, 50–51
Planner, 205
Power distance, 12, 110
Programming, 194–197
Project management, 101

Q

Qualitative behaviors, 137
Quality of life, 111f
Quantitative parameters, 137

R

RAMR, 251
Rehabilitation, surgical robots/robots used in, 44–45
Remote-controlled/autonomous machines, 248
Remotely operated vehicles (ROVs), 247–248
Research and development (R&D), 252–253
Responsibility, 71
Rights-based ethics, 61
Robots, 63–72
    autonomous, 26–28, 26f
    section, 122
    videoed encounters, 159–161
Robot use selfefficacy (RUSH), 46
Rotter Interaction Analysis System (RIAS), 142
Royal College of Nursing (RCN), 4

S

Safety, 68–69
Sample size, 148
Scientific objectives, 90–92
Selfdriving cars prototypes, 279
Selflocalization, 195, 198
Sense, Model, Plan, Act (SMPA), 26–28, 26f
Sensing, knowledge, planning, and acting, 203–207, 204f
Service Robotics Market, 284–285
Shared decision-making, 64–65
Simultaneously localization and mapping (SLAM) paradigm, 195, 199b
Smart Robots Market, 282
Social contact substitution, 69–70
Socially assistive robots (SARs), 2
    animal-like socially assistive robots, 42–44
    autonomy, 63
    avoidance of harm, 68–69
    caregivers, 63–72
    care recipients, 63–72
    CARESSES project, 43, 47, 62–63
    common good approach, 61
    consequentialism, 61
    data protection and privacy, 65–66
    deception and attachment, 66–67
    deontology, 61
    dignity, 64
    ethical frameworks for, 60–62
    ethics of care, 61
    fairness approach, 61
    false expectations, 67
    governance, 72–74
    health inequalities, 67–68
    health professionals, 48–49
    humanoid, 42–44
    human–robot interaction (HRI), 45–47
    implementation, enablers and barriers to, 50–51
    informed consent, 64–65
    labor replacement, 71–72
    legislation, 72–74
    nurses, 48–49
    Patient Reported Outcome Measurement (PROM data), 43
    person-centered approach, 50–51
    rehabilitation, surgical robots/robots used in, 44–45
    responsibility, 71
    rights-based ethics, 61
    robotic innovations, 60
    robots, 63–72
    robot use selfefficacy (RUSH), 46
    safety, 68–69
    shared decision-making, 64–65
    social contact substitution, 69–70
    social robotic technology, 42–43
    stigma, 70–71
    transcultural ethics, 61–62
    Unified Theory of Acceptance and Use of Technology (UTAUT), 46
    virtue ethics, 61
Social robots, 85–88
Sociodemographic frequencies, 231t
SoftBank Robotics, 281
Specific Affect Coding System (SPAFF), 142
Stigma, 70–71
STRIPS (Plan), 29
Subconscious/hidden cultural elements, 146

T

Task-based conversation, 183
Terminological Box (TBox), 174–175, 177
Theory of Mind (ToM), 86
Transcultural AI robotics, 247–264
    AI devices and robots, 251–264
    disaster robots, 247–248
    ebola virus outbreak, 251–253
    emergency carers, 249–251
    existential disaster, transcultural robots in, 262–264
    geographic information systems (GIS), 258
    health informatics, 258–259
    human–robot interaction (HRI), 249
    information and communication technology (ICT), 252
    knowledge, 267–268
    legal and ethical issues, 268
    MHDs robotics, 253–262
    MHD training curriculum for, 267–268
    National Health Service (NHS), 257
    operation, 268

Transcultural AI robotics (*Continued*)
  personal protective equipment (PPE), 254—255
  preparing, 265—268
  prevention, 255
  RAMR, 251
  remote-controlled/autonomous machines, 248
  remotely operated vehicles (ROVs), 247—248
  research and development (R&D), 252—253
  Robots to rescue, 249
  socially assistive robots, 260—262
  spiritual care, 262—264
  training, 265—268
  ultraviolet-C (UVC) light, 255
  unmanned surface vehicles (USVs), 248
  9/11World Trade Center (WTC), 249
Transcultural ethics, 10—13
  health and nursing, 11
  principles, 11—12
Trial design, 218—225
  allocation and blinding, 220
  data collection tools, 223
  ethical issues and considerations, 223—225
  interventions, 220—221
  participants, 219
  testing procedures, 222—223
  trial preparation, 220
Trial feasibility, 225—230, 226t—228t
Triggers
  certainty/uncertainty, 145
  daily living routines, 145
  formal/informal caregiver's behavior, 145
  health, 145
  receiving news (personal or global), 146
  wellbeing, 145

U
Ultraviolet-C (UVC) light, 255
Uncanny Valley theory, 201
Uncertainty avoidance, 12, 110
Underpinning values, 10—13
Unified Theory of Acceptance and Use of Technology (UTAUT), 46
Unmanned surface vehicles (USVs), 248
Use of stories, 109
User Interface (UI), 207—208
User satisfaction, 235t, 237—240

V
Values, 13, 111f
Verbal communication, 143—144
  affective communication, 144
  artifacts, 144
  care and health communication, 144
  dressing, type of, 144
  encounter communication, 144
  laughter, 144
  lifestyle and feeling communication, 144
  other elements, 144
  religious ornaments, 144
  silence, 144
  social communication, 144
  taking turns in conversation:, 144
  tone of voice, 144
  use of humor, 144
Verona Coding Definitions of Emotional Sequence (VR-CoDES), 142
Virtue ethics, 61
Vocabulary, 168—169

W
Wild robots, 32—35, 35f
Work packages (WPs), 103f
World Health Organization (WHO), 245—246
9/11World Trade Center (WTC), 249
Writing computer programs, 22—25, 24f

Z
Zen garden, 188

9780323904070